Praise for Miles Harvey's

T
KING of

D0403756

A TALE OF UTOPIAN DREAMERS, FRONTIER SCHEMERS, TRUE BELIEVERS, FALSE PROPHETS, AND THE MURDER OF AN AMERICAN MONARCH

Longlisted for the 2021 Andrew Carnegie Medal for Excellence in Nonfiction

A *New York Times Book Review* Editors' Choice

A CrimeReads Best True Crime Book of the Year

"A jaunty, far-ranging history…Despite the frontier setting, there is something eerily contemporary about Harvey's portrait of a real estate huckster with monarchic ambitions, a creative relationship to debt, and a genius for mass media…Harvey deploys small scraps of knowledge to great effect…This approach amounts to a sort of historical pointillism, bringing the manic, skittering mood of the era into focus. It is a style of history well suited to the antebellum decades, when American culture was most unabashedly itself…Harvey's wonderfully digressive narrative is interspersed with news clippings, playbills, land surveys, and daguerreotypes, as if to periodically certify that all of this madness is really true…Rather than a biography of a single man, he offers a vivid portrait of the time and place in which a character like Strang could thrive."

—Chris Jennings, *New York Times Book Review*

"Deeply researched, artfully written, and splendidly compelling…Great writers deserve great subjects, and Miles Harvey, who has proven himself a great writer in two previous books, has found another subject worthy of his skills…A riveting book." —Rick Kogan, *Chicago Tribune*

"Harvey is a skillful writer and thoughtful researcher...He examines the bedeviled society [of antebellum America] through the life of James Jesse Strang, a strange man of many parts—most of them bad."
—Howard Schneider, *Wall Street Journal*

"Miles Harvey's meticulously researched tale *The King of Confidence* brings alive the bizarre and chaotic arc of Strang's life...America's history is rich with tales of frauds and fakers who successfully bamboozled their fellows. In Harvey's lively and insightful book, he shows why Strang deserves to be remembered as a prime exemplar of the type."
—John Reinan, *Minneapolis Star Tribune*

"A riveting tale told in lively prose and gripping anecdotes...Harvey is a master storyteller, and his skills are in full display."
—Benjamin E. Park, *Salt Lake Tribune*

"The story of James Strang—a messianic con man who wreaks havoc on an island community of his own devising—is amazing in itself. But it is the telling of the tale—think Herman Melville meets Mark Twain—that makes *The King of Confidence* a masterpiece. This book has talons that sink into you and won't let go."
—Nathaniel Philbrick, author of *In the Heart of the Sea* and *Mayflower*

"A ludicrously enjoyable, unputdownable read—a book with unsettling (but also weirdly comforting) parallels to our time. By illuminating this forgotten moment in American history, where a group of rational adults fell under the spell of a charismatic madman, Harvey reminds us of the endlessly repeating nature of history and humanity."
—Dave Eggers, author of *What Is the What*

"Harvey delivers a vivid account of the life and times of American sect leader, lawyer, newspaper editor, and con man James Jesse Strang...He paints antebellum America as a time of 'excesses and delusions' and skillfully explores the era's technological advances, rising immigration, political violence, religious fervor, and leading literary figures. This evocative tale will astonish and delight fans of American history."

—*Publishers Weekly* (starred review)

"*The King of Confidence* is that rarest of gems: gorgeously written, impeccably researched, and completely addictive. Miles Harvey has written one of the best books of the year. But don't take my word for it. Read it!"

—Jonathan Eig, author of
Luckiest Man: The Life and Death of Lou Gehrig

"Vividly portrayed...Miles Harvey specializes in true stories of audacious individuals, here attaining new heights of wonderment...Writing with electrifying pleasure in discovery, Harvey zestfully captures 'the carnivalesque atmosphere' of antebellum America...Deftly performing a fresh and telling analysis of the timeless power of the con man over Americans who worship those who invent their own rules and 'their own truths,' Harvey brings to galloping life a forgotten, enlightening, and resounding chapter in America's tumultuous history of searchers and charlatans." —Donna Seaman, *Booklist* (starred review)

"Is James Strang the most infamous American con man you've never heard of? That's the question animating Harvey's biography of the opportunist prophet king, a convert who persuaded the Mormons who did not follow Brigham Young to Utah to join him on Michigan's Beaver Island. Strang's authoritarian rule may have done him in, but Harvey's marvelous rendering of this con man in fraught antebellum America may have a particular resonance today." —*National Book Review*

"*The King of Confidence* reads akin to the best of thriller fiction. The true nature of the book renders the events all the more shocking and makes for an impactful read. Miles Harvey has done a masterful job bringing the past to life, narrating the whirlwind rise and fall of a true confidence man." —Philip Zozzaro, *San Francisco Book Review*

"Perfect for fans of *Devil in the White City*...Harvey's narrative is a page-turning exercise in popular history...A nicely spun yarn of religious chicanery on the frontier in a nearly forgotten historical episode."

—*Kirkus Reviews*

"Flip this book open, read page one, and then try to stop. *The King of Confidence* is mesmerizing all the way through—a quirky, rollicking ride through an America marked by upheaval, tumult, and religious fervor. It feels like one of those dystopian futures that Hollywood keeps warning us we're hurtling toward, but it's actually our own forgotten past. What this startling book cleverly illuminates, though, is our own perilous present, where so many of us still yearn for con men and kings."

—Dave Cullen, author of *Columbine*

"In tracing Strang's rise and fall, Harvey creates a colorful portrait of this society that served as backdrop to his subject's doings...Harvey's skillfully crafted story splits the difference between outright skeptic and full-on believer, getting us close enough to ground level—through newspaper reports, court documents, letters, journals, and so forth—to wonder."

—Donald G. Evans, *Newcity Lit*

"Wooly and wild, as artful as scrimshaw, *The King of Confidence* literally had me at the table of contents, and never let go. What an immense pleasure to be in the hands of so deft a storyteller, to be swept away by the richest kind of story, one that veers back to a historical moment while capturing America today, our pixie dust delusions and national gullibility in the face of old-fashioned hucksterism. Miles Harvey is a literary treasure; he's added his best yet to a growing heap of masterpieces."

—Michael Paterniti, author of *Driving Mr. Albert*

"James Strang is my new favorite ne'er do well of history: a con artist for the centuries...Please read this book. It's the most fun you'll ever have reading about the 1840s...Enjoy this wild tale."

—Molly Odintz, *CrimeReads*

"Over several hundred exhaustively researched pages, Harvey presents an account of Strang's life that plays out like a classic narrative of ambition, transgression, success, and, ultimately, failure."

—Patrick Sullivan, *Northern Express*

"Brilliantly summed up by its subtitle...Harvey does an excellent job of not only detailing Strang's peripatetic life, and those of some of his more outlandish followers, but also of placing their lives in the context of the turbulent 1850s." —Jessica Howard, *Shelf Awareness*

"Fascinating...Harvey, in a nonjudgmental style, sorts out reality from myth when recounting Strang's bizarre life."

—Bill Castanier, *Lansing City Pulse*

"Miles Harvey masterfully relates one of the great unknown chapters of our nation's history, one of those peculiarly American tales where faith, madness, and old-fashioned flimflammery converge to stunning effect. The story of James Strang, con man extraordinaire, is wildly amusing in its exposure of the stone-cold gullibility of our forebears, but also unsettling in its eerie echoes of our current national landscape, and the realization that very little has changed. *The King of Confidence* is a marvelous read." —Scott Anderson, author of *Lawrence in Arabia*

"In this year of remote work and canceled vacation plans, the most engrossing virtual trip I've embarked on transported me to a Mormon kingdom on a Lake Michigan island during our nation's antebellum era. And it's an outstandingly entertaining excursion."

—Margaret Fosmoe, *Notre Dame Magazine*

"A spirited, entertaining read with a twist of insight and a tang of scandal...Harvey has penned a tour de force of popular history."

—*Library Journal*

THE KING of CONFIDENCE

A Tale of Utopian Dreamers, Frontier
Schemers, True Believers, False Prophets,
and the Murder of an American Monarch

MILES HARVEY

BACK BAY BOOKS
Little, Brown and Company
New York Boston London

Little, Brown and Company
Hachette Book Group
1290 Avenue of the Americas, New York, NY 10104
littlebrown.com

Originally published in hardcover by Little, Brown and Company, July 2020
First Back Bay trade paperback edition, September 2021

Back Bay Books is an imprint of Little, Brown and Company, a division of Hachette Book Group, Inc. The Back Bay Books name and logo are trademarks of Hachette Book Group, Inc.

Little, Brown and Company is a division of Hachette Book Group, Inc. The Little, Brown name and logo are trademarks of Hachette Book Group, Inc.

The publisher is not responsible for websites (or their content) that are not owned by the publisher.

The Hachette Speakers Bureau provides a wide range of authors for speaking events. To find out more, go to hachettespeakersbureau.com or call (866) 376-6591.

ISBN (hc) 9780316463591 / 9780316463607 (pb)
LCCN 2019952531

Printing 1, 2021

LSC-C

Book design by Marie Mundaca

Printed in the United States of America

———

Passing stranger! you do not know how longingly I
   look upon you,
You must be he I was seeking, or she I was seeking,
   (it comes to me, as of a dream,)
I have somewhere surely lived a life of joy with you...

—Walt Whitman

Contents

THE
KING
of
CONFIDENCE

Prologue

In which an angel watches a man fall from a window in Illinois, then flies to Wisconsin with pressing business

I don't blame anyone for not believing my history. If I had not experienced what I have, I would not have believed it myself.

—Joseph Smith

AN ANGEL WATCHED THE MOB EMERGE FROM THE WOODS AND steal single file along an old rail fence toward the town jail. Although the men, more than 100 strong, attempted to hide their muskets and rifles by keeping the long barrels close to the ground, the angel was not deceived. Nor was he fooled by the mud and gunpowder with which they had blackened their faces in disguise. Whether the murder that these men were about to commit was an act of sacred purification or an abomination against God, whether it would earn the killers an exalted place in heaven or instead secure their eternal damnation—these were celestial mysteries to which the angel alone on earth knew the answers.

History, however, must adhere to the facts. It was Thursday, June 27, 1844, in Carthage, Illinois, some dozen miles from the banks of the Mississippi River. The time was around five o'clock in the evening. When the men reached the jail, they surrounded it and a host of them rushed the entrance. One of the guards fired shots from the front steps but no one in the mob fell, after which the men pushed past the guards and stormed up the stairs, blasting their weapons as they stumbled toward a second-story room. Barricaded inside, along with three associates, was the one they had come to kill.

In the instant before the assailants reached his room, that man readied a six-shooter, smuggled in by one of his supporters. While the angel was no doubt able to peer through the walls of the jail and deep into the man's soul—his fears, his regrets, his thoughts about his rapidly dwindling time on earth—history can record only that his name was Joseph Smith, that he was thirty-eight years old, and that he was the founder of the Church of Jesus Christ of Latter-day Saints.

Bullets ripped through the wooden door. Splinters flew. One of the other prisoners slumped to the floor, uttering, "I am a dead man." And now the mob pushed into the room, and now the one they had come for fired his gun, and now his bullets were spent, and now he rushed to an open window, and now he flexed to jump, and now he was shot in the back and then, from below, in the chest, and again in the back.

"O Lord, my God," he yelled as he plummeted toward the earth.

Let us stop him there for a moment, frozen in time, arms outstretched, eyes wide open to take in his fate. And if the image of a doomed man suspended in midair seems somehow implausible, is it any less plausible than the rest of Smith's life? Is it plausible, for instance, that a down-and-out drifter—a person with only a rudimentary education, who spent much of his time hunting for buried treasure with a divining rod, who was described by those who knew him as "indolent," "ignorant," "prevaricating," and "shiftless"—would be the one man singled out by God to found a new church, to produce a radically new holy book, and to ready the way for Christ's return to earth? Is it plausible that angels fluttered about the American wilderness watching over this man? Or that one of them, a celestial being with the unlikely name of Moroni, had suddenly appeared at his bedside in rural New York one night to reveal the existence of golden tablets that would change the course of history? Or that those tablets—containing a heretofore unknown account of the ancient inhabitants of the Americas, as well as a detailed chronicle of mankind's future—just happened to be buried a few miles from the man's house? Or that these prophecies were written in "Reformed Egyptian," a language unknown to scholars, and absent from the historical record, before or since? Or that the man was miraculously able to read this lost language, thanks to a supernatural pair of seer stones called the Urim and Thummim? Or that he was somehow able to produce this new bible, nearly 600 pages long, in less than three months? Or that after he was done translating the golden tablets, he gave them back to the angel Moroni, thus eliminating any means of independently verifying his own story?

Is it plausible, moreover, that despite the fact that the Book of Mormon was full of faulty grammar and anachronisms, despite the fact that it repeated the phrase *and it came to pass* an estimated 2,000 times, despite the fact that many readers found it impossibly dull ("chloroform in print," in the words of Mark Twain), despite the fact that even Smith's own hometown newspaper called it "the greatest piece of superstition that has come to our knowledge," the man soon began gaining large crowds of enthusiastic followers? Is it plausible that, even as he hurtled toward the ground, his new religion, not yet fifteen years old, could claim at least 25,000 converts in America and Europe? Or that just twenty miles from this lonely jailhouse his people had built their own city—a city from which a huge Greek revival–style temple was beginning to rise over the Mississippi River, a city with more than 10,000 residents, many of them all the way from England, a city that at the moment of its founder's death rivaled Chicago as the most populous in Illinois?

And what of Smith's own transformation? How had this "most ragged, lazy fellow," in the words of one of his earliest supporters, managed in just a few short years to metamorphose into a prophet, seer, and revelator, as well as the mayor of the city of Nauvoo, the supreme justice of its court, and the general of a powerful militia? What were the odds that he would take as many as forty women as polygamous wives? Or that, at this very moment, he would be a candidate for president of the United States? Or that he would make so many enemies at every juncture that his people would be driven from their settlements first in Ohio, then Missouri, and, in the very near future, from Illinois, so many enemies that those waiting for him below the window would not be satisfied until they filled his lifeless body with more bullets than even the angel could count?

No, none of it is the least bit plausible. But in the antebellum era—that tempestuous period of American history leading up to the Civil War—plausibility was about as fashionable as three-cornered hats. It was possibility that filled the air, possibility that spewed from the smokestacks of factories and steamships and locomotives, possibility that shot off the printing presses, possibility that gleamed through the stained-glass windows of churches and flapped the tents at revival meetings, possibility that glimmered in the eyes of transcendentalists, possibility that rapped on the séance tables of spiritualists, possibility that keened its siren song to immigrants across the globe, possibility that shone like the North Star to escaping slaves and to the 2.5 million still in bondage in the South, possibility that spilled across the map in what would soon be called Manifest Destiny, possibility that barked like a street vendor to passersby in booming cities and howled like a coyote to restless loners in desolate frontier outposts, endless possibility.

The mid-nineteenth century was a time when everything—even time itself—seemed indeterminate, malleable, open to new rules. Just five years earlier, a Frenchman named Louis-Jacques-Mandé

Daguerre had announced an invention with the magical power to freeze time, to capture light and shadow, to suspend an object in motion the way that Smith, our falling man, now hangs above the earth. And just in the previous month—May of 1844—an American named Samuel F. B. Morse had demonstrated an equally incredible invention, this one with the ability to speed up time by allowing instantaneous communication across long distances. When Morse sent the first message on this astonishing medium, the electrical telegraph, he selected a question from the Old Testament, a question that seemed to underscore all the promise and anxiety of this frenzied age: *What hath God wrought?*

The falling man proclaimed to his followers that God had wrought a new kind of chosen people—Latter-day Saints—who were specially commissioned to usher in the restoration of the Kingdom of God, right here on the North American continent. He told them that time would stop—perhaps within their own lifetimes—that the wicked would perish, and that Christ would "reign personally upon the earth," which would be "renewed and receive its paradisical glory." He insisted that angels existed, some of them "having bodies of flesh and bones," and that regular people were able to converse with them. He maintained that God was "once a man like us," and that, in turn, they could all become gods.

If these ideas were heretical to most of the falling man's contemporaries, they nonetheless reflected the spirit of the age—a time of geographic mobility, of frantic canal and railroad construction, of westward expansion and Manifest Destiny, of drifters with no fixed profession or status, of seers and seekers and swindlers and speculators, of religious fevers and apocalyptic dreams and economic collapses; a time when the fastest rate of urban growth in American history, before or since, and fraying ties of kinship and community had created a nation of strangers; a time when as much as half the paper money in circulation was thought to be

counterfeit; a time when a nobody, a shape-shifter such as Joseph
Smith, could suddenly rise to godlike heights and just as suddenly
crash back to earth.

Indeed, as Smith completed that final plunge, the inglorious conclusion to his own story was about to institute the beginning of an
equally epic and unlikely saga. Because even as the prophet hit the
ground, even as his last words drifted across the plains, the angel
was taking flight. With Smith dead, this celestial messenger had
important business in Wisconsin.

As he flew north from Carthage, the angel passed over vast
stretches of prairie that were quickly giving way to squared-off
farm fields. He passed over little towns with squat wooden buildings. He passed over dusty roads that had once been Indian trails
and, before that, buffalo paths. The buffalo were long gone, but
just twelve years earlier Native Americans and federal troops had
still been slaughtering each other in the Black Hawk War, which
ended with the Sauk and Fox nations giving up 1.3 million acres in
northern Illinois. Angling northeast along the course of the Rock
River, the angel flew over the hamlet of Grand Detour, where a
blacksmith from Vermont named John Deere had invented a steel
plow that was much better at slicing through the thick prairie
soil than its cast-iron competitors. In the future, this device would
become known as "the Plow That Broke the Plains," but for now
this region, still the frontier, was considered the American West.
(It wouldn't become known as the "Midwest" for another half
century.) Wisconsin, which the angel now spied ahead of him, was
still a territory, four years from statehood.

Just over the border, the angel reached his destination, a settlement
at the junction of the White and Fox rivers, forty miles southwest
of the site of Milwaukee, still two years away from incorporating.
There the angel came upon one of the local denizens, a short man
with intense brown eyes. As the man would later report, the angel

anointed his bald head with oil, sanctified him as the successor to Joseph Smith, and issued him a sacred commission:

> God blesseth thee with the greatness of the Everlasting Priesthood. He putteth might, and glory, and majesty upon thee.... Thou shalt preach righteousness and the sublime mysteries in the ears of many people, and shall bring the gospel to many who have not known it and to the nations afar off.... While the day of the wicked abideth, shalt thou prepare a refuge for the oppressed and for the poor and needy. Unto thee shall they come, and their brethren who are scattered shall come with them, and the destruction of the ungodly shall quickly follow, for it already worketh. Go thy way and be strong.

And then the angel disappeared, never to be seen again.

History does not record this celestial messenger's name, nor does it establish whether he was an actual divine or a figment of the imagination or an outright lie—only that the bald-headed man's name was James Jesse Strang, that he was thirty-one years old, that much like Smith he would rise from obscurity to fame, and that he too would meet a violent end. And in an age when the showman P. T. Barnum was perhaps the most famous person in the country—an age when, as one contemporary put it, "larceny grew not only respectable, but genteel" and "swindling was raised to the dignity of the fine arts," an age that gave birth to the term *confidence man*—Strang would come to embody a constantly repeating character in American history, a kind of figure whose grip on our collective imagination is as tight today as ever. But before all that, he would reign as King of Earth and Heaven.

One

In which we meet a man who isn't there

———◦◦◦———

Ours is an age of suicide and mysterious disappearance.
—Arcturus, *A Journal of Books and Opinion*, 1841

IN AUGUST OF 1843—TEN MONTHS BEFORE THAT ANGEL FLEW TO Wisconsin—a man from a small town in western New York vanished into the night.

Such disappearances were not uncommon in those days. The Panic of 1837—the deepest and longest-lasting economic crisis the young country had ever faced, to be rivaled only by the Great Depression a century later—had hurtled countless average Americans into sudden financial ruin. For some, the humiliating prospect of having the sheriff take possession of their goods and real estate to satisfy a creditor's claim was simply too much to bear. As one Pennsylvania man who owed "two hundred and fifty dollars—gone I can't tell where" put it in his 1842 suicide note: "I am gone and forgotten—numbered with the dead, where the creditors call upon me no more."

But for others there was a way to end one's miseries without putting a bullet in one's brain, to lose one's life without actually dying. For years, those who hoped to outrun creditors had sought refuge on the fast-expanding western frontier. The man who disappeared from the

New York town of Randolph, sixty miles south of Buffalo, at the tail end of the summer of 1843 had faced mounting debts for years, putting off his creditors with increasingly ornate ruses, until at last his only hope was to get out of town. In many other periods of history, the missing man might never have been heard from again after his disappearance. But he lived in an era of sudden transformations, an era when you could be broke one day and rich the next, anonymous one day and famous the next, an era when wild dreams and lunatic fantasies could quickly metamorphose into hardened facts. At that exact moment in history, for example, as many as 50,000 followers of a prognosticating preacher named William Miller were convinced that the Second Coming of Christ would take place within the next seven months. Such a precarious time, when nothing felt stable or certain anymore, favored chameleons like the man who was no longer there.

Although he was physically unimposing—a few inches over five feet, and bald, with an oddly bulging forehead—he did possess one distinguishing feature: his dark brown eyes, which one acquaintance described as "rather small but very bright and piercing, giving an extremely animated expression to his whole countenance." Another claimed that they seemed "as though they could bore right through a person." But more than any tangible attribute, the vanished man possessed an invisible, ineffable aura called *confidence*. And in those days before electrical power, confidence was what made antebellum America hum. Confidence was black magic, good fortune, and hard cash combined. Confidence could turn worthless paper into glittering gold, cow towns into cities, empty lots into bustling businesses, losers into winners, paupers into millionaires. Confidence was a charm deployed by bankers and merchants, philosophers and politicians, clergymen and card sharps alike. Confidence was "the soul of trade," in the words of a leading financial publication. Without it, added Herman Melville, "commerce between man and man, as between country and country, would, like a watch, run down and stop." In an age before the federal government began printing paper money, an age when people had to trust in privately issued bank notes—glorified IOUs—confidence was the de facto national currency.

But if the missing man's gift for confidence enabled him to gain people's trust, to make them believe the most absurd stories, it also got him into serious trouble. Just before dropping out of sight, he had allegedly attempted to pull off a swindle involving a farm he "pretended to own in the interior of Ohio," in the words of one newspaper near his hometown. He managed to sell this nonexistent property to an unsuspecting purchaser, who then "removed to Ohio, but was unable to find the farm he had bought." Finding no evidence that the seller owned any land in the county, the enraged buyer returned to New York, procured a warrant, and had him arrested. Shortly after being detained, however, the man reportedly escaped by making up "some excuse for he wished to step up stairs, and was permitted to do so, since which the officer has not seen him." This fugitive's name was James Jesse Strang, but the local paper had another sobriquet for him: "the greatest scoundrel in all the land."

One day, his name would be on the lips of the president of the United States. But for the first thirty years of his life, Strang had lived an obscure existence in western New York, which in those decades was a place of seismic demographic shifts, dizzying social upheavals, and frenzied enthusiasms. What sparked these cultural explosions was the construction of the Erie Canal, one of the engineering marvels of the nineteenth century. Completed in 1825, this 363-mile ditch, chiseled by brute force through the rocky wilderness between Albany and Buffalo, connected the Great Lakes with the Atlantic Ocean via the Hudson River. In the days before the arrival of railroads, it allowed merchandise to move west and raw materials to flow east at a fraction of the previous time and cost, making New York City, which stood at the eastern end of the waterway, the financial capital of the United States. Perhaps even more important, the canal opened the vast interior west of the Appalachian Mountains to settlement. In the 1820s, as Strang was entering adolescence, no region of the United States saw a more rapid rise in population than that of western New York.

But the canal also became what historians have called a "psychic highway," transporting migrants not just through space and time but into a kind of alternate universe where rigid traditions could lose their social form and moral clarity, radical ideas could be tested, unconventional lifestyles could be embraced, wild ambitions could be realized, and dark fears could run rampant over the collective imagination. Many of the great social movements of the nineteenth century—abolition, women's suffrage, and temperance among them—were already taking root in the fertile intellectual soil of western New York. But the region was becoming even better known for its seething religious passions. So many different spiritual wildfires lit up the landscape that the place would become known as the Burned Over District. And for the first three decades of his life, James Strang was never far from the blistering heat of those flames.

His parents, Clement and Abigail Strang, were charter members of a Baptist church in Forestville, New York, where the young man was raised on a farm with his older brother, David, and his younger sister, Myraette. By the time he reached his late teens, the region had gained widespread fame as the scene of "the greatest revival of religion throughout the land that this country...ever witnessed," in the words of the nationally famous itinerant preacher Charles Grandison Finney, who in 1830 and 1831 waged an epic evangelistic crusade in the Burned Over District. During six feverish months of nonstop preaching, proselytizing, and prayer meetings in Rochester, for example, Finney managed to convert 800 people. As one witness put it, "You could not go upon the streets and hear any conversation, except upon religion."

But the Burned Over District also produced a more radical species of preacher—zealots with unconventional ideas and apocalyptic murmurings, men and women who founded their own sects, convinced that they alone spoke for God. In the summer of 1831, for instance, an erratic, unemployed carpenter named Robert Matthews received a divine revelation. Henceforth he would call himself Matthias the Prophet and preach of an imminent cataclysm, in which 1,800 years of Christian misrule would come to an end, "all real men" would enter paradise, and all disobedient wives and outspoken women would be damned, along with "clergymen, doctors and lawyers." In some other age, this eccentric preacher—dressed in his trademark green frock coat, crimson sash, and tight pantaloons—might have been ridiculed, arrested, or institutionalized. But in an era when almost any oracular claim seemed possible, he soon found a devoted following.

"Here and there in the midst of American society you meet with men full of a fanatical and almost wild spiritualism, which hardly exists in Europe," wrote the French political scientist Alexis de Tocqueville, who visited the Burned Over District in 1831 as part of a nine-month tour that resulted in his landmark book, *Democracy in America*. "From time to time strange sects arise which endeavor to strike out extraordinary paths to eternal happiness. Religious insanity is very common in the United States."

Yet of all the groups stumbling down "extraordinary paths," none caused more of an uproar in the Burned Over District than Joseph Smith and his Latter-day Saints. Like many homespun holy men, Smith insisted that God spoke through him; unlike his competitors, however, he produced a massive sacred text to support his claim. The Book of Mormon told the story of a centuries-long fratricidal struggle between two branches of an ancient Israelite clan that fled Jerusalem just before the Babylonian captivity, eventually winding up in the Americas. One of those tribes (the idolatrous, dark-skinned Lamanites) subsequently wiped out the other (the righteous, fair-skinned Nephites), but not before a Nephite prophet named Mormon managed to compile the history of his doomed people on some golden plates. Left with the melancholy task of safeguarding this record of destruction, Mormon's son and fellow scribe Moroni, the last Nephite survivor, buried the plates beneath a hill in what would one day become western New York, where they remained for 1,400 years until Joseph Smith unearthed them.

Smith's translation of those plates, 588 pages long and selling for $1.25, finally rolled off the presses in 1830, the year James Strang turned seventeen. The initial reception to the book was brutal. The *Rochester Daily Advertiser and Telegraph* described it as a "blasphemous work" and a "fraud," adding that "a viler imposition has never been practiced." The *Fredonia Censor,* a paper published about ten miles from the Strang family farm, called Smith a "miserable impostor" and predicted that "the deluded followers of Jo Smith's Bible speculation" would soon come to their senses "and reason [would] resume again." Yet despite such forecasts of the sect's early demise, Mormonism had by then found a fervent group of followers numbering in the hundreds in western New York.

Strang himself, however, was not among them. At the age of eighteen he wrote in his diary about a growing distaste for religion: "It is all a mere mock of sounds with me for I can no longer believe the nice speculative contradictions of our divine theologians of our age. Indeed it is a long time since I have really believed these dogmas." Although he continued to take an active part in the local Baptist church and to "pray and talk on religious subjects," he did so only "to please the people." Already adept at dissembling, he believed not a word of what he professed. "I am," he wrote, "a perfect atheist."

This sense of standing apart from the normal flow of life, from other people, and even at times from himself was nothing new. It had been with Strang since a sickly childhood, when he once came so close to death that his parents made plans for his burial. For the rest of his life, he would feel "a kind of creeping sensation akin to terror" when he recalled that lonely existence: "Long weary days I sat upon the floor, thinking, thinking, thinking!...My mind wandered over fields that old men shrink from." In those early days, he rarely attended school, and even when he did teachers paid him scant attention, convinced he was "scarcely more than idiotic." But all that isolation, all that *thinking, thinking, thinking,* left him with an overwrought fantasy life. He began to imagine a new self, began to construct a future in which a lonely farm boy would inspire love and adulation, a youth small in stature would loom large, and an absolute nobody would become a legend.

My mind has always been filled with dreams of royalty and power. The nineteen-year-old diarist recorded that revelation, as he recorded all of his darkest desires, in cipher—early evidence of a lifelong fascination with cryptography. It was as if he already viewed his persona as two separate selves: the anonymous James Strang of the present, who could be described in plain English, and the exalted James Strang of the future, who required an entirely new language, one that looked on the page like magical runes.

(Beinecke Rare Book and Manuscript Library, Yale University)

In this secret code, he sketched out plans to marry thirteen-year-old Princess Victoria, heir to the British crown. "I shall try," he wrote, "if there is the least chance." In this secret code, he vowed to become "a Priest, a Lawyer, a Conqueror and a Legislator." In this secret code, he predicted a civil war between the North and the South—one he hoped to use to his advantage. "Amidst all the evils of the disturbances of our national affairs," he wrote, "there is one consolation: that is if our government is overthrown some master spirit may form another. May I be the one. I tremble when I write but it is true."

He dreamed of being the American version of Napoleon, the soldier of humble origins who rose to become the emperor of France. Six months before describing his "dreams of royalty and power," Strang noted that he had just purchased the *Life of Napoleon*. Although we don't know which one he read—several books at that time had the same title, owing to the French leader's popularity—we can guess what he learned from it. One widely circulated *Life of Napoleon*, for example, described the emperor's brilliant use of "those principles of duplicity and dissimilation which are commonly called Machiavellian. Never were trickery, falsehood, cunning, and affected moderation put into requisition with more talent or success." Another book with the same title praised Napoleon for "the insincerity with which he could use words to mislead those who treated with him."

But if books taught the young man how to exploit his fellow human beings, they also enabled him to imagine a future society where people acted on their better instincts. One of his favorite texts was *Queen Mab*, Percy Bysshe Shelley's book-length poem, which takes readers on a journey to a utopian seascape of "bright garden-isles," a paradise where "green woods overcanopy the wave" and a new moral, social, and economic order arises from the ruins of history. Banned in England and published in a series of black-market editions, the poem would become, in the words of one scholar, "*the* inspirational underground text" for nineteenth-century political re-formers. In his diary, Strang noted he'd had a hard time obtaining a copy of this scandalous book, which attempts to demonstrate that,

as Shelley put it, "there is no God!" The young atheist must have
derived pleasure from the poet's denunciation of believers as "human
dupes." But he also seems to have been enchanted by Shelley's
depiction of the possible future of civilization.

Strang was but one of thousands of young dreamers to fall
under the spell of this incendiary fairy tale, which calls for equality
of the sexes, lambastes financial competition as morally corrosive,
and advocates an economic system based on a "commerce of good
words and works" rather than on money. Even more alluring to
the growing number of people alienated by the dislocations and
injustices of the industrial revolution was the poem's idealistic vision
that "human things [would be] perfected," and that the world was
on the verge of a glorious millenarian era, a time

> *When poverty and wealth, the thirst of fame,*
> *The fear of infamy, disease and woe,*
> *War with its million horrors, and fierce hell,*
> *Shall live but in the memory of time,*
> *Who, like a penitent libertine, shall start,*
> *Look back, and shudder at his younger years.*

Strang would never forget Shelley's vision of a utopian society
set on a verdant island. Yet nor would he forget Napoleon's lessons
in how to hide your real feelings, how to manipulate other people,
how to deceive the world at large in order to achieve your own
ends. For the rest of his life, he would be torn between two opposite
impulses—a passionate idealism and a corrupting ambition—each
of which would drive him to extremes.

———

"Fame, fame alone of all the productions of man's folly may survive,"
Strang wrote in his journal, and it isn't hard to imagine why he
believed that. The young man grew up in an unprecedented age of

self-invented celebrities, unlikely heroes whose renown would not have been possible even a single generation earlier, when the world was still "governed by inheritance, fixed social rank and ordained life courses," in the words of one historian. There was Andrew Jackson, an orphan born into poverty who became the first western president of the United States. There was Henry Clay, the powerful senator from Kentucky who rose from relatively obscure roots and is often credited with coining a term that would come to embody the era's ultimate idea of success: "self-made man." And there was Davy Crockett, the legendary frontiersman from Tennessee whose exploits had made him a national folk hero and whose much-quoted motto was "I leave this rule for others when I'm dead, Be always sure you're right—THEN GO AHEAD!"

Those last two words had powerful resonance in the nineteenth century. When Strang's contemporaries spoke of the "go-ahead" spirit or principle or method, they were talking about a kind of headlong, can-do approach to life and commerce. Daring entrepreneurs were known as "go-ahead men." By the time he vanished, James J. Strang had attempted, at many times and in many ways, to go ahead. So far, however, he had managed only to go bust.

When he was a few months shy of his twentieth birthday, Strang had begun studying law with a local attorney, learning the profession by performing clerical tasks in exchange for the opportunity to read law books in the lawyer's library and to observe him in court. With this hands-on legal education, not uncommon at the time, he was admitted to the New York bar, in 1836, after which he opened his own law practice. "He possessed a wonderful memory, and as an orator he had few equals. He had a great command of language and could apply it in a wonderful manner," according to a man who knew him in those days. But after seven years in the profession, as the man recounted, Strang lost "the confidence of people who knew him and had little practice."

For a few years, perhaps owing to the fact that his law practice was failing, he also worked as a U.S. postmaster, a part-time patronage job he received for supporting Democratic candidates. For ambitious young men of the day, the position of postmaster offered "an excellent vantage point from which to observe the workings of American commerce and public life," according to one scholar. Among those who had used the job to launch their political careers was Abraham Lincoln, who, while serving as postmaster of New Salem, Illinois, was elected to the state General Assembly at age twenty-five. But Strang's time in office was marred by accusations of corruption, and in 1841, after the Whigs took control of the White House, he was one of more than 1,000 postmasters appointed by Democrats who were unceremoniously removed from office. To make matters worse, the U.S. Treasury informed him that he owed the government $14.41 for overpayments during his time in office.

By then he was in an unhappy marriage. Since his teen years, Strang had been "inclined to a certain evil which is easier avoided than corrected," as he described his intense sexual appetite. One affair with an older woman had almost certainly involved sex, and there may have been similar intimacies with other girlfriends. But as for his wife, Mary, the daughter of a construction contractor, Strang professed no "violent passions." Instead, he seemed more interested in control. At one point in their courtship, she had called off the engagement, informing him that "when we meet again it must be as total strangers." He was devastated but refused to give up. "By heavens she is mine," he insisted. "I will steal her heart in an hour she thinks not. I know she can and must and will love me."

Somehow he coerced her into marriage, but it appears to have been a disaster from the start. Years later, one of the couple's daughters would describe the 1836 wedding, "ushered in by rain and sleet and snow, and November wind and gloom," as "a fit precursor for the tragic life of Mary Abigail Content Perce. Who could have imagined, as they walked up the aisle to the altar that Sunday morning, the sorrow and trouble, the heartache, and woe and pain the years were holding for her?" When the couple climbed into a wagon and left town seven years later, they had two children in tow, but Strang's plans to make Mary adore him were, it seems, already a failure.

He was also deep in debt. In the early 1830s, Strang had tried to make himself into a real-estate mogul, joining thousands of other Americans who had gambled their life savings on rising land values. This boom began in 1830, when the federal government started one of the most massive sales of public assets in U.S. history. By 1836, some 72,000 square miles of land had gone from public to private hands, much of it in territory opened to settlement after the ouster of Native Americans. More than two-thirds of that property—50,000 square miles, an area roughly the size of England—sold in the final two years of that stretch, from January 1835 to December 1836. This "mania for obtaining land," as one paper put it, fueled inflation. From 1830 to 1836, land prices rose 150 percent across the country. One tract in Buffalo, worth $500 an acre in 1835, sold the following year for $10,000 an acre.

As long as those prices kept climbing, and as long as new players kept getting in on the action, small-time speculators such as Strang could dream of making a fortune. But the Panic of 1837 brought this frenzy to a dead stop. Hundreds of banks closed their doors. Hundreds of thousands of Americans lost their jobs. Countless people went bankrupt, as prices plummeted and credit dried up. The boom years had been built on IOUs, and once the bubble burst everybody owed everybody and nobody had the hard cash to pay. *Shuffling*—a term for the evasions, obfuscations, dodges, and deceptions employed by debtors—suddenly became the national pastime, infinitely more popular than "base ball," which in the early 1840s was just taking shape as a formalized sport.

Strang was a shuffler of the first order, paying one creditor with a bank note from a bank that no longer existed while attempting to convince another that somebody had stolen a payment after he'd put it in the mail. To support this claim, he not only offered a probable route the letter had traveled but a theory about where the presumptive theft had taken place. He had a gift for telling stories, for convincing other people of even the most outlandish assertions, but over time, as one after another of those claims proved to be false, fewer and fewer locals were willing to take him at his word.

His final job in the area, as editor and publisher of a weekly newspaper called the *Randolph Herald,* lasted less than a year. Only one copy from that period has survived. Four pages long and replete with typographical errors, it contains an item titled "HOW TO MAKE MONEY," full of practical financial wisdom that the editor himself had either ignored ("think twice before you throw away a shilling") or botched ("buy low, sell fair and take care of profits"). The key to success, the story tells readers, is go-ahead tenacity: "Should a stroke of misfortune come on you in trade, retrench, work harder, but never fly the track—confront difficulties with unflinching perseverance and they will disappear at last....Shrink from the task, and you will be despised."

Days after that story appeared in print, Strang stopped publishing the newspaper. Six weeks later he was gone. "The next that was heard of him," noted the local paper that reported on his disappearance, "a coat, hat and some papers containing his name and residence were found in the weeds, in one of the eastern counties of the state, and the leaves so stirred up as to convey the impression there had been a severe struggle, and the suspicion of murder."

But the missing man was not dead. In fact, he was about to begin one of the most improbable stories of rebirth in American history. The next time his creditors in western New York heard anything about him, he was living 600 miles to the west and practicing a new profession: prophet of God.

Two

In which we encounter a mermaid
and witness the birth of another imaginary being

———⊨⊨◈⊨⊨———

Out of old materials sprang a new creature.

—Herman Melville, *The Confidence-Man*

ON JULY 9, 1844, A LETTER FROM A DEAD MAN ARRIVED AT THE post office in Burlington, Wisconsin, forty miles southwest of Milwaukee. Addressed to "Mr. James J. Strang," it had been postmarked three weeks earlier in the Mormon city of Nauvoo, Illinois. The dead man was Joseph Smith, founder of the Church of Jesus Christ of Latter-day Saints. He had written the letter nine days before his murder, but already he could see what fate would soon befall him. "The wolves are upon the scent, and I am waiting to be offered up," he confided to Strang, whom he addressed as "My Dear Son."

Indeed, it was the prophet's premonition regarding his imminent demise that had prompted him to write. "In the midst of darkness and boding danger the spirit of Elijah came upon me," he explained, "and I went away to inquire of God how the church should be saved." According to Smith, God's voice came in reply: "My servant James J. Strang."

This mysterious epistle would go down as "one of the most important—and controversial—documents in the history of the

Mormon religion," in the words of one modern observer. If the letter was to be believed, thirty-one-year-old James Strang—who had disappeared from western New York less than a year earlier, with creditors close on his heels—was now the rightful heir to a church of more than 25,000 members worldwide.

How had this seemingly impossible turn of events come to pass?

One thing seems certain: Strang had not gone west with the goal of becoming a prophet of God. His original intention, he later told an interviewer, was to make a fortune in what had been one of the era's fastest-growing industries, the construction of canals. The success of the Erie Canal, completed in 1825, had set off a canal boom in the United States, with more than 3,000 miles of these inland waterways constructed by 1840. Strang hoped to use a family connection to get work as a contractor on the Illinois and Michigan Canal, an ambitious effort to link the Great Lakes and the Mississippi River.

That family connection was his father-in-law, the redoubtable William L. Perce, a longtime canal contractor with a remarkable record of graft and profiteering at public expense. Because canal projects were so massive, they were usually funded by individual states and run by political appointees, making the system ripe for corruption. As a superintendent of repairs on the Erie Canal in the late 1820s, for example, Perce was able to hand out contracts to his cronies and to himself. Even by the standards of a business notorious for its fraud and graft, he binged at the trough with impressive gluttony. A New York lawmaker later summarized a state investigation into Perce's tenure as a superintendent, which concluded that

> fraud and profusion in the expenditure of moneys...had been fully
> proved and established; [and] that such fraud and profusion had
> not been moderate and occasional, but systematic and frequent and
> varied. Sometimes the fraud was "ingenious and covert," at other

times "bold and barefaced"; and that such fraud mingled in almost every considerable transaction done by that superintendent.

Consequently, in August of 1828 Perce was arrested, and "not being able to procure bail, he was committed to the [jail] of the county of Cayuga," according to the New York State attorney general. Six months later, he was ordered to pay $40,000 in damages—more than $1 million in today's dollars—"for monies which he had fraudulently obtained from the public treasury...by means of false and double vouchers." But being "utterly unable to pay the judgment, or any part of it," he was still behind bars a year and a half after his arrest.

Perce, in short, was a scoundrel—the first of many colorful charlatans who would soon gravitate toward Strang, like rats to rotten meat. During almost any other age, the contractor's well-publicized arrest might have meant a quick end to his career in the canal business. But the antebellum era was full of figures with a special gift for slipping back and forth between disrepute and respectability. By 1835, Perce was once again working as a contractor, this time on the James River and Kanawha Canal in Virginia, where he appeared to be "getting rich," according to Strang. It wasn't long before the unregenerate cozener took the money and ran. But somehow that didn't stop him from landing yet another job as a contractor, on the Illinois and Michigan Canal—with predictable results. Soon, a newspaper in Illinois would publish a story about Perce under the ironic headline "A Distinguished Character." The article's purpose, according to the editors of the *Ottawa Free Trader*, was "simply to let numerous strangers, who are now locating on the line of the canal, know something about a notorious swindler," whose name was "synonymous with fraud and knavery." So abysmal was Perce's reputation, the paper added, that "there is hardly a farmer or day laborer who has ever dealt with him but can testify to his villainy."

This, in sum, was Strang's father-in-law and the man he'd been counting on to help him find work, and maybe a fast fortune. But the fact that those plans fell through appears to have had less to do with Perce's bad reputation than with Strang's own bad luck. While his in-laws had preceded him to Illinois, his own arrival there with his family in the fall of 1843, at the age of thirty, happened to coincide with a two-year suspension of work on the Illinois and Michigan Canal, due to financial problems in the state. Once again, Strang had failed in a career—this time, even before it could begin. When the canal work that Perce had long promised failed to materialize, Strang apparently saw no reason to settle with his in-laws in Illinois. Instead, he moved the family north to Burlington, Wisconsin, where both the town and its newest resident would soon be utterly transformed.

———

Located at the confluence of two beautiful rivers, Burlington had been settled by a group of pioneers from Strang's home area of western New York. Arriving in 1835, before Congress had incorporated Wisconsin as a U.S. territory, these newcomers took over land that, until a recent treaty, had belonged to Native Americans. There they set about building their own community in the wilderness, fifteen miles north of the Illinois border. Like Strang, who had years earlier declared himself a champion of "universal liberty," many of these settlers were abolitionists, some of them having already established a semi-secret organization for assisting escaped slaves. Unlike Strang, however, they were Mormons—early converts to the faith whose religious enclave in Wisconsin now included about 100 members, including one of Strang's closest childhood friends.

Benjamin Perce—the younger brother of the corrupt canal contractor and the uncle of Strang's wife, Mary—had done fairly well for himself on the frontier, speculating in land, opening a store, and serving as a justice of the peace. He also owned one of the area's few frame homes, which he now opened to Strang and his family. After settling in, the newcomer quickly set up a law practice with a fellow attorney named Caleb P. Barnes, whom he had known back in New York. The frontier offered Strang a reprieve from the past and a new start. Free from the stain of his previous misdeeds and failures, he attempted to revive his legal career, arguing cases in both Wisconsin and Illinois. One judge would later recall him as an attorney of "great shrewdness," who was "continuously bringing up unexpected points in law cases, and using arguments that would have been thought of by no one else. I think he liked the notoriety that resulted from that sort of thing."

Strang might never have had a career as a holy man, in fact, had a legal case not required him to travel to Ottawa, Illinois. There he happened to meet up with one of his Mormon neighbors from Burlington, who persuaded him to make a 175-mile detour to Nauvoo to hear Joseph Smith preach. The journey came at a difficult time in Strang's life. Shortly after the family's arrival in Burlington, his eldest daughter, just five years old, had become ill and died—an event that "seemed to wear heavily on him," in the words of his sister. But if this loss had put him in a reflective mood, it seems not to have brought him any closer to God. When he arrived in Nauvoo in February of 1844, Strang was, by his own estimation, "an inveterate unbeliever and opposer of the Mormon faith."

———

It must have been exhilarating for Strang to emerge from the prairie into the bustling metropolis of Nauvoo. With two sawmills, a flour mill, a foundry, a brewery, a brick factory, a tannery, a bookbindery, and a match factory, the city was "growing like a mushroom (as it were, by magic)," according to a local resident. Founded just five years earlier, after Joseph Smith and his disciples had been forced to flee earlier headquarters in Ohio and Missouri under the threat of violence, Nauvoo now rivaled Chicago as the most populous city in Illinois. All over town, people from as far away as England were erecting houses of brick, stone, lumber, and logs. A huge new temple was half-finished, and a three-story Masonic Hall was nearly complete. Also under construction was the Nauvoo House, a hotel and tourist center for travelers.

Like Strang, most visitors came to Nauvoo in hopes of meeting the famous prophet. One man who arrived in town around that time described Smith as a "sturdy self-asserter" who had "a strong mind utterly unenlightened by the teachings of history." Another pilgrim characterized the founder of Mormonism as "a mixture of shrewdness and extravagant self-conceit, of knowledge and ignorance, of wisdom and folly." A third visitor maintained that Smith was "a great egotist and boaster" whose "language and manner were the coarsest possible," while a fourth found him to be "a compound of ignorance, vanity, arrogance, coarseness and stupidity and vulgarity."

Strang didn't record his own impressions of the prophet. Nonetheless, something extraordinary happened at their meeting, perhaps even something miraculous—something that altered the course of Strang's life and has confounded historians ever since. Strang himself would have little to say about what did in fact transpire between the two strangers, other than to tell one journalist that he "contended with Smith for a considerable time, but was at last converted to the faith."

What was behind this conversion? Why did a skeptic like Strang suddenly open his mind to the Mormon message? How could it be that a man who had spent his entire adult life lifting his "puny arm in rebellion against the Most High God," in the words of his devout Baptist sister, would suddenly drop to his knees with the zealotry of a true believer? Was he, as that same sister would suggest, hoping to fill a spiritual void caused by the death of his daughter? Did he, like so many others before him, succumb to the force of Smith's personality, the allure of his words, the charisma that circled him like a silvery halo, the mysteries and mystifications that enveloped him like the cigar smoke of a card sharp? Or was a more complicated dynamic at work? Could it be that in this inventor of a new bible, a new religion, a new city, and a new self, in this empire builder who was running for president of the United States, James Jesse Strang recognized, at long last, a way to realize his own dreams of royalty and power?

Many years later, an acquaintance would insist that the whole thing began as a simple real-estate swindle, set up by Strang and two other men—childhood friend Benjamin Perce and law partner Caleb Barnes. According to this witness, Barnes once confided that the initial intent of the scheme was to draw Mormon pilgrims to Burlington, thus drastically inflating local property prices and making the three men rich. "Their aim, in the first place," claimed the friend, "was to have Joseph Smith appoint a gathering place, or Stake, on their lands, but as Smith was killed about this time they changed their plans and concluded to make Strang Smith's successor."

Whether this version of events, recounted more than forty years after the fact, has any validity is one of the many mysteries surrounding Strang's conversion to the faith. What we know for certain is that on February 25, 1844, Strang went to the basement of Nauvoo's unfinished temple, where, in a wooden font resting on twelve wooden oxen, he was baptized by Joseph Smith. We know that a week later, on March 3, he was ordained as an elder of the church by Hyrum Smith, the prophet's older brother. We know that during Strang's visit, which ended in late March or early April, long-simmering antagonisms between city residents and their neighbors reached full boil, with anti-Mormon agitators demanding decisive action against what the *New York Sun* called "a great military despotism...growing up in the fertile West." We know that Nauvoo was also the scene of internal strife, thanks in part to the worst-kept secret in town—the practice of polygamy by Smith and other church leaders. We know that in June of 1844, Mormon dissidents published a paper called the *Nauvoo Expositor,* which accused the prophet of introducing "false and damnable doctrines into the Church." We know that after a single issue of this new journal, the Nauvoo City Council, at Smith's behest, ordered the printing press destroyed, precipitating an armed standoff between Smith and Illinois authorities. We know that on June 24, the prophet surrendered to officials in the nearby town of Carthage on charges of inciting a riot. We know that Smith informed bystanders that he expected to be murdered by anti-Mormon mobs—and that three days later his premonition came true. We know that he died without publicly naming a successor. And we know this, too: in July of 1844, James Jesse Strang started telling all those who would listen that the martyred prophet had secretly placed him in charge of the church. For anyone who doubted this sensational claim, Strang was prepared to offer physical evidence as proof.

—

Until that letter from Joseph Smith arrived at his door, Strang's life had been one long string of failures. But in a strange way, all those stumbles and missteps had prepared him for this pivotal moment, making possible everything that was to follow. Growing up in the Burned Over District's frenzied atmosphere had not only exposed the young atheist to the rhetorical powers and crowd-manipulation techniques of revivalist preachers; it had also imbued him with a millennial sensibility and opened him to a variety of nontraditional religious sects and self-made messiahs. Working as a frontier lawyer taught him how to navigate the legal system, how to argue persuasively, how to make even the most absurd case seem plausible. Editing a newspaper honed his already strong writing skills and granted him an insider's view of a communications revolution that was beginning to reshape American culture. And serving as a U.S. postmaster—well, that was perhaps the most useful training of all.

Modern researchers have identified the letter from "Joseph Smith" as a forgery. The main body of the text is written in print lettering rather than in cursive script—a style of penmanship so unusual for the prophet and his secretaries that no other examples are known to exist, according to one scholar. The signature, moreover, "bears no slightest resemblance to that of Joseph Smith," in the words of another expert. And the two sheets of paper used in the letter are from different kinds of stock.

But in some ways, the fraud is quite a clever one. Envelopes and postage stamps were not yet common in 1844, so letter writers often left one side of the outer sheet blank, then folded it in such a way that it could be used for the address and postmark. And in the case of "the letter of appointment," as Strang soon began calling it, the postmark, hand-stamped in red ink, appears to be authentic. This seems to indicate that someone did indeed send the cover sheet to Strang from Nauvoo on June 19, 1844, even if the inside sheet was a total fabrication. And who, after all, would know better how to pull off such a fraud than someone who had spent several years as a U.S. postmaster?

Strang was asking Joseph Smith's faithful followers to believe the all-but-impossible—that the prophet had handpicked a complete outsider, a neophyte unknown inside the church, as his successor. But in antebellum America, reality was porous. The seeming impossibility of a proposition did not always prevent its acceptance as truth. Indeed, in many ways Strang's ensuing career would parallel that of the famous showman Phineas T. Barnum, who in 1842 and 1843 drew thousands of customers to his American Museum in Manhattan to witness "the greatest curiosity in the world," the preserved corpse of a mermaid. In reality, this "fabulous creature" was an expertly crafted hoax, pieced together from the torso and head of a juvenile monkey and the tail of a fish. Barnum, of course, knew that the object was not genuine. But as he made clear in a conversation with a scientist he consulted before purchasing the mermaid, possibility—not authenticity—was his article of faith:

> I requested my naturalist's opinion of the *genuineness* of the animal. He replied that he could not conceive how it was manufactured; for he never knew a monkey with such peculiar teeth, arms, hands, etc., nor had he knowledge of a fish with such peculiar fins.
>
> "Then why do you suppose it is manufactured?" I inquired.
>
> "Because I don't believe in mermaids," replied the naturalist.
>
> "That is no reason at all," said I, "and therefore I'll believe in the mermaid."

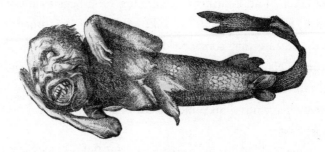

In the months to come, James J. Strang would ask thousands of Americans to believe in the possibility of an object no more authentic than Barnum's outlandish monstrosity. But something strange was happening to him now. He, too, was transforming into a new kind of creature, a stitched-together composite of the man he'd always been and the man he'd always dreamed of becoming. Other puzzling occurrences would soon follow.

Three

In which one shining city falls and another begins to rise from the prairie

In commercial affairs he was a bold speculator. In plainer words he had a most distinguished genius for swindling.

—Charles Dickens, on "an admirable man of business" in antebellum America

IN LATE SEPTEMBER OF 1845, A TALL, SLIM MAN WITH SAD EYES and a faraway look visited the new Mormon settlement in southern Wisconsin. His name was Christopher Latham Sholes, and he "possessed a remarkable inventive genius," according to one contemporary. Sholes would one day go down in history as the creator of the first practical typewriter and the QWERTY keyboard, still a standard feature of personal computers today. But for the time being, he was merely the editor of a small-town Wisconsin newspaper, the *Southport Telegraph*. The purpose of his journey was to meet another remarkable inventive genius, "the gentleman alluded to as Seer or Prophet," as Sholes called him.

It had been fourteen months since Strang received what he called the "letter of appointment," and his efforts to establish himself as Joseph Smith's successor had so far met mostly with frustration. After traveling 200 miles by foot to a Mormon conference in Florence, Michigan, for instance, the would-be messiah had received a decidedly cool reception. One elder grilled him on the plausibility of his tale, claiming later that he forced Strang, whom he described as a "false spirit," to concede that he "had no authority to act as a prophet." Another concluded that the letter "carried on its face the marks of a base forgery." Perhaps this humiliation had made Strang reluctant to take his case directly to Nauvoo, where anti-Mormon violence was on the rise and the Illinois legislature had stripped the city of its special legal protections. Instead of attempting to take advantage of this chaotic situation, Strang chose to stay away and bide his time.

By January of 1845, when the upstart prophet and a small band of followers held their first church service in Burlington, it was becoming clear not only that he faced long odds of success but also that the letter alone would not be enough to sway opinion in his favor. Strang did not abandon the cause, but during the bleak winter of 1844–45, he complained:

> I am delivered over to the buffetings of Satan, yet when I pray God answers. I lay hands on the sick and they recover. I can speak in new tongues.... Is it not rather strange if God gave such gifts to men who believe not in him and blaspheme his name continually.... If I'm not what I profess to be, I am of all men most wicked.

And now another remarkable event had transpired, one that was already causing "much talk" in southern Wisconsin, according to Sholes, the local newspaper editor who had come to Burlington on that fall day in 1845 to ascertain the truth about a story so incredible, so outlandish, that it was enough "to stagger ordinary credulity." Two weeks earlier, on September 13, Strang had gathered a group of his closest followers to report that "it had been revealed to him in a vision that an account of an ancient people was buried in a hill south of White River bridge." After leading the men up that rise to an oak tree, he instructed them to examine the ground carefully for signs of tampering. "The tree was surrounded by a sward of deeply rooted grass...and upon the most critical examination we could not discover any indication that it had ever been cut through or disturbed," according to the diggers' subsequent sworn testimony.

As James Strang stood aside, the men dug to a depth of about three feet, eventually setting aside their spades and hacking away at hard-packed clay with a pickax, until suddenly they struck something—a flat stone about one foot wide and three inches thick, which they pried from the soil. Underneath it, they discovered "a case of slightly baked clay containing three plates of brass," covered with various symbols, including a man with a crown on his head and a scepter in his hand, along with "what appear to be alphabetic characters, but in a language of which we have no knowledge." That language would also prove to be unknown to scholars. In fact, only one man in the world possessed the power to translate it. Luckily, he happened to be the same person who had seen the vision and brought the men to the hillside near the White River. Strang took the brass plates into his palms and headed back down the hill to begin deciphering the mysterious script.

In this effort he was assisted by a pair of seer stones called the Urim and Thummim, a combination of magical glasses and crystal balls, which he claimed an angel had loaned him specifically for the task. Thanks to these miraculous devices—just like the ones that had enabled Joseph Smith to translate the Book of Mormon—Strang finished the work in a mere five days. On September 18, 1845, he declared the plates to be the work of a certain Rajah Manchou of Vorito, who in some distant age had fallen in battle at the site where the plates were discovered. The word "rajah" normally refers to a king or prince from India, but Strang didn't venture to explain what an ancient royal from the subcontinent might have been doing in southern Wisconsin, or how his story connected to the larger Mormon epic. In fact, in the years to come he would never have much to say about the mysterious Rajah Manchou. What was important about this enigmatic figure from the past was the message he delivered to denizens of the nineteenth century.

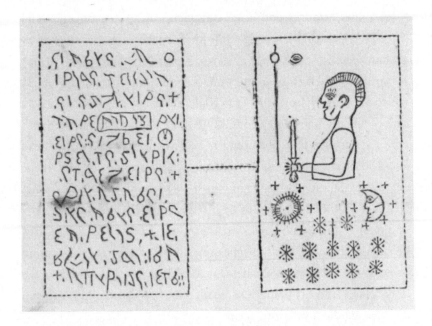

A contemporary broadside depicting the Rajah Manchou plates. (Church History Library, The Church of Jesus Christ of Latter-day Saints)

"My people are no more. The mighty are fallen, and the young slain in battle," lamented the rajah, who added that "the word of God came to me while I mourned." After informing the dying noble that "other strangers shall inhabit thy land," God told him to record and bury these words: "The forerunner men shall kill, but a mighty prophet there shall dwell. I will be his strength, and he shall bring forth thy record."

For Strang's small but devoted group of followers, the meaning of this prophecy was self-evident. Just as Joseph Smith had unearthed the "golden plates" that became the Book of Mormon, James Strang had now stumbled upon a second holy text, a sign from God about the true heir to the church. Could the "forerunner," after all, be anyone but Joseph Smith? And the "mighty prophet"? Well, wasn't this the final proof that it must be Strang?

For many longtime Mormons, however, the Rajah Manchou plates would seem as blatant a fraud as the angel that Strang claimed had visited him on the day of Smith's death or the letter in which Smith supposedly named Strang his successor. "Is it not surprisingly strange," wrote one church leader, "that Joseph Smith should appoint a man to succeed him in the presidency of the church some seven or ten days before his death, and yet not tell it to the High Council, nor any of the authorities of the church?"

The author of those words was Brigham Young, a rough-spoken former carpenter from the Burned Over District who had risen to the top of the Mormon hierarchy following Smith's murder. Although he lacked the charisma of some rivals and the family connections of others, the shrewd and ruthless Young had used his position as president of a crucial governing body, the Quorum of Twelve Apostles, to establish himself as the de facto head of the church. Anxious to protect his grip on power, he had quickly excommunicated Strang, whom he recognized from the start as a serious threat.

It was in fact the growing controversy over Strang (whom Young called a "wicked liar") and his revelations (which Young called "pretended") that had brought Sholes to Burlington on that day in late September of 1845. The editor found Strang to be "a very intelligent man, devoid of anything like enthusiasm; and, so far as we could judge, honest and earnest in all he said." But even after examining the plates with his own eyes and visiting "the spot from which they purport to have been taken," Sholes didn't know what to make of the prophet's improbable tale. "The popular opinion will doubtless call it a humbug," he conceded. "So should we from the natural impulse of our mind." Still, Sholes hesitated. After all, he explained, the men who supported Strang's version of events "are said to be among the most honest and intelligent in the neighborhood." For the moment, Sholes was reluctant to either believe or disbelieve.

"We are content," he wrote, "to have no opinion about it."

Sholes's story appears to have been the first newspaper coverage of a new Mormon colony near Burlington, which Strang called Voree, a word that supposedly meant *garden of peace*. But many more articles would soon follow. Within months, papers all over the country were publishing reports about the settlement and its previously unknown prophet.

Strang's sudden rise to national prominence came amid a communications revolution—one so sweeping that scholars sometimes compare it to the Information Age of the twenty-first century. Technological advances—notably, the use of steam engines to power printing presses—allowed publishers of big-city newspapers to drastically lower their costs, enabling them to reach mass audiences. But small-town papers were thriving too. In the 1830s, there were some 900 newspapers in the United States; in 1840, the U.S. census counted more than 1,600; by 1850, that number topped 2,500. This proliferation of media outlets, combined with the emergence of steam and rail transportation, meant that news now moved with remarkable speed across previously unimaginable distances to reach ceaselessly expanding readerships.

Strang would prove a genius at exploiting these changes. He shrewdly perceived, for instance, that before he could have a colony, he must have a newspaper. Although the *Voree Herald* attracted fewer than a dozen subscribers for its first edition, in January of 1846, the publication was not really aimed at a local audience. Strang understood that Americans were now interconnected.

Already the telegraph, invented just two years earlier, was beginning to transform the way information was gathered and disseminated. James Gordon Bennett, editor of the *New York Daily Herald*, predicted that the new technology would have a "prodigious" influence on the republic, instantaneously linking disparate regions and peoples. "The whole nation is impressed with the same idea at the same moment," Bennett wrote. "One feeling and one impulse are thus created, and maintained from the center of the land to its uttermost extremities."

But information and "impulse" flowed the other way as well. Strang was quick to recognize that in this new media landscape, he was just as well situated to reach a national audience from the "uttermost extremities" of America as he might be from a major city. And thanks to his experiences as a postmaster and newspaper editor in New York, he knew exactly how to game the system to get his own name in headlines.

In the nineteenth century, papers got most of the news stories that came from outside their immediate region through a network of "exchange papers"—what we might think of as a primitive forerunner of the internet. In the 1792 Post Office Act, Congress had stipulated that "every printer of newspapers may send one paper to each and every other printer of newspapers within the United States, free of postage." In the fifty years since the act had gone into effect, this system of exchanges had evolved into, if not exactly an information superhighway, a complex grid of news gathering and dissemination that moved, for the time, at a furious pace. In 1843, for example, each newspaper in the country received an average of 364 exchanges in a single month.

Editors of the era, like scouts for news, scoured exchange papers and reprinted stories from around the country for local audiences. Sometimes they would credit the journal from which an item originated, but often they would simply set the story in type without identifying its source, much less verifying its accuracy. At its best, this system provided "a vast national conversation through the frictionless transmission of voices from equal nodes in an unlimited network," according to one modern scholar. But like the decentralized world-wide web of a later era, it was also vulnerable to the spread of facts that weren't true, news that wasn't real. In April of 1846—a little more than half a year after Strang had deciphered the Rajah Man-chou plates—papers around the country began to publish versions of a dispatch from the distant frontier of Wisconsin: "The city of Voree, where the new Mormon prophet Strang has established his head quarters, is rapidly filling up. Its inhabitants already number ten thousand. It is represented to be a most beautiful place, and its water power is immense; sufficient to make it the first manufacturing place in the West."

One of the papers to receive a copy of this story was the *American Freeman* in Prairieville, Wisconsin, a town (soon to be renamed Waukesha) a scant twenty-five miles from Voree. Unlike their counterparts in other regions of the country, the editors there could see the piece was full of falsehoods. "The 'city of Voree,' for aught we know, might be 'rapidly filling up,'" they wrote, "but it is very certain that its present population does not reach more than the *fiftieth part* of ten thousand." Of those 200 people, moreover, most lived in "miserable tenements." And as for that "immense" water power? A gross exaggeration—or, in the nineteenth-century parlance of the *American Freeman,* "all gammon." The editors questioned the origin of the piece, which they had taken from an exchange paper. "Whence it originated does not appear," they wrote, then added, "Probably from the Prophet himself."

It's quite possible that they were right. As a former U.S. postmaster, Strang understood how the exchange system could be manipulated in the "manufacture of public opinion," as one prominent nineteenth-century newspaper editor put it. And as a former publisher, he knew just what local news would grab the attention of editors around the country—most notably, stories about bizarre occurrences on the frontier.

Like P. T. Barnum, Strang had discovered that there was no such thing as bad publicity, that once a story was reprinted enough times, it took on a life of its own—one which an astute manipulator of media could constantly find new ways to exploit. Not long after that exchange-paper article on Voree began to circulate, for example, Strang visited the offices of the *Milwaukee Sentinel*. The editors there found him to be "a shrewd, active, well-informed man" who was careful to urge caution about one of the more outrageous claims being made about his town. "He tells us that Voree is 'going ahead' rapidly, and daily receiving recruits from Nauvoo," the *Sentinel* reported, "but it is not yet the city of 'ten thousand inhabitants' which the Eastern papers represent it." Of course, the eastern papers might well have received that population estimate from the same judicious and reasonable man who was now calling it preposterous.

———

In time, mass media became Strang's blue smoke and mirrors. He was adept at using it to project the image of a seductively indistinct dreamland on the imaginations of would-be followers. Nonetheless, these attempts to conjure up a floating city in the clouds, no matter how sophisticated, might have failed if not for events in a real-life city on the Mississippi.

On September 30, 1845, the same day that C. Latham Sholes published that initial story on Voree, a man arrived in Nauvoo, nearly 300 miles distant, on a much different mission. Unlike the lanky Sholes, this visitor was only five feet four inches tall, but he would leave a huge footprint on history. Elected to Congress two years earlier as a representative from Illinois, Stephen A. Douglas was already known as the "Little Giant" for his oversize political skills and soaring oratorical powers. In the near future, he would gain national celebrity as the fierce political rival of fellow Illinoisan Abraham Lincoln. But today he was matching wits with another shrewd politician, the Mormon leader Brigham Young.

During the previous few weeks, long-standing tensions between Nauvoo residents and their non-Mormon neighbors, on the rise since the murder of Joseph Smith a year earlier, had erupted into outright war, with more than 200 Mormon buildings torched and many people killed on both sides in various raids and reprisals. With little hope for a peaceful solution, Illinois governor Thomas Ford had appointed Douglas to head a delegation to travel to Nauvoo with the express goal of persuading the Mormons to leave the state. To provide Douglas and his colleagues with some leverage, the governor had sent them on their way with an armed militia of more than 300 men.

The official reason those troops were entering the city was to search for the bodies of two men allegedly killed by Mormons. The actual reason was to allow Douglas and his delegation a chance to negotiate directly with Brigham Young about a brokered peace, in which local vigilantes would cease their violence in return for the Mormons' leaving Nauvoo by springtime. After Douglas assured Young that the federal government would have no objection if the Mormons were to settle in the Far West, the two sides came to an agreement. As Young wrote in his diary that night: "It was decided that all the council [of church leaders] were to go west with their families, friends and neighbors." City residents began making plans for the monumental task of emptying out one of the largest cities in Illinois in a few short months.

And so it happened that just as Young and his followers were abandoning Nauvoo, Strang and his disciples were busy establishing what one newspaper described as "the El Dorado of their hopes."

Strang's "garden of peace" began to take root in an age when America was teeming with utopian experiments. "We are a little wild here with numberless projects of social reform," the essayist Ralph Waldo Emerson had joked to a Scottish friend in 1840. "Not a reading man but has a draft of a new Community in his waistcoat pocket." Just 100 miles to the north of Voree, for example, was a colony called Ceresco—one of twenty-three loosely affiliated social-ist communes scattered throughout the United States, all of them inspired by the French utopian philosopher Charles Fourier. "Our ulterior aim," wrote a member of one such commune in 1844, "is nothing less than Heaven on Earth, the conversion of this globe, now exhaling pestilential vapors and possessed by unnatural climates, into the abode of beauty and health."

If such dreams strike modern readers as quaintly idealistic, they nonetheless had a strong hold on the antebellum mind. As historian Daniel Walker Howe puts it:

> We would err to dismiss these aspirations as a trivial, lunatic fringe. In a time of rapidly changing means of communication and systems of production, when everything from race relations to banking practices came under challenge, there was no sharp distinction between the mainstream and the marginal.

In the midst of this concussive period of change, Strang offered his followers—many of whom were losers in mid-nineteenth-century America's economic, demographic, and social convulsions—a sense of belonging and purpose, a belief that they alone could purify an unclean world and that he alone could show them how. He furnished them with simple solutions to their problems, scapegoats for their miseries—assuring them, for instance, that the collapse of Nauvoo was due to the "mal-administration of the corrupt usurpers who have recently exercised authority there." Theirs, he insisted, was a righteous victimization. It was "hardly possible at this time," he maintained, "to serve God faithfully until one has become thoroughly reconciled to live and die hated." Yet he promised his followers that they would one day rule the world.

He provided two other crucial enticements as well. The first was a safe haven. As the departure of the anxious citizens of Nauvoo drew nigh, he addressed them directly in the *Voree Herald*: "Many of you are about to leave the haunts of civilization & of men to go into an unexplored wilderness among savages, and in trackless deserts to seek a home in the wilds where the foot print of the white man is not found. The voice of God has not called you to this." That must have struck a nerve among the more than 10,000 residents of Nauvoo whom Brigham Young had ordered to prepare to leave the city. Many of them were indeed worried that, as Strang described it, they would have to concern themselves with "saving their daughters from Indian prostitution and their sons from the tomahawk." Not even Young knew where they would wind up, having made only vague plans to settle near the Great Salt Lake, a landform only recently mapped—incorrectly, as it happened.

Strang's second inducement had less to do with fear than with faith: he offered church members a figurehead. The *Voree Herald*'s pronouncement that "the voice of God" had not called residents of Nauvoo to go west reminded readers that he, James Strang, was the only one who could hear that voice. When Brigham Young had taken control of the Nauvoo church, he had told the faithful they were now without a prophet, perhaps not wanting to be seen as supplanting Smith, even after his death. But Strang knew that a prophet was exactly what the people wanted—that they had joined the church precisely because they believed its founder spoke to God. The very last item of the very first edition of the *Voree Herald* was the lyric to a familiar Mormon hymn:

A church without a Prophet, is not the church for me,
It has no head to lead it, in it I would not be.

In response to such provocations, Young issued a letter in late January of 1846, warning that Strang's claim to be the true heir to the church was "a lie—a forgery—a snare.... Flee from it, and save yourselves from the snare of deception and the Devil." But as things turned out, it was Young himself who soon had to flee. Recently indicted by a federal grand jury in Illinois on counterfeiting charges, and fearing not only his own arrest but also more mob action against his people, he decided to abandon Nauvoo earlier than expected. On February 2, 1846, Young acknowledged to fellow Mormons in the city that the utopian experiment there was over, declaring it "imperatively necessary" to head west as soon as possible. "If we are here many days," he said, "our way will be hedged up. Our enemies have resolved to intercept us."

Soon the exodus of the Latter-day Saints from Nauvoo was in full swing, with thousands crossing the Mississippi in the dead of winter. On February 15, Brigham Young himself departed, joining other evacuees at a temporary encampment in Iowa. Three weeks later, a resident who remained in Nauvoo noted that "many are turning away from the Church...to follow a new prophet that has risen up," while another member of the faith from nearby Knoxville, Illinois, agreed that many Mormons were "filled with the notion that J. Strang is the man to lead the Church," a situation that was bound, he believed, to "cause the greatest split that ever has been made." Strang had still not set foot in Nauvoo since the death of Joseph Smith, yet many residents of that doomed city had somehow come to view him as their savior.

———

In addition to his cunning use of the printed word, Strang had "an earnest, energetic manner" in the pulpit, showed "considerable talent [and] great shrewdness," and was "very persevering in his efforts to convince others of the truth," according to a journalist who saw him deliver a sermon around this time. These powers of persuasion were on full display at an event where Strang matched wits with one of Brigham Young's closest allies. Shortly before leaving Nauvoo, Young had dispatched a man named Reuben Miller to northern Illinois to organize local Mormons for the journey west. In the town of St. Charles, Miller crossed paths with Strang, there to recruit converts to his own cause. The two men agreed to a debate.

Strang spoke first, exhorting onlookers for four straight hours "in his rapid manner," according to a later account. When it came time for the rebuttal, however, something unexpected happened. Instead of going on the offensive, a dazzled Miller praised Strang's knowledge of Mormon doctrine, then conceded that he "was not able to contend against the force" of his opponent's arguments. Strang returned to Voree with a list of 300 new recruits, while Miller went back to Nauvoo "considerably bewildered by Strang's new fangled revelation," in the words of a frustrated Young, who found Miller to be "almost devoid of reason" in the aftermath of his encounter with Strang.

But what, exactly, was this upstart prophet's allure? How could someone without any of the traditional trappings of power or influence—money, formal education, family connections, stature within the elite strata of society—have attracted such feverish followers? Historians point to the economic, cultural, and demographic upheavals of the antebellum era. As Karen Halttunen observes in

Confidence Men and Painted Women: A Study of Middle-Class Culture in America, 1830–1870:

> The clear authority exercised within the hierarchical social institutions of seventeenth- and eighteenth-century America was giving way to the more tenuous authority possible within the egalitarian social organizations of the nineteenth century. In the emerging social system, authority could be seized by any charismatic figure who emerged from the masses as a man of magnetic personal power.... These men held the fascinated attention of the American people because, in the absence of a clearly defined, hierarchical authority structure, they used the power of charisma to bend others to their will.

To many people of Strang's time, however, this "power of charisma" was not the result of remote historical factors but of something more immediate and mysterious. In the late eighteenth century, German physician Franz Anton Mesmer had postulated that human beings are susceptible to unseen gravitational forces, just like those that steer the sun, moon, and planets. According to Mesmer, an invisible "fluid" permeates the nervous system, surging through and among people. Proponents of mesmerism believed that by learning how to harness this force—known as "animal magnetism"—a person could exert control over other human beings.

The theory, which began to take hold of the American imagination in the 1820s, had by the mid-1840s reached the "meridian of its glory," in the words of one journal. Audiences turned out by the thousands to hear lecturers describe animal magnetism and demonstrate its powers by putting people into trance states. If such ideas seem laughable to us now, scholars note that by drawing attention to the inner workings of the mind, mesmerism helped lay the groundwork for the formal scientific study of psychology in the late nineteenth century.

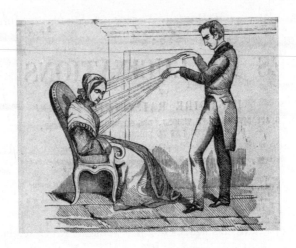

But in the mid-1840s, with Sigmund Freud's birth still a decade away, the deepest explorations of the human psyche were undertaken not by phrenologists or mesmerists but by poets, who took it upon themselves to help people navigate "the path between reality and their souls," as up-and-coming writer Walt Whitman put it. In his visionary masterpiece, *Leaves of Grass,* Whitman would soon take readers down that path for a disturbing glimpse at the era's fascination with charismatic figures:

Are you the new person drawn toward me?
To begin with, take warning, I am surely far different from
 what you suppose;
Do you suppose you will find in me your ideal? . . .
Do you think I am trusty and faithful?
Do you see no further than this façade, this smooth and tolerant
 manner of me?
Do you suppose yourself advancing on real ground toward a
 real heroic man?
Have you no thought, O dreamer, that it may be all maya,
 illusion?

More than forty years after the discovery of the Rajah Manchou plates, one of Strang's former confederates would claim that the relics had been part of an elaborate fraud perpetrated by the would-be prophet and two collaborators—his old friend Benjamin Perce and his law partner in Wisconsin, Caleb Barnes. According to this witness, Barnes once confided that the plates had been made out of an old brass kettle, which the men engraved with a file saw, then treated with acid to give them an "ancient appearance." After that, they used an auger to bore a long, slanting hole in the hillside, after which they carefully placed the plates beneath the earth and tamped down the surrounding soil, "leaving no trace of their work visible," according to the man's account. The motivation for this ornate hoax, he said, was simple: selling property owned by Strang and his associates in Burlington to unsuspecting Mormons.

Such rumors had hung over the prophet since the earliest days of his colony in Wisconsin. By May of 1846—just eight months after the discovery of the Rajah Manchou plates—he had already managed to make a group of enemies in Voree, some from the local community and others from inside the church. These detractors alleged that he was the "owner of a large tract of land" and that his real goal for establishing the church was to get rich on speculation—a charge the *Voree Herald* angrily denied. Strang, the paper declared, "owns two acres and a half of unbroken prairie, in the outskirts of Voree...and BESIDES THIS HE DOES NOT OWN A FOOT OF LAND ON THE FACE OF THE BROAD EARTH." The paper did not mention the prophet's long and checkered career as a real-estate speculator. Nor did it bring up the allegations that he had once swindled an unsuspecting rube by selling him a fictional farm in Ohio, or make clear that much of the land in Voree happened to belong to his best friend and fellow speculator, Benjamin Perce.

During a tour of the United States a few years earlier, the celebrated British novelist Charles Dickens had visited a similar frontier outpost—the town of Cairo, Illinois, at the confluence of the Mississippi and Ohio rivers. Like Voree, Cairo was marketed to outsiders as "a mine of Golden Hope," as Dickens put it in *American Notes and Pictures from Italy*. Many of his fellow countrymen had speculated from England on plots of land, sight unseen, "on the faith of monstrous representations." But when Dickens visited Cairo, in 1842, he found nothing but "a dismal swamp, on which the half-built houses rot away: cleared here and there for the space of a few yards; and teeming, then, with rank unwholesome vegetation, in whose baleful shade the wretched wanderers who are tempted hither, droop, and die."

Although investments in the town led "to many people's ruin," Dickens was surprised to discover that those responsible for the scheme, instead of being condemned by the public, received only praise. He attributed this fact to a strange American "love of 'smart' dealing: which gilds over many a swindle and gross breach of trust...and enables many a knave to hold his head up with the best." As Dickens explained:

> The merits of a broken speculation, or a bankruptcy, or of a successful scoundrel, are not gauged by its or his observance of the golden rule, "Do as you would be done by," but are considered with reference to their smartness. I recollect, on both occasions of our passing that ill-fated Cairo on the Mississippi, remarking on the bad effects such gross deceits must have when they exploded, in generating a want of confidence abroad, and discouraging foreign investment: but I was given to understand that this was a very smart scheme by which a deal of money had been made: and that its smartest feature was, that they forgot these things abroad, in a very short time, and speculated again, as freely as ever. The following dialogue I have held a hundred

times: "Is it not a very disgraceful circumstance that such a man as So-and-so should be acquiring a large property by the most infamous and odious means, and notwithstanding all the crimes of which he has been guilty, should be tolerated and abetted by your Citizens? He is a public nuisance, is he not?" "Yes, sir." "A convicted liar?" "Yes, sir." "He has been kicked, and cuffed, and caned?" "Yes, sir." "And he is utterly dishonourable, debased, and profligate?" "Yes, sir." "In the name of wonder, then, what is his merit?" "Well, sir, he is a smart man."

No doubt this same love of scoundrels accounted for some of Strang's appeal. In the anxious climate of antebellum America, where a sense of powerlessness ran as rampant as typhoid fever, people were drawn to those who succeeded at writing their own rules, inventing their own truths. And by the fall of 1846—just a year after he and a few cronies had plucked those mysterious brass plates from a lonely hillside—the prophet could claim approximately 500 followers in Voree. Never mind that the place still looked, even in Strang's own estimation, "like an encampment rather than a town." In the colony's newspaper, he wrote that inhabitants of this ramshackle community "dwell in plain houses; in board shanties, in tents, and sometimes many of them in the open air." Nonetheless, he added, "The place is more prosperous than could have been expected in the present impoverished state of the church. All who come here find plenty of employment at good wages and a bountiful supply of all the necessities of life at low prices." Strang went so far as to trumpet Voree as "undoubtedly the best location ever occupied by the saints," a claim that just months earlier would have struck even the most sympathetic reader as absurd.

But that same month the once-thriving city of Nauvoo finally collapsed, as the remaining Mormons surrendered unconditionally to a mob of vigilantes. Those fleeing, according to newspaper reports, were "in destitute condition," many of them having "embarked on steamboats going up the river, probably with the view of attaching themselves to the church at Voree." New converts were also beginning to arrive from other parts of the country, thanks to the tireless recruiting efforts of Strang and other emissaries of the sect. With only a handful of followers one year earlier, the prophet could, by the fall of 1846, confidently boast that Voree was "destined to make a flourishing town."

But Strang had never aspired to rule over a mere town, flourishing or otherwise. Already he was making plans to lay claim to a kingdom all his own.

Four

In which a kingdom is born

—————⸺◉⸺—————

Methinks an island would be the most desirable of all landed property, for it seems like a little world by itself.
——Nathaniel Hawthorne, *The American Notebooks*

DUE TO THE GEOGRAPHY OF THE GREAT LAKES, THE STEAMBOAT that brought Strang back to Wisconsin in the fall of 1846 had to take a circuitous route. After a westward journey on Lake Erie from Buffalo to Detroit, the vessel veered north for hundreds of miles to the Straits of Mackinac, a narrow waterway that connects Lake Huron to Lake Michigan. It was there, after navigating those straits and starting the journey south, that the steamer cruised past a remote spot that would alter the course of J. J. Strang's life and career.

That place was Beaver Island, an isolated landmass in the northern-most waters of Lake Michigan. Thirteen miles long and six miles wide, it had long been populated by the Odawa and Ojibwe (also known as the Ottawa and Chippewa), culturally and linguistically related Native American groups who referred to themselves as Anishinaabeg, or "original people." Over the previous two decades, the federal government had made life increasingly difficult for the Anishinaabeg. In 1830, Congress passed the Indian Removal Act, which gave U.S. presidents power to negotiate the ouster of Native Americans living east of the Mississippi in exchange for lands to the west. After coming to the conclusion that their people would soon be forced out anyway, Odawa and Ojibwe representatives signed a treaty in 1836 that ceded Beaver Island, along with another thirteen million acres of land in northern Michigan, to the United States. The agreement allowed Native Americans to remain on the island only until 1841, but when Strang's steamboat arrived five years after that, a small community of them still lived there. A handful of white pioneers, meanwhile, had established fishing and trading posts, and the government had begun surveying the island for future settlement.

According to one account, the prophet's first glimpse of the island came when his steamer was forced to take refuge in its deep natural harbor during a storm. "When my eyes first rested on Beaver Island, I thought it the most beautiful place on earth," Strang was quoted as saying. In this version of events, the prophet was then hit by a sudden jolt of inspiration: "This is where I will come to build up my kingdom."

The first part of that story may be true: Beaver Island was indeed beautiful. The largest island in Lake Michigan, it was thickly wooded, a lush burst of green above the glimmering water. But the second part—that Strang's decision to move there came in a flash—was almost certainly false. Even before leaving on this trip two months earlier—a major recruiting and fund-raising effort, in which he made "alarming progress toward capturing the Mormon strongholds from Illinois to the Atlantic," according to a later historian—he had probably discussed the island with associates. By the time Strang saw it from that steamboat, in fact, one of his aides had already written to the commissioner of the General Land Office in Washington, D.C., about the possibility of purchasing the distant landform, part of an archipelago in northernmost Lake Michigan known collectively as the Beaver Islands. Soon, that same aide was reportedly telling his friends not to waste their money on land in Voree.

—

Islands held a special place in the collective imagination of mid-nineteenth-century Americans. Readers of the period had an insatiable appetite for maritime adventure stories, such as *Two Years Before the Mast,* Richard Henry Dana Jr.'s popular 1840 account of his time as a common seaman, which inspired a few dozen books with similar titles. Such volumes often romanticized islands as primitive Arcadias, untouched by the corruptions of the industrial revolution and unbound by the rigid sexual strictures and codes of self-restraint endlessly elucidated in etiquette books, another wildly popular antebellum literary genre.

In 1846 and early 1847, as more followers arrived in Voree and Strang began making plans for his kingdom on Lake Michigan, two new books about islands were attracting a wide readership in the United States. One of them was by a previously obscure British naturalist named Charles Darwin, whose account of his five-year, round-the-world voyage aboard the H.M.S. *Beagle* was out in a first American edition. Although full of the scientific data Darwin would one day use to support his theory of evolution, the text was also a riveting adventure yarn that only added to the mystique of exotic islands. "I do not doubt," Darwin wrote, "that every traveler must remember the glowing sense of happiness which he experienced when he first breathed in a foreign clime, where the civilized man had seldom or never trod."

The other book was a debut novel by a twenty-six-year-old adventurer named Herman Melville. A fictionalized account of Melville's own travels in the South Seas, *Typee* tells the story of a young man who has become weary of the "evils" of civilization: "the heart-burnings, the jealousies, the social rivalries, the family dissentions, and the thousand self-inflicted discomforts of refined life." He joins the crew of a whaling ship, but by the time it reaches the Marquesas Islands in Polynesia, after fifteen months at sea, he has grown disillusioned with the hardships of the work and the company of his fellow crew members; sick of being surrounded by "dastardly and mean-spirited wretches," he resolves to flee to the nearest island shore. "Having made up my mind," he recalls of that pivotal moment, "I proceeded to acquire all the information I could obtain relating to the island and its inhabitants, with a view of shaping my plans of escape."

That passage sums up what must have been going through Strang's mind as he leaned over the rail of a steamboat on his return to Wisconsin. Back in Voree, he had been feeling more and more trapped, foiled at every turn by his own version of dastardly and mean-spirited wretches. Notwithstanding Strang's unearthing and translating of the Rajah Manchou plates the year before, a growing number of residents were starting to question his bona fides as a man of God, and now that the shepherd had been apart from his flock for the first extended period, some of its leading members had begun to stray.

One of the defectors was Reuben Miller—the prominent Mormon leader who just a year earlier had become so beguiled by Strang that it seemed to Brigham Young as if he had lost all reason. After breaking with Young, Miller had published a widely circulated pamphlet that rallied support for the new prophet within Nauvoo and in other Mormon communities. He then purchased a small farm near Voree and was named by Strang to a leadership position in the church. Over time, however, Miller had begun to second-guess Strang's claim on authority.

What caused him to lose faith was the story Strang frequently told about how an angel had visited him upon Joseph Smith's death. Miller couldn't help noticing that the details of this account had shifted over time, as Strang adapted it to various audiences. For many observers, such embellishments might have seemed minor, especially when compared with some of Strang's even more implausible yarns, but Miller was a rigid categorical thinker whose worldview allowed no middle ground. For him, the conflicting stories constituted a spiritual calamity. "I came to the conclusion, irresistibly, that I had embraced an error, a delusion," he declared. Far from seeing Strang as a messiah, Miller now believed the prophet and his church would go "down on the pages of history, as a monument...of the corruption and wickedness of the human heart." So fervent was his opprobrium that he would eventually organize local opposition to the prophet.

It was becoming obvious to Strang, in short, that the flatlands of southern Wisconsin—too easy for supporters to depart, too easy for enemies to stay—were not the ideal locale for the kind of colony he had in mind. If he was going to maintain control over his followers, he would need to get them out of town and lead them to a new promised land.

"The whole landscape seemed one unbroken solitude...and as we advanced through this wilderness, our voices sounded strangely in our ears, as though human accents had never before disturbed the fearful silence," the narrator of *Typee* recalls about arriving on the island with a fellow deserter from the ship. As the scholar Andrew Delbanco has observed, the escape into that unbroken solitude, that fearful silence, "was Melville's version of [the] American dream—not the dream of raising one's status in the world as it is, but the dream of starting over, getting out from under, and putting it all away to discover life anew." And now it was the prophet's dream as well.

———

The mastermind of plans for a kingdom on Beaver Island was Strang's second-in-command, "the greatest scamp in the western country," in the words of Illinois governor Thomas Ford, the same governor who had dispatched Stephen Douglas to rid Illinois of Brigham Young and the other Mormons of Nauvoo. Even in an age of what one newspaper called "bare-faced impudent corruption and public plunder," John C. Bennett stood out as an unprincipled schemer, a Machiavelli of the frontier.

Bennett began his career as a physician, having granted himself the titles *M.D.* and *LL.D.*—the first self-fabrication in an entire career built on "gilded hopes and fairy dreams," as one critic put it. In the 1830s, despite having never received a formal degree in medicine, Bennett launched a crusade to champion the health benefits of the tomato, countering the widespread belief that the fruit was poisonous. Although a number of his claims—including that the tomato could prevent cholera—"savor[ed] of the most arrant quackery," in the words of one publication, his efforts helped to popularize the plant in the United States.

When not promoting tomatoes or practicing medicine, Bennett worked as an itinerant Methodist preacher. He also created what is sometimes considered the country's first "diploma mill"—an Indiana college that sold degrees in medicine, law, and other disciplines to "students" who never received training or took exams. And despite his complete lack of military training, he managed to get himself named brigadier general of the Invincible Dragoons, a unit of the Illinois Militia. Officers in the state militia also elected him quartermaster general, making him responsible for arms and munitions across Illinois.

In 1840 Bennett converted to Mormonism and moved to Nauvoo, telling Joseph Smith he had decided to devote his "time and energies to the advancement of the cause of truth and virtue, and the advocacy of the holy religion which you have so nobly defended and honorably sustained." He quickly rose through the leadership ranks, with Smith appointing him to the church's highest governing body and awarding him the prominent positions of mayor of Nauvoo, chancellor of the University of Nauvoo, and general of the Nauvoo Legion, a Mormon militia of 2,000 men. By 1842, he was "the Prophet's great gun," according to a *New York Herald* article, which Bennett may have written himself.

The only known likeness of this remarkable man, who sometimes signed his name "J. C. Bennett, Prince," comes from his heyday in Nauvoo. It shows him in an ornately embroidered military uniform with a high collar, elaborate braid fastenings, and oversize epaulets. His Roman nose, delicate mouth, and somber sideward glance are reminiscent of portraits of Napoleon Bonaparte, as is the placement of his right hand inside his jacket—the trademark gesture of the famous French general nicknamed the Man of Destiny. When Bennett posed for this portrait, he clearly saw himself as just such an individual.

Those glory days were short-lived, however. In the summer of 1842, Bennett was forced to flee Nauvoo amid a sexual scandal. Already married to someone in Ohio, he was alleged to have had sex with several local women after assuring each one that such intimacy was sanctioned by the church under what Bennett described as the "spiritual wife doctrine," a term he seems to have introduced to Nauvoo. He was not, of course, the only man in town to engage in such behavior. Smith and other church leaders had been quietly practicing polygamy since at least the year before. By the time of Smith's death, in fact, the prophet would have as many as forty wives, one of them only fourteen years old. Nonetheless, Smith was determined to keep the practice secret. And with the conspicuousness of Bennett's reckless and predatory behavior, he had simply become too much of a threat.

After his ouster from the church in 1842, Bennett fought back that same year with a tell-all book, *The History of the Saints; or, An Exposé of Joe Smith and Mormonism,* which charged that leading members of the church were "guilty of infidelity, deism, atheism; lying, deception, blasphemy; debauchery, lasciviousness, bestiality; madness, fraud, plunder; larceny, burglary, robbery, perjury; fornication, adultery, rape, incest; arson, treason, and murder." Scorned by literary critics, who variously described it as "a heap of monstrosities" and "too stupid...ever to be read by anybody," the book managed to stoke anti-Mormon passions around the country and earn Bennett the lasting hatred of many members of the faith. One church leader compared him to Judas.

By 1845, the year Strang would unearth and translate the plates in Wisconsin, Bennett was in Cincinnati, having accepted an appointment as a lecturer at a medical school, the Literary and Botanico-Medical College of Ohio. This quaintly named institution had recently come under attack in the *Boston Medical and Surgical Journal,* which claimed that it left students ill prepared to practice medicine and preyed on "western dolts, who are duped out of [their] precious time...duped out of their money, and made a laughing stock of the community." Some local physicians were likewise scandalized by the presence of Bennett, whom the *Western Medical Reformer* referred to as "that notorious personage," reminding its readers he had once sold bogus diplomas "to every ignoramus who could raise ten dollars to buy one." He managed to keep his job despite these attacks, but his time in the city offered little peace of mind. "I have not been myself," he conceded in a letter, "for my spirits have been depressed and gloomy."

Bennett was a man of intense cravings—for attention, for money, for status, and for sex. The only place he'd ever been able to meet those needs was Nauvoo, where, by his own estimation, he had "possessed power, wealth and the means to gratify every passion or desire." Ever since falling out with Joseph Smith, he'd felt oppressed by daily life, but news of Strang's "glorious movement" had made Bennett feel "like a young lion let loose." The forty-one-year-old wrote Strang with a proposition: the two men, he proclaimed, should combine their talents and invent a kingdom together. While Strang assumed the position of "Crowned Imperial Primate," Bennett proposed to be his "General-in-Chief."

An independent kingdom on American soil—perhaps even to Strang it seemed initially a lunatic scheme. But hadn't he always hoped to accomplish "one great thing," as he'd long ago vowed in his diary? Hadn't he written in that same book about "dreams of empire"? Thanks to his new partnership with John C. Bennett, this grand course of action was open to him at last.

If there was one unchanging thing about the chameleonic Strang, it was the reports of his physical appearance. "In person, Strang is rather below the ordinary size [and] very plainly dressed [with a] red face, bold *prominent* forehead, large eyes and mouth, and cheek bones," one newspaper correspondent observed in 1846. "In fact, I may as easily describe him by saying he is a diminutive, ill-favored, insignificant-looking man." But as he paced the deck of that steamboat and peered out at Beaver Island, eye level with other men's shoulders, Strang possessed a secret knowledge that made him a giant.

Unbeknownst to anyone but a few confederates, he already reigned as Sovereign Lord and King on Earth.

At a series of candlelit ceremonies in Voree over the summer of 1846, before Strang started on his trip, his closest followers had gathered in private to join a clandestine organization known as the Order of the Illuminati. They learned the secret handshake (three fingers within three fingers), the secret sign (three fingers of the right hand to the mouth), and the secret passwords they would need to identify one another. They received noble titles: *viceroy, lord, duke, earl, chevalier, marshal, marquis, cardinal, illuminatus.* They swore an oath "ever to conceal, and never to reveal, any of the ceremonies, secrets and misteries" revealed to them. At the climax of these induction rites, the men promised their absolute obedience to Strang, not only as "the Prophet of God, Apostle of the Lord Jesus, and Chief Pastor of the Flock" but also as "the Imperial primate and actual Sovereign Lord and King on Earth." Then they entered their signatures in a record book, an act that some of them would later claim was done with their own blood.

As Bennett's correspondence makes clear, the Order of the Illuminati was his idea. He borrowed the group's ornate rites, as well as its solemn pledges to secrecy and obedience, from Freemasonry, the centuries-old fraternal organization with which Bennett had been affiliated for much of his adult life. In 1841 he had played an important role in founding a Masonic Lodge in Nauvoo and—more significantly—in introducing Joseph Smith to the organization, which the prophet soon embraced with a passion, incorporating Masonic symbols and practices into the most sacred of Mormon rituals. Although Bennett was eventually ousted from the Nauvoo Lodge for seduction, adultery, lying, perjury, embezzlement, and "illicit intercourse with a Master Mason's wife," he knew better than anyone how Masonic initiation ceremonies might be adapted to create cohesion, isolate members from outside influences, inhibit independent thinking, and cultivate dependence on authority. According to those with inside knowledge of the Order of the Illuminati, each individual member vowed to treat Strang's dictates as "the supreme Law, above and superseding all laws, obligations and mandates of any other person, authority or power whatsoever." Nonetheless, a significant number of Strang's followers refused to join this new order, claiming not only that its practices were contrary to their religious beliefs, but also that the group was nothing less than a secret government, whose members had placed the word of Strang above local laws and the Constitution of the United States.

The fiercest criticism was aimed at Bennett himself. During his three short months in town, the self-proclaimed Pontiff Premier and General-in-Chief had managed to stir up a remarkable amount of resentment. Enemies claimed he had cajoled people into joining the Order of the Illuminati by "picking out his victims—those whom he could gull the easiest." As chief architect of the group, they argued, Bennett had subjected Strang's followers to "abject slavery, binding us by horrid oaths to obey all edicts, mandates and commands of the absolute sovereign and pontiff, leaving us no alternative but to become dupes and accomplices of wicked men and oppression."

But that wasn't all. In an apparent repeat of his misdeeds in Nauvoo, Bennett was accused of having illicit sex with a fifteen-year-old girl. For the dissenters, this was the breaking point. On October 4, 1846, while Strang was on the last leg of his return trip, dissident leaders called a meeting, at which they charged Bennett with "teaching false doctrine," including "polygamy and concubinage, and attempting to carry them into practice." Having "unanimously agreed that the charges against him were sufficiently sustained," they promptly took it upon themselves to excommunicate Bennett.

But the controversial physician, certain that Strang would come to his rescue, did not give up power, much less leave town. Perhaps, however, he should not have been quite so confident. For the prophet, who arrived back in town eight days later, Bennett's continued philandering posed a huge political risk. From the very start, Strang had been trumpeting himself as the anti-polygamy alternative to Brigham Young, telling anyone who would listen that he opposed "spiritual wifery." By offering a purer vision of Mormonism, unstained by the doctrine of plural marriage, the upstart prophet hoped to show the public he was a moderate reformer, while at the same time convincing disaffected members of the faith that he would return the church to its true path. Strang even issued a curse against those who preached the "damning, soul-destroying doctrines" that "polygamy, fornication and adultery are required by the command of God," and left no doubt as to the fate he believed should befall them:

> May their bones rot in the living tomb of their flesh: may their flesh generate from its own corruption a loathsome life for others: may the blood swarm with a leprous life of motelike ghastly corruption, feeding upon flowing life, generating chilling agues burning fevers & loathsome living corruption. May peace and home be names forgotten to them; & the beauty they have betrayed to infamy, may it be to their eyes a crawling mass of putridity & battering corruption, a loathsome ghastliness, its delicate hues a sickly light that glares from universal corruption; its auburn tresses the posthumous growth of temples crawling with worms, its fragrant breath the blast of perdition.

In the end, however, Bennett's faith in his own impunity proved correct. Strang spared his lieutenant from the rotting bones, chilling agues, burning fevers, and crawling worms. Calling the excommunication an illegitimate attempt to "destroy a man of distinguished talent and faithfulness," he overruled the edict. Bennett, it seems, was simply too important to the prophet's plans for his future.

———

Strang arrived in Voree with a story about a strange vision. During his trip to the East, he said, he was visiting a town on the Monongahela

River south of Pittsburgh when suddenly, via second sight, he was transported to an entirely different landscape:

> And lo, I beheld a land amidst wide waters, and covered with large timber, with a deep broad bay on one side of it. And I wandered over it upon little hills and among rich valleys, where the air was pure and serene, and the unfading foliage, with its fragrant shades, attracted me till I wandered to bright clear waters, scarcely ruffled by the breeze. And Indians in canoes glided about, and caught fish, and sat down to eat; and they gathered in assemblies, and were taught words of truth and ways of holiness, and they hearkened. And I beheld many wonders there.

Baffled by the sight of this lush and mysterious island, Strang stopped one of the Native Americans along the river to ask, "What meaneth all this?" The man, apparently conversant in the seventeenth-century English that people seemed to speak in Strang's visions, replied, "Thou art carried away in the spirit, and brought to this land in the midst of waters, in the north country, that the Lord might show thee what he will do hereafter." The Indian then prophesied that before Strang returned to Voree, he would see with his own eyes the future home of his kingdom, a place of "abundance in the riches of the forest, and in the riches of the earth, and in the riches of the waters; and there shall the children of God learn his law."

Around the time that Strang publicly described this apparition, the *Voree Herald* announced plans to "establish a mission among the Indians." This "small settlement" would allow the prophet's followers to "devote themselves to the improvement and salvation of their less favored fellow creatures." Moreover, "*the place for such a work has already been pointed out by the finger of God,* and measures for its occupation are now far advanced.... The situation is a most delightful one, in the immediate proximity to vast numbers of Indians, and secure from molestation of any kind."

Proximity to Indians was important to Strang's followers, because the Book of Mormon foretold that Native Americans would have a central part in the preparation for Christ's millennial reign and the establishment of a New Jerusalem, playing "a significant role in building that new city and its temples," according to one historian of the church. Whether Strang believed such prophesies is uncertain: what's clear is that the supposedly noble idea of an Indian mission on Beaver Island was, from the beginning, little more than a ruse. Not only were Strang and Bennett proposing to establish this beneficent undertaking on a piece of land that no longer belonged to Native Americans, but all their plans hinged on this very fact. Responding to Bennett's repeated inquiries, for example, a federal official had offered written assurances that "in the absence of authorized occupation of the island by the Indians," the place was up for grabs under the Preemption Act of 1841—a law that allowed squatters living on government-owned property to buy the land at a very low price.

Always alert to the possibility of making a buck, the prophet could see many practical advantages of a move to Beaver Island. Because railroads had not yet connected the Eastern Seaboard to the western boomtowns of Detroit, Milwaukee, and Chicago, steamboats were still a flourishing business on the Great Lakes. Located directly on those heavily trafficked routes, Beaver Island, with its large natural harbor and plentiful supply of timber, was an ideal refueling stop for those vessels, most of which still burned wood instead of coal. Outlining his plans to pursue "the vigorous prosecution of the wooding business," Strang noted that "the Beaver Islands have over fifty thousand acres of wood of the superior quality" and were "easily accessible at all times and in all weathers to the steamboats passing both ways, daily from Buffalo to Chicago." He foresaw many other profitable undertakings for his people as well, including fishing, boat-building, farming, and trading with the Native Americans. Beaver Island's "easy and rapid access to the principal cities of the United States, and the numerous towns on the lakes," he concluded, would "secure the highest advantages of society, trade, and the arts."

But there was another potential advantage to the island, one that Strang failed to mention in the gushing reports he published in his own newspaper, many of which were soon reprinted elsewhere. Even at this early stage, the prophet and his scheming lieutenant, John C. Bennett, must have known their future kingdom would be ideally situated for other business enterprises—the kind you don't brag about in newspapers.

Islands, wrote Edgar Allan Poe, loom in the stormy seas of the psyche as places of "perfect security," where "freedom from all restraint [can] be enjoyed." Tiny cosmos where normal laws, normal rules of conduct, and normal systems of logic don't apply, they are frequent locales for experimental communities (including the original Utopia, which Thomas More set on an island in his famous sixteenth-century book), as well as sanctuaries of the oppressed (such as the island deep in the Great Dismal Swamp along the Virginia–North Carolina border, which escaped slaves defiantly controlled from 1680 until the Civil War).

But islands also make ideal bases of operation for criminal enterprises. Around 1840, for example, three islands on the Mississippi River between Memphis and Vicksburg were taken over by "a large number of counterfeiters, gamblers, negro stealers and inland pirates," as one newspaper put it. Another paper noted that despite "repeated instances of their passing counterfeit money and robbing the honest citizens of their property," the thugs remained at large, having "fearlessly announced their intention to assassinate everyone who took any steps towards bringing them to justice." Finally, in August of 1841, a local sheriff organized a posse of between forty and seventy men, who raided the islands, rounded up the criminals, "placed them on board a trading boat, took her to an unfrequented place, so that there might be no witnesses, *and shot and drowned them all!*," in one paper's breathless description. According to various other newspaper reports, as many as twenty-three outlaws died at the hands of this mob and had their bodies "cast upon the bosom of the mighty Mississippi, to find a grave in its dark and turbid waters." Although many observers expressed outrage at the lynchings, some conceded that attempts to stop the gang through legal means had completely failed. "The daring impunity with which the land pirates who infest the borders of our river perpetrate their outrages upon orderly members of society," observed the *North Alabamian,* "would seem to indicate that the arm of the law is too short or too feeble to punish them."

This was precisely why so many makers of fake money and other antebellum criminals operated in frontier regions "along geographical and political fault lines," in the words of the historian Stephen Mihm, author of *A Nation of Counterfeiters: Capitalists, Con Men, and the Making of the United States.* By the mid-1850s, vigilante violence, including those killings on the Mississippi, had largely discouraged counterfeiting operations in the Deep South but not in the Middle West, where "the machinery of policing and social control was weaker than almost anywhere else in the country." One group of counterfeiters and horse thieves, for example, had a hideout amid a vast tract of marshland in Indiana, just half a mile from the Illinois border. Accessible only from one side along a perilous road of submerged logs, the place was known as Bogus Island. "In states like Ohio, Michigan, Illinois, and Missouri, counterfeiters flourished on the outer reaches of the nation, their reputations reaching mythical proportions," Mihm writes. "They thrived thanks to lax law enforcement and a growing tolerance for illicit money-making of all kinds." Among the most notorious of these asylums, in fact, was a town where unique legal protections helped counterfeiters, horse thieves, and other miscreants ply their trades with relative impunity—the Mormon city of Nauvoo.

———

In his role as lobbyist, Bennett had played a key part in the passage of the 1840 Nauvoo Charter, which in many ways made the town an independent state-within-a-state. "Bennett managed matters well for his constituents. He flattered both sides with the hope of Mormon favor; and both sides expected to receive their votes," wrote Illinois governor Thomas Ford, who, despite considering the influence peddler a complete scoundrel, could not help admiring his political skills. A young state legislator named Abraham Lincoln also praised Bennett's work in lobbying for the charter, which protected Mormons from prosecution in other jurisdictions and eventually made the town "a happy hunting ground for fugitives from justice elsewhere," according to one historian. As one mayor of Nauvoo wound up conceding, the place was crawling with "thieves, robbers, bogus makers, counterfeiters and murderers."

Some of those thugs were outside opportunists, there to take advantage of naive converts. But many of them were Mormons who had come to believe that preparing the world for the Second Coming entitled them to break laws when necessary, especially if it involved stealing from the gentiles, as they called all non-Mormons. On January 27, 1844—not long before Strang's only visit to Nauvoo—the *New York Tribune* had wryly described city residents as "a set of fanatics whose fundamental doctrine is, that the Earth and all its good things are theirs, and that they will shortly inherit them; many of whom are not willing to await the appointed time, but proceed to take their portion from the Gentiles in advance."

A Mormon commandment known as the Law of Consecration stipulated that the faithful should voluntarily deed their own property to the church—but in Nauvoo, criminally inclined zealots soon began using this doctrine to justify the involuntary consecration of other people's property. Even Joseph Smith's brother, Hyrum, once admitted that Nauvoo was home to residents who believed it was "right to steal from anyone who does not belong to the church," provided the thief gave two-thirds of his plunder to the building of the Mormon Temple.

Such behavior, of course, only inflamed anti-Mormon sentiment in Illinois. In the end, Nauvoo's quasi-autonomous status had neither protected Joseph Smith from the mob nor staved off the city's downfall. But Strang and Bennett could see that a colony in the middle of Lake Michigan would give them something even better than a special charter: mile upon mile of water between their sect and all potential enemies.

———

Perhaps at this point in his career, the prophet would have done well to consider the warning of a favorite poet from his youth:

> *Look to thyself, priest, conqueror or prince!*
> *Whether thy trade is falsehood.*

No doubt Percy Bysshe Shelley's vision of an island utopia—a "paradise of peace" where humanity finally frees itself from social and political oppression—still lingered somewhere on the distant horizon of Strang's imagination. But along with it, he now nourished a darker vision of a refuge rising from the waves, a place beyond the reach of the law. Strang the visionary idealist versus Strang the misanthropic opportunist—it must have become hard for even the prophet to tell them apart anymore. Because now all his ambitions, sincere and cynical, pure and tainted, had converged into one obsessive dream: a "golden island," in the words of Percy Shelley, "gleaming in yon flood of light."

And so it happened that the next spring, in mid-May of 1847,

Strang and four followers found themselves searching the rain-sogged forest floor of Beaver Island for something to eat. The men had run out of funds during their journey to the island from Wisconsin and were forced to sell their blankets in order to complete the ship passage. They came ashore, as Strang would later report, "with less than two days [of] provisions, and not one cent of money." Encountering a chilly reception from the few settlers of this sparsely populated outpost, they built a makeshift shelter out of hemlock boughs and began to forage for food. The kingdom on the lake was not getting off to a glorious start.

For the next two weeks, the men traveled all over Beaver Island, surviving mostly on wild leeks and beechnuts until they found enough work—perhaps by chopping wood for local residents—to buy provisions. Eventually, they arranged for the use of a boat and explored several smaller islands nearby. Then, after building a cabin and leaving behind a pair of men to establish a permanent Mormon presence, Strang and his other two followers headed back to Voree by steamboat.

It had been a grueling journey. Nonetheless, the prophet quickly dashed off an ecstatic report on Beaver Island for the June 1, 1847, issue of his newspaper: "The advantages of [Beaver] and the adjacent Islands for settlement are far greater than we anticipated, furnishing as they do a large amount of land of a superior quality for agricultural purposes, an abundant supply of the best timber, and surrounded by the most extensive inland fisheries in the world." This paradise on earth, he wrote, was now just "waiting for occupants."

Five

In which one charlatan is run out of town, only to be replaced by an even greater scoundrel

---

"Old man," said the young one, "I reckon we might double-team it together; what do you think?"

"I ain't undisposed. What's your line—mainly?"

"Jour printer, by trade; do a little in patent medicines; theater-actor—tragedy, you know."

—discussion between the Duke and the King,
Mark Twain, *Adventures of Huckleberry Finn*

ON MAY 26, 1847, SHORTLY AFTER RETURNING FROM HIS journey to Beaver Island, the prophet issued a cryptic pronouncement:

> I have received information of some proceedings of a very grave nature seriously affecting the interest of the church and pecunarily some of its most worthy members, not at all authorized by any instruction from the *proper source*. More I will not say lest injustice might be done on mere surmise, but I do hope the brethren will not follow the instructions of every man who sets himself up as director.... Instructions from me are generally written, *always* signed by *my own hand*.

The guilty party, it seems, was the man who called himself Pontiff Premier and General-in-Chief. Although the details of his transgressions have been lost to history, it's clear that while Strang was away,

John Bennett had somehow attempted to seize power. On June 7, the prophet announced that Bennett "has been removed from all official standing in the church" for, among other offenses, "suppressing letters addressed to Pres. Strang," and "giving instructions to the Saints, purporting to be by the authority of the First Presidency, which were entirely unauthorized." Having stubbornly stood by Bennett amid charges of heresy and sexual misconduct, Strang now drew the line at siphoning off money without permission and undercutting the prophet's own authority.

Bennett packed up his military uniform and medical supplies and departed Voree after just one tumultuous year in town, in much the same manner as he had left Nauvoo. He was soon to be officially excommunicated in absentia, and then, according to church records, "delivered over to the buffetings of Satan."

———

The man whom Strang selected to replace Bennett as his top lieutenant was once described by the *New York Times* as "qualified to take the position of chief of all the confidence men on the face of the earth." For better or for worse, few people would have a more profound impact on Strang than this "deceiver of the first class," George J. Adams.

A couple of years older than Strang, Adams was born in Oxford, New Jersey, around 1811. Trained as a tailor, he wed his wife, Caroline, in his early twenties before switching careers to become an itinerant "Methodist exhorter," preaching around Boston. "Possessed of a certain rude eloquence," the *Times* wrote, "he soon became a shining light of the religious community, and his converts were many." Impressed by his charisma, the manager of a local theater solicited him to perform *Richard III* and other Shakespearean roles. But according to the *Times*, Adams was "as poor an actor as ever spoke," not to mention a notorious drunk and "an exceedingly negligent, even dirty man," who "would borrow garments from his actors and return them in such a soiled condition that they must be thrown away."

Newspaper lampoon of George J. Adams perfoming onstage in 1847. (American Antiquarian Society)

He did not, in short, seem like an ideal candidate to join the Church of Jesus Christ of Latter-day Saints, which required its members to practice personal cleanliness and abstain from intoxicants. Nonetheless, in 1840 George Adams became a "red-hot convert," according to the *Times*. The following year, church leaders dispatched him to England, where, in his spellbinding style, he forewarned rapt audiences that the second advent of the Messiah was nigh. Thanks to the fiery Adams and his fellow missionaries—as well as to crippling economic conditions in England, which left many out of work—nearly 3,000 British converts sailed for Nauvoo during 1841 and 1842.

Adams's success during the thirteen-month mission raised his status in Nauvoo and earned him the respect of Joseph Smith, who granted the preacher a prominent place in the Mormon hierarchy.

So strong was Adams's influence, in fact, that after Smith's murder in June of 1844, church leaders dispatched him on a delicate mission to consult with Mormon leaders on the East Coast about the future of the church. Once there, however, Adams began drinking heavily, "begging money" and "running all over the rights" of local Mormon elders, according to one account. He also started to teach "the Kissing Women spiritual wife" doctrine as a means of cajoling women into casual sex, reported the church official who monitored his exploits.

At the beginning of October 1844—a few days before the official filed his report—Brigham Young already had nine wives. By the end of the month, he would add six more. Nonetheless, Young—who would not publicly acknowledge the practice for another eight years—was in no position to tolerate the overt and vulgar way Adams exploited polygamy, stripping "celestial marriage" of its supposedly lofty religious ornamentation as a sacred means of helping men and women achieve greater glory at Christ's return. In 1845, Young kicked Adams out of the church, citing the controversial preacher's "diabolical conduct."

By February of the following year, Adams was reported to be in St. Louis, managing a theater under the assumed name of Young—a jab, perhaps, at the man who had just excommunicated him. It was around this time, apparently, that he renewed a correspondence with John C. Bennett, whom he had known in Nauvoo. The two men could not exactly be described as friends. Just three years earlier, Adams had publicly denounced "the vile, polluted, the corrupt, the crafty, the licentious, lustful" physician, whose footsteps were "marked by treachery." But now that both of these ambitious schemers were on the outs with Young, they decided to form an alliance and offer their services to Strang. On March 24, 1846, Bennett wrote the prophet to recommend Adams and propose a power-sharing agreement. Strang would be "first in all things," followed by Bennett and Adams as "equal councilor[s]." Three days later, Adams followed up with a letter of his own, assuring Strang that reports of his womanizing were untrue and that any story of his drinking was "a base phalshood." Although spelling was clearly not his strength, Adams knew he had a talent that would be immensely valuable to Strang: "I draw crowds whereaver and wheneaver I lift up my voice," he wrote—and for once, it appears he wasn't exaggerating.

After Adams joined Strang's sect, he became its chief recruiter, proselytizing to enthusiastic audiences all over the country. One observer described him as "all fire, all feeling," with a "forensic eloquence" and "nothing dull, monotonous or prosy about him." Another noted that "when he came to dwell on the second resurrection...the whole congregation seemed for a moment to forget that they were listening to a poor despised Latter-day Saint or Mormon, and tears of joy fell from their eyes."

The charismatic preacher had regularly shared the pulpit with Strang during the prophet's recent recruiting mission to Philadelphia, New York, and Boston, where the pair met with considerable success, significantly increasing the population of Voree. Whether Strang might have already had Adams in mind when he kicked Bennett out of the church, we can't be sure. But Adams expressed neither surprise nor sadness at the news. "I am glad he has showed himself as he is," he wrote to Strang from Portland, Maine, in July of 1847. "He is a corrupt man—he is all self—has injured you very much."

The selfless Adams, of course, knew just the man to replace Bennett: "I am a sinner; but I am a honest man, a true man, a faithful friend. True until death," he told Strang. Before long, "a certain rattle brained Elder...well known as the walking satire of depravity and humbug," in the phrasing of one journalist, had secured the uncontested position of second-in-command in the future utopian colony on Beaver Island.

The two of them made a strange pair. Adams was tall, unkempt, and unpredictable; Strang was short, self-possessed, and, by his own account, "cold, stern, uncommunicative, petulant, and exceedingly difficult to please." Adams could barely spell; Strang was bookish. Adams was endlessly falling off the wagon; Strang was a teetotaler. What the two men had in common, other than oversize ego and ambition, was almost superhuman stamina.

In the late summer of 1847, for example, not long after divesting himself of Bennett, Strang completed another recruiting trip to the East, his first since the preceding summer. During the journey he attended five religious conferences, preached thirty-one sermons, and traveled more than 3,800 miles by steamboat, railroad, stagecoach, and foot. Along the way, he "visited nearly all the principal places between Wisconsin and the Hudson River, and many of the principal men," reported Strang's newspaper, which boasted that the prophet "made converts to the cause and friends to himself wherever he went." Strang also claimed that in the previous three years he had traveled over 16,000 miles in all, and had visited every state north of the Carolinas except for three, many of those several times.

Adams lived, if anything, an even more peripatetic existence, wandering from city to city on the East Coast, where he would recite the tragedies of William Shakespeare one night and preach the gospel of James Jesse Strang the next. In New York, he performed *Richard III* (casting his own young son as the doomed child-prince, the Duke of York). In Philadelphia, he was called a "shining light Shakespearean and ecclesiastical." In Baltimore, he was "deemed a better preacher than an actor," even though he was said to be "making money rapidly." In Boston, "feeling greatly scandalized by a report of one of his sermons," he hunted down the journalist who had mocked him and horsewhipped the man on the street before a crowd of 100 people. In Washington, he spoke, with revealing hypocrisy, at a "Grand Temperance Rally" and was named an officer in a group that advocated total abstinence from alcoholic beverages, then opened a saloon up the road in Baltimore, where he also set himself up as the manager of a theater, advertising a performance of *Hamlet* by one of the great actors of the nineteenth century, Junius Brutus Booth (father of ten-year-old John Wilkes Booth, future presidential assassin). But the show was abruptly canceled when performers refused to take the stage, claiming Adams had not paid them and had "made all sorts of promises, which in every respect he has failed to keep." He wound up in jail ("confined for debts," according to the *Baltimore Sun*) but got out in time to become manager of another theater.

He also made headlines as the star witness in the 1847 case *Cobb v. Cobb*, the sensational divorce trial of a Boston society matron who abandoned her husband of twenty-one years to become one of Brigham Young's plural wives. Adams, who had observed the woman in Nauvoo with Young, testified he had warned her that polygamy "would lead to the devil," but that "she was led away by religious frenzy" and believed "persons had a right to live together in unlawful intercourse." As for his own views on the matter, Adams swore under oath he would remain an unwavering foe of plural marriage, even if it meant death, and claimed that the Mormons, outraged at his opposition to the doctrine, had in fact tried to kill him numerous times. Not long after that testimony, he began sharing the pulpit with another preacher, a man described by various newspapers as an "unmitigated scoundrel" who "has already three wives living in various parts of the U.S., and who has been preaching temperance throughout the country, [and] recently ran away with a respectable widow in Charleston, South Carolina." The talks of Adams and his companion had titles such as "lecture on love" and "lecture on the passions."

All this in one manic two-year stretch: No wonder the tragedian could not make time to visit Voree or Beaver Island. Nonetheless, "I long to be with you," he assured the prophet in late 1847, "and, if necessary, suffer with you, that I may also reign with you." In the meantime, the charismatic preacher continued to attract new converts to the fold. As the new year approached, Adams sent Strang an update from Philadelphia:

> I am preaching here every Sunday to overflowing houses. And saints and sinners said I preached last Sunday with more power, spirit, eloquence and energy than I ever did before, even in my most palmy days, particularly in the evening, when I was bearing testimony to the truth and divinity of your mission, priesthood and calling as the successor to Joseph. I suppose, from everyone that was present says, that for a few minutes toward the end of my testimony no power in language can describe the feelings of the entire audience, it was so intense. I had over 300 young men between eighteen and twenty-five years of age to hear me, and what is still better they believed me. When I bore testimony to your labor, toil and hardships for the cause of truth, there was hardly a dry eye in the house.

Beaver Island, in Lake Michigan, has become the chosen spot of the Mormons, under J. J. Strang.... Voree, Wisconsin, his present place of residence, contains about 1,000 followers. His power is almost unlimited.

Thus did one newspaper sum up the prophet's fortunes late in 1847. But in truth, Strang's hold over his flock had never been so tenuous. Church records from this period are full of excommunications. Apostasy, departing from the faith, un-Christian conduct, slander, adultery, lasciviousness, believing in the spiritual-wife system, indulging in the practice of intoxication, "various immoralities"—the list of charges against citizens of Voree grew longer by the week. Some of the defendants entered a perfunctory guilty plea, citing "no desire to remain in the church." Others didn't even show up for their trials, having long since lost interest or left town. One paper reported that due to internal "divisions" only 400 people remained in Voree—down by more than half from the 1,000 reported to have resided there the previous year.

The Beaver Island scheme wasn't going well, either. All that autumn, Strang had been attempting to secure his claim on the promised land by rallying his supporters to move north to the island before cold weather made the trip impossible: "Well, brother, do you wish to settle there?" he wrote in his newspaper. "Now is the time. Navigation soon closes, and then, except a monthly mail drawn by dogs, you will be shut out from the rest of the world till spring."

Perhaps unsurprisingly, the idea of being trapped for months in a frozen wasteland hadn't inspired a stampede of volunteers. By the prophet's own account, "several families moved to the Island, but became dissatisfied with the prospects and left. At the setting in of winter the Mormon population consisted of five men and their families, in all eighteen persons." And there was more bad news. By the end of 1847, reports were trickling in that an advance party of Mormons under Brigham Young had reached the Great Salt Lake, where they planned to establish a homeland. For two years, Strang had been predicting disaster for the Mormons who were migrating west. But suddenly it looked as though Brigham Young would beat him in the race to establish a viable permanent colony.

The prophet's personal life was likewise in turmoil. His marriage to Mary Perce Strang, troubled from the start, now seemed to be in shambles. By all indications, Mary—who had a tendency to "harbor melancholy," as her mother once put it—was a conventional middle-class woman of her time, more interested in domestic matters than in worldly affairs, distrustful of the bewildering changes going on in antebellum society, traditional in her views on religion, gender relations, and sexuality. She was not, in short, the ideal partner for a mercurial self-styled prophet. Strang would later confide that after the untimely death of their firstborn, in 1843, Mary largely refused to have "wifely relations" with him. And while the three children born to Mary since that time offered evidence of some physical intimacy, the prophet and his wife seem to have been mostly at odds, even when it came to religion. Although Mary became a Mormon herself, she did not permit any of her three children to be baptized into their own father's church.

Strang had also recently lost his close childhood friend (and Mary's uncle), Benjamin Perce, who left Voree in 1846, never to return. One of the first Mormons in Wisconsin, Perce had lived in the area for more than a decade, and was the one who had urged Strang to move west, opening his home to him and, according to a later account, conspiring with him to counterfeit the Rajah Manchou plates. The reason the two men parted ways is unclear, but if there was a rift between them, it could not afterward be mended. In September of 1847, Perce died in Boston as the result of a construction explosion.

Having lost the companionship of his closest friend, the affection of his wife, and the shrewd political mentorship of Bennett, the prophet was in a grim frame of mind as 1847 came to a close. In one particularly reflective moment, he wrote that his "mind was dark" and that his "ideas seemed lost in the bottom of a deep, dark well." Yet even in his angst, Strang was once again exhibiting an uncanny gift for embodying the zeitgeist, a word that had recently entered the English language. All over the country, it seems, Americans were starting to feel what one contemporary called "an almost universal apprehension"—a collective fear that "great changes were at hand." As always, the prophet was prepared to turn other people's anxiety to his own advantage.

Six

In which the end of the world approaches
and a sea monster is spotted off Beaver Island

⸺⊙⸺

It needs a wild steersman when we voyage through Chaos! The
anchor is up! farewell!
—Nathaniel Hawthorne, *The Blithedale Romance*

IN 1848 A GROWING NUMBER OF AMERICANS CAME TO BELIEVE
the world was on the verge of an apocalypse. Although they had
wildly divergent views about the nature and exact timing of this cataclysm, they had become increasingly convinced that a wave of
extraordinary events was crashing down upon them—events that
could be interpreted only as signs that the human race had stumbled
onto a pivotal moment in cosmic history.

In France, Germany, Italy, and the Austrian empire, republican re-
volts against long-ruling monarchies caused many people to conclude
that the old political, religious, and economic order was collapsing
before their eyes. In Ireland, a potato famine of biblical proportions
killed more than a million people and prompted another two million
to flee their homeland; more than half of those ventured to America,
where the surge of ragged, impoverished immigrants unleashed a
counter-surge of nativist hatred against foreigners and Catholics. In
Mexico, the United States came out victorious in its first foreign
war, but not without a death toll of almost 13,000 soldiers, a bill to

taxpayers of $97 million, and an angry backlash against President James K. Polk, who opted not to run for reelection. Across the United States, the debate over whether slavery should be prohibited in the vast new territories acquired in the conflict with Mexico sharply divided Americans and helped set the stage for the looming civil war. And in one of those new territories, gold was discovered at Sutter's Mill near San Francisco, causing hundreds of thousands of fortune seekers to scurry to California.

Combined with the era's other upheavals, the bewildering developments of 1848 filled many Americans with anxiety and anticipation. "Events are occurring in the world that are surprising and unexampled," wrote the well-known Presbyterian minister Albert Barnes in May of that year. "They amaze us by the rapidity with which they succeed each other, and the facility with which they are accomplished. At no period of the world's history have changes so important taken place in so brief a period of time." Like many other Americans, Barnes believed that in such tempestuous times, the instinctive "promptings of all minds" were to examine scripture in order to "see whether these very events may not be there shadowed forth in some symbol till now not understood, and whether the ultimate bearing and results may not be found foretold." Another observer, writing the following month, noted that "a universal impression exists upon the minds of men, that wonderful and important events are about to transpire.... The wisest of men asks, in wondering anxiety, 'What will the end of these things be?'"

Strang, too, spent the summer of 1848 pointing to what he described as "ominous" signs, including the revolutions in Europe, the war in Mexico, and rising tensions between North and South. For months he'd been urging his followers to prepare for the end: "Let me warn you that the time draws near. Prophetic events are crowding close upon one another." Hesitation was no longer an option, he told members of the Mormon diaspora who remained undecided about joining one of his colonies at Voree or Beaver Island. "Come up to the places God has appointed," he implored, "for the Lord delayeth not his coming."

Strang's newspaper even reported that Mormons and local fishermen had spotted a huge sea serpent off the coast of the island—one of many such sightings around the world during the portentous years of 1847 and 1848. From a twenty-first-century perspective, of course, it's hard to know what to make of such an outlandish claim. But one possibility is that Strang intended to equate his Lake Michigan monster with the "Beast from the Sea," whose appearance heralds the apocalypse in the Book of Revelation. Knowing that Joseph Smith had claimed such beasts symbolize "the degenerate kingdoms of the wicked world," Strang may have hoped to underscore the idea of Beaver Island as the new Zion of prophecy—that promised land where, according to Mormon teachings, the Latter-day Saints would gather to help usher in the Second Coming of Christ and the advent of His 1,000-year reign on earth.

Illustration of a sea serpent supposedly spotted in the South Atlantic in 1848.

The trouble was that as of 1848, only about sixty true believers had heeded the prophet's call to pull up stakes and move to Beaver Island. Even Strang himself remained in Voree, where he was now occupied with formulating a new system of governance through which to assert control over his ever more fractious followers.

———

Amid the furor and foreboding of 1848, a small underground political group issued a short pamphlet that changed the world. Published in German, the 9,600-word document was at first almost completely ignored. Nonetheless, it was "destined to have a greater effect than all previous prayers, commandments and laws, greater than the Lord's Prayer with its 56 words, than the Ten Commandments with 297, and the American Declaration of Independence with its 300," wrote essayist Fritz J. Raddatz. The authors, two German revolutionaries living in exile in Brussels, began the work by describing the sense of anarchic and uncontrollable change that so many people around the globe were experiencing. The emerging industrial age was a time of "uninterrupted disturbance of all social conditions [and of] everlasting uncertainty," they wrote, adding that "all fixed, fast-frozen relations, with their train of ancient and venerable prejudices and opinions, are swept away.... All that is solid melts into air."

The pamphlet offered a solution to this chaos—one that, as the authors explained, "may be summed up in the single sentence: Abolition of private property." They blamed society's ills on economic competition and private ownership of the means of production. But they also believed that some social reformers' dreams of establishing individual utopian colonies—which they called "isolated... editions of the New Jerusalem"—were doomed to fail. In contrast to these romantic schemes, which they dismissed as "castles in the air," the authors put forward a self-styled scientific socialism, based not on wishful thinking but on "historical facts" and "inevitable" outcomes.

Yet despite their claim of objective certainty, the authors were not immune from the apocalyptic fevers of their times. They, too, envisioned an imminent cataclysm (a revolution in which the working class overthrew its capitalist oppressors), which would help pave the way for the perfect society (a stateless global communism).

The names Karl Marx and Friedrich Engels were, of course, completely unfamiliar to Strang. Nor could he possibly have read the *Communist Manifesto*, which would not be published in an English translation for another two years. Nonetheless, just as that tract was beginning to circulate, he issued a kind of communist manifesto of his own. It appeared in a June 1848 edition of the Voree newspaper, now called the *Gospel Herald*. Unsigned but almost certainly written by Strang himself, the article began with an overview of the revolutions in Europe, which, the author insisted, were being fought "not against the despotism of monarchy or aristocracy, but against the tyranny of the almighty dollar":

> Money governs the world. The systems existing among men cast everything else beneath its power. Crowns and sceptres are but sand and dust before it. It makes love false, justice a farce, and truth a fable. Men, to obtain it, will slay their mothers; betray brothers to death; sell sisters to infamy, and wives to prostitution.

The alternative to this false and destructive way of living? The answer, the article insisted, was socialism, "a generic name for all the various parties who hold to the necessity of a new social organization of society, in which the goods of the whole community should in some sense be made a fund for the ultimate wants of all men." Strang, it seems, had once again donned a new mask. So it was that this go-ahead man, this reckless speculator, this erstwhile enthusiast of what he'd once called the "money business," became a champion of the socialist cause.

True, he would not go down in history as a brilliant political theorist. But in at least one important respect, the prophet was more farseeing than Marx and Engels. In the view of these thinkers, communism would lead inexorably to liberation of the disenfranchised; or, to quote a soon-to-be-famous line from their manifesto, "the proletarians have nothing to lose but their chains." But Strang saw from the start that things were more complicated. Like countless autocrats and apparatchiks who would follow him—the people who constructed sprawling gulags, enforced brutal five-year plans, and committed mass murders in the name of forced collectivization—he recognized that communist principles could be used not to break chains but to strengthen them, not to do away with a central authority but to make it less vulnerable, not to liberate one's followers but to reestablish control over them just when it appeared one's power was beginning to slip away.

Strang's grand experiment in communism was called the Order of Enoch. Founded in January of 1848 by the members of twelve families in Voree, it effectively replaced the controversial Order of the Illuminati, while making even bigger demands on participants. Members pledged to give up all money and belongings, and to combine their property together in one large household, with Strang as the presiding patriarch. By the end of 1848, the Order of Enoch had some 150 members. They agreed to live a Spartan life—eschewing the use of coffee, tea, and other stimulants, as well as abstaining from sugar, spices, and dried fruit. They also consented to wear unostentatious uniforms: the women's matching dresses made of durable cotton, the men's clothing of flannel.

It was not long, however, before the experiment began to go awry. Some members of the new order left almost as soon as they had joined, taking with them their property, including materials and livestock vital to the prosperity of the group. Others hesitated to sign up, unwilling to relinquish not just their belongings but also their sense of individual identity. Increasingly, the prophet expressed frustration with those who were "slow to enter" the group. With the Second Coming just around the corner, he said, believers faced a stark choice: only those who were willing to hand over their worldly goods—or, as Strang put it, to "make a consecration of all they possess"—could hope to become exalted beings in Christ's heavenly church. Those who clung to their belongings and freedom would be doomed. "I admonish you to come out of Babylon and separate yourselves from her uncleanness," he wrote in a pastoral letter. "For the day of God's wrath upon her is near, and the time is at hand when his vengeance will be poured out."

———

Today we use the word *cult* to describe a small group of extremists cut off from contact with the outside world by an all-controlling leader. People in antebellum America, however, struggled to find language for the phenomenon, largely because they had never seen anything quite like it before. As recent scholars have attested, "The historical record indicates that utopian and apocalyptic cults and communes first appeared as a major form in the United States during this epoch."

As Strang attempted to tighten control of the Order of Enoch, for example, another self-styled prophet was establishing his own colony 200 miles southwest of Voree, in Bishop Hill, Illinois. Eric Jansson, who claimed to be the "vicar of Christ on earth" and "the restorer of true doctrine," maintained that "since the time of the Apostles, there has been found no true preacher before me." Arriving from Sweden in 1846, he and 400 followers were forced to dig underground "mud caves" in order to survive their first winter in the United States. But despite the group's enduring a near-endless string of hardships (including almost 150 deaths in a cholera epidemic), Jansson managed to maintain order through a combination of charisma and fear. "All authority has been given unto me in heaven and on earth," he once proclaimed. "If I so willed, you should at once fall dead at my feet and go to hell." When Jansson was gunned down by a former follower in 1850, many true believers of Bishop Hill expected him to rise from the dead.

But how did people wind up in such groups? As was so often the case before the emergence of psychology and sociology as formal studies, the secrets of the antebellum mind revealed themselves less through science than through literature. And few people grasped the complex relationship between leader and follower better than novelist Nathaniel Hawthorne, himself a charter member of a famous utopian colony.

Hawthorne's community—Brook Farm, in West Roxbury, Massachusetts—was falling apart just as the Order of Enoch was getting off the ground. Doomed by a ruinous fire and dwindling membership, Brook Farm was sold at public auction in 1849, after which it was turned into an almshouse. During its glory days in the early and mid-1840s, however, this community had garnered national attention as the pet project of the transcendentalist community in New England. Although the reclusive Henry David Thoreau steered clear of the 175-acre site, declaring that he would "rather keep bachelor's hall in hell than go to board in heaven," many other prominent intellectuals were regular visitors to the farm. Guests included brilliant woman of letters Margaret Fuller, journalist Horace Greeley, philosopher Bronson Alcott, and essayist Ralph Waldo Emerson, who observed that despite the community's demise many who lived there had considered it "the most important period of their life."

As a founding member of Brook Farm, the thirty-seven-year-old Hawthorne lived on the property full-time for six months, an experience that would inspire his 1852 novel, *The Blithedale Romance*. In his introduction to that book, Hawthorne wrote that he did "not put forward the slightest pretentions to illustrate a theory, or elicit a conclusion, favorable or otherwise, in respect to Socialism." He was much more interested in group dynamics—the day-to-day power relationships that big-picture theorists such as Marx and Engels largely failed to take into account.

One of the darkest and most complex characters in the novel is a charismatic social reformer named Hollingsworth, whom the narrator—a stand-in for Hawthorne himself—initially describes as having a "divine power of sympathy." This gift can sometimes make him seem like "the tenderest man and the truest friend on earth," but eventually the narrator realizes his own feelings of fellowship are not reciprocated. "I loved Hollingsworth," he acknowledges, but "it impressed me, more and more, that there was a stern and dreadful peculiarity in this man, such as could not prove otherwise than pernicious to the happiness of those who should be drawn into too intimate a connection with him. He was not altogether human."

Most members of the colony are idealists whose sole purpose is "showing mankind the example of a life governed by other than the false and cruel principles, on which human society has all along been based." But as the novel progresses, the narrator becomes increasingly aware that Hollingsworth "was never really interested in our socialist scheme." A cynic among dreamers and a man of action among triflers, Hollingsworth turns out to be a single-minded manipulator who plans to take over the colony for his own purposes. He is, in short, much like a number of real-life figures who succeeded in exploiting the utopian idealism of the era, "men of iron masquerading in Arcadian costume," as one commentator has called them. Eventually the narrator comes to understand that such men "have no heart, no sympathy, no reason, no conscience. They will keep no friend, unless he make himself the mirror of their purpose; they will smite and slay you, and trample your dead corpse under foot."

In a time when, as Marx and Engels memorably put it, "all that is solid melts into air," the Hollingsworths of the world—and the

Strangs—offered firmness and strength; in a time when "all fixed, fast-frozen relations...are swept away," they offered a sense of connection; and in a time of "everlasting uncertainty," they offered absolute confidence.

—

By the time Strang established the Order of Enoch and began to push for a mass migration to Beaver Island, underhanded manipulators like Hollingsworth were becoming omnipresent figures, insinuating themselves into every level of antebellum society. One writer noted, for example, that Wall Street was overrun with "respectable, princely, bold, high-soaring 'operators,' who are to be satisfied only with the plunder of a whole community." Many other small-scale "operators," meanwhile, plied their trade on the sidewalks of New York, using their dagger-sharp powers of inducement to pick off victims one at a time. One such individual—described as "a man of genteel appearance"—had gone by many names: Samuel Thompson, Samuel Thomas, Samuel Powel, Samuel Willis, Samuel Williams, William Evans, William Davis, William Brown, William Thompson, James Thompson, and Edward Stevens. But he would soon become famous across the country for a brand-new sobriquet: the Confidence Man.

People of the nineteenth century had a flair for finding evocative language to describe the chaotic new economic realities that Marx and Engels identified in the *Communist Manifesto*. "Almighty dollar," for instance, reflected the fact that money had been elevated to a "great object of universal devotion throughout our land," in the words of novelist Washington Irving, who is often credited with coining the term. A "businessman," meanwhile, was not just a craftsman who made goods or a merchant who traded them, but a more fluid kind of capitalist, constantly finding new ways to turn a profit. ("If you ever perceive a man setting up as a merchant or a manufacturer...he's an ass," declares the title character in

Edgar Allan Poe's satirical short story "The Business Man.") But until mid-century, no phrase had quite captured the fundamental quality of what had become a "ubiquitous personage" in American society, as one newspaper aptly put it. Then one day the perfect phrase bolted into being, as if waiting in the collective unconscious for just the right moment to form on people's tongues. On July 8, 1849, a story appeared in the *New York Herald*:

> *Arrest of the Confidence Man.*—For the last few months a man has been traveling about the city, known as the "Confidence Man;" that is, he would go up to a perfect stranger in the street, and being a man of genteel appearance, would easily command an interview. Upon this interview he would say after some little conversation, "have you confidence in me to trust me with your watch until to-morrow;" the stranger at this novel request, supposing him to be some old acquaintance not at that moment recollected, allows him to take the watch, thus placing "confidence" in the honesty of the stranger, who walks off laughing and the other supposing it to be a joke allows him so to do. In this way many have been duped.

The term would spread with astonishing speed, because it so precisely described a type of person increasingly familiar to Americans of all classes. Within a matter of months the phrase *confidence man* was in common usage, often preceded by an indefinite article, referring not to a specific person but to any "ingenious man of persuasion" who uses "the gift of speech" to dupe his victims, in the words of the *New York Daily Herald*. During the latter half of 1849, *confidence trick* and *confidence game* also entered the lexicon. "And so," writes psychologist Maria Konnikova, "the 'confidence man' was born: the person who uses others' trust in him for his own private purposes. Have you confidence in me? What will you give me to prove it?"

On October 8 and 9, 1849, the trial of "Samuel Thompson,

alias Thomas, alias Williams, alias the Confidence Man," took place in New York. The jury came to a quick guilty verdict, and the defendant was sentenced to two and a half years in state prison.

Strang happened to be in the city at that time, proselytizing with George Adams about "the commandment to gather to Beaver Island, where the Lord has promised to deliver his saints." It seems likely, in fact, that he would have followed the Confidence Man's trial in the *New York Daily Herald,* where it received prominent coverage. Perhaps he even read the testimony of a "thunderstruck" victim who expressed bafflement that a man who seemed "so very much a friend...should steal my watch."

But by then the prophet was attempting to pull off the most audacious confidence trick of his career—one so bold that it made swiping a watch seem like child's play. He was asking people to ignore not just their better judgment but their own eyes.

Seven

In which we meet J. J. Strang's mysterious nephew

Who knows, my dear sir, but for a time you may have taken
yourself for somebody else? Stranger things have happened.
                          —Herman Melville, *The Confidence-Man*

THE YOUNG MAN STARED INTO THE CAMERA, TRYING NOT TO
blink. It was the autumn of 1849, and he was about to have
his portrait taken at a daguerreotype studio in Buffalo, New York.
Although this photographic process had been invented in Paris a
mere decade earlier, the technology had spread with stunning speed
throughout the United States. "In our great cities, a Daguerreotypist
is to be found in almost every square; and there is scarcely a county
in any state that has not one or more of these industrious individuals
busy at work," one magazine reported earlier in the year.

Now the lens opened, and the young man's body tensed, one hand
draped over a book, index finger pointing down, the other folded
into a fist on his lap. "All you have to do," one contemporary writer
explained about the trick to posing for a portrait, "is to place yourself in an easy, well-cushioned chair, assume the position in which
you desire to be perpetuated and look steadfastly at a given object,
for the matter of half a minute, and your features, expression, every
thing connected with your countenance, are caught and stamped
with a vigor and similitude that are unsurpassable."

(Clarke Historical Library, Central Michigan University)

And now the wait was over and the exposure was done and the sheet of silver-plated copper had captured for eternity the handsome face of Charles J. Douglass, teenage nephew and private secretary of the Mormon prophet James Jesse Strang. "Creating man's perfect image and identity"—that's how one contemporary described the magic of this new technology. But as the curious case of Charley Douglass demonstrates, a man's image and his identity are sometimes two very different things.

———

For the first time in months, things seemed to be going well for Strang. On the way to Buffalo he had stopped at Beaver Island with his wife and three children—the seventh visit he'd made there in the previous year and a half. These nonstop efforts to recruit pilgrims, both from eastern cities and from Voree, were finally paying off. Mormon settlers had already started work on a new tabernacle and a road into the island's interior. They'd also begun to clear land for farms and set up homesteads, though few of them appear to have bothered paying for the land. The federal government, Strang argued, had no right to sell uninhabited tracts to wealthy speculators "while so many are homeless." Whether enticed by the prospect of free land or by the hope for eternal salvation, Strang's followers were now starting to feel "a more favorable impression of the place, and confidence in its prospects," as he put it. On this trip, he had escorted about thirty followers who planned to settle on the island permanently, bringing the number to a respectable total of approximately 250 souls. "We left things prospering at Beaver, and emigrants are arriving by nearly every boat," the prophet reported. "A family landed from Virginia a few minutes before I left."

The mood also seemed to be improving somewhat in Voree, thanks in part to the prophet's recent institution of a practice known as baptism for the dead. This rite, first performed by the late Joseph Smith, allowed Mormons to be baptized on behalf of deceased relatives in order to ensure those ancestors a chance at everlasting life. In a precarious period of history, when white men had a life expectancy of only about thirty-six years and white women thirty-eight years, such baptisms offered a considerable amount of comfort, linking them to lost family members and to past generations. But it also gave Strang more control over his flock, since God had ordered that only members of the Order of Enoch and other parishioners who weren't behind on their tithes to the church qualified for the privilege. Although baptism for the dead was supposed to take place in a temple, the Prophet Elijah, Strang claimed, had personally paid him a visit to let him know that because the church in Voree was still under construction, a section of the White River, "from the bathing-pool unto the water wheel," had been miraculously sanctified for the purpose. Just days before departing on his journey to the East, Strang had led a great many of his followers to the water's edge, where they lined up to be baptized by immersion, acting as proxies for their own ancestors, as well as for such deceased luminaries as U.S. president James K. Polk, English statesman Oliver Cromwell, poet Lord Byron, and the prophet's boyhood hero, Napoleon Bonaparte.

Thanks to the recent departures of Reuben Miller and other enemies of the prophet, Voree was no longer quite the snake's nest for Strang that it had been in the past couple of years. Nonetheless, it was becoming clear that he no longer saw the prairie town playing the central role in his future kingdom. Henceforth the "garden of peace" would be a second-class colony. Some members of the church would remain there—including, for the time being, Strang himself—but from now on, Beaver Island would be the focus of every dream and intrigue, every hope and fabrication.

After his stopover on the island, Strang attended a church conference in Michigan, then traveled to his parents' house in western New York, where he dropped off his wife and children before heading on to Buffalo alone. In this port town, he met up with his nephew Charley Douglass, an intelligent and capable youth who would serve as the prophet's private secretary for a tour of major East Coast cities aimed at attracting more converts—and future denizens of Beaver Island. While in Buffalo, Douglass had his picture taken at that daguerreotype studio. Then uncle and nephew likely returned to their lodgings, where they shared a room for the night before traveling together to a church conference in New York City.

For the next six months, the two would go almost everywhere together. But it would not be long before those who encountered Strang began to gossip about the man he described as "a traveling friend." Have you noticed, they whispered, that something seems a little odd about this Charles Douglass? Maybe it was the slope of his shoulders or the tenor of his voice, maybe it was the way he walked or laughed, maybe—well, it was hard to put into words. Or maybe it wasn't so hard after all. "I am informed," wrote one follower, that "your clerk was in the habit of wearing petticoats until very recently."

———

The prophet's wife, Mary, had never wanted to take part in this trip. After all, she had three children in tow—ages nine, four, and eleven months—and even with recent improvements in transportation, antebellum travel remained exhausting and often dangerous. The steamboat that the family had taken from Beaver Island to Detroit, for example, hit rough waters and practically everyone aboard got seasick, according to Strang.

Attending to such problems always seemed to fall on Mary. Although her husband had apparently told her before leaving Voree that he would help with the childcare, as she bitterly reminded him afterward in a letter, he'd wasted no time in breaking that promise. He had initially mentioned plans to take Mary and the children with him on his tour of eastern cities, but then he'd waltzed off to Buffalo alone. It was bad enough that she found herself stranded at the home of her in-laws, but shortly after her husband's departure, the baby came down with whooping cough—a terrifying disease in an age before vaccines, when one-third of all white children and more than half of black children died before adulthood. Having already endured the loss of one child—five-year-old Mary Elizabeth, their firstborn, in 1843—the prophet's wife had good reason to feel anxious about the sick baby, especially after her other daughter, the nine-year-old, developed a case of bilious fever, a nineteenth-century phrase for a variety of illnesses involving fever and nausea or vomiting. "I have had two of them at the same time so sick that I feared they would die," she wrote to her husband.

Strang, however, largely ignored her letters. Although Mary kept herself "in constant reddiness for traveling," as she reminded him, he did not send for her. Weeks went by, then months. She sent mail to the wrong city, no longer sure of the prophet's movements or plans.

"Do write something [about] what you are intending to do," she pleaded in one letter, adding angrily that "if I had money I would take the children and go home."

But Mary Strang couldn't go home. Like most women of her generation, she had almost no real power in her marriage, much less anything resembling autonomy. Although a few states such as New York had passed laws that granted limited economic rights to married women, most jurisdictions still held that a husband owned his wife's body, her property, her earnings, and her offspring. And unlike some women of her generation, who were beginning to demand more power in marriage, the prophet's wife had always found herself in a dependent and submissive role—never more so than now. If Strang's intention had been to cut her off from the outside world, he could hardly have devised a better prison than his parents' house, where Mary could neither get news of his travels nor be exposed to gossip back in Voree.

"There exists in the minds of men a tone of feeling toward women as toward slaves," wrote noted antebellum essayist and journalist Margaret Fuller in her 1845 book, *Woman in the Nineteenth Century*, described by one later historian as "the boldest and, in a real sense, the first statement of American feminism." Fuller argued that the place women of the era occupied was "so narrow" that any attempt to break out would cause them to "become outlaws." Men, too, were stunted by the rigid gender divisions of the antebellum period, which, in Fuller's view, imprisoned members of both sexes and suppressed their true selves from soaring free. She looked forward to a time when false borders between the two genders faded away. "Male and female represent the two sides of the great radical dualism," she wrote. "But, in fact, they are perpetually passing into one another. Fluid hardens to solid, solid rushes to fluid. There is no wholly masculine man, no purely feminine woman."

"Charley's a gal!" That's how the writers of one letter, a husband and wife, summed up rumors that were beginning to blow like "whirlwinds" among Strang's followers by the time he and Douglass reached Philadelphia in November of 1849. One man claimed to recognize Douglass as a young woman he had seen on Beaver Island. Another added up the clues—including the feminine contours of the young man's rear end and chest—to conclude that "from the crown of his head to the soles of his feet," Strang's secretary was "every whit a woman." Still another follower, who had allowed Strang and his assistant to stay in her lodgings, reported that when she washed Douglass's laundry, she discovered "a mess of bloody cloths, which <u>women</u> sometimes use, all rolled up....O Gemini, thought I. The cat's out of the bag sure enough. O dear! This Pseudo Charley turns out to be a <u>filthy & abominable...hussey</u>! But when I examined the bed—O dear!...<u>O Strang, Whang-Strambang, hocus pocus-pocus!!!</u>"

Strang angrily defended his private secretary—and himself—against such allegations. In response to a follower who had noted Douglass's "physiological peculiarities," for example, the prophet took a combative tone:

> Don't you know that the mere suspicion, no matter how unfounded, that I traveled with a female in disguise would be taken up by a thousand tongues each of whom would assess it strong as holy writ? Are you so ignorant of human nature as not to know that the mere suggestion that a traveling friend of mine had one single feminine Physiological peculiarity must inevitably fall upon me as a distinct charge of keeping a concubine?

Unlike many of the allegations made against the prophet in recent months, however, this last charge was false. The young woman who wore men's clothes and went by the name of Charles J. Douglass was not Strang's concubine. She was, in fact, his new wife.

———

"I now say distinctly, and I defy contradiction, that the man or woman does not exist on earth, or under the earth who ever heard me say one word, or saw me do one act, savoring in the least of *spiritual wifery*, or any of the attending abominations," Strang wrote in 1847. "My opinions on this subject are unchanged, and I regard them as unchangeable."

But the following year, something happened that altered everything for Strang. Her name was Elvira Field, female alter ego of the future Charles Douglass. Intelligent, attractive, and gutsy, she had first come to Voree not long before her eighteenth birthday, arriving with her family from Michigan for a church conference in April of 1848. After her parents returned home, she and her nineteen-year-old brother remained in town and joined the Order of Enoch before returning home in the fall. By March of 1849, when the entire family moved to Beaver Island, she would have had ample opportunity to interact with Strang, though it's unclear how well acquainted they were or whether their contact up to that point ever went beyond the normal bounds of a preacher-parishioner relationship.

What's certain is that by July of 1849, when Strang arrived on the island for a church conference, he had come to a pivotal decision. First, he dispatched George J. Adams—who had made his first journey to Beaver Island after spending the previous two years preaching in the East—to "sound out" Elvira. Then Strang approached her himself with "certain proposals." On July 13, a few days after the conference disbanded, the thirty-six-year-old prophet and his nineteen-year-old disciple were married in a secret ceremony performed by Brother Adams. After a brief honeymoon—during which one of Strang's supporters received reports that the prophet had been spotted on a "frigging spree"—the newlyweds parted company for a few weeks, only to be reunited in Buffalo as uncle and nephew.

⸺

The girl who grew up to become Charles J. Douglass had loved to hunt. Born in northeast Ohio in 1830, she soon became an "expert in the use of a rifle" who "could kill a hawk on the wing," according to the recollections of relatives. In 1844 her family moved to central Michigan, where she trained to become a tailor. That skill would one day come in handy when she needed to equip her alter ego with a man's suit, but it did not hold her interest for long. Instead she became a teacher—one of the very few occupations that allowed antebellum women any degree of financial independence or geographic mobility. Before the 1840s the profession had been dominated by men, but soaring immigration and rapid western expansion helped cause a shortage of good teachers, creating opportunities for a new generation of women like Elvira Field. True, her salary was around only a dollar a week plus board—about what she would have made as a domestic worker. Yet despite the low pay, teaching allowed Field to live out of the house and learn to rely on her own resources. Even before meeting Strang, she was already something of a trailblazer.

Antebellum women who transcended rigid gender barriers, as Margaret Fuller observed, had no choice but to "become outlaws," but Elvira Field seems to have embraced the role. It may be true, as she later insisted, that she agreed to the secret marriage with Strang because she viewed his proposition as a command from God. But it's also true that their attraction to each other seems far more complex—and far more intense—than either of them fully put into words. Whatever reservations she may have had about playing the part of Charles Douglass, moreover, she proved herself to be a skillful and savvy confidence woman. What's surprising about her deception is not that a few people saw through it, but that so many others were apparently taken in.

Though perhaps it shouldn't be surprising after all. The annals of the period are full of such deceptions. In October of 1848—a year before Douglass posed for that daguerreotype in Buffalo—the U.S. Army had discharged a soldier named Bill Newcom after he was "discovered to be a disguised woman," according to government records. Private Newcom, whose real name was Elizabeth, had enrolled in Company D of the Missouri Mounted Volunteers at Fort Leavenworth in 1847. Although her unit didn't see any direct action in the Mexican War, she served for more than a year, during which time she withstood "the fatigues of the campaign as well as or better than most able-bodied men of the battalion," according to one newspaper account. Nor was her story all that unusual. In the Civil War, more than 400 women would somehow manage to masquerade as soldiers, observes historian Gayle V. Fischer, author of *Pantaloons and Power: A Nineteenth-Century Dress Reform in the United States*. "Anecdotal evidence," writes Fischer, "suggests that the nineteenth-century United States teemed with women who dressed 'outside their sex.'"

A key factor in all of this was women's fashion, which reinforced sharp distinctions between the sexes through elaborate displays of femininity. Under the antebellum ideal of "true womanhood," fashionable ladies were by the 1840s expected to wear six or seven petticoats beneath bell-shaped dresses that hung all the way to the ground. Decorum also demanded that they adorn themselves with bonnets, belts, shifts, corsets, tight sleeves, and jackets, all of which served both to restrict the wearer's movements and to hide her form from public view. In the words of one later historian: "There never was a period when women...were more completely covered up."

Paradoxically, in Fischer's view, "a woman achieved 'true womanhood' by disguising herself." And the irony of such disguises, such ornate signifiers of femininity, was that they only made it easier for Elvira Field to become Charles Douglass. According to Fischer, women attempting to pass as men found that other people's "entrenched ideas about gender roles often aided...in their charade." In antebellum America, in other words, the very idea that a woman might dare to adopt men's clothing and manners was so alien that many people found it almost impossible to believe—even when staring in the face of just such a gender outlaw.

"We would have every arbitrary barrier thrown down," Margaret Fuller wrote in *Woman in the Nineteenth Century.* "We would have every path laid open to woman as freely as to man." Thanks to her transgressive confidence game, Field had suddenly seen at least a few of those barriers thrown down, those paths laid open. In the guise of Douglass she was able to perform tasks normally done by men, including answering the prophet's correspondence and writing articles for the *Gospel Herald.* She also assisted in religious rites, such as administering the sacrament to members of the congregation, baptizing new converts, and healing the sick.

In her novel *The Hermaphrodite*—probably written in 1846 or 1847 but not published until 2004—suffragist Julia Ward Howe wrote that because antebellum gender roles were so restrictive, some people "wore disguises so they might act the truth." By playing the part of Charles Douglass, it seems, Elvira Field discovered something of her own truth—a sense of power and agency that few women of the era were able to experience. But as the weeks wore on, this masquerade must have begun to exact a huge emotional toll. Because Field had hidden the ruse even from her own family members, they had no idea what had become of her. As far as her loved ones knew, she had simply vanished. For months, in fact, her brother had been on an epic search for her, roaming Michigan on foot for several months in an ever more desperate effort to find his lost sister. "He is quite anxious to learn where she is...I cannot imagine where she has gone unless it is Voree," one baffled resident of Beaver Island informed Strang. If Strang should come upon any information about the young woman's whereabouts, the correspondent added, "I wish you would let me know."

That trust in Strang's goodwill, of course, was misplaced. By the fall of 1849, as the prophet and his "nephew" toured the East to raise money and recruits, his disguise was perhaps even more complete than hers. Whatever was left of his true self—if there ever had been such a thing—was quickly disappearing, as Strang the opportunist crushed Strang the idealist.

But there was one topic, it seems, on which he had never lost his moral center. And so it was that the man who always seemed to have history bearing down on him suddenly found himself forced to take a public stand on the greatest issue of the day.

Eight

In which our protagonist faces a choice between the diabolical and the divine — and, for once, does not place himself on both sides

———◉———

I am eternally tired of hearing that word caution. It is nothing but the word of cowardice.

—John Brown

THE MEN WERE LOST IN THE WOODS: "NO FOOD, NO GUN, NO blanket nor overcoats," as one of them later summed up their plight. Tourists from New England, they had embarked a day earlier on what they thought would be a six-hour hike in the Adirondack Mountains of upstate New York, only to lose their bearings at sunset in a "limitless expanse of forest." After a desperate night, the hungry men spent the following morning struggling through "fallen timber, hillsides, swamps and undergrowth." But then they spotted something in the distance that gave them hope—a modest house.

It was June of 1849—a couple of weeks before J. J. Strang and Elvira Field's secret marriage on Beaver Island—and though the men didn't know it yet, they had stumbled upon one of the many utopian colonies cropping up all over the American wilderness. This one, as they soon discovered, was even more remarkable than most. Its populace was largely black, while the owner of the cabin, "kind of a king among them," was white. Informed that he was not at home but would soon return, the "worn, wearied, black-fly-bitten travelers" lay in the grass beside the house and waited.

They soon learned that the townspeople were "mostly fugitive slaves" who had come there via the Underground Railroad. In fact, this unlikely hamlet in the mountains—located near the Canadian border, the final destination of many of those who escaped bondage—was a terminus for that abolitionist system of secret routes and safe houses. Nationwide, as many as 100,000 slaves had already made their way to freedom through this network, and in recent times rescue efforts had become bolder than ever. The previous year, for example, the largest known nonviolent escape attempt by slaves in U.S. history had been thwarted only when a steamboat carrying a posse of armed white men caught up with a ship called the *Pearl,* carrying seventy-seven fugitive slaves on the Potomac River near Washington, D.C. After the plot was foiled and the intricate organization behind it revealed, outrage among pro-slavery contingents in the South intensified, and a mob rioted through the nation's capital, menacing local abolitionists.

The episode touched off a controversy that reached all the way to Voree, where the *Gospel Herald* lamented the fate of the ship's "unfortunate slaves" and lashed out at "very pious" Christians who "have become rich by trading in the souls of men." In Ohio, meanwhile, the *Pearl* affair inspired Harriet Beecher Stowe to begin writing the anti-slavery melodrama *Uncle Tom's Cabin,* which would sell 10,000 copies in its first week of publication and 300,000 in its first year, becoming the great American bestseller of the nineteenth century and a crucial catalyst of the Civil War.

But the owner of this lonely house in the Adirondacks would play an even bigger role in bringing about that cataclysmic conflict. He arrived in the late afternoon, walking behind a long buckboard wagon that carried some of his black fellow colonists. One of the lost travelers who greeted him that day was Richard Henry Dana

Jr., author of the bestselling maritime memoir *Two Years Before the Mast*, who later described his "grave, serious" host as a "tall, gaunt, dark-complexioned man" who had "a marked countenance and a natural dignity of manner." The stranger's name was John Brown.

In retrospect, 1849 turned out to be a pivotal year for the antislavery movement. Until then, many abolitionists had clung to the concept of "moral suasion"—the belief that good intentions, rational arguments, and righteous appeals to the conscience of white Americans might someday bring an end to slavery. But Brown was among a growing number of radical emancipationists who had come to believe that their aims would never be achieved through talk alone.

As the essayist Henry David Thoreau angrily lamented, "There are thousands who are *in opinion* opposed to slavery...who yet in effect do nothing." Such citizens, Thoreau recognized, would "wait, well disposed, for others to remedy the evil." These words are from his famous essay "Civil Disobedience," first published in 1849 under the title "Resistance to Civil Government." In later generations, it would become one of the most influential works of American philosophy, helping to shape the thinking of such visionaries as Mahatma Gandhi and Martin Luther King Jr. But at the time it was a desperate cry for action, an urgent call for "honest men to rebel":

> How can a man be satisfied to entertain an opinion merely, and enjoy it?...Action from principle,—the perception and the performance of right,—changes things and relations; it is essentially revolutionary....It not only divides States and churches, it divides families; aye, it divides the *individual*, separating the diabolical in him from the divine.

Strang had always had more trouble than most people in sorting out those two intermingled parts of his persona. But in 1849, the issue of race forced him to choose, once and for all, whether to embrace the diabolical or the divine.

Strang's interest in abolitionist politics dated to at least 1836, when the twenty-three-year-old attorney wrote New York representative Abner Hazeltine, an outspoken opponent of slavery in the U.S. Congress, to declare his support for "universal liberty." Hazeltine replied that it was "truly refreshing" to find someone who had the "courage and the inclination" to stand by his principles. By then, of course, Strang had already perfected his talent for telling other people just what they wanted to hear, so a dose of skepticism is in order for any belief he professed—a double dose for the ones he professed passionately. There's no evidence, for instance, that the young attorney ever took action on Hazeltine's suggestion that he join an effort aimed at getting abolitionist newspapers into the hands of people in the South, where such publications were banned.

But if Strang's opposition to slavery was only theoretical in 1836, it seems to have become hardened by firsthand experience in the summer of the following year, when he traveled from the Burned Over District to Virginia as an emissary for his father-in-law, the corrupt canal contractor William L. Perce. In what had become a pattern of fraud, Perce had recently fled Virginia with his work on the James River and Kanawha Canal unfinished. Perhaps fearing he would be arrested if he returned, just as he had been under similar circumstances in New York a few years earlier, Perce dispatched Strang south to mop up the mess.

On canal projects north of the Mason-Dixon Line, the back-breaking work was largely done by Irish laborers and other new immigrants, but on the James River and Kanawha Canal, contractors such as Perce counted on slave labor. Local plantation owners, cash-strapped because of plummeting cotton prices, were anxious to maximize profits on the backs of their black workers. And men like Perce also saw utility in renting slaves, not only because they could be forced to work longer and harder than whites but also because they were thought to better tolerate the southern heat and to resist disease.

When Strang arrived at Perce's construction site, however, he found a feeble and malnourished workforce living amid unspeakable conditions. "The cause of so much sickness here is perfectly obvious," he informed his father-in-law in an outraged letter:

> The men were fed on corn bread and bacon three times a day and coffee once and nothing else. The water for washing and <u>cooking</u> was taken from a <u>mud hole</u> in one side of which...[were] six or eight hogs. The manure in the stable was thrown in a pile before the door. The kitchen slop all went in front of the door and large ponds of green water were suffered to accumulate...near the houses....After reading this...far from being surprised that half [the] good hands are sick...you will better be astonished that three-fourths are not dead.

One of Perce's associates at the site, Strang observed, "attributes all misfortune" to the slaves. But Strang himself insisted that any lack of production on their part was due to sickness and squalid conditions. When able to work, he wrote, "they are better than whites."

Strang would not soon forget the image of infirm and underfed slaves cracking rocks in the fierce July heat or wallowing knee-deep in mud amid swarms of malaria-carrying mosquitoes. For the rest of his life, he would be an outspoken abolitionist. But until 1849, it seems, he had never been faced with the need to act on those convictions.

———

When Strang arrived in New York City on October 7 of that eventful year, shortly after reuniting with Elvira Field in Buffalo, he found his followers torn over the issue of whether to admit a black man to the priesthood—a title normally conferred on all male members of the Mormon Church.

The late Joseph Smith had sent mixed signals on the status of African Americans. In the Book of Mormon, for example, dark skin is a sign of God's curse. That text tells the story of the Lamanites, members of a lost tribe of Israel who hardened their hearts against God, and "because of their iniquity...the Lord God did cause a skin of blackness to come upon them." But Smith's views had evolved over time. Although he remained an opponent of interracial mixing, he came to believe that African Americans "have souls & are subjects of salvation." At his death in 1844, he was campaigning for president on a platform of emancipation, in which freed slaves would be sent to Mexico.

Brigham Young, by contrast, had taken an increasingly racist position. In 1847, for example, upon receiving a report about a black man being married to a white Mormon woman—a union that resulted in a child—he had responded, "If they were far away from the Gentiles [i.e., non-Mormons], they would all have to be killed." The farther into the wilderness Young and his flock traveled, the more hardened his views on race became. An outsider who spent the winter of 1849–50 in Salt Lake City reported that church leaders were assuring followers "the Negro is cursed...and must always be a servant wherever his lot is cast." According to this same witness, a system of black "involuntary labor" was already in place in Utah. In 1852, Young declared himself "a firm believer in slavery" and officially banned African Americans from the priesthood, proclaiming that "negroes shall not rule us." But in practical terms, that ban was already in place when Strang arrived in New York in 1849.

Perhaps it was no wonder, then, that Strang's followers in New York were unsure what to do about a black man named Moore Walker who had applied for ordination in the church. This was apparently the same Moore Walker who had long been active in abolitionist circles, serving on the board of the American Moral Reform Society, a group of black leaders devoted to boycotting goods produced by slave labor and employing all other available means in the struggle for emancipation. During its existence, from 1835 to 1841, this organization was "visionary in the extreme," in the phrasing of one contemporary—so much so that it had passed a resolution (seconded by Walker) denouncing any reference to a person's skin color as a gratuitous form of racial discrimination. The group had also worked to promote equal rights for blacks in white-dominated churches, leaving open the question of whether Walker, who later joined a Protestant congregation, was a true believer in Mormonism or had come only to see if the sect would grant a black parishioner membership.

Whatever the case, Strang rose to the occasion. According to minutes of the conference—apparently written by the capable Charles J. Douglass—the prophet began by noting "the impression had gone forth that a colored man could not hold the priesthood." But this, he said, was "not true." While conceding that Mormon theology taught that "color was a curse," he insisted that this fact posed "no bar" to admitting blacks to the priesthood. Then, in a display of his rhetorical powers, he asked followers to look inward. "Who is there that does not labor under a curse?" he asked. "Death is the fate of all men, and is a curse incurred by sin."

So it was that Strang's wing of Mormonism ordained an African American elder—a full 129 years before Brigham Young's branch finally lifted its ban on blacks in the priesthood and 164 years before the Utah-based church offered a full disavowal of "the theories advanced in the past that black skin is a sign of divine disfavor or curse."

Four days before Strang welcomed a black man into his flock, a paper on the Eastern Shore of Maryland published a notice offering a $300 reward for the capture and return of three escaped slaves. One of those fugitives was a woman identified as "MINTY, aged about 27 years," and described as being "of a chestnut color, fine looking, and about 5 feet high." Born into bondage under the name Araminta Ross, she adopted a new name—Harriet Tubman—when she showed up in Philadelphia in the autumn of 1849, having reached freedom along the Underground Railroad. Under her new identity, Tubman soon gained international acclaim as a leading abolitionist and Underground Railroad operator, secretly returning to Maryland again and again to help liberate about seventy other slaves.

THREE HUNDRED DOLLARS REWARD.

RANAWAY from the subscriber on Monday the 17th ult., three negroes, named as follows: HARRY, aged about 19 years, has on one side of his neck a wen, just under the ear, he is of a dark chestnut color, about 5 feet 8 or 9 inches hight; BEN, aged about 25 years, is very quick to speak when spoken to, he is of a chestnut color, about six feet high; MINTY, aged about 27 years, is of a chestnut color, fine looking, and about 5 feet high. One hundred dollars reward will be given for each of the above named negroes, if taken out of the State, and $50 each if taken in the State. They must be lodged in Baltimore, Easton or Cambridge Jail, in Maryland.

ELIZA ANN BRODESS,
Near Bucktown, Dorchester county, Md.
Oct. 3d, 1849.

☞The Delaware Gazette will please copy the above three weeks, and charge this office.

Notice in a Cambridge, Maryland, newspaper for Harriet Tubman's capture.

Tubman's daring flight to freedom was just one of many brave escapades of its kind in 1849—"the year of remarkable slave escapes," according to Manisha Sinha, author of *The Slave's Cause: A History of Abolition*. On March 24, for example, a heavy wooden box labeled "dry goods" had arrived at the headquarters of the Pennsylvania Anti-Slavery Society. Inside was a fugitive slave named Henry Brown, who, with the help of friends, had packed himself into the crate the day before in Richmond, Virginia, then had himself shipped to freedom as cargo. The stunning odyssey—described in a book published as Strang began his tour of eastern states—had already made Henry "Box" Brown famous, inspiring abolitionists and igniting new fear and rage among slave owners.

Another recent escape, meanwhile, had made a mockery of the "scientific" justification for slavery—a widely held belief in the fixity of biological differences based on skin color. As one prominent slave-holding physician from Alabama put it, whites and blacks were two entirely different species, "originally and radically distinct." Like the boundaries between men and women, the theory went, these lines were impermeable. On Christmas morning of 1848, however, when a gentleman from Georgia and his African American valet stepped down from a train in Philadelphia, everything began to blur. Over the previous four days, the pair had journeyed about 1,000 miles by rail, coach, and steamboat, traveling in luxury. In Charleston, South Carolina, they had stayed in an excellent room at the city's best hotel, where they were paid "the attention and homage [the proprietor] thought a gentleman of his high position merited." But unbeknownst to the obsequious innkeeper (or to any of the other Southerners with whom this wealthy traveler had come in contact), the young gentleman wasn't white. Nor was he wealthy. Nor was he a man. He—or rather she—was Ellen Craft, a fugitive slave, the light-skinned daughter of her own white master. The valet was also a runaway—her husband, William Craft.

In the months since their ingenious deception, the Crafts had become celebrities, their escape hailed as "an incident of courage and noble daring" by prominent abolitionist Wendell Phillips, who predicted that "future poets and historians would tell this story as one of the most thrilling in the nation's annals; and millions would read it with admiration." Even in an age when it could sometimes seem that everyone was wearing a disguise, Ellen Craft's metamorphosis—not just from woman to man, but from racially tainted to racially pure, from an object of scorn to one of fawning esteem, from slave to master—had the power to astonish, arousing both fascination and terror. If the two races were "originally and radically distinct," how could the lines smudge so easily?

Nineteenth-century illustration of Ellen Craft disguised as a man.

———

We don't know whether the woman who called herself Charles J. Douglass read about the much-publicized adventures of Ellen Craft, confidence woman extraordinaire. Nor do we know whether "Charley" felt a tinge of envy for the fugitive slave who had to disguise herself as a man for only a few days, rather than for months on end. What we do know is that the longer Strang's tour of the East wore on, the more exhausted his private secretary grew of her part in the masquerade.

The first week of February 1850 found Elvira Field in a melancholy mood. By then she had been playing the role of Charley Douglass for more than four months, and several weeks still remained before she could return home and resume her life as a woman. To make matters worse, she found herself apart from Strang, who was in Washington, D.C., while she waited in Baltimore, fighting a nasty cold. On February 4, she wrote the prophet to report that she was enduring "some rather lonesome evenings" without him. But something else was also bringing her down. Having recently learned of her brother's desperate efforts to locate her, she was reckoning with the profound emotional consequences of her unexplained disappearance. "[It] make[s] me a little sad to heare [*sic*] of other people's sadness," she told Strang. "You know what I mean."

Meanwhile, as the prophet's personal secretary waited for him in Baltimore, sick and gloomy, his legal spouse was still stranded at the home of his parents in upstate New York. She too was glum. Writing Strang to tell him that his brother David's wife had been felled suddenly by one of the many deadly diseases that regularly raged through antebellum America, she added, "Her death has shocked me beyond my power of expression." The letter was short and curt—evidence of Mary's exasperation with a mate who had contacted her only sporadically and largely kept her in the dark about his travels. By now she knew her husband had an assistant named Charley, though she was apparently still unaware of the unusual nature of that relationship. But that didn't make her any less bitter. "I have neither the time or strength to write more," a businesslike Mary declared, closing the letter with the less than affectionate valediction "yours, etc."

Strang took his time in replying, explaining to his long-suffering wife that he had hesitated to write because of his own bouts with illness and depression: "I have not been well...and my spirits begin to lag. I have only kept up by the exercise of an iron will and if that gives way I shall sink." As for Charley, the prophet told his wife that the young man "can scarce help me at all," due to the fact that he, too, was "sinking rapidly."

———

Sinking was a term that applied to many others beyond Strang and his assistant. It was a catchall antebellum expression of anxiety, suggesting not just a loss of health or physical strength but also a decline in economic or social status, a failure of the will, a collapse of the spirit, a descent into chaos. Tocqueville had once commented on this American obsession with "not sinking." As the first few months of 1850 unfurled, people across the nation felt the ground give way as the body politic reached the point of no return on the issue of slavery. In mid-February, for example, South Carolina senator John C. Calhoun—a fierce proponent of the peculiar institution—declared that the South "cannot safely remain in the Union, as things now stand," and that "there is little or no prospect of any change for the better."

Many of Calhoun's enemies shared this sense of doom. Among them was Frederick Douglass, who in recent months had abandoned his moral-suasion stance and begun openly to advocate the use of violence, thanks to a newfound conviction that "slavery can only end in blood." It was a view echoed by Douglass's friend John Brown, who had started to make secret plans for an armed insurrection against the U.S. government, convinced that God had selected him "for the emancipation of the negro race." In fact, the anti-slavery zealot had already zeroed in on a target: the U.S. arsenal at Harper's Ferry, Virginia.

Many years after his accidental encounter with John Brown in the woods of upstate New York, Richard Henry Dana Jr. looked back with wonder at that June day of 1849:

> It would have been past belief had we been told that this quiet frontier farmer, already at or beyond middle life, with no

noticeable past, would, within ten years, be the central figure
of a great tragic scene, gazed upon with wonder, pity, admiration or execration by half a continent! That this man should
be thought to have imperiled the slave empire in America,
and added a new danger to the stability of the Union! That
his almost indistinguishable name of John Brown should be
whispered among four millions of slaves, and sung wherever
the English tongue is spoken, and incorporated into an anthem
to whose solemn cadences men should march to battle by the
tens of thousands! That he should have done something toward
changing the face of civilization itself!

The incident caused Dana to reflect, in his exclamatory fashion,
upon the elusory nature of destiny. "How mysterious," he wrote, "is
the touch of Fate which gives a man immortality on earth!"

James Strang, too, had spent his whole life waiting to feel that
touch. "Fame, fame alone of all the productions of man's folly may
survive," the ambitious young man had written sixteen years earlier.
Now, as he concluded his tour of the East in March of 1850,
Strang's dreams of a place in history seemed far more realistic than
those of John Brown, with whom he had much in common. Both
were headstrong men who had gone broke in the Panic of 1837,
having speculated recklessly in land. Both had failed in a number of
professions before stumbling into careers as prophets of God. Both
had a gift for gaining the confidence of devoted followers. Both
would soon make headlines for standoffs with the U.S. government.
And both would get themselves killed.

But for the moment, Strang's long-held "dreams of royalty and
power" finally seemed within reach. On the way home from his tour
of the East, the prophet apparently parted company with his devoted
"traveling friend," Charles J. Douglass. The young man was never
seen again, evanescing into the mists of history as suddenly as the

long-vanished Elvira Field would soon reappear on Beaver Island. In western New York, Strang rejoined his wife of thirteen years and their three children, departing with them for the island, but the reunion proved brief. When Mary and the children came down ill again, the restless prophet abandoned them once more, this time in Buffalo, and pressed ahead to the island—where, thanks to the recent influx of Mormon settlers, he and other leaders of his sect now planned to move their families and set up permanent residence.

Even the prophet's own mother was shocked by this latest desertion. "We felt very bad to think that Mary and the children were left at Buffalo, unwell, and among strangers & very little money," Abigail Strang wrote to her son, adding with obvious exasperation, "I would like to know what engaged your attention last winter to keep you so long absent from your family. I hope you will endeavor to be with them more." Aware of her son's wild ambition, she closed with some motherly advice: "Do not let [your] whole soul be taken up in trying to make yourself great in the eyes of man."

But it was far too late for that. Strang was about to crown himself king.

Nine

In which the King of Earth and Heaven
is inaugurated with a crown made
of paper on a throne stuffed with tree moss

————))((◉))((————

"But the emperor has nothing on!" said the little child.
—Hans Christian Andersen, "The Emperor's New Clothes"

AT THE CORONATION OF QUEEN VICTORIA ON JUNE 28, 1838, an unprecedented crowd of 400,000 people had lined the streets of London to see the procession. Some, like Charles Dickens, rented rooms along the route for a better view of the monarch as she rolled past in her ornately gilded coach, pulled by eight horses and weighing four tons. The ceremony took place in Westminster Abbey, the setting of every coronation since 1066, with its 500-foot-long chapel and 100-foot-high nave, tallest in England. The young queen sat on a magnificent oaken throne, carved in 1300 and fitted with an ancient relic known as the Stone of Destiny, which, according to legend, the biblical patriarch Jacob had used as a pillow when he dreamed of a ladder to heaven. Victoria's crown, made specially for the event, contained more than 3,000 gems, including the legendary Black Prince's Ruby, which Richard III was said to have been wearing when he was killed at the Battle of Bosworth Field in 1485.

At the coronation of King James on July 8, 1850, a couple of hundred people gathered on a mosquito-infested island 3,696 miles from London and 218 miles from the nearest town of even 20,000 people. The grand event took place in a half-finished building called a tabernacle—in reality just a crude structure of hewn lumber, completed to the height of seven or eight feet with a piece of drapery stretched across the ceiling to hide the fir joists from view. The throne on which the king would receive his rites was made of boards, covered with painted cloth and stuffed with tree moss. The crown, made of paper and decorated with gold tinsel stars, was designed by the king himself with the help of the former Charles J. Douglass, who had returned to Beaver Island as her true self, Elvira Field, and was, on this historic morning, celebrating her twentieth birthday.

As a young diarist, Strang had dreamed of marrying Victoria and assuming the English crown. The elusive empress had, of course, slipped through his grasp, but now he was gaining something even greater than the British empire. He was about to take the throne as the King of Earth and Heaven.

———

Ever since the founding of the Order of the Illuminati in 1846, many of Strang's disciples had been swearing obedience to him as their "Imperial Primate and Absolute Sovereign." But those secret rites, conducted in cramped dark rooms in Voree, fell far short of the magisterial fantasies that had long haunted Strang's imagination. Now that he was in charge of an actual kingdom, he planned to announce himself to the world as an actual king. True, the kingdom was tiny and isolated. And true, his control over it was tenuous at best. But in an era of manic go-aheadism and audacious wish fulfillment, Strang intended to become the ultimate self-made man. As Edgar Allan Poe observed in a posthumous story collection published a few months before the coronation, people who "dream by day are cognizant of many things which escape those who dream only by night." Whatever else might be said about him, James Strang dreamed by day.

One of the few people who could match him in this extravagant urge to make fantasies come true—a trait Poe attributed to a "disease of thought"—was the master of ceremonies for the day's event, George J. Adams. Having spent years trolling the East for recruits, the mercurial preacher finally planned to be a more permanent resident of Beaver Island now that the glorious kingdom was taking shape. Arriving in late April of 1850, about ten days after Strang, he quickly established himself as an oversize force in the religious and political life of the tiny colony. Nonetheless, a newspaper correspondent who saw him preach on the island a month before the coronation came away less than dazzled. Adams, he wrote, was a "regular tearer" who spoke "long and loud concerning this God-forsaken generation" and "maintains there is no redemption for this black hearted Government from the sink of iniquity into which it has fallen, short of entire destruction, and boldly declares the sooner the better."

And yet it was precisely this scaremongering that seemed to draw people to Adams. He may have been an object of ridicule among the learned, but in a turbulent age he was an expert at playing on the public's fear and anger. Just five days before this coronation ceremony, for instance, the tragedian had set off a sudden furor on the island, going before the faithful to announce that he had learned a mob was going to be gathered "for the purpose of breaking up our assemblies and also to drive us from the island." With his usual bravado, the preacher threatened that "every person who [is] not of this church and are found in the ranks of our enemies or with mobs shall die!"

The recent flood of Mormon immigrants to the island had caused a backlash among other residents of St. James, as Strang and his followers had recently renamed Beaver Island's main settlement. Some frustrated locals had gone so far as attempting to stop newcomers from setting foot in the town. "A dozen men would generally surround a family of emigrants and order them back on the boat, telling them that they were preparing to drive off and kill all the Mormons," Strang would later remember. But as the colony continued to grow, with the prophet's followers now far outnumbering the small number of original white settlers, Strang had become more bellicose. Vowing that his people would "no longer submit to injury and insult," he declared that from now on they would "return blow for blow." Until Adams sounded the alarm of an imminent raid, however, the violence had been limited to isolated incidents.

For the next two days after Adams's warning, residents of the colony went into a state of high alert, convinced that assailants from the island, as well as from nearby Mackinac Island and the mainland, were planning an attack during Fourth of July celebrations. One Mormon who took part in an all-night vigil remembered running into Strang, who warned that everyone needed to be prepared for bloodshed and showed his own weapon—a frontier version of nunchucks, consisting of a thick length of string from which dangled "a piece of lead of the shape & size of an egg."

But no raid ever materialized—a fact that the prophet later attributed to cannon blasts he fired as warning, which made his would-be attackers "not a little alarmed." He also claimed to have committed acts of sabotage—destroying gunpowder and poisoning barrels of whiskey—while on a late-night mission to the nearby trading post where his foes were allegedly massing. But modern observers can't be blamed for questioning whether the entire crisis was manufactured by Adams and Strang in order to unite followers against a common enemy and to convince them, in those days before the coronation, that it would be necessary to surrender themselves to the will of the king.

In preparation for the coronation, Adams had put his theater training to good use, designing costumes, buying Masonic regalia for the royal wardrobe, and overseeing construction of the set. "There was

a curtain drawn in front of the stand so as to conceal from view anything that might occur behind," one audience member later recalled.
"But as George Adams was a play actor, we expected to see some
great performance." The man was not disappointed:

> When ready to exhibit, the curtain was drawn aside and to our
> great astonishment we beheld Strang sitting in a large chair with...a
> scepter in his hand....Then George J. Adams became animated with
> some powerful spirit and began to testify that he knew Strang was a
> prophet and that if he ever denied it he hoped God Almighty would
> send a thunderbolt and knock his brains out, that his tongue might
> cleave to the roof of his mouth.

When Adams was done, audience members leaned forward in
nervous anticipation. "Such a scene," the man in the audience would
one day remember, "has never presented itself before nor since." It
was, in fact, just like something from a fable.

———

One day a couple of swindlers, who called themselves weavers, made
their appearance in the imperial town of _____. They pre-
tended that they were able to weave the richest stuffs, in which not only
the colors and pattern were extremely beautiful, but that the clothes
made of such stuffs possessed the property of remaining invisible to
him who was unfit for the office he held, or was extremely silly.

So goes "The Emperor's New Clothes," a tale just then reaching
American audiences for the first time, with newspapers across the
country excerpting an English translation published in 1846. No
doubt Hans Christian Andersen's fable of deception and delusion
had special resonance for antebellum readers, who increasingly encountered con artists in their everyday lives. Now, with the help of

Adams, Strang was about to offer his own retelling of that parable, but with a twist: in his version, swindler and emperor were the same man. And somehow this man, this fabulist, this king, had managed to convince the 235 lonely souls gathered in the tabernacle that his paper crown was a dazzling royal diadem, that his wooden scepter hummed with occult energies, and that his floor-length red robe, stitched together by ladies of the church, enveloped him in righteousness and splendor. But did he believe it himself? Had he become so masterly at spinning cloth from thin air that now, perched on his moss-stuffed throne, he had finally become both the deceiver and the deceived?

One person who seemed to have doubts about the whole spectacle was the prophet's wife Mary, who, according to a later report, "did not attend as she was not a believer in his doctrine." Assuming this secondhand account is accurate, Mary Strang was missing out on the sight of her husband seated on a raised stage, with more than a dozen church officials seated behind him. Then there was Adams, who, according to another witness, "towered over the short-statured King, who, however, made up in intellect what he lacked in frame." As the ceremony began in earnest, all eyes were on the little bald man who now claimed that his lineage traced directly back to David, the first monarch of all the tribes of Israel. Aware of the Mormon belief that one of David's descendants would rule in the last days, Strang had covered himself head to foot in robes that, according to a firsthand account, "were made to resemble the Ancient Jewish High Priests."

———

Strang's new clothes weren't the only garments that had been causing a stir on Beaver Island in the buildup to the day's ceremony. About a month earlier, a visiting correspondent had been surprised to observe "large numbers of lady saints" sporting a "new style of dress which the ladies here are bringing into vogue." Namely, breeches. Because of the period's rigid codes for female dress, the idea of women in pantaloons—loose-fitting trousers, gathered at the ankles—was as shocking and salacious to Americans of the mid-nineteenth century as the idea of women in bikinis would be a century later. The newspaper correspondent didn't seem sure whether to be amused, outraged, or aroused. Noting that the women of Beaver Island "have not entirely discarded dresses, but wear them coming just below the knee," he ventured that the ones sporting pantaloons "looked quite comical," though he was quick to qualify that he could "hardly say, however, that they looked bad."

Another visitor, a Mormon who had come to the island shortly before the coronation, was also taken aback. One morning soon after his arrival, the man ran into a young woman with short black hair who was "dressed in drawers & skirts coming to the knees which looked odd," he recalled. "I made some remarks about the oddity of her dress, which she seemed to resent, & replied to with spirit. Her name was Elvira Field."

The young woman's return to Beaver Island, it seems, had been as enigmatic as her departure. The date and manner of her arrival are lost to time, as are several other crucial details, such as how she managed to account for her absence and how she was received on the island by family and friends. Also missing from the historical record are the circumstances under which the king informed Mary Strang that he had taken a second wife, though by all indications she was not pleased with the news. However these emotionally charged events may have played out, Field does not give the impression of having been particularly deferential, either to Mary or to anyone else. Perhaps emboldened by her long masquerade as Charles J. Douglass, she had abandoned neither the habit of wearing trousers nor, judging by her interaction with the stranger that day, the habit of speaking her mind.

In both traits, she was ahead of her time. Indeed, pantaloons would soon become a symbol of the national women's movement. The following spring, a social reformer named Amelia Bloomer made headlines for wearing short skirts and "Turkish trousers" and for encouraging other women to throw off "ten or fifteen pounds of petticoat." In the ensuing public furor, such legwear became known as the "Bloomer costume," or simply "bloomers." But almost a year before Amelia Bloomer herself adopted the style, Field and other women on Beaver Island were wearing breeches in public.

By all indications, the force behind this radical new costume was Strang himself, who may have borrowed the idea from another controversial utopian colony, the Oneida Community in central New York. This group of "Bible communists" practiced a system of "complex marriage," in which men and women frequently exchanged sexual partners. It was part of Oneida's revolutionary rethinking of gender relations, which also included what one insider called "semi-masculine attire" for female members. Strang may have had many reasons for instituting a similar dress code, but as the historian Gayle Fischer points out in *Pantaloons and Power,* one was obvious: "social control." According to Fischer, "Standardized apparel enabled Strang to limit and regulate the clothing choices available to women and reinforce his dominance."

Modern cult experts list the use of special uniforms among tactics that leaders use to isolate members from the outside world, establish a separate social universe, and enforce conformity. It's probably no coincidence, then, that Strang's new dress code emerged as he attempted to consolidate power, pressuring almost every man, woman, and child on Beaver Island to sign a loyalty oath. In the lead-up to the day's coronation, followers as young as nine had sworn allegiance to Strang "in preference to the laws, commandments and persons of any other Kings, Potentates, or States."

———

After Adams placed the crown on Strang's head that momentous morning, he knelt before his new king. Raising his royal scepter—a wooden stick about a foot and a half long—the monarch tapped Adams on the head, thereby ordaining him as prime minister. After christening several other nobles with the same rite, "James, the Anointed" sat on his throne and brandished his scepter while "with uplifted hands," as one observer put it, the faithful bore witness "that the Kingdom of God is set up on Earth."

To make that kingdom a reality, Strang and Adams had recently composed a "testimony to the nation." Addressed to President Zachary Taylor, the U.S. Congress, and the American people, the document formally requested that the prophet and his followers be granted the right to "settle upon and forever occupy all the uninhabited lands of the islands of Lake Michigan." Though the pols and bureaucrats in Washington may have scoffed at the idea, those gathered in the tabernacle seem to have truly believed they were, at that very moment, establishing an independent nation-state on U.S. soil.

Near the end of the coronation, Adams led the faithful in a cheer: "Long live James, King in Zion!" they chanted as one. Then, after Strang asked the congregation to rise, Adams closed the ceremony with an "eloquent discourse," in which he revealed a miraculous dream he'd had, one that foretold a glorious future in which he and Brother Strang were "to be together and take the lead in the great work of the last days." And with that, the remarkable events of the day had finally come to an end.

A century later, a psychologist would coin a memorable term for the way human beings rationalize inconsistencies in their experience. In the 1950s, while studying members of an apocalyptic cult, Leon Festinger used *cognitive dissonance* to describe the means by which people are able to maintain logically impossible beliefs. The subjects of Festinger's study had convinced themselves that superior beings from the planet Clarion would swoop down in a flying saucer and save them just before the end of the world. But was that belief any more improbable than the faith of Strang's followers that this plain-looking little man with the paper crown on his head and a costume straight out of some traveling sideshow would soon rule heaven and earth?

Avoidance of facts that might contradict the group's belief system—Festinger called it *cognitive dissonance,* but long before he came up with a phrase for such magical thinking, Hans Christian Andersen had described it in a fable. That tale—a parable about how we convince ourselves not to believe our own eyes—so closely approximates Strang's coronation on Beaver Island that we need not try to come up with a new moral for this story. We can capture the final moments of that gathering simply by appropriating the last lines of Andersen's marvelous allegory: *But the emperor and the courtiers—they retained their seeming faith, and walked on with great dignity to the close of the procession.*

Ten

In which the inhabitants of Beaver Island evolve into what Charles Darwin might have called "a different set of beings"

Was [he], then, a pirate, sir?—for they who make free with the goods of others on the high seas are neither more nor less than pirates.

—James Fenimore Cooper, *The Sea Lions*, 1849

IN THE IMMEDIATE AFTERMATH OF HIS CORONATION, STRANG made two bold moves. One was to announce that God had given the islands of the Great Lakes to him and his followers. No longer did the land on Beaver Island belong to the federal government or to the original Odawa and Ojibwe inhabitants, or to anybody else—and no longer did the Mormons have to worry about paying for it. God had blessed Strang with the power to assign parcels of land to Mormon pilgrims, who, in return for these "inheritances," would give the king a tenth of all they possessed. Thus did the colony abandon its great experiment in socialism, the Order of Enoch, to become instead a theocratic kleptocracy, with Strang as Squatter-in-Chief.

The other bold move was to purchase a boat. The prophet paid $1,000 for it—about $34,000 in today's dollars—a huge outlay for the cash-strapped kingdom. But the monarch had big plans for the schooner, a vessel known for its speed and agility. Such a boat, of course, would have many practical uses for the colony, including

fishing and transporting people and goods to and from the mainland and nearby islands. But schooners were notorious for other
uses as well. Fast and maneuverable, they could make quick escapes
and launch sudden attacks, navigating easily in shallow waters and
shoals. They were, in other words, the perfect vessels of pirates.

———

Get rich quick. That phrase—and, in no small part, that spirit—is
a lasting legacy of the antebellum period. But when King Strang assumed his throne in 1850, it seemed as though everyone was making
a fast buck except the denizens of Beaver Island. In that year alone,
miners extracted $42 million worth of gold from California—more
than the entire annual U.S. federal budget—and the nation was
consumed with "gold fever," as tens of thousands of people packed
up their possessions and scrambled toward the promised land. "The
frenzy continues to increase every day," wrote an observer in New
York. "It seems as if the Atlantic Coast was to be depopulated, such
swarms of people are leaving it for the new El Dorado. It is the
most remarkable emigration on record in the history of man since
the days of the Crusades." One newspaper went even further in
describing this mania: "The coming of the Messiah, or the dawn of
the Millennium could not have excited anything like the interest."

On Beaver Island—the precise spot where that millennium was
due to transpire—the prophet worried his followers would succumb
to gold fever. In the *Gospel Herald,* he warned that those who
went to California would inevitably find themselves "surrounded
by desperadoes, where the rifle and the bowie knife are the only
protection to life, [and] will necessarily and inevitably fall into the
same practices. The country will have more gold robbers than gold
diggers." Luckily, "gold fever has seized on so very few of the saints,"
reported Strang, who assured his flock that the way to strike it rich
was by sticking with him. "We look forward with confidence," he
wrote, "to the time when the chosen ones of God shall possess not

merely the [rivers and streams] where men wash sands for hidden gold dust, but the mines, the mountain masses from which these particles have been abraded."

The trouble was that Strang's followers couldn't wait for the millennium to feed their families. From the very start of his reign, the king faced overwhelming financial pressures. True, his recent tour of the East had brought in some much-needed cash. But how long would it last? And how would Strang feed and house all the new converts arriving at Beaver Island, where temperatures sometimes dropped to twenty-five below zero and an icy lake prevented commerce with the outside world for months on end? How, in short, would the monarch pay for his new kingdom?

Just one year earlier, some residents of Voree had gone to desperate lengths in order to keep "men, women & children shod for the winter," as one follower put it. In a time when 90,000 gold-seekers from all over the world arrived in California, a small group of Mormons undertook their own mining venture in western Wisconsin, near the shores of the Mississippi River. They were in quest not of gold but of lead—a key antebellum commodity, used to make everything from pipes to gutters to bullets.

A few of their fellow church members saw the undertaking as dangerously speculative, based more on wishful thinking than on any solid chance of success. But faced with mounting debts and the onset of cold weather, the men felt they had no better hope. For months they dug from morning until night in the cold and wet, using shovels and pickaxes to sink shafts into the rocky soil—all for nothing. No lead, no luck. In despair, one of the miners wrote Strang to beg for divine intervention. Couldn't the prophet simply look into his seer stones—those magical glasses that received revelations from God—and pinpoint the exact location of the lead? Strang, it seems, did not reply. Finally, after months of futile digging, the men abandoned the mining operation early in 1850. "Our enemies think that we are down," one church leader wrote. "And unless God delivers us we are. We are worse off now than we were a year ago."

Yet there were other ways of getting rich quick—schemes that had been employed by Mormon vigilantes in Nauvoo, schemes that were even better suited to Beaver Island, which afforded Strang strategic advantages he couldn't have dreamed of on dry land. "The 'consecrating' of 'Gentile' property, or, in other words, the robbing of those who were not Mormons, was a recognized and established practice, from the earliest settlement of the island," a local historian named Morgan Lewis Leach wrote in 1883.

Leach based his assertion on interviews with surviving witnesses, including Mormons who had lived on the island at the time. The prophet's own correspondence from the period also seems to support the claim. In February of 1850, for example, Adams had boasted to Strang about teaching new recruits how to consecrate property. "We are going into the gentiles with a rush," he reported from Baltimore, while both men were still touring the East. Although Adams used coded language, his meaning seems almost unmistakable: "We will send you—or I mean we will bring you some 'rocks' so keep cool—all is good—all is straight—everything is going ahead." The justification for such "plundering operations," wrote Leach, was that they were "the natural and legitimate sequence of the doctrine that the Mormons are God's peculiar people, who alone had a right to the earth and were eventually to possess it."

———

Almost three decades later, in a newspaper from the port town of Oswego, New York, a salty old sailor would tell a tale so riveting it sounded like something out of a pirate novel, a genre hugely popular among antebellum readers. Unlike most of those yarns, however, this one did not take place in the Caribbean or on the Barbary Coast of North Africa. The setting was an island in Lake Michigan, and the events supposedly transpired in the autumn of 1849, as Strang was in the midst of his adventures back east with his putative nephew. The sailor had apparently been encountered by the newspaper writer at a shop where this "weather beaten hulk," who was never named in the article, was regaling other customers with yarns from his shipboard days.

"The lakes have had pirates in their day," declared the ancient mariner. Then he launched into a suspenseful account of a passage from Chicago to Buffalo aboard a small brig, a sailing vessel with two square-rigged masts, which encountered strong northerly winds as it approached Beaver Island. At first, the captain "thought we could breast out the breeze," the sailor recounted, but the men soon realized that the seas, "too 'bumpy,'" were causing the little brig to make "dives that would do credit to a loon." With night approaching and the sky threatening snow, the captain decided to cast anchor near the coast and remain there "until the storm had spent its fury." After dropping both anchors and paying out the chains to ensure the ship was secure, the crew turned in. Around midnight, however, they were awakened by the screams of the man standing watch. "On reaching the deck," the old man remembered, "we could see by the lights of the Mormons' houses that we were drifting fast toward the beach." Springing into action, the crew managed to unfurl the sails just in time. "When the canvass filled, the brig picked up her feet and clawed off the shore like a green turtle...digs back to the water."

What had caused the ship to drift? Sabotage, according to the sailor. The crew soon discovered that someone had rowed into the lake late at night, snuck up to the bow of the brig, and cut the chains holding its anchors. "It was evident that the Mormons had been at work," the seafarer recalled, "and had it not been for the timely discovery we would soon have been ashore and murdered."

All those years later, he still considered himself lucky to have survived: "Several vessels disappeared in that vicinity in mid-summer, and neither they nor their crews were ever heard from," he claimed.

"It was said that the Mormons boarded becalmed vessels, murdered the crews, discharged the cargoes on the island and burned or scuttled the craft."

Perhaps this outlandish yarn, recounted thirty years after the fact by a witness of possibly questionable lucidity, was simply a sea story, a few half-remembered half-truths mixed with a massive amount of legend and bravado. Or perhaps the old man never existed at all, none of the events actually transpired, and the *Oswego Palladium* correspondent who wrote the piece made the whole thing up for the sake of amusement. Either might be just as likely as the tale itself. And yet the mariner's story was far from the only allegation of piracy by Beaver Islanders. Nor, it turns out, was buccaneering the only crime rumored to be taking place at the colony.

The king placed the coin in the young man's palm and invited him to examine it. One side was stamped with a seated Lady Liberty surrounded by a circle of stars, while the other was emblazoned with a bald eagle clutching an olive branch in the talons of one leg and three arrows of war in the other. Above the eagle's head stretched the words UNITED STATES OF AMERICA, and beneath its feet ran the inscription HALF DOL., for half dollar.

The young man studied the coin, turned it over, felt its cool surface.

It was bad, the king told him. Counterfeit. And he gave the young man a conspiratorial glance while he held up two other coins. As soon as the proper supplies arrived, he said, there would be more where these came from.

It was the autumn of 1850, and this conversation allegedly took place in the tabernacle on Beaver Island. The young man hadn't intended to run into the monarch that morning, he would later say, much less to learn about his counterfeiting scheme; he'd come only to pick up a misplaced umbrella. Or at least that's what he would soon testify in a deposition for a federal criminal case against

Strang. The young man would also swear that Strang tried to recruit him: "He wanted men to go off on a consecrating expedition and a-passing counterfeit money."

———

By the second half of 1850, a new sense of reality had begun to overtake the island slowly but inescapably, like the onset of winter. The biggest change, Elvira Field later wrote, was that "church and state were united," with Strang now securing complete power as "law-giver," along with his previous roles of apostle, prophet, seer, and revelator. Field's own status in the new kingdom, by contrast, was less well-defined. On the one hand, Strang was not yet willing to acknowledge her as his plural wife or to embrace polygamy as an official practice of the church. On the other, their relationship was now an open secret, with Elvira listed in the 1850 census as a resident of both Strang's household and that of her own parents. She appeared arm in arm with the king in public and, in the aftermath of the coronation, apparently took up residence under his roof. If her presence in that house was a source of outrage and embarrassment to Mary Strang, it seems to have been a point of pride to the prophet, who liked to call his new love "Charley" in front of others, a none-too-subtle reference to their sexual escapades in the East. "He made a great joke of this," one island resident later wrote, "and boasted 'Charles' was the best worker he ever had."

This, of course, made Field the target of endless speculation and gossip. One visitor to the island described her as a "lewd woman," adding that Strang was "guilty of gross corruption." Appalled by their "shameless" relationship, as well as by the sight of some of Strang's top lieutenants involved in a roguish game of cards, he made a hasty departure, opting not to join members of his family who had moved to the island. But other followers seemed to adjust themselves to their strange new existence, learning to accept as commonplace many aspects of life that might have previously seemed shocking, including a new form of government, a new style of dress, and a new (though still unofficial) system of marriage. The monarch, moreover, promised even more radical changes. He was, he said, translating a *second* set of sacred metallic plates, consisting of "hidden truths" with enormous ramifications for his followers.

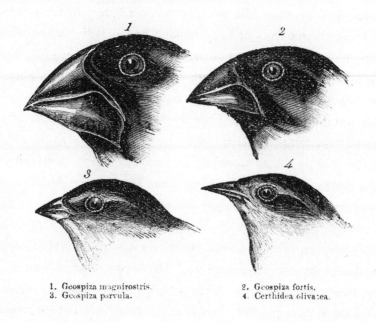

1. Geospiza magnirostris.
3. Geospiza parvula.

2. Geospiza fortis.
4. Certhidea olivacea.

Finches of the Galápagos Islands, from a book by Charles Darwin.

The ability of Strang's followers to acclimate themselves to his ever-changing whims and dictates would have come as no surprise to naturalist Charles Darwin, who in 1850 was still formulating his monumental manuscript on the process by which organisms adapt to new environments. As he confided to a friend around that time, he continued to "defer my species-paper." But the longer he worked on his theory of natural selection, the more Darwin came to believe that islands were crucial to understanding how plants and animals had evolved. After studying specimens of various species of finches he collected in the Galápagos Islands, for example, Darwin became convinced that despite their superficial differences all these birds had come from a single ancestor and had evolved separately in the isolation of their protected environments. "Different islands, to a considerable extent, are inhabited by a different set of beings," he wrote.

Isolation, of course, changes human cultures, too. By the autumn of 1850, the residents of Beaver Island had already become what Darwin might have called a different set of beings, as their kingdom fast became "a little world within itself," to borrow another phrase the naturalist used in describing islands. A scientific observer's field notes on this "little world" from the fall of 1850 might have catalogued three distinct species.

The first of those, according to historian Leach, consisted of "the sincere believers in the original and fundamental doctrines of Mormonism, and in [Strang's] divine mission and offices as the successor of Joseph Smith." To this group, Leach wrote, Strang "was really prophet, priest and king. His advice was sought and followed in all matters, temporal and spiritual. His word was law. No sacrifice was too great to be made, if the prophet advised it; no crime too revolting to be committed, if the king commanded it. In their view it was no crime."

A second group—the smallest and least influential, at least for now—was made up of those whose faith had been "shaken or wholly destroyed by the doctrines and practices taught by Strang and his minions," according to Leach's taxonomy, while a third, also "comparatively small in numbers,"

consisted of unprincipled men, whose adherence to Mormonism arose, not from conviction of its truth as a religious system, but from the opportunities it afforded for unbridled license under the pretended sanction of religion. These men were the willing tools of

Strang. Without being themselves deceived by his profession of having a divine commission, they helped to fasten the deception upon others. The most important trusts were sometimes committed to persons of this sort, and they were usually chosen for leaders in the execution of projects likely to be distasteful to persons of a tender conscience and large philanthropy.

But the trouble with all such species of "unprincipled men" is that they tend to devour their own. It should come as no surprise, then, that the perilous ecosystem of Beaver Island was soon to experience a fierce struggle for survival of the fittest.

Eleven

In which a melodrama is performed, and the curtains fall on one of the players

Does all the world act? Am *I*, for instance, an actor? Is my reverend friend here, too, a performer?
— Herman Melville, *The Confidence-Man*

THE TRAGEDIAN STOOD BEFORE THE AUDIENCE, TRYING TO remember his next line. The footlights glared up at him, casting shadows on his lined face, high cheekbones, hawkish nose, and deep-set eyes. Somewhere in the distance a bullfrog croaked. Farther off, the waves washed slowly in on Beaver Island. And still George Adams couldn't remember his line.

He'd been acting for years, often at big theaters in major cities. Just a few weeks earlier, the *Brooklyn Daily Eagle,* commenting on his reputation on the stage and pulpit, had described Adams as an "eccentric genius." True, the intention of that remark wasn't exactly clear. And true, the tragedian's acting career had often been less noteworthy for his theatrical triumphs than for the frequent occasions when he "was taken suddenly drunk," in the words of the *New York Times,* "and would have to be dosed with salt brine inside, and drenched with buckets of pump-water outside, to sober him sufficiently to enable him to 'get through' his part."

But sometimes all the salt brine and pump water in the world couldn't bring back a phrase that had stumbled round the bend. So what was an eccentric genius to do? Every now and again the tragedian would resort to improvisation, offering a clever substitute for whatever forgettable bit of verbiage the playwright had put in the script. But that approach, in the words of one young actress who had shared the stage with him, "was anything but pleasing to those who depended upon him for their cue."

Now here it was happening again, even though he had performed this play—Richard Brinsley Sheridan's *Pizarro*—countless times. Adams tried to think back over the script of that melodrama now, but everything blurred together like a three-day bender.

What was the line? What was that wretched line?

Exactly three months had passed between King Strang's coronation on July 8, 1850, and the performance of *Pizarro* in the yet-unfinished tabernacle. In that time the prophet had enforced a rigid ethical code on his followers. "The discipline of the Church in the matter of temperance and morals was very strict," Elvira Field later recalled. "The use of tea, coffee and tobacco, as well as liquors, was prohibited," and "no betting or gaming was permitted, but the rules were very liberal in the manner of amusements."

Fortunately for Adams, chief among those amusements was theater. Since coming to the island, he had set up something of an amateur thespian troupe, staging such popular nineteenth-century plays as *The Lady of Lyons,* a melodrama about an impostor who passed himself off as a prince. In recent weeks, however, things had not gone well for Adams, whose reign as prime minister was threatening to be as short and tragic as that of the doomed Richard III, another of his favorite roles.

The trouble had begun even before the coronation, when Adams showed up with a rich widow named Louisa Cogswell, whom he introduced as his new wife. To those who inquired about his *old* wife, Caroline—who was, in Adams's own words, "one of the best women that ever lived"—the tragedian employed his prodigious gift for bathos to announce that she had died of consumption. Given his reputation as an adulterer and polygamist, this news must have raised a few eyebrows even before one of the islanders received a letter from Caroline Adams, who reported that she was still alive, though very sick and almost completely destitute. Her husband, she revealed, had sent her a grand total of two dollars in the months since he had kidnapped their son and absconded to Beaver Island with his "prostitute." This letter was read in public—a further blow to Adams's prestige. Then came one last plot twist: the first wife finally died, this time for real, bitter about Adams's betrayal until "she breathed her last."

Strang had appointed Adams prime minister despite the scandal, perhaps owing to the tragedian's ability to inspire crowds and attract new recruits. But given the gargantuan egos of both men, not to mention their mutual penchant for backbiting, the partnership was perilous from the very beginning. What brought it to the verge of collapse was the enigmatic woman who called herself Louisa Cogswell. Strang later claimed that *Cogswell* was merely an alias and that the woman's real identity was Louisa Pray. Assuming the prophet was correct, she may well have been a woman by that name who made her living as a dancer, entertaining audiences with everything from ballets to polkas between acts of theatrical performances.

It seems likely that this "graceful and popular danseuse," as one newspaper described her, would have known Adams through entertainment circles in Boston, where he preached and performed during the winter of 1849–50. Such was her reputation in that city that one scandalmongering publication, which claimed to expose the secret lives of "the gambler, the thief...the harlot, [and] the licentious *coryphée de ballet*," mentioned Louisa Pray by name among a group of dancers who were "not savagely virtuous" and "had an 'orful' good time with the boys." Nonetheless, she was married (or soon would be) to George F. Browne, a diminutive actor whom Adams had once swindled out of a paycheck during his disreputable days as a theater manager.

Newspaper ad depicting the "beautiful and accomplished" Louisa Pray. (Rock Island County Historical Society, Moline, Illinois)

Only three things are certain about this mysterious figure—first, that she was a gossip; second, that she gossiped about the love life of James J. Strang; and third, that her indiscretions had pushed the prophet into a furious rage. With this knowledge weighing on his mind, who could blame poor Adams for not remembering his line? But...wait, hold on! Yes, yes, it was coming to him now, teetering off the tip of his tongue the way a happy drunk bursts from a barroom after a night of riotous carousing. For the moment, at least, everything was right for the man whose booming voice shook the tabernacle.

The play Adams was performing that night—*Pizarro in Peru; or, The Death of Rolla*—would go down in history as "a literary embarrassment," according to one modern critic, who cites as evidence "the bombast of its speeches and the improbability of its actions, scenes and outcome." But nineteenth-century audiences, as Adams had learned during his many years of treading the boards, adored this melodrama, which told the tale of a noble Inca warrior's doomed battle against an evil conquistador.

The play had proved especially popular among Mormon theatergoers. In fact, in April of 1844, two months before the murder of Joseph Smith, Adams had codirected and starred in *Pizarro* in Nauvoo, the first Mormon theatrical production in that city. Brigham Young had a walk-on part as an Inca high priest, calling fire down from the heavens to light his offering at the altar—a trick he pulled off with the help of amateur stagehands. The *New York Daily Tribune* was one of several papers around the country to run "a most irresistibly ludicrous account" of the production. The writer did not comment on Adams's performance but took gleeful note of his reputation as a polygamist, with a sneering reference to his "'spiritual babies' by Miss ******—Oh shame! where is thy blush?"

If the cosmopolitan readers of New York were amused by that account, the faithful in Nauvoo had found the performance itself deeply moving. "At times nearly the whole audience would be affected to tears," recalled one young woman in attendance. "Joseph [Smith] did not try to hide his feelings, but was seen to weep a number of times." The reactions in Nauvoo may have been so intense because Mormon audiences seemed to recognize something of their own story in the play. The Book of Mormon, after all, tells the story of a righteous people, the Nephites, who are exterminated by their rivals, leaving behind the Book of Mormon to be discovered by Joseph Smith. Similarly, *Pizarro* is a tale of the honorable Incas, who perish tragically and pass down their empire to a virtuous European—a Spaniard named Alonzo who, like Smith, founds a new society on the ruins of the lost realm. These thematic resonances were so powerful to Mormons that when the first theater opened in Utah in 1852, its inaugural performance would once again be *Pizarro,* which eventually became known as the "Mormon national play," mounted annually in Salt Lake City from 1863 to 1874.

Although few details about the production of *Pizarro* on Beaver Island have survived, we know that the cast included Mary Strang, who played the Peruvian heroine, Cora. Full of "youth...loveliness and innocence," as another character puts it, Cora embodies antebellum notions of virtuous motherhood—the cult of the true woman amid the fall of the Incan empire. But the play has another heroine, a doppelgänger to the pious and pure Cora. She is, of course, a fallen woman, albeit one of "noble family," who has surrendered her home and good name to become the consort to "a licensed pirate" who treats "the world as booty." That pirate is Pizarro, but Beaver Island theatergoers might have noticed certain similarities between his character and that of another "ignobly born" adventurer who found himself "encamped in a strange country" with a band of fanatical followers, a man who was "ferocious and unpolished, though cool and crafty." And it must have been nearly impossible for even the most oblivious members of that crowd to avoid exchanging arched glances at an awkward coincidence: in the script of this melodrama, the name of Pizarro's whore is Elvira.

The real-life Elvira was not, apparently, performing the part; she may not even have been in the audience. (Neither of the two people who offered eyewitness accounts of the performance recalled the prophet's paramour being present at the event.) As for Mary Strang, who was not only in the tabernacle but on the stage, she must have winced every time someone recited a line containing that name. (*Fie, Elvira!*) The prophet's affair with Field was, after all, an open secret on the island. (*Why dost thou smile, Elvira?*) And it was widely rumored that the younger woman now lived under the same roof as James and Mary Strang. (*Elvira, leave me!*)

Nineteenth-century illustration of the character Cora from Pizarro. *(National Portrait Gallery, London)*

The prophet still insisted, at least in public, that "one man shall have but one wife," which made him both an opponent and a practitioner of polygamy. ("Oh, King! torture me not thus!" declares the long-suffering Cora.) But can it have been anything other than humiliating for Mary to stand before everyone on Beaver Island and spit out lines such as *Can you wish that I should break my [marriage] vow?* and *Give me my husband?* During the performance, Mary started to become ill, a condition that worsened as the play went on. At some point she could no longer continue in her role. A doctor who examined her that night described her as being "extremely feeble, low, and in a critical state." Perhaps she was suffering from a virus—or perhaps it was simply the stress of being onstage with all those eyes, full of judgment, fixed on her.

As for the absent Elvira, it's quite possible that her reason for missing this performance was that she, too, felt incapacitated, as women often do in the early months of pregnancy. Her waist was growing steadily—right along with the gossip about her relationship with James Strang. But when her baby boy came into the world six months later, it wouldn't be his famous father whom Field chose as his namesake. Instead, she honored the other great man in her life—the prophet's personal secretary. Like an actress reprising her own greatest role, Field called her newborn Charles James, after the vanished Charles J. Douglass.

———

To many people of the antebellum era, daily existence itself had begun to seem more and more like theater. "The exterior life is but a masquerade, in which we . . . use language suited to the characters we assume," lamented *Godey's Lady's Book,* a leading fashion magazine of the period. Everyday interactions, the journal observed, took on the quality of a performance, in which "with smiling faces, [we] mask aching hearts; address accents of kindness to our enemies, and often those of coldness to our friends. The part once assumed must be acted out, no matter at what expense of truth and feeling." This culture of commonplace deception, in turn, had given rise to a pandemic of distrust. In a world where everyone put on an act, how could anyone be sure where they stood with anybody else? Loved ones could turn into strangers overnight, allies into antagonists.

Anyone who saw Strang and Adams sitting side by side at a church conference a few days before the performance might have assumed that the two men were still, to use a nineteenth-century expression, *thick as thieves.* But in fact tensions between the two men had reached a crisis point. Their already strained relationship took a turn for the worse a few weeks after the July coronation, when Adams briefly left the island and traveled to Voree, still home to a significant number of Strang's supporters, and immediately began to stir up trouble. One local disciple reported back to the king that Adams was claiming Strang had two wives and was surrounding himself with "corrupt men." Perhaps aware that word had gotten back to Strang, Adams desperately tried to convince the king he deserved his trust. While still away from Beaver Island in August, a month after the coronation, he wrote Strang from the road:

> Oh! James, be wise, a thousand snares surround you—all are not true men that they appear to be. God protect you—men will come to you with tales about me—yes! and women too—listen not to their slander—you know I am a true man but you don't realize how true I am and what I will do to serve you.... May my King live foreaver; yours in love, truth and everlasting fellowship.

But that "everlasting fellowship," it seems, was already doomed. By the time Adams stepped onstage to perform *Pizarro* two months later, word had reached Strang that the tragedian's paramour, Louisa Cogswell (née Pray, or perhaps vice versa), was spreading rumors about him. Not satisfied with two wives, she said, the king had designs on the fifteen-year-old daughter of a follower. The prophet would later claim that Adams and his mistress went so far as to forge affidavits in order to prove their accusation and circulated those documents on the island. Their reasons for turning against him aren't known, but as happens to all lead characters in tragedies, they would author their own ruin.

"His fate is sealed," says one character in *Pizarro*. And whether or not Adams knew it as he stood onstage that night, so was his. Within a few days, the tragedian, along with his paramour, would be banished from Beaver Island, cast out like Bennett before him, exiting the stage with his usual mix of bluster, venom, fraud, and farce. In his place, another enigmatic rogue had already made a quiet entrance—one that would eventually have fatal consequences for Strang.

———

In October of 1850, as Adams took his final bow on Beaver Island, the novelist Nathaniel Hawthorne was in Lenox, Massachusetts, hard at work on a new book. His departure from Brook Farm, the ill-fated utopian community near Boston, was nine years distant, and ever since that fiasco Hawthorne had been struggling to make his name as a writer. For most of this time, he was, even by his own estimation, "the obscurest man of letters in America." But now, after years of feeling "like a man talking to himself in a dark place," Hawthorne had suddenly scored a huge success.

The Scarlet Letter, published in March of 1850, sold out an initial press run of 2,500 copies in less than two weeks and gave Hawthorne, at the age of forty-five, his first commercial hit. What seemed to fascinate antebellum readers, perhaps as much as the salacious story of an illicit affair in seventeenth-century New England, was the novel's obsession with what Hawthorne called "the inmost Me behind its veil." In a time when it seemed more difficult than ever to tell truth from fraud, audiences were drawn to the book's theme of masked identities. One of the central characters, for example, is a preacher, adored by his fanatical followers, who can't reconcile his public and private personas. "No man, for any considerable period, can wear one face to himself, and another to the multitude," wrote Hawthorne, "without finally getting bewildered as to which may be the true."

In his new novel, however, Hawthorne turned his attention from characters who masked "the inmost Me" to those who seemed entirely void of that core persona. More and more common in everyday antebellum life, such shadowy figures were constantly "putting off one exterior, and snatching up another, to be soon shifted for a third," as Hawthorne put it in his new book, *The House of the Seven Gables*. To embody this emerging breed of formless men, Hawthorne created a character who is "continually changing his whereabout, and therefore responsible neither to public opinion nor to individuals." An itinerant daguerreotype artist, the character calls himself Holgrave—though, as readers will eventually learn, that is not his real name. Nothing else about him is fixed, either:

> Though now but twenty-two years old, (lacking some months, which are years, in such a life,) he had already been, first, a country school-master; next, a salesman in a country store; and, either at the same time or afterwards, the political editor of a country-newspaper. He had subsequently traveled New England and the Middle States as a peddler, in the employment of a Connecticut manufactory of Cologne water and other essences. In an episodical way, he had studied and practiced dentistry, and with very flattering success, especially in many of the factory-towns along our inland-streams. As a supernumerary official, of some kind or other, aboard a packet-ship, he had visited Europe, and found means, before his return, to see Italy, and part of France and Germany. At a later period he had spent some months in a community of Fourierists. Still more recently he had been a public lecturer on Mesmerism....His present phase, as a Daguerreotypist, was of no more importance in his own view, nor likely to be more permanent, than any of the preceding ones.

At some point in the spring or summer of 1850, a similarly amorphous figure showed up at Beaver Island—a character so remarkable and mysterious that he, too, seemed to be the invention of some fiction writer. Like Holgrave, he was, or soon would be, a traveling photographer, though he seemed to have had other professions as well—possibly including saboteur and spy. He called himself Dr. J. Atkyn, but both the title and the name were probably made up. (Strang would later insist that the visitor "assumed a new name once in a few days" and was "ever on the move.") The stranger's reason for coming to the island was murky—if, in fact, he had one. (Strang would later claim the man was dropped off by a steamboat for refusing to pay his passage.) He may have been tall. He may have been a drinker. He may have been a Freemason. He may have been, by turns, ingratiating and abrasive. He'd soon get the nickname Dr. Akenside, an apparent euphemism for "pain in the ass." His first name, if he ever mentioned one, would be lost to history.

In physical appearance, general demeanor, and modus operandi, Atkyn seemed much like a man described in an 1845 notice in the New Orleans *Times-Picayune,* which cautioned its readers with the headline "Look Out for the Scoundrel." "The public are hereby warned against a man named _____ AIKEN, about 5 feet, 11 inches high, stout built, 28 or 30 years of age, brown hair, bland and insinuating manner, and usually well dressed," the notice began. This stranger had appeared one day in East Feliciana Parish, north of Baton Rouge, and told anyone who asked that he was a native of Ohio. Talking his way into a job as a teacher, he was "treated as a gentleman" by the locals, "whose hospitality he returned by borrowing a gold watch and divers sums of money." Then one day he "concluded to go to New Orleans," and promptly disappeared, leaving the people he duped to pay his debts.

Atkyn and *Aiken* were, of course, variations of the same name, but it hardly matters whether the man who vanished from Baton Rouge in 1845 was the one who appeared on Beaver Island in 1850. Individuals of this kind were as interchangeable as the various identities they assumed. Their stories all had the same plot and came to the same ending as that episode in Louisiana: "He has not been heard of since."

It hadn't taken long for Dr. Atkyn and Brother Adams to become rivals. No doubt the tragedian recognized something of himself in this man of many characters, but the two had diametric theatrical styles. Adams preferred classical parts, such as Richard III, whereas Atkyn invented his own roles and wrote his own scripts. Adams loved being onstage; Atkyn disappeared into the crowd. "He is a mirror, with no face of its own, but a smooth surface from which each man of ten thousand may see himself reflected," wrote Henry Ward Beecher, whose 1846 description of an emergent brand of American rogue hinted at a truth about this stranger—assuming there were any truths to be found.

What filled Adams with bitter resentment, however, was not the newcomer's different approach to confidence games. It was that he saw Atkyn as a competitor for the affections of Louisa Pray, the *danseuse* Adams had brought to the island earlier in the year, introducing her as his new wife. Exactly what action might have prompted the prime minister to become "jealous of Dr. Akenside," as Strang put it, was uncertain. But by the time Adams embarked on a brief journey to Ohio in the late summer of 1850, not long after Strang's coronation, his fears of losing Louisa, whom he had left behind on Beaver Island, had begun to consume him. An August 14 letter to the prophet—full of the tragedian's singular spellings and punctuation—made his anguish all too apparent:

> My Sufferings, are beyond what I can Bare. I am Growing Gray—and Breaking down under them…James!! I love!! Louisa!!! My *Dear Wife*!!!! *Yes love her* to MADNESSS—I have not treated her Verry well of late—it is true; I have not—I am Sorry…She has Sacrifised much for Me, Verry much, more James than I ever told you—James She must be saved.

And of the people who were "Seeking her ruin," there was "one in particular" who obsessed Adams: "I mean *a tall man under* the Garb of friendship, if he Suckceeds I am lost ruined undone…Should that Man or any other take advantage of my friendship I Swear by the king of Zion I will have his hearts Blood…no Matter how it is done." Did the tall man ever "suckceed" with Louisa Pray? Or was the whole love affair a product of the tragedian's overstimulated imagination? Once again, history would keep its secrets. What the episode did reveal, however, was the increasingly agitated state of Adams's mind, just when Strang had started to lose faith in his prime minister.

In the end, the troubled tragedian had to choose between his new leading lady and his king. Tensions between Louisa Pray and Strang had been on the rise for weeks, ever since the prophet learned from an informant that Adams's new wife was not a rich widow but an impostor from Boston. At one point Strang allegedly went so far as to tell Pray that her life would be in danger if she remained on the island. In response, she produced a bowie knife and declared she would plant it in the prophet's heart if she ever got the chance.

The conflict came to a crisis on October 10, 1850, two days after the performance of *Pizarro,* when a Mormon court on Beaver Island found the *danseuse* guilty of "gross slander and personal insult" to Strang, as well as conspiracy against the church. Her sentence was to be "all penalties, curses and maledictions" naturally invoked by the breaking of her sacred covenant with the church, an oath of punishment that all members were required to swear against themselves in advance, in the event that they erred: *May disease rot my bones with me; parched and thirsty may I die without friends or succor; unloved by the good, cursed of evildoers.* Three days later, Adams was stripped of all his powers because, in Strang's words, "the church would not countenance his wife in her devilish actions."

The tragedian did not go without drama. Grabbing up all the curtains and other theatrical fixtures, an outraged Adams caught a boat off the island with Pray, vowing "an eternal war and a war of extermination" against his fellow Mormons and former confederates.

As for Atkyn, he spent only a few weeks on the island, where he "obtained a precarious subsistence," as Strang's newspaper would later report, by "going back and forth between Mormons and Gentiles, and offering his service to each as [a] spy upon the other." Then one day, forgotten by posterity, he was gone, "a continually shifting apparition...vanishing too suddenly to be definable," as Nathaniel Hawthorne put it in *The House of the Seven Gables*.

In the future, the enigmatic Atkyn would rematerialize to help doom Strang. But for now the king found himself with a far more concrete antagonist to worry about: the president of the United States.

Twelve

In which the country's chief executive can't make up his mind

———◦◦◦———

I was not born to fortune, name [or] influence. I was never the
favorite of accident or chance.

—James Strang, *Diary*, 1835

I was just an apprentice with little hope of being anything but
a mechanic.

—Millard Fillmore, letter to a friend, 1872

IN HINDSIGHT, MILLARD FILLMORE AND JAMES STRANG SEEM
like doppelgängers—shadowy counterparts of each other,
twins of fate and fortune. Both came from the same rural county in
New York; both were the sons of backwoods farmers; both had little in the way of formal education; both taught in country schools
before deciding to take up the law; both were admitted to the state
bar at age twenty-three; both saw politics as their way out of obscurity (Strang as a member of the Democratic Party, Fillmore as a
Whig). And in one last quirk of happenstance, both came to power
at almost exactly the same time.

Fillmore was still vice president of the United States when James
Strang anointed himself King of Earth and Heaven on July 8, 1850.
But the very next night, a messenger arrived at Fillmore's residence
in Washington, D.C., with an urgent communiqué from members of
the Cabinet: "Sir, The melancholy and most painful duty devolves

on us to announce to you that Zachary Taylor, late president of the United States, is no more. He died at the President's mansion this evening at half-past ten o'clock."

And with that, Millard Fillmore was in charge of the entire country—an idea that would have seemed absurd to the late president Taylor, who had apparently cultivated no relationship whatsoever with his colorless running mate before the election and had made a point of excluding him from the inner circle at the White House. "My advice has neither been sought nor given," Fillmore once complained—and it looked as if he would be fated to spend four years as the administration's resident nonentity. But then, on July 4, 1850, the normally robust Taylor, a war hero whose nickname was Old Rough and Ready, began to feel ill after attending a ground-breaking ceremony for the Washington Monument. Within hours, the president was racked by nausea, cramping, diarrhea, and dehydration. His death—the exact cause of which has never been determined—came after just sixteen months in office.

"The shock is so sudden and unexpected that I am overwhelmed," Fillmore declared upon receiving the news. And who could blame him? Like Strang, he now found himself the protagonist of a success story too preposterous to be true in any other historical setting but the carnivalesque atmosphere of antebellum America. The King of Earth and Heaven and the president of the United States—"His Majesty" and "His Accidency," as the press would soon call them—had until now been walking parallel paths. But like all doppelgängers, their destinies would soon intersect.

Two men were instrumental in bringing Strang to the president's attention. The first was George J. Adams, who wasted no time in attempting to exact vengeance upon his former ally. After his furious parting from Strang, the tragedian and his paramour stormed straight off to Mackinac Island, fifty miles east of Beaver Island by boat and the nearest Anglo settlement of any significant size. There they immediately set about stirring up trouble, with Adams calling Strang a "self-confessed impostor" and accusing him of a variety of crimes. The prophet's erstwhile lieutenant found a receptive audience among the locals, who had already come to believe, in the words of one resident, that Strang and his followers were "more like a gang of pirates than any apostle of the Lord." Not long after the county sheriff at Mackinac filed charges against the prophet, articles such as this began to appear in newspapers all over the country:

> THE MORMON COMMOTION.—*Adams and Strang.*—The diffi-
> culty among the Mormons on Beaver Island, Lake Michigan, by which
> elder Adams, the actor, had to flee for his life for having caused the arrest
> of Strang, the prophet, it is stated, arose from revelations to Strang,
> that a certain woman was to be his spiritual wife; but the consent of
> all parties could not be obtained, and consequently this "anointed of
> the Lord" waxed wroth. Adams left, taking with him the theatrical
> curtains and fixtures from the Church, and went to Mackinac, where
> he is going to play "tragedy." Strang was taken to Mackinac, tried
> and convicted, and sentenced to six months' imprisonment. It was
> supposed that the Mormons would attempt a rescue.

That "rescue," however, would prove unnecessary. Set free on a technicality, Strang was re-arrested and re-released three more times in the ensuing weeks. This failure to keep him behind bars was partially owing to the fact that Strang understood the intricacies of the law much better than the bumbling justice of the peace who kept trying his cases, Charles O'Malley. At one point, the prophet mockingly assured O'Malley, a native of Ireland who had been educated as a priest, that "your ignorance has shielded me from malice." But Strang's skill as an attorney may not have been the only reason for his legal success. Critics charged that his deliverance from the jail cell was a quid pro quo, purchased from local Democratic politicians in exchange for a promise of Mormon votes in the upcoming elections. But whatever the real reason, Strang managed to remain beyond the reach of justice—at least for now.

The second man who set Strang and Fillmore on a collision course was yet another of those bigger-than-life figures that the antebellum era seemed to spawn. George C. Bates shared with His Majesty and His Accidency an upbringing in the Burned Over District, where, like both of them, he passed the bar. He then headed west for Detroit and rose through the legal ranks to become the U.S. district attorney for Michigan. In that powerful post, Bates embodied some of the most ostentatious qualities of the other two men. Like Strang, he was, as one biographer put it, "a brilliant public speaker and a fine ready writer," almost a match for the prophet in self-invention and self-promotion. Like Fillmore—whom Queen Victoria was quoted as calling the best-looking man she had ever met—Bates was "a decided favorite with the ladies." Now nearing forty, he had once been "considered the handsomest man in the state," according to another biographer.

> His face was of classic mold, with a rather high forehead, bright blue eyes, light auburn hair, a flexible, handsome mouth, a finely-molded chin, a fresh and healthy, but not rosy, complexion, and small, aristocratic hands and feet. In manner, he was frank, genial and bubbling over with animal spirits, but always gentlemanly, and in conversation was witty, mirthful and captivating.

Yet for all those strengths, the biographer observed, Bates was also "unstable in purpose, fond of change and excitement, and in his actions never seemed to feel the weight of moral responsibility." He was also extremely ambitious, having recently run an unsuccessful campaign for the U.S. Congress as a member of Fillmore's Whig Party. A fiery orator, he had become "famous all over the country" for making speeches on behalf of the Whigs and against the rival Democrats, "arousing the enthusiasm of his audiences in a remarkable degree." Bates was a political animal, in short, and as even he would later concede, his partisanship played a role in his decision to prosecute Strang. With the prophet's supporters voting as a solid block for the Democrats, he wrote, "this Mormon element had become an important faction in the elections of Michigan." In a close contest, Strang's followers "would determine the success of parties in the State." Bates was determined to stop that from happening.

In March of 1851 he wrote U.S. attorney general John Crittenden—the country's chief law-enforcement officer—to announce that he'd been "credibly informed" of Strang's involvement in a number of federal crimes. "Without purchasing any land," he wrote, the Mormons had "taken possession of nearly the whole island" and were "cutting and selling all the wood and timber." They were also, he alleged, operating a "large establishment" for counterfeiting. The only way to bring Strang and his compatriots to justice was through the federal system, and the only way to arrest them was to raid the colony by warship. "No vessel, except an armed one, could land there with a posse," Bates wrote, claiming that Strang's followers had vowed to resist arrest with the force of arms.

The U.S. district attorney for Michigan, in other words, was advocating nothing less than a military invasion of Beaver Island. But to make it happen, he needed the approval of the president.

———

Millard Fillmore "means well," wrote the *New York Tribune*, "but he is timid, irresolute, uncertain." Many Americans agreed with the paper's assessment that the president "lacks pluck" and "wants backbone." Even when it came to the defining issue of the day, Fillmore managed to be on both sides at once. "God knows that I detest slavery," he said, "but it is an existing evil, for which we are not responsible, and we must endure it." Fillmore had enraged abolitionists, including many members of his own party, by signing into law the Fugitive Slave Act, which authorized the seizure and return of runaway slaves who sought refuge in a free state. Whig senator William H. Seward of New York, for example, called the president a "man of hesitation and double opinions," overmatched by a job in which "decision and singleness are indispensable."

Perhaps not surprisingly, when Bates went to the White House with evidence of Strang's wrongdoing, Fillmore equivocated. "Being a very cautious, cold, and calculating man," Bates later wrote, the president "hesitated and halted for a long time." Bates would blame this delay on the president's desire to keep his job. According to the prosecutor, Fillmore was worried about offending Beaver Island's small but united block of Mormon voters, who, in a tight race, could cost him the election in Michigan. Fearing this outcome, the indecisive president took time to consult with members of his own party, including Secretary of State Daniel Webster, as well as Democratic leaders such as Stephen A. Douglas, who since his days of getting the Mormons evicted from Nauvoo had become the senior senator from Illinois.

In the meantime, public pressure had begun to mount on the president over his policies toward Mormons in another part of the country. Fillmore's predecessor in the White House had been openly antagonistic toward the Mormons of Utah, whose population had swelled to more than 11,000. During his presidency, Zachary Taylor was quoted as calling these pioneers "a pack of outlaws" who "were not fit for self-government." Taylor vowed to veto any legislation that would grant the settlement status as a state or territory, a concept he viewed as "an absurdity." This stand, of course, did not earn Taylor many friends along the Great Salt Lake. After the president's sudden death, Brigham Young declared that Taylor had gone to hell. When someone asked him how he knew, Young replied, "Because God told me so."

Fillmore, by contrast, had reversed Taylor's policies toward Young and his followers. Not only did the new president support Utah's admission as a territory under the Compromise of 1850—the sweeping legislation aimed at averting a crisis between North and South—but he also named Young as Utah's first governor, effectively giving the church and its leader political control over the new territory. One later observer credited the president with "a religious tolerance few possessed at that time in history." And perhaps it's true that Fillmore's roots in upstate New York had left him with less of the fear and distrust many Americans felt toward Mormons. But it's also true that his policy toward the church seemed transparently driven less by moral conviction than by political calculation. As with the issue of slavery, Fillmore appears to have determined that it would be more expedient to endure Mormon control of Utah than to oppose it. By granting Young the governorship, he hoped to calm rising tensions between the church and the U.S. government—at least until after the 1852 election.

Within weeks of Young's inauguration in February of 1851, however, newspapers across the country began to carry salacious stories about his domestic life. One editor, who republished a widely circulated report that Young had admitted to having "only" twenty-six wives, sneered, "This is the Governor of Utah!" Soon another observer reported that "some of the opposition presses in the country are blaming President Fillmore for appointing such a man as Brigham Young to be Governor of the Territory."

Did this growing public backlash against Fillmore for cozy relations with the Mormons in Utah play into his deliberations on whether to attack the Mormons in Michigan? It's impossible to say, since those deliberations seem to have taken place in secret. What's certain is that after weeks of waffling, the president finally made up his mind. As Bates later put it, at last the president decided to "lend the power and process of the United States to the arrest and conquest of King James the First."

On April 30, 1851, Fillmore formally authorized legal action against the Mormons on Beaver Island. By then, however, the prophet was already in hiding—not from federal authorities but from local vigilantes. Throughout the winter, the frozen lake had served as a natural barrier between Strang and his foes. But shortly after the ice broke up in early April, the sheriff from neighboring Mackinac descended upon Beaver Island with an armed posse. Along with "eight or ten drunken Irishmen," the angry mob included "thirty intoxicated Indians," according to Strang, who added that the remaining local Odawa and Ojibwe had now declared "war and annihilation against the Mormons." The prophet managed to evade apprehension, thanks to a harrowing escape through icy waters in a leaky fishing boat. But there was currently a $300 reward for his arrest, with bands of bounty hunters, whose numbers reportedly ranged from 45 to 350 at various times, hunting him down dead or alive. And unbeknownst to the beleaguered king, he would soon face a far more lethal force.

———

On May 16, Fillmore and several top members of his Cabinet gathered inside a steamboat on Lake Erie. The cruise was part of a series of public events to mark the completion of the New York and Erie Railroad, a 450-mile stretch of track that linked the Atlantic Ocean to the Great Lakes. The boat ride to Buffalo was full of feasts and toasts and "interchange of civilities," in the words of one newspaper. But there also might have been a covert agenda: to make final arrangements for the raid on Beaver Island.

Scholars have puzzled over the apparent disappearance of almost all documents related to the planning of the attack. The editor of Fillmore's collected papers, for example, observed that although "it would seem probable that President Fillmore engaged in considerable correspondence in the matter," just a couple of brief letters have survived, including an April 30 missive from Fillmore authorizing the operation.

One explanation for this mystery could be that Fillmore and his advisers had largely formulated their plans during private conversations. And the gathering on that steamboat, which came just days before the planned raid, would have afforded them a perfect opportunity to firm up details. Accompanying the chief executive were the two Cabinet members who would have been vital to plotting the strategy for any such attack, Attorney General Crittenden and Secretary of the Navy William A. Graham. Also present was the officer assigned to carry out the operation, Commander Oscar Bullus.

Bullus and Graham, in fact, began the journey aboard the U.S.S. *Michigan*—the vessel that was to be sent to raid Beaver Island—which, on that day, was escorting the president's ship to Buffalo. An hour into the journey, however, a curious event transpired. The two ships pulled alongside each other, and Secretary Graham boarded the president's steamboat. Then, after the *Michigan* fired a salute to the president and his entourage, the vessels parted company. These circumstances suggest that the secretary of the Navy was acting as an intermediary between Fillmore and Bullus on a final course of action for the raid.

On the following day, the *Buffalo Commercial* offered the first public hint of those plans:

> The *Michigan* reached the mouth of our harbor around 4 p.m. Another national salute was fired, and the *Michigan*, after a delay of an hour or two only, and without coming to an anchor even, left for the upper lakes, she being under orders to assist the government authorities in quelling disturbances at Beaver Island, the Mormon settlement.

And so the *Michigan* steamed on, its roundabout route through the Great Lakes connecting the legacies of Fillmore and Strang like the twisting plot of some nineteenth-century doppelgänger narrative as it built to an inevitable climax.

Thirteen

In which many people feel trapped

I am no bird; and no net ensnares me; I am a free human being
with an independent will; which I now exert to leave you.
                                    —Charlotte Brontë, *Jane Eyre*

ON MAY 19, THREE DAYS AFTER THAT U.S. NAVY WARSHIP
departed from Buffalo, a messenger arrived in the town of St.
James with a note addressed to "M.A.P. Strang." The prophet's wife,
Mary Abigail Perce Strang, must have instantly recognized this familiar scrawl, which had been etched into her psyche ever since she
received her first love letter from a young small-town lawyer fifteen
years earlier. Perhaps, as she opened this new note, her mind drifted
back to one that she had received as a newlywed, containing a poem
from her husband:

My spirit bows before thee,
To listen and adore thee;
With full but soft emotion,
Like the swell of summer's ocean.

Maybe she now wished she'd never opened that note and maybe
she hesitated before unfolding this new one. Summer's ocean, after

all, had long since dried up. For many months, every word from her husband had brought another heartache.

(Beinecke Rare Book and Manuscript Library, Yale University)

It wasn't just that the king had taken a second wife but that he behaved as though determined to flaunt that relationship in public. Strang "seemed very affectionate" toward the new woman in his life, one island resident would later recall. "Every pleasant day they were walking about together.... Most of the time he called her 'Charles,' and sometimes Elvira." And if all that wasn't humiliating enough for Mary, there had been another development—one that reportedly put her in such a desperate frame of mind that she was contemplating violence. On April 6, Elvira Field had given birth to J. J. Strang's son.

Now there was even more trouble. For the past six weeks—since just after the birth of that new son—the prophet had been in hiding, on the run for his life from heavily armed mobs of vigilantes and bounty hunters. But even in his absence, the man who had betrayed Mary in a thousand different ways couldn't quite leave her alone. What could he possibly want from her this time?

Before his latest troubles, Strang had spent much of the winter of 1850–51 aboard a stranded steamship, the *Lexington*. Sent to rescue another steamer that had been shipwrecked on a nearby reef, the vessel had encountered a fierce storm and ended up washing ashore, at the end of November, in the Beaver Island harbor. The crew, anxious to catch the last boat off the island before the lake turned to ice, left the *Lexington* under the care of Strang, who turned it into his private headquarters, a kind of island sanctuary within an island sanctuary. In the privacy of this hideout, he spent much of the winter translating the Plates of Laban—eighteen brass tablets, mentioned in the Book of Mormon, which, according to the prophet, contained one of the lost books of the Bible. So important was this text, said Strang, that it had been "kept in the Ark of the Covenant, and was held too sacred to go into the hands of strangers." At some point in the ancient past, the plates had mysteriously vanished from that holiest of vessels. And now, just as mysteriously, they had wound up on Beaver Island. Strang, who claimed the enigmatic text was written in Egyptian, demanded the strictest secrecy for his translation efforts. Even in correspondence with close associates, he insisted on referring to the plates by a code name. For reasons perhaps known only to him, he called them "the Swedish work."

By his own estimation, Strang had spent the winter "rising early and sitting up late and frequently missing meals for want of time to eat." When he wasn't on the *Lexington,* bent over the Swedish work with the Urim and Thummim, those magical seer stones that allowed him to read the otherwise indecipherable text, he was at the new printing office, typesetting the translation. In late winter or early spring of 1851, the prophet published 200 copies of an eighty-page document that, according to the historian Milo Quaife, provided "a complete framework of government...applicable to any population, however great, and laying down regulations for the most important relations of human society." Entitled the *Book of the Law of the Lord,* it was nothing less than a constitution for the new kingdom.

Under this document, Strang, as the kingdom's divinely appointed ruler, received absolute powers: maker, interpreter, and enforcer of laws; distributor of property and patronage; overseer of infrastructure and internal revenue; military commander, chief justice, and supreme pontiff all rolled into one, with authority "over the princes and rulers, and over all that sit in judgment." In Quaife's memorable words, "A more centralized autocracy, it is safe to say, the mind of man never devised."

The *Book of the Law of the Lord*—or the *Book of the Law,* as it was often afterward called—stood as Strang's magnum opus of self-invention. Half a lifetime ago, a nineteen-year-old farm boy in the Burned Over District had imagined himself as a "master spirit" capable of forming an entirely new government. "I tremble when I write but it is true," he had scribbled in secret code. And now, through the force of his will and the power of his prose, he had made it happen—the ultimate wish fulfillment for that ambitious former self who'd always dreamed of royalty and power.

This extraordinary text also offered the first official, if somewhat tacit, sanction of polygamy within his sect. This should have been good news for Elvira Field, who until this point had existed in a kind of limbo—her marriage to Strang an open secret, despite his official opposition to the system of plural wives. And now Field was a mother, her son born on the most holy day of the Mormon calendar, April 6, the anniversary of Joseph Smith's founding of the church. With so many blessings, she had every reason to be happy. Still, something appeared to stop her. "She was very sweet and seemed very fond of her baby," one witness observed, "yet her face seemed sad when not smiling."

In February of 1851, around the time the *Book of the Law* was being published on Beaver Island, American newspapers were abuzz with a surprising story from the literary world: Currer Bell, the man who had written the wildly popular 1847 novel *Jane Eyre*, was not a man at all. In an article published that winter in the *New York Tribune,* Charlotte Brontë revealed why she and her two sisters, Emily and Anne, had begun publishing books under the gender-neutral names Currer, Ellis, and Acton Bell: "We did not like to declare ourselves women because—without at that time suspecting that our mode of writing and thinking was not what is called 'feminine'—we had a vague impression that authoresses are liable to be looked on with prejudice." But now, with both sisters suddenly taken from her by tuberculosis, Charlotte Brontë no longer cared so much what people thought. Still unwed at thirty-four and frustrated by both the "piteously degrading" marriage market and the "wretched bondage" of traditionally feminine occupations such as teaching and being a governess, she had come to believe that women "suffer from too rigid a restraint, too absolute a stagnation."

To a remarkable degree, Strang's second bride had thus far managed to resist that restraint, to escape that stagnation. Little more than a year earlier, after all, Elvira Field had been traveling freely under the guise of Charles J. Douglass, assuming responsibilities reserved for men and, like Charlotte Brontë, publishing her own newspaper articles under a masculine pen name. Even after arriving on the island, she had pioneered a radical new style of dress, donning pantaloons and urging other women to throw off their heavy petticoats. But now—caring for the infant she had named Charles, a nostalgic tribute to the persona she would never again fully inhabit—Elvira found herself thrust back into a more traditional and constricted role, one not too far from the antebellum ideal of "true womanhood." And as if attending to the endless needs of a newborn wasn't challenging enough, she faced another harsh reality:

a few days after the baby was born, his father had gone into hiding, fearing for his own life. History does not reveal whether mother and child joined the king on the lam, or even whether she had any direct access to Strang during this time. But as his forced exile dragged on for six weeks, she must have begun to experience doubts about her relationship with the prophet, nagging apprehensions "that come up and fill me with wonder," as she put it.

She couldn't understand why it was, for example, that although Strang proselytized all over the country, he had "never tried to bring his own relatives into the church." Nor did he seem interested in requiring his three children by Mary to become Latter-day Saints, despite the fact that his eldest daughter, ten-year-old Nettie, was now of a sufficient age to be baptized into the faith. Did they have some special place in the prophet's mind and heart that her child with him could never hope to attain?

And what about her own status? Up to this point she'd had every reason to see her position as a privileged one within the sect. Just as God had singled out Strang, so the prophet had singled out her, selecting Field (with what one local resident called "an eye to the beautiful") to be his confidante, adviser, lover, and wife. But now there were rumors—whispers that Field had already heard, or soon would hear—that Strang was sleeping with other women on the island, women he didn't deem important enough to recognize as plural wives, women he thought of simply as "concubines." Did Elvira feel that she must ignore these women, pretend they didn't exist, even though they would likely bear her new husband children; even though she would one day look back and realize she "was always mad" about them; even though she would never stop believing that what they shared with the prophet was "nothing but whoredom"; even though she knew all too well that some people viewed her own situation in exactly the same way?

In *Jane Eyre*, Brontë railed against the idea that women "ought to confine themselves to making puddings and knitting stockings, to playing on the piano and embroidering bags." So far, Field had done everything within her power to avoid such a fate. But now, with one child in tow and no doubt more soon to be on the way, she increasingly found herself in a situation less like that of the plucky, independent heroine Jane than that of the novel's most tragic character—that woebegone woman in the attic, locked away by a husband who wanted to move on to a new chapter with another wife.

As for Mary Strang, her time on the island was coming to an end and perhaps she knew it, even as she unfolded the note containing whatever bad news her husband had in store for her. According to one later report—said to be based on the recollections of a close friend—Mary had become more and more antagonistic toward her husband and his cause in recent months, "having no faith in the revelations he claimed to have." Yet the more she pushed herself away from the prophet, the more determined he seemed to pull her back. Just last month, the same one in which his child with Field was born, he had appointed Mary to his governing council—a move that came more than 150 years before Brigham Young's branch of the church allowed women into high-level leadership positions. Still, the appointment seemed to stem less from Strang's feminist leanings than from a desire to keep Mary in his orbit, or to mollify her over his misdeeds.

The note, written in a rush, found the prophet in a desperate mood—one at odds with his defiant public posturing. In his newspaper (which he'd once again renamed, this time as the *Northern Islander*), Strang had boasted that he and his confederates would never "huddle up like frightened sheep," and if it came down to a fight, "the aggressors would be wiped off the face of the earth." But now, after being on the run for weeks, he was contemplating a secret mission to the mainland to speak with Michigan's governor about "the enormities which have been and still are practiced on us." True, he confided to Mary, "I don't feel at all well about going and had much rather have a fight & put my life in the scale," but he was aware that he was "no benefit here if I remain hid up."

Strang wrote that he intended to leave for the mainland "immediately," but if anyone could clearly see that he would never follow through on those plans, it was his longtime wife. The current moment was, after all, a microcosm of her entire marriage to a man who was never quite present but never seemed to leave, a man who, as far as Mary was concerned, had always been in hiding. Within weeks, the fragile fifteen-year relationship would reach a breaking point. But before that rupture the residents of Beaver Island would be rocked by an even more unsettling event, when an armed warship swooped out of the night.

Fourteen

In which one fanatic hunts a white whale and another tracks down a missing monarch

Those grand fresh-water seas of ours,—Erie, and Ontario, and Huron, and Superior, and Michigan,—possess an ocean-like expansiveness, with many of the ocean's noblest traits; with many of its rimmed varieties of races and climes. They contain round archipelagoes of romantic isles, even as the Polynesian waters do.

—Herman Melville, *Moby-Dick*

THE SHIP SENT TO CAPTURE STRANG WAS NO ORDINARY VESSEL. As the first U.S. Navy steamer built with an iron hull, the U.S.S. *Michigan* constituted "the missing link between wooden battleships and fully armored iron and steel warships," in the words of maritime historian Bradley A. Rodgers, author of *Guardian of the Great Lakes: The U.S. Paddle Frigate* Michigan. According to Rodgers, the vessel was nothing less than

a revolutionary new ship—a ship that, when fitted out, would combine new-type weapons, propulsion, and hull material; a ship that could outrun the fastest sailing frigate or devastate wooden warships, with shells from new pivoting shell guns mounted on its centerline....Though comparable in appearance and layout...to the newest wooden frigates, the U.S.S. *Michigan* was not a conventional ship any more than the first iron projectile points were conventional to the late Bronze Age. Both advancements signaled the end of one era and the beginning of another.

In service since 1844, the *Michigan* was charged with patrolling the Upper Great Lakes of Erie, Huron, Michigan, and Superior—about 87,000 square miles in all. (Only Lake Ontario remained out of the ship's range, due to the impossibility of navigating Niagara Falls.) Powered by two paddle wheels, one on each side, the vessel was "designed to outgun most contemporary warships and outrun those it could not outgun." Although the *Michigan* had originally been armed with eighteen powerful guns, the United States had greatly reduced the ship's firepower in order to ease tensions with Great Britain, which had vital commercial and strategic interests on the Great Lakes, the scene of fierce battles between the two nations during the War of 1812.

Armaments taken from the vessel had been stored in Erie, Pennsylvania—the *Michigan*'s first stop, as it happened, on the way to Beaver Island. Rodgers speculates that the ship's commander, Oscar Bullus, might have "used this opportunity in Erie to remove and mount his battery guns from storage." Loaded up with fuel and supplies—and perhaps fitted out with extra artillery—the ship departed Erie on May 20, setting course for the Mormon kingdom on Lake Michigan.

U.S. District Attorney George C. Bates—the man whom President Fillmore had placed in charge of the Beaver Island operation—boarded the ship the following day in Detroit, along with other federal officials. Bates also brought along forty "well armed and equipped" deputy marshals and the senior officer of the state militia. Beneath the pomp of his official duties, however, was a brutal reality: the prosecutor, a stalwart of the Whigs, was about to launch an all-out military operation against a member of a rival political party. And if that might strike those of later generations as extreme, such fanaticism had by 1851 become a defining quality of American life. Across the country, political parties of all stripes had organized "paramilitary bands to rally voters, claim the public streets and intimidate the opposition," according to one historian.

Newspapers in mid-century America were also unabashedly partisan, eschewing even the slightest pretense of neutrality or objectivity. The two leading papers in Detroit, for example, were offering radically different perspectives on the planned raid. In its May 22 edition, the *Advertiser*—a Whig paper closely allied with Bates—portrayed the operation as a patriotic mission:

> The U.S. steamer *Michigan* sailed from this port yesterday for Beaver Island, the seat of Empire of Strang the 1st... who is charged with the commission of sundry offences against the laws of the United States.
>
> His majesty has long set all civil authority at defiance, and he will now have a due opportunity to try his spunk.

But the *Detroit Free Press*—a Democratic Party organ—provided a different view:

> We were certain from the beginning that the hue and cry against the Mormons was all moonshine. Violations of the law may have taken place among them, and it would be strange, indeed, if they did [not] now and then occur in a community numbering some seven hundred souls. But every instance of the kind has doubtless been greatly exaggerated, until finally it was thought politic to send a large force to make arrests.

Without actually naming him, the *Free Press* was accusing Bates of putting political ambition above principle, and even above the law. *Party hack*—on most days that phrase, another of the antebellum era's colorful contributions to the American lexicon, fit the dandyish prosecutor like a fine suit. But simple opportunism couldn't account for the extreme measures that Bates had undertaken in this unusual quest. Something about the prophet had apparently turned the fun-loving, skirt-chasing Bates—a "devotee of Venus and Bacchus," as one biographer put it—into a single-minded hunter who couldn't rest until he had captured his prey. Such was the strange power of James J. Strang that he seemed to bring out the zealot in everyone, for or against.

—

By the morning of May 23, having traveled more than 200 miles north on Lake Huron since its departure from Detroit, the warship closed in on the Straits of Mackinac, a small channel between lakes Huron and Michigan. From the deck, Bates and his companions could see the densely forested shores of northern Michigan, where 200-year-old conifers soared high into the air, enlivening it with their fresh, resinous smell. But the prosecutor knew those trees were more than just beautiful; they were also big business. By the mid-nineteenth century, lumbering had become the country's second-largest manufacturing industry—behind flour and grist but ahead of cotton, the controversial enterprise threatening to split the nation in two. So valuable was this natural resource, in fact, that by the end of the century the total worth of Michigan's lumber industry would be $1 billion greater than that of the Gold Rush in California. The state's timber—especially the much-prized white pine, known for its straightness, strength, and soft texture (making it easy to saw)—had already started to play a crucial role in the westward expansion of the United States by allowing pioneers to build houses on the treeless prairies.

Given the value of what some scholars now refer to as "green gold," it's no surprise that tree poaching on government property was "fast becoming epidemic in the upper lake states," according to a later historian. This was one of the most serious federal charges against Strang—that he and his followers had been trespassing on public land and illegally harvesting timber, which they then sold to steamboats. Bates also accused Strang and several of his followers of obstructing the U.S. mail and assaulting a postal carrier with dangerous weapons, charges that centered around a February 1851 incident in which a Mormon posse allegedly tried to intercept a man attempting to carry U.S. mail across the frozen lake by dogsled.

In addition to those two main charges, Bates accused Beaver Islanders of several other crimes. These included counterfeiting U.S. coins, an allegation stemming in part from a recent incident soon to be covered by papers across the country. On April 16, according to this account, Strang and his "gang" had arrived by boat at a community on the mainland in Grand Traverse Bay, where he "purchased goods, for which he paid in bogus half dollars." The fraud was quickly discovered, however, and a posse, led by the local sheriff, gave chase across the water. But when they caught up with Strang, according to the story, the king and his men "turned and took deliberate aim at their pursuers with fire arms, and drove them back."

If the story was true, it would have meant that Strang had attempted to pass the counterfeit coins while already on the run from local authorities. But the prophet insisted the incident had never taken place, calling it "the boldest and most far fetched pretense on which to charge a gentleman with a felony I ever heard of."

Bates, unsurprisingly, viewed matters differently. One big reason "King James and his infatuated brethren" had not been brought to justice for this and other offenses, he insisted, was that they had used their electoral advantage over non-Mormons to gain control of the "entire machinery of the county government." An important cog in that apparatus was a Strang crony named James M. Greig, who had recently been elected as a judge for Michilimackinac County—an entity that at the time encompassed much of the northern part of the state, including Beaver Island. Now, as the military operation finally began in earnest, the district attorney had selected Greig as his first target.

The U.S.S. *Michigan* was not the first warship to have trained its guns on Mackinac Island. This strategically important outcropping, located in the narrow waterway between lakes Huron and Michigan, had been the site of a fort for nearly three-quarters of a century. Originally built by the British, in 1781, the stronghold was taken over by U.S. soldiers following the American Revolution, only to be recaptured by its original owners during the War of 1812. The fort—described by Herman Melville as "the goat-like craggy guns of lofty Mackinaw"—had since reverted to U.S. control, but by 1851 it had become a sleepy outpost, occupied by only a skeleton crew of soldiers. The center of activity on the island was the ramshackle town of Mackinac, a hub of the local fishing industry and the county seat.

Nineteenth-century painting of Mackinac Island. (U.S. Senate Collection)

In midafternoon of May 23 the *Michigan* steamed up to this settlement, anchored just off the coast, and aimed its artillery at the courthouse. With the on-deck troops mustering arms in a show of force, Bates went ashore with two other men and entered the courthouse, which was but a "half musket shot from the war steamer and her grinning guns," he later wrote. Apparently, notwithstanding the reports in various papers along the way, the prophet and his associates had received no advance notice of the *Michigan*'s objective, since Bates found Greig, the Strang acolyte and county judge, "sitting without his coat or cravat on the seat of justice." When the prosecutor presented his warrant for Greig's arrest, the stunned jurist not only refused Bates's command to come aboard the *Michigan* but threatened to arrest the intruders for contempt of court. Bates, in turn, invited Greig to glance out at the guns of the warship, adding that any lack of cooperation "would result in the destruction of the building and his own death."

But not even this threat impressed Judge Greig. In the end he had to be "taken by violence" to the awaiting ship, still "threatening his captors with every kind of punishment." By nightfall the *Michigan*, having navigated the Straits of Mackinac and entered Lake Michigan, was "steaming gently away toward the Beaver Island with the Hon. J. M. Greig, as prisoner, confined below decks." But the U.S. district attorney's plans for his captive had only just begun to unfold. After ordering the ship to proceed slowly, Bates went to the judge and presented him with a pair of ultimatums:

First, he demanded that Greig write a letter to Strang, urging him to surrender.

Second, he ordered his captive to reveal the exact location of the king, who had been in hiding from law-enforcement officials for more than a month.

The intransigent judge, however, "positively refused" to obey either of those orders.

It was at this moment that Bates revealed just how single-minded his pursuit of Strang had become. Sitting down next to Greig to command his attention, the prosecutor told him "in the most solemn manner possible...that unless he gave such a letter within one hour, he should swing from the yard-arm as certain as the stars twinkled above it." He then stormed off, leaving the judge "in utter amazement." Greig was so rattled by this threat that when the ship's commander visited him later, the captive demanded to know whether Bates was "drunk or crazy."

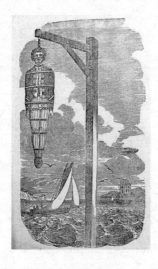

"Crazy Ahab"—that's what Herman Melville called the antihero of his unfinished novel, which he was attempting to complete just as the raid on Beaver Island reached its climax. For the past fifteen months, Melville had been feverishly drafting what he called "a strange sort of book," unlike anything he'd ever written. Now, as he had recently informed his friend and fellow author Nathaniel Hawthorne, the end was in sight. Even by his own estimation, Melville's stature in the literary world at that point was "horrible." Desperate for money, he had cranked out three books in quick succession, but sales had been dull—and criticism sometimes sharp. After the cool reception for his 1849 novel, *Mardi,* for example, Melville told a friend it was as if he'd been "driven forth... like a wild, mystic Mormon into shelterless exile."

The initial reception to *Moby-Dick* would only heighten his feelings of failure. Mocked by critics, the novel's first printing earned barely $500 in American sales, significantly less than Melville had made from any previous book. Nonetheless, as future generations came to understand the author's achievement, *Moby-Dick* would secure him a place in the literary canon. In the figure of Captain Ahab, with his single-minded obsession of hunting down and destroying the white whale, Melville had created a conduit for all the monomaniacal currents that crackled through the antebellum era. One scholar, commenting on the political and spiritual fever of the mid-nineteenth century—"a disease specific to a society of uprooted and driven men"—observed that "Ahab embodied the dangers facing America in 1850." Another called him "the personification of the very essence of fanaticism... in other words, the American dreamer gone mad."

It's not hard to imagine that those same mad dreams powered the U.S.S. *Michigan* toward its target now. Maybe what carried the vessel across the dark waves was not its roaring engines, eighty-eight tons in all, but the fanaticism of the age—the same fanaticism that drove slaveholders to dream of civil war and abolitionists to cry for righteous bloodshed and doomsday preachers to yearn for end times; the same fanaticism that had transformed a normally hedonistic prosecutor into a frontier vigilante; the same fanaticism that had brought hundreds of what Melville might have called "wild, mystic Mormons" to a remote island where they now slept, the night silent save for the faint sound of an approaching ship.

Fifteen

In which a tragedy opens in Detroit, and a drama comes to its climax on Beaver Island

Where is that viper? Bring the villain forth.

—William Shakespeare, *The Tragedy of Othello*

As U.S. District Attorney Bates and his armed posse moved in on Beaver Island, with Judge Greig under guard, a different kind of drama was getting under way back in Detroit. On May 23—the very day of the judge's abduction—the *Detroit Free Press* announced that a local theater had "entered into a short engagement with the celebrated and far famed Elder G. J. Adams, known as the 'Preacher Player, and uncompromising defender of Legitimate Drama,' who will appear this evening for the first time before a Detroit audience."

Having lost his previous post as viceroy for the Kingdom of God, the tragedian had returned to his former line of work. The theater's management was only too happy to "engage Mr. Adams at this time, owing to [publicity surrounding] the Beaver Island difficulties, and the energetic and determined part he has taken in the overthrow of King Strang," noted the *Free Press*. "We predict a full house, and shall go and see if the 'Elder' is as great as fame reports." According to an ad published in that day's paper, the entertainments would include a polka-dancing performer named "Mademoiselle Louise"—possibly yet another alias for Adams's paramour, Louisa Pray. For his own part, the notorious actor would be portraying what the paper called "his great character of 'Othello, the Moor of Venice.'"

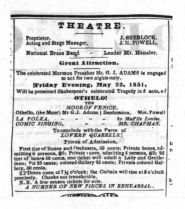

(Burton Historical Collection, Detroit Public Library)

His main reason for coming to Detroit, however, was not to perform at the National Theatre but to testify against Strang in federal court. Before Adams could do that, however, Bates and his posse would need to hunt down the prophet, who had by then been hiding from authorities for six long weeks.

On the night of that performance in faraway Detroit, an increasingly terrified Judge Greig implored the commander of the U.S.S. *Michigan*, Oscar Bullus, to tell him the truth: Could the kidnapped judge really be put to the noose for refusing to assist the manhunt? And would the commander actually obey those absurd orders to execute him?

Yes, Bullus assured his incredulous captive. If instructed to do so by U.S. District Attorney George Bates, he "should be bound to swing him from that yard-arm."

With that Greig cracked, supplying his captors with what Bates called "a long letter for King Strang, urging him to come on board at once." If the prophet failed to turn himself in by sunrise, the letter added, Bates would not hesitate to hang his hostage. Greig also supplied "specific and minute directions, with a pen chart, how to reach Strang."

(*Archives of Michigan*)

That hand-drawn map, which would be lost to history, was probably quite accurate, since Greig happened to be a self-described "draftsman" and amateur cartographer. The following year he produced another map, this one destined to survive, which would provide historians with a clear notion of the scope and speed with which Strang and his followers had laid claim to Beaver Island. In the northeast corner of that map is the natural port of Paradise Bay, around which curls the town of St. James—the target of the evening's military operation. As Greig detailed it, a road ran south from the harbor town into the island's interior; it had opened early in 1851 and was still under construction as the U.S.S. *Michigan* approached. Off that main thoroughfare shot smaller roads leading to plots of land that Strang had apportioned to his followers, despite the fact that most of the island officially remained U.S. government property. What the map does not make clear, however, is just how much of the island's terrain was still covered by thick woods and dense cedar swamps—ideal places of shelter for a man who did not want to be found.

At 2:00 a.m. on May 24 the *Michigan* anchored off St. James and the crew quietly lowered a rowboat into the bay. To avoid detection, Bates and a small group of men muffled their oars and covered their lanterns before rowing to the beach. Armed with Navy revolvers and cutlasses and guided by Judge Greig's map, they advanced single file toward their target. Presently they arrived at "a long hewn log building two stories high," as the prosecutor described the prophet's place of residence. A light gleamed from an upper window.

What Bates would remember, a quarter of a century later, about storming up the stairs and into the king's private chambers that night was a "long low room, where wide berths, heavily draped with stunning calico, shielded beds like the berths and state-rooms of steamers, which proved to be occupied by Mormon women four to a bed." Although that extravagant description, which made Strang's rustic abode sound like an Ottoman harem or a Parisian bordello, was almost certainly inaccurate, his description of what happened next generally corresponds with Mormon accounts. Upon rushing toward the glow of the lamp they had spotted from outside, the prosecutor and an assistant found a man asleep in bed, only to discover it was not Strang but one of his top advisers, a certain Samuel Graham. The past few days had been rough for Graham, who had suffered a fractured skull and a broken arm in an assault by Strang's enemies. According to the Mormon version of events, a pair of local fishermen had attacked Graham with a heavy cane, shouting, "Kill him!" Now he was waking to the sight of gun-toting strangers, even as his head was still "covered with clotted blood," as Bates put it.

The news that Bates delivered to Graham must have been even more disorienting. Forty armed men were waiting offshore, he said, ready to attack. They had a Mormon hostage. They would kill him by sunrise unless they got their man. *Where was Strang?* Bates demanded to know. *Where was the king?*

After "some hesitation and parley," in Bates's telling, Graham finally affirmed that the monarch was nearby and agreed to send a messenger to him. Then came the wait. As a courier rushed to Strang's place of hiding, Bates and his deputies passed the time by chatting with Graham, reading the Book of Mormon, and wandering around the house.

At length, Bates heard someone approaching in the dark. Then Strang, "with a cotton collar spread all over his shoulders, like a Catholic cardinal, with a lithe form...heavy projecting forehead, and a swinging gait, shot into the room." Assailing Bates with "anathemas long and loud," Strang demanded to see the arrest warrant.

"The papers are aboard," the prosecutor replied, "and if you will step aboard for a few minutes, I will show them to you."

Perhaps realizing he had little choice—and apparently convinced he would get better treatment from federal authorities than from the local posse that, the king had come to believe, was set not just on his capture but on his murder—Strang finally agreed to surrender. Around 3:30 a.m. he climbed aboard the U.S.S. *Michigan,* the first "foreign potentate," as Strang himself put it, on whom the U.S. government had "conferred the distinguished honor of bringing him into the country in a national vessel."

Less than twenty-four hours later the curtain came down on the second and final Detroit performance of the "great attraction" otherwise known as "the celebrated Mormon Preacher Mr. G. J. Adams," in the words of the National Theatre's playbill. After performing *Othello* the previous evening, the tragedian closed this two-night stand with a reprise of his Beaver Island staging of *Pizarro in Peru; or, The Death of Rolla.* The actor's appearance in town had been quite a curiosity. But in the antebellum era, such sensations never lingered long in the public imagination. Puppeteers, lecturers, phrenologists, ropewalkers, fire-eaters, magicians—the traffic of novelty was endless, spurred on by transportation and media revolutions, as well as by what P. T. Barnum called "that insatiate want of human nature—the love of amusement." Two weeks from now, in fact, Adams would return to Detroit with an entirely different attraction, one that the *Detroit Free Press* would describe as "perhaps the most exciting pageant on record"—a giant painting, 3,000 feet of canvas in all, portraying scenes related to the history of Mormonism. As vignettes from this "moving panorama" spooled past the audience, Adams, a "very talented lecturer," planned to offer thrilling commentary on the "cheatry practiced by this formidable body of hypocrites."

But before that, an even more remarkable curiosity would come to town. On May 26, a large crowd gathered to catch a glimpse of the renowned figure who had just arrived aboard the U.S.S. *Michigan*. The *Detroit Advertiser* described the "well-proportioned" man who stepped off that ship at about 9:30 a.m. as possessing "an open countenance, indicating some cunning and shrewdness," though perhaps not the "malicious character" attributed to him in some quarters. The *Free Press,* meanwhile, declared that the "hardy look-ing" newcomer "would pass, readily, for an unassuming, intelligent well informed farmer."

When J. J. Strang had surrendered to federal authorities, he instructed thirty-one other Mormons to turn themselves in as well. Strang would later claim that Bates and his colleagues, who had expected armed resistance from the islanders, "expressed them-selves quite astonished at the frank and generous manner they were received." The prosecutor released most of those arrested, pending further legal action, but he ordered Strang and three other leaders sent to Detroit. An exultant Bates recalled that as the prophet and his fellow prisoners walked from the wharf to the jail, "the streets were lined with amazed and amused spectators." Soon these "novelty hunters," to use another expression born in the antebellum era, would be treated to a spectacle unlike any they'd ever seen: the trial of an American king.

Sixteen

In which a murderous mood
descends upon the kingdom

———⟫⟪———

In every community persons are to be found who are fond
of indulging and cultivating a love for what is marvelous, and
who are ready to believe that a supernatural agency is involved
in whatever transcends their comprehension. Such tendencies
are by no means found in connection exclusively with low
intellectual powers, and small attainments. On the contrary,
it is not infrequently the case that persons of education, of
reflection, and even of superior mental endowments in some
respects, are led astray.

—*Buffalo Medical Journal,* 1851

M RS. McCULLOCH, YOU ARE AN EDUCATED, ACCOMPLISHED
lady, born in Baltimore, and reared in the very best society.
Can it be that you are a Mormon?"

"Yes, sir. I have that honor, sir."

"Madam, will you please allow me to look you directly in the
eye, when I interrogate you? I always like to watch a witness when I
examine them."

"Yes, Mr. District Attorney; you may stare at me if you choose. I
have seen greater men and better than you are. Go on, sir."

It was the third week of June 1851, and lawyers for both the
prosecution and the defense had come to Beaver Island to collect

depositions for Strang's upcoming criminal trial, due to begin in Detroit at the end of the month. Inside the rough-hewn temple where the prophet normally delivered his sermons, U.S. District Attorney George C. Bates was taking testimony from a prominent follower named Sarah McCulloch.

"Can it be possible, madam," Bates continued, "that so accomplished a lady as you are can believe that that fellow Strang is a prophet, seer, and revelator?"

"Yes, Mr. District Attorney, I know it."

"Perhaps we do not comprehend each other, madam; what do you mean by a prophet?"

"You know well enough, Mr. District Attorney. I mean one who foretells coming events, speaks in unknown tongues, one like Isaiah and the Prophets of the Old Testament."

"Ah, madam, how do you know that Strang speaks in unknown tongues and foretells coming events?"

"Because I have heard him—and witnessed those events thus foretold."

In Bates's account of this exchange—like many of his reminiscences, quite possibly exaggerated—he describes how Mrs. McCulloch, irritated by his badgering, angrily called him an impudent fool, causing even his fellow officers of the court to explode into laughter. For his own part, the normally confident Bates admits to feeling "utterly abashed at the energy of this accomplished and beautiful Mormon."

It was true that Sarah McCulloch seemed out of place on Beaver Island. Unlike most fellow residents, who had come from the ranks of the poor and working class, she had grown up on a 500-acre farm on the outskirts of Baltimore. The daughter of a military officer, she was married to an accomplished physician, Hezekiah D. McCulloch, who, before joining Strang's sect, had given public lectures on chemistry. Cultivated and cosmopolitan, the McCullochs were not the sort of people who, in normal times, might be expected to surrender themselves to supernatural beliefs. But these were not normal times. Strang's trial arrived at a moment in history when tens of thousands of Americans—many of them educated and wealthy—had suddenly come to believe in unseen worlds beyond the scope of scientific understanding.

The past three years, for example, had witnessed the rise of a wildly popular new movement called spiritualism, which traced its roots to a series of uncanny events at a farmhouse in the famous Burned Over District, about ten miles from where Joseph Smith had founded Mormonism. There, in 1848, the Fox sisters—eleven-year-old Kate and fourteen-year-old Margaret—proclaimed they had made contact with a ghost, who used knocking sounds to communicate from the beyond. Their older sister Leah soon declared that she, too, had the gift, and in short order, 400 people crowded into the largest hall in Rochester to hear the mysterious noises and witness the sisters in conversation with departed souls. Since then the movement had gained adherents with blinding speed. The list of true believers included many prominent Americans—business and religious leaders, journalists, judges, physicians, and scholars. Just three years after the Fox sisters had held their first séance, there were now an estimated 100 spirit mediums in New York City alone. "If ever the world was afflicted with arrant humbugs of any age, it is the present," declared a frustrated writer for *Scientific American*.

The furious emergence of spiritualism coincided with another phenomenon that seemed to offer evidence of a country losing its grip on rational thought and action. Since the late 1840s, murder rates had "exploded across the nation," according to historian Randolph Roth, who notes that some parts of the country that had been previously among the "least homicidal places in the Western world suddenly became the most homicidal." For years, worried observers of American culture had noted a "growing disposition to...the wild and furious passions" of "savage mobs," as

Abraham Lincoln put it in 1837, and by mid-century, superstition, alienation, and bloodlust seemed to be prevailing over reason and the rule of law.

Early in 1851, for example, the radical abolitionist John Brown formed what we might today call a terrorist cell. Convinced he was directed by God, Brown recruited forty-four African Americans to join the League of Gileadites, a secret organization in Springfield, Massachusetts, committed to taking up arms against slave catchers and other enemies. "Let the first blow be the signal for all to engage; and when engaged do not do your work by halves, but make clean work with your enemies," he instructed these would-be killers. Although the group split up before committing any violence, its establishment marked a turning point for Brown. From now on, he would be under the spell of a murderous dream, one that seemed to be seducing more and more people from all walks of life.

In his book *American Homicide*, Roth notes that in the 1850s "aggression and vitriolic language invaded personal as well as political relationships and turned everyday encounters over debts or minor offenses like trespassing into deadly ones." Fellow citizens, he writes, "killed each other over card games, races, dogfights, wrestling matches, and raffles." In the same month as Strang's arrest, a teenage girl from Rhode Island was charged with murder in a case that the *Hartford Courant* called "one of the most singular on record." Claiming the power to communicate with the spirit world, fourteen-year-old Almira Beazely had predicted the imminent death of her younger brother. Then, in what defense attorneys portrayed as a "morbid excitement" brought on by her conversations with the dead, the girl laced his milk with a fatal dose of arsenic.

Had a similar sort of "morbid excitement" taken hold of Strang's followers? Was his power over them so complete that they would break laws to obey his commands? And to what lengths were they willing to go? Those questions would dominate the federal trial in

Detroit. But even before it got under way, shocking news arrived from Beaver Island. An enemy of the prophet had been shot dead. And one of the two men charged with his murder was the husband of that "educated, accomplished lady" who had just testified to her faith in Strang's supernatural powers.

———

Until his arrest, Dr. Hezekiah D. McCulloch had built a seemingly distinguished career, serving as an Army surgeon and later as the health officer for the City of Baltimore. Nonetheless, he had sometimes exhibited erratic, even violent, behavior. In 1846, for example, McCulloch was convicted of assault and battery in his hometown, and then fined fifty dollars, for punching a fellow physician whom he had accused of stealing one of his patients. He had also been in financial trouble, facing a pair of foreclosure suits in 1848 and 1849, not long before he moved his wife and sons—ages five and six—to the Michigan wilderness. The McCullochs might indeed have believed Strang to be a prophet, but desperation as much as faith may have motivated their decision to begin life anew. Dr. McCulloch, it seems, had a weakness for drink. One later account asserted that he had fled Baltimore because "intemperate habits had brought him into disgrace." According to this version of events, Dr. McCulloch had "taken refuge with the Beaver Island colony, where liquor was unknown, in order to protect himself from temptation."

Whatever his personal demons, McCulloch brought valuable expertise to the Great Lakes, where a deadly cholera epidemic was then raging. Indeed his main responsibility as the health officer for the City of Baltimore had been to keep the citizenry safe from disease—no easy task in the nineteenth century. At one point the city council had asked Dr. McCulloch to determine whether the pigs that roamed freely through town, feeding on the garbage left behind by human beings, should be "excluded from the streets, as in some northern cities." McCulloch responded that the animals were indeed "offensive and unsightly" and had "vicious habits," but until a better system for taking care of the city's mess was put in place, the swine "must be esteemed as useful."

Strang appears to have taken a similar attitude toward the doctor, ignoring any of the newcomer's faults because of his proficiency and intelligence. George Adams had been deeply resentful of the erudite newcomer, whom he considered "mean," and once the tragedian was out of the picture, it didn't take long for the doctor to become one of the king's closest advisers. In addition to being the only physician on the island and the co-owner of a local store with a near monopoly on Mormon business, McCulloch assumed "a preeminent position in the Church," according to the *Northern Islander.* But the combative physician also became enmeshed in the escalating animosity between Mormons and local fishermen—a feud that, for the first time, had turned deadly.

———

In *American Homicide,* Roth attributes the sharp spike in murder rates during the late 1840s and 1850s to the fact that "Americans could no longer coalesce.... Disillusioned by the course the nation was taking, people felt increasingly alienated from both their government and their neighbors."

This pervasive sense of estrangement provided the psychological subtext for the killing that took place at Beaver Island on June 7, 1851. Members of Strang's church, who had journeyed to this far corner of the world to isolate themselves from American society and government, now accounted for the vast majority of the island's population. The influx of these newcomers, in ever-burgeoning numbers, had meant that other residents—especially the local fishermen—felt more and more marginalized. No longer welcome in the town of St. James on the north end of the island, many of the fishermen settled in and around Cable Bay, near its southern tip. A large number of these fishermen had been born in Ireland—early arrivals in the great wave of migration that would bring more than 1.5 million survivors of the Irish potato famine to America from 1845 to 1855. Beaver Island, in short, had already become the scene of a heated turf war between two groups alienated from, and persecuted by, the culture at large. Caught between them was a third marginalized group, the local Native Americans. Having fled Beaver Island when Strang established his colony there, a number of them now lived on Garden Island, a couple of miles north of the Mormon kingdom. And by 1851, the Ojibwe and Odawa residents of this neighboring island had sided with the prophet's adversaries.

The fishermen complained that Strang and his followers were stealing their property, harming their business, pressuring them to obey the laws of the kingdom rather than those of the United States, and forcing them to pay "tithes" to the church. Perhaps the prophet's most outspoken enemy among these malcontents was a man named Thomas Bennett, who, as the *Northern Islander* asserted in April of 1851, had vowed "to have the life of Mr. Strang before another harvest." Strang reportedly returned this threat, telling Bennett that if he did not pay taxes in the form of tithes, "mark my words, that you will be sorry." Apparently he wasn't bluffing. Another witness later testified McCulloch had declared "that Bennett was the cause of much of the disturbance at Beaver Island, and that they were bound to get him out of the way."

A few days after allegedly uttering those words, McCulloch joined about three dozen members of a posse that surrounded the house where Bennett resided at the south end of the island. The mob had come to arrest Bennett and his brother, Samuel, who owned the house, for an earlier incident in which they'd supposedly threatened the life of a Mormon constable. But upon seeing the armed intruders approach, the brothers slammed the front door and, as Samuel Bennett later testified, "told them we would not obey Mormon law, King Strang's law or any other law but the laws of our country."

In the coming weeks the two sides would tell sharply divergent stories about what happened next. The Mormons claimed that someone inside the house fired three shots at them, grazing one man in the head. Samuel Bennett, meanwhile, insisted that only one shot was fired—by accident, when his wife tried to wrest the gun away from him—and that it could not have hit anyone. The only points both sides agreed upon were that the members of the posse then rushed the house, firing through the windows and the door, and that when the onslaught was over, Thomas Bennett lay dead.

A few days later, the *Detroit Advertiser* ran this headline:

FURTHER OUTRAGES AT BEAVER ISLAND!
BRUTAL AND DELIBERATE MURDER BY THE
FOLLOWERS OF STRANG!!

By that time, Dr. McCulloch, along with several other Strang associates, had been arrested for the killing. It wasn't just the doctor's role in the fatal attack, however, that had suddenly made him notorious, with newspapers all over the United States, and even as far away as England, republishing the *Advertiser*'s sensationalistic accounts of the murder. What really enraged critics were McCulloch's alleged actions right afterward, when, as the island's lone physician, he performed an autopsy on the body. The *Advertiser* accused McCulloch of "butchery," claiming that after removing the dead man's heart, he had held it aloft and twirled it around on his finger. "Blood was then scooped from the cavity of the chest from where the heart was taken," the paper claimed, "*and by the same hand was daubed with bitter derision on the face of the corpse!*"

McCulloch denied these charges, which his wife, in an open letter published in papers across the country, dismissed as "slanderous reports which have emanated from a few perjured men." But the macabre accusations, coming less than two weeks before the start of Strang's trial, only added to the widespread perception that the prophet wielded such sinister influence over his followers that they were capable of any crime.

———

In the depositions collected by Bates on Beaver Island in preparation for the trial, Strang's disciples regularly described him as "a prophet, gifted by divine inspiration, and clothed with miraculous powers," as the *Advertiser* put it. But miraculous or not, those powers no longer held one key member of the colony in thrall. Amid the chaos of the prophet's arrest and extradition to Detroit, Mary Strang, his wife of fifteen years, packed up her bags and left the island in May of 1851, taking with her the couple's three children. The exact circumstances of her departure, including whether it was voluntary or forced, are lost to time, but Strang's correspondence indicates the prophet had exiled her from the kingdom.

Nineteenth-century illustration of a Mormon woman escaping her polygamous husband.

According to a later account, purportedly based on the testimony of one of her friends, Mary had become so opposed to her husband's regime that she eventually began to operate as a kind of Harriet Tubman of the northern wilderness, smuggling disaffected followers off the island in birchbark canoes with the help of Native Americans. There's good reason to be suspicious of this story, which sounds like something straight out of *Uncle Tom's Cabin,* the abolitionist melodrama whose first serialized installment was published the same month as Strang's trial. What seems clear, however, is that Mary did something to make her husband angry—so angry that he finally felt compelled to banish her from the kingdom.

It may be that he had simply come to believe "Mary was jeopardizing Strang's hold on his followers," as one biographer put it. But there is another possible explanation, one more ominous and more in keeping with the homicidal mood of mid-century America. The lone clue for this scenario—a cryptic notation scribbled in the margin of a Strang family scrapbook—would not be discovered until a researcher happened upon it more than a century and a half later. The handwriting of the notation matched that of Charles James Strang, born the month before Mary's leave-taking: "Mary tried to kill the writer of this, when he was an infant."

———

On the same day the *Advertiser* ran that screaming headline about the "brutal and deliberate murder by the followers of Strang," the prophet, who was still awaiting trial in Detroit, sat down to scratch out a letter to the governor of Michigan, John S. Barry: "I write you under the most painful apprehensions…"

Things had never looked worse for Strang. Not only did he face the possibility of years in prison, but his name had been ridiculed and reviled in newspapers across the country, his closest aides had been arrested for murder, and his lawful wife had left him. Strang implored the governor to protect "the little settlement of Mormons on Beaver Island" from "a set of lawless renegades on the borders [who] have defied the administration of the law there." Without intervention, he feared, the colony would "be annihilated."

Governor Barry placed the letter in his "under advisement" box.

Seventeen

In which the prosecutor wishes he had a bit more evidence, and the defendant wishes he had one true friend

The plan of "counting the chickens before they are hatched" is an error of ancient date, but it does not seem to improve by age.

—Phineas Taylor Barnum, *The Life of P. T. Barnum*

ALTHOUGH THE EXACT SEQUENCE OF EVENTS IS SOMEWHAT ambiguous, it appears that on July 8, 1851—the first anniversary of his coronation as king—Strang stood before a jury to make closing arguments at his own federal trial in Detroit. Members of that jury had just heard several days of testimony against Strang and twelve codefendants for obstructing the U.S. mail and assaulting a postal carrier with dangerous weapons—the prosecution's first set of charges. Star witness George J. Adams described how by the fall of 1850 the prophet had become obsessed with keeping critics on the island from communicating with the outside world. Strang, the tragedian testified, had vowed that once winter came and ship traffic ceased, he "would have control of the mail, and that communications should not leave there unless he knew what they were, and from where they went."

Adams added that he had once asked Strang how he planned to stop the wintertime postal carriers who took mail to and from the island once a month by dogsled. The prophet, he said, had replied that "dead men told no tales," and that it would be "very easy to cut a hole in the ice" in order to dispose of a corpse. Other witnesses recounted an ambush on the frozen lake, in which a dozen Mormons had tried to intercept the dogsled carrying the mail to Mackinac. The attempted theft failed, thanks to the intervention of Indians from nearby Garden Island, who headed off the posse and hid the mail in one of their homes. "The evidence was quite clear against them," Bates would later say about Strang and his codefendants.

From day one, the odds seemed against them as well. Only two members of the jury were Democrats (Strang's party), while ten were Whigs (the party of Bates and the *Detroit Advertiser*). Now Strang began to address those men, staring them down with his intense brown eyes. The transcript does not survive, but other accounts of his verbal fireworks allow us to imagine what members of that jury might have experienced. In a different setting, one observer described the prophet's oratorical skills as being "of the fervid, impassioned sort that would carry his audience with him every time. His words came out in a torrent; he could work himself into emotional spells at will, the sincerity of his words being attested by tears when necessary to produce that effect, or by infectious laughter when his mood was merry. He had what is known as magnetism." Even Bates came away impressed with the prophet's performance that day. "Strang's speech to the jury was very strong, full of bitterness and dramatic points," he would later remember. "He compared himself to Christ, his prosecutors to the lawyers and Pharisees who persecuted him."

It took only a few minutes for jurors to return with a verdict—acquittal of all thirteen defendants. Bates, who had sunk enormous amounts of time and tax dollars into the arrest and unsuccessful prosecution of Strang, blamed his failure on the notion that "the jury seemed to have imbibed the idea that these men were on trial for religion's sake." He faulted the judge, a Democrat, for steering jurors in this direction. But the prosecutor conceded that the prophet's speech had also played an important role. In Bates's version of events, jurors were just the latest victims of Strang's spellbinding powers.

The *Detroit Free Press*, however, offered a very different view of the proceedings. Skeptical of the case from the start, the paper placed blame for the verdict on Bates, who had badgered witness after witness about what the *Free Press* called "the question of King Strang's gifts prophetical" rather than about any actual violations of the law.

> The evidence was of the most dim and shadowy nature. Most of it related to anything else but the charge of obstructing the mail, and seemed designed rather as a general *exposé* of Mormon credulity and the peculiarities of the Mormon faith than as testimony upon which a prosecutor could seriously ask conviction by a jury.... That the defendants were Mormons was the only crime fully substantiated.

Modern experts agree. One legal scholar, for instance, has wondered why the district attorney did not open his case with accusations that the defendants trespassed on public land to illegally harvest wood, since "the timber theft charges were sounder factually and...prosecuting timber cases had always been a priority for Bates." But whatever his motivation, the district attorney's decision to start the case with the sensational charge of obstructing the U.S. mail would prove a fatal miscalculation. Two months after the verdict, prosecutors in Detroit quietly dropped all remaining federal charges against the Mormons. Of the alleged crimes that had prompted the U.S.S. *Michigan*'s spectacular raid on Beaver Island—including counterfeiting—not a single one resulted in conviction. And despite repeated attempts by Strang's enemies to apprehend Dr. McCulloch and others accused in the murder of Thomas Bennett, none of the men charged in that case were ever brought to trial. The *Detroit Free Press* concluded that Strang's followers had been victims of

> a systematic effort...to stamp upon the public mind an indelible impression of the guilt of the Beaver Islanders.... That they were guilty was *assumed* at the outset, and without one particle of proof they were branded as felons and murderers—as being so sunk in infamy and crime, as to be without the pale of human sympathy, or common justice.

———

It appeared that the cloud of suspicion that had hung over Beaver Island like a dense lake fog was finally beginning to lift. But then, less than two weeks after those charges were dropped in Detroit, four men invaded a home in Koshkonong, Wisconsin, a town about sixty miles west of Milwaukee where Strang had a group of about twenty local disciples. On October 10, 1851, around midnight, a husband and wife awoke to find the assailants in their room. "While one of the ruffians stood over the bed with a cocked pistol," a local newspaper reported, "the other three proceeded to rob the house." Although the gunmen got away with only eleven dollars in cash and some of the family's possessions, the incident outraged the surrounding community, which raised a posse of about 100 citizens. Eventually ten or twelve suspects were rounded up, all Mormons. "The proof against these men," reported another local newspaper, "is of the very strongest character.... The whole Mormon community at Beaver Island are implicated in crimes, sufficiently numerous and black to send them to the penitentiary."

One of those arrested was an island resident named David Heath, a true believer who saw non-Mormons as "the enemy." In a letter sent from Cleveland shortly after Strang's federal trial in Detroit,

Heath had expressed joy at the prophet's acquittal. "I heard that you was to be hanged by the neck until dead! dead!! dead!!!" he told Strang, boasting he had known from the start that the prophet's enemies "would not hurt a hair on your head." Yet for all his bravado, Heath could not disguise his concern that he had fallen from the king's good graces, having quietly fled the island during the tumultuous weeks leading up to Strang's arrest. Some members of the sect, he conceded, might think he "was frightened away by the mobocrats" who had been launching vigilante raids on the island, but the truth was that he had departed for health reasons—two bad legs that left him unable to fight. Instead of surrendering to the "shoulder grabbers"—a quaint antebellum expression for officers of the law—Heath had opted to retreat to the mainland for a full recovery. Though he would have to "keep [his] legs bandaged for several months yet," he looked forward to rejoining Strang in the battle against "wicked rulers" who "fill the cup of their iniquity previous to their overthrow." In the meantime, he yearned for a letter containing a few kind words from the prophet. Upon leaving Beaver Island, he confessed, "I felt as if I had not a friend on earth."

Heath's letter leaves the impression of someone with an apocalyptic worldview, someone who sees himself as part of a persecuted minority deserving justice and retribution, someone whose group identity is so strong he feels lost on his own, and someone with deep anxieties about his place within that group and a desperate need to prove his loyalty to its leader. It's the mind-set of a fanatic, a man who harbors "such indignation against the enemy" that he can justify almost any crime as legitimate self-defense of his own people, who have been chosen by God for a sacred purpose. Not all Beaver Islanders held such beliefs, of course, but for an unknown number of hardened zealots, criminal activity had become a kind of sacrament. In that same letter to Strang, for instance, Heath wrote cryptically about plans to travel to Baltimore for "business there which will benefit both me and the Church." It's not clear if this is a reference to a planned robbery, but there can be little doubt that he was involved in the raid on that home in Wisconsin three months later. In November of 1851, Heath and another Mormon man were found guilty and sentenced to four years in state prison.

Around that same time, someone wrote anonymously to one of the papers covering the case in Wisconsin to report that on Beaver Island "the Mormons are continually going and coming, and their business is stealing, which they call 'consecrating.'" The correspondent added that the thieves "generally go in bands, furnished with all kinds of burglary tools, keys, &c., prepared for anything that may occur, and armed to the teeth with revolvers, dirks, swords, &c." The letter appears to have been written by one of Strang's fiercest opponents on the island, a man named Eri J. Moore, who had testified against the prophet at his recent federal trial in Detroit and had plenty of reason to cast Strang in the worst possible light. Nonetheless, the most startling allegation his letter contained would turn out to be true. The king, he said, had left Beaver Island on a secret mission "in search of another place of refuge for his people." The prophet's plan, according to the letter, was to establish a new hideout north of the border, from which he and his "band of pirates" could launch raids on targets in Michigan and Wisconsin, then retreat with impunity into Canada, "and there laugh at those in chase of them."

Strang's own correspondence makes clear that this was the exact scheme he had in mind. In late October of 1851, he penned his brother, David, a letter from Detour Township, on the eastern tip of Michigan's Upper Peninsula, a couple of miles from the Canadian border, where he had been on an "exploring expedition." He and his colleagues, James wrote, were looking "to purchase a large Island of the British, and see if we cannot obtain the liberty of conscience in that Empire which is denied us in our own country."

The two siblings do not appear to have been close, and David Strang, a plainspoken farmer who had remained in western New York, seems to have been singularly unimpressed by his brother's grand ambitions. ("I fear," he had told Strang years earlier, "you are unsteady minded.") Nonetheless, the prophet apparently viewed his brother as a kind of confessor, someone to whom he could air his grievances, gloat over his triumphs, or offer justifications for his actions. This letter found Strang feeling particularly sorry for himself. During their journey to the wilderness, he wrote, he and his fellow travelers had suffered through freezing temperatures, fierce winds, and almost constant rain and sleet. Not only was he short on provisions, but he'd also had "a severe attack of inflammatory rheumatism," which had caused him to seek shelter at what passed for a hospital in this tiny village. During the wait, his mood had darkened.

"Truly, David, this is a hard life I live," wrote the prophet, who could not see how things would change for the better. Although he had "struggled manfully against [his] enemies," triumphing in federal court, he lived in constant fear of being arrested once more "and sent to prison and to death." Adding to his anxieties, he confided, was the fact that Mary and their three children had left Beaver Island—though he didn't acknowledge having exiled her himself. "So many hopes have failed me that I work on mechanically, my heart is crushed and a settled melancholy is stealing over me," he wrote, adding that "the one sole question is shall I ever have one friend, true and unchanging?"

Not even the compassion he imagined eliciting from his brother could "heal my sorrow, no, no.... You have never lived in the wild scenes that have given their peculiar tempest to my feelings."

The King of Earth and Heaven felt entirely alone. "The snow is flying and the ground is nearly covered," he added. Winter had "descended early."

Eighteen

In which the King of Earth and Heaven runs for elective office

Beaver Island is a very handsome spot.... As it rises before you with its shores clad with green foliage, the cedar, the fir, the tamarack, you are reminded of the Island bowers of Calypso.

—Visitor to Beaver Island, 1852

Is it possible that man's heart can harbor, amid such ravishing natural beauty, feelings of hatred, vengeance, or the desire to destroy his fellows?

—Leo Tolstoy, "The Raid," 1852

THIS IS MY REVENGE."

It was November of 1852, thirteen months after Strang wrote that sorrowful letter during his expedition to Canada, and once again the prophet was sitting down to update his brother on recent events. This time, however, his mood was euphoric. Strang had just been elected state representative for a sparsely populated district occupying a quarter of the landmass of Michigan. Instead of moving to Canada to flee the law, he had, through shrewd manipulation of the ballot box, put himself into a position to *make* the law. Even in a life full of dramatic reversals, this was a stunning twist, and one that had left the prophet—in despair while writing that letter the previous year—feeling invincible.

Strang had managed to pull off the victory by winning, suspiciously enough, all 165 votes on Beaver Island—enough to easily defeat the other four candidates, who split the remaining 200 ballots. This low turnout had been intentional on the part of the prophet, who ran a covert campaign, making no announcement of his candidacy until the day of the election. In an era before standardized ballots, few voters were even aware that Beaver Island was part of their legislative district, much less that the controversial Mormon leader had entered the race.

Yet despite the underhandedness of his victory, the election had given Strang a sense of "triumph" over those who had "sought and well-nigh accomplished my ruin," he told his brother. In 1832, as a nineteen-year-old farm boy, Strang had vowed to become "a Priest, a Lawyer, a Conqueror and a Legislator." Now, two decades later, he was on the verge of achieving all of those goals. "I have made my mark upon the times in which I live, which the wear and tear of time in the unborn ages shall not be able to obliterate," he confided to his brother. "Like Moses of old my name will be revered, and men scarcely restrained from worshipping me as a God."

It wasn't just his election to the Michigan legislature that had him feeling ebullient. The year 1852 had already been a very good one for Strang, who in the wake of his acquittal had managed to consolidate control over Beaver Island. His followers had taken over all the posts in local government, with Strang elected as town supervisor and Dr. McCulloch serving as clerk and health officer. With these power bases in their hands, the Mormons made life miserable for the prophet's foes, tormenting non-Mormons with petty lawsuits, many of which happened to fall under the jurisdiction of a certain James J. Strang, justice of the peace. Strang would later boast that some of his "most violent persecutors" had no choice but to come before him and receive judgment. And thanks to his acute knowledge of the law, those rulings were hard to overturn. Although some of his decisions were appealed to higher courts, none, he claimed, were ever reversed.

The practical effect of all this, according to one island resident, was that "everyone whom he didn't like...became an outlaw."

Strang had also taken advantage of a state legislation, passed a year earlier, requiring traders who sold alcohol to post a large bond to local authorities. This had few negative consequences for Mormons, all of whom were, in theory at least, teetotalers. But for non-Mormons—who sold so much alcohol to fishermen, steamboat travelers, and Native Americans that the northern part of the harbor was known as Whiskey Point—the new rules were devastating. Shortly after the state law went into effect, Strang and other Mormon officials began issuing heavy fines to violators who could not, or would not, post the bond, thereby further harassing the king's adversaries.

With their financial and legal status undermined and their physical safety increasingly threatened, a steady stream of non-Mormons had packed their possessions and left the island during the course of 1852. By the late summer, the *Northern Islander* asserted that Strang's followers now outnumbered non-Mormons by approximately 1,000 to 20. Strang frequently exaggerated the population of his kingdom, so those numbers should be weighed with skepticism. Nonetheless, it was clear that the tide had turned. Even "the blindest can see that we have an entire victory," the paper proclaimed, adding that the days of "mobbing the Mormons" were gone for good. Strang could now go among his enemies "alone and unarmed" and not fear "molestation or danger."

For the last remaining non-Mormons, by contrast, the situation was growing more perilous by the day. Those who "refused to affiliate with Mormondom, and refused to be participators in the crimes and enormities which have...shocked the moral sense of the entire country," the *Green Bay Spectator* reported, were being driven from the island "in a state of destitution and misery." As one island resident later recalled, the purge soon reached completion: "One morning about the first of November a messenger came to every Gentile family with a letter from the king, saying every Gentile family must come to the harbor and be baptized into the Church of Zion or leave the island within ten days after receiving the notice signed by the King, James J. Strang." Not coincidentally, the presumptive date of this crackdown—November 1, 1852—was just one day before that same election in which a unanimous vote from Beaver Island carried Strang to a seat in the Michigan state legislature.

Elizabeth Whitney Williams, a non-Mormon resident who was eight years old at the time of these events, later recounted, "Within twenty-four hours after receiving the notice every Gentile family had gone but ours. They had taken what they could in their fish boats. Our boat being small, father thought best to wait for a vessel to come and take us away." Nine "anxious days" followed, in which Mormon men patrolled the beach, "each carrying a gun, but none ever spoke to us." Finally, the rescue vessel arrived—but when "all was loaded except a few boxes and two large trunks," the family returned from the awaiting ship to discover their remaining possessions surrounded by a number of men bearing firearms. "This was enough," Williams wrote. "Father knew the rest of our goods must be left." Years later she could still remember her sadness at glancing back on the open door of the now-empty house her father had built, as well as "how happy we all felt that night" upon reaching the mainland, where there were no longer any "Mormons to be afraid of."

Strang would soon boast that his authority on the island was now so complete he was even able to make peace with local Native Americans, who, until recently, "excited by liquor, and allured by the offer of a reward for my head," had been "armed and hunting me for my life," as he wrote in a letter to the *New York Tribune*. But now the Indians were like "members of my family," having been saved from drink and poverty by the prophet—or so he claimed. It gave him satisfaction, he said, to see "a few of the vast race of red men, redeemed from utter annihilation, and to be able to say, 'This is my work.'"

It wasn't only his political and economic control over the island that Strang extended during the course of 1852. He had been increasingly bold in imposing a new social order as well. In January, a few months after that forlorn letter to his brother from the Canadian border, Strang had taken a third wife. Thirty-one-year-old Elizabeth "Betsy" McNutt was a true believer with a penchant for betraying the confidences of close friends in order to prove her loyalty to the king. Yet even if it were true, as one of those friends charged, that she wielded "poisonous arrows of slander" against others, Strang clearly placed importance on her devotion to him. After a private marriage ceremony, she moved into his modest home, joining Elvira and baby Charles, then just nine months old. Samuel T. Douglass, a member of the Michigan Supreme Court who visited the island around this time, wrote that Strang "lived in a log house with four rooms and two wives; rooms upstairs led us to believe that he slept with them on the [every] other night plan."

But if certain outsiders pictured Strang's homelife as an endless orgy at a backwoods brothel, at least some of his followers were starting to see polygamy as a sign of piety, a practice commanded by God. "At first it was talked of quietly and secretly among the leaders and afterward publicly and openly among the people," Elvira later recalled. "It was not looked upon favorably, and there were never over twenty cases of plural marriages." Strang never explained his shifting stance on this controversial topic, but his public statements on polygamy became more assertive and candid over the course of 1852. In March, for example, the *Northern Islander* published a strongly worded defense of plural marriages among Mormons in Utah. "Does not the constitution of the United States guarantee freedom of religion to all citizens?" the newspaper asked, adding that "nothing can be found in the common law against polygamy; nothing in the civil law; nothing in the Old or New Testament against it."

Such arguments were apparently lost on a defiant Mary Strang, who, after departing the previous year, would never again return to the island. In her absence, the prophet and his other two wives began a grand experiment in cooperative housekeeping, one inspired by both scriptural precedents of the ancient past and futuristic utopian schemes that called into question basic assumptions about family structure, sexual relations, and gender roles. Inside the Strang home—less a palace than a royal cottage—Betsy took over many of the traditionally feminine domestic chores, while Elvira continued as the prophet's private secretary. Both women, meanwhile, underscored Strang's radical reimagining of society by adopting a style of dress that had by now become one more powerful emblem of loyalty to the king.

Though it may be hard to imagine distant Beaver Island as a vanguard of fashion, pantaloons had become a national cause célèbre in the two years since those first sightings of women in strange apparel in Strang's kingdom. For proponents of the women's movement, the wearing of these loose trousers under a skirt that reached only to the knees—an outfit sometimes known as the "freedom dress"—had become a symbol of liberation, convenience, and comfort. But for other Americans, including many women, it was a source of anxiety, animosity, scorn, and confusion.

Nowhere had this collective anguish been more evident than in various cartoons published around the country during 1851 and 1852. One depicts a complete gender reversal, with a bearded man in a dress caring for his infant while a take-charge woman in trousers deals with a business matter. A second shows a gathering of feeble-looking men modeling a "New Costume for Males," an absurd version of the freedom dress. A third portrays "The Great Bloomer Prize Fight," in which a female boxer, wearing only a see-through tunic and a pair of pantaloons, strikes an aggressive pose before a crowd of leering male spectators.

Man in his Natural Position, and Woman where she ought to be.

Mr Booby delivering his Lecture on and upon the New Costume for Males

THE GREAT BLOOMER PRIZE FIGHT FOR THE CHAMPIONS BELT.

For the time being, Strang's new wives must have felt somewhat akin to the pantalooned pugilist in that illustration—ascendant and invincible. But the cartoon contains the image of another woman, that swaggering prizefighter's opponent, who cowers in fear or revulsion, her face buried in both hands. She too wears pantloons, but the picture seems to suggest that she has no choice in the matter, that she's been forced to take part in this spectacle for the amusement and titillation of the male onlookers. Much like the reluctant contestant of that cartoon, some women on Beaver Island wanted no part of Strang's new social order, whether it came to pants or plural marriage. One day these skeptics would come out swinging. But for now they had no choice but to hide their eyes. After years of swindle and struggle, Strang had finally become master of every sphere of human thought and action on Beaver Island.

By the time he wrote that second, exultant letter to his brother in November of 1852, the prophet seems even to have achieved something of a détente with his first wife. When Mary Strang fled the island a year and a half earlier, she first moved in with family members in Illinois, where her father was still a contractor for public-works projects. But in 1852 she returned to Wisconsin, where she planned to live alone in Voree with her three children, ages twelve, seven, and four, at their old house, which the prophet still owned. This didn't guarantee her complete autonomy, of course, but since the social stigmas and restrictive laws of 1852 made divorce almost impossible, she probably lacked a better option. As feminist firebrand Lucy Stone observed at a women's rights convention in September of that year, once a woman "has taken the sacred marriage vow, her legal existence ceases. We are asked to trust our husbands, fathers and brothers still, when, having trusted them, they have made such havoc of our rights."

A similar conclusion may have prompted Mary to sequester herself in Voree, beyond the immediate reach of her husband. But the

move also had the beneficent effect—intended or not—of enabling
the prophet to save face. From then on Strang had a ready response
to "the implication that my first wife is a 'runaway wife,' or a
separated woman." Whenever anyone asked why she no longer
lived on the island, he would reply that he still owned a large farm
in Wisconsin. "It is convenient," he'd add, "to have some person
there who has more than a hireling's interest in the success of my
business."

In that same triumphant missive to his brother, the prophet predicted
that his own legend would live on, even after "it is forgotten that
Millard Fillmore...was ever President of the United States." To poor
David, it must have seemed like the maddest of mad boasts, proof
of why he had once called his brother "unsteady minded." But compared to Strang's other megalomaniacal prognostications, this one
landed surprisingly close to the mark, at least for a time. Fillmore, in
fact, had already begun to fade into irrelevance, having failed to win
his own party's nomination for the presidency during the summer of
1852. Deeply divided on the issue of slavery, the Whig Party itself
would soon self-destruct—happy news for the prophet, who viewed
Whig politicians such as U.S. District Attorney George C. Bates as
his private persecutors.

As far as his own political fortunes went, by contrast, Strang saw
only glory ahead: "Frankly, brother, I intend to rule this country; and
it will be a hard struggle if I do not make myself one of the Judges
of the Supreme Court, within one year." It's hard to know what to
make of this outlandish claim. One expert argues that by *country*
Strang simply meant the Beaver Island region, and that by *Supreme
Court* he was referrring to the state court in Lansing, not the federal
one in Washington. But whatever the true nature of his ambitions,
Strang's enemies were determined to make sure he never achieved
them. Even as the prophet dashed off the final line of the letter to his

brother, they were making plans to prevent him from assuming his seat in the Michigan legislature—by force, if necessary.

Strang's critics had long accused him of election fraud. In 1850, for example, the pro-Whig *Detroit Advertiser* reported that "the faithful were commanded to vote the Democratic ticket." This decree, the paper claimed, was the result of a divine revelation experienced by Strang, who supposedly threatened that anyone who failed to cast a Democratic ballot "would be struck dead." According to a "reliable source" on the island, the story added, "women dressed in men's clothes, youths, aliens &c., &c., boldly walked up to the polls, and deposited their ballots, without objection and without scrutiny." Predictably, critics were mortified by the 1852 Beaver Island vote totals, which demonstrated what even the prophet's own newspaper called a "unanimity probably nowhere else seen."

With the Michigan House—which met only once every two years—set to start a new session in early January of 1853, Strang's antagonists attempted to have him arrested on an old warrant shortly after his arrival in the state capital of Lansing. The freshly minted state representative's response was to stall for time and to ask his fellow Democratic lawmakers to intervene. Relying on his impressive legal knowledge and superb oratorical skills, the new legislator made a persuasive case that the arrest had nothing to do with justice but was based solely on "private malice." Even the prophet's skeptics were impressed. " 'King Strang' pled his right in a masterly and convincing manner," observed one paper from the south-central Michigan city of Jackson. "He is a talented man, equal to any other man in debate and information."

Not only did the Michigan House vote overwhelmingly to allow Strang to retain his seat, but he also quickly managed to become a respected member of that body. By the end of the 1853 legislative session, even the *Detroit Advertiser*—the driving force behind that long-running crusade to put "the miscreant Strang" behind bars—had come away impressed. As a correspondent for the paper put it:

> Mr. Strang's course as a member of the present Legislature, has disarmed much of the prejudice which had previously surrounded him. Whatever may be said or thought of the peculiar sect of which he is the local head, throughout this session he has conducted himself with a degree of decorum and propriety which have been equaled by his industry, sagacity, good temper, apparent regard for the true interests of the people, and the obligations of his official oath.

And so it was that one of the nineteenth century's greatest shape-shifters undertook yet another startling transformation. In less than two years since his trial in Detroit, Strang had rehabilitated his public image from reviled criminal to esteemed statesman. And now he had an even bigger metamorphosis in mind.

Nineteen

In which the King of Beaver Island visits his old
haunts, contemplates eating poison, and loses a
machine that can predict the future

———— ⸎ ————

There's no place like home!
There's no place like home!

—Popular antebellum song

IN EARLY MARCH OF 1853, THREE WEEKS AFTER THE MICHIGAN
House adjourned its biennial legislative session, a noteworthy
visitor turned up in the southeastern corner of the state. "Hon. J. J.
Strang passed through our city a few days since on his way to Washington," reported a paper in the little town of Adrian. "We
understand he would like to be Governor of Utah." The article appeared just days after Franklin Pierce's inauguration as the
fourteenth U.S. president, an event that caused thousands of Democrats, including the King of Earth and Heaven, to set out for
Washington in search of jobs with the new administration.

Spoils system—that phrase, coined in the antebellum era, described
the practice of awarding government posts to partisan cronies,
which by 1853 had become the driving force in American politics.
"There never were before so many pure and disinterested patriots
who were willing to serve their country in any capacity or station,"
joked one paper on March 9, as Strang made his way east to join
the scramble. "Like the frogs of Egypt, they not only fill the streets

of Washington, but come up even into the houses of those who have patronage.... 'Office,' 'office,' 'office,' is their constant cry."

Strang, who might have appreciated the biblical metaphor, knew the rules of patronage as well as he knew the Old Testament, having been a beneficiary of the spoils system in his days as postmaster in the Burned Over District. If he was soon to become one of those frogs plaguing the nation's capital, at least he could console himself that he was attempting to catch a very big fly. The governorship of the Utah Territory was currently held by Strang's archrival, Brigham Young, who owed the job to outgoing president Millard Fillmore. But Young's four-year term would end in 1854, and his reappointment seemed less and less likely, especially since he was in the midst of a heated feud with federal officials sent to the territory to keep an eye on him. Young had further hurt his own cause in the previous year by deciding officially to acknowledge the long-standing practice of polygamy in the church, an announcement that caused widespread condemnation outside Utah. As one emissary for the church in Washington, D.C., conceded, "It is considered a settled matter that Governor Young is to be removed."

In his quest to fill this powerful post, Strang had at least three things going for him. First, as a longtime and loyal Democrat, he could count on access to powerful party members in Washington, including U.S. senator Charles E. Stuart and Secretary of the Interior Robert McClelland, both of whom hailed from Michigan. Second, during his brief time in Lansing, he had already established himself as "the most talented and ready debater in the House," one who was "equally ready on any subject, political, commercial, financial, judicial, educational," according to one newspaper. And third, he could offer the new administration a means of undercutting Young's grip on Utah by promising President Pierce that if appointed he would devote himself to "the uprooting of Brighamite Mormonism in the Salt Lake Valley," as Elvira Field would later put it.

The governorship of Utah would not only make Strang the top political official in a fast-growing territory. It would also allow him to challenge Young for control of the entire church. Reflecting on his chances of success, the *Battle Creek Journal* observed that it would be "a delicate matter to attempt to dethrone Governor Young; but the King is competent to any emergency. Bold, energetic, and cunning; and...reliable under all circumstances, he will probably be appointed." As he traveled to Washington, Strang must have felt confident—so confident, it seems, that he decided to stop for a triumphal return to his hometown.

———

It had been a decade since James Strang vanished from the western New York village of Randolph, with critics claiming he had faked his own death in order to flee creditors and avoid criminal prosecution. Now the prodigal son had returned, anxious to recover his pride and rebuild his reputation. In a letter to his brother, David, four months earlier, Strang had acknowledged that "there are many there who look on me as ruthlessly as though I had been a worm in the dust." Yet despite this antipathy, or perhaps because of it, he had become obsessed with the idea of a glorious return. In a letter suffused with nostalgia for "the place of my childhood," Strang confessed to David that "it is there, more than here that I should feel an honest pride in my success."

Upon his arrival in town, it appeared as though the prophet would get his wish. Welcomed as "the hero of the hour," in the words of one eyewitness, he gave a series of lectures at the local schoolhouse, during which "he claimed that the true believers had no fear of serpents nor deadly poison and that by laying on the hands they could heal the sick though in the agonies of death." While unable "to secure any converts," he "displayed no little talent" and generally captivated the curious citizenry.

Sheet music of "Home, Sweet Home," 1854. (The Lester S. Levy Sheet Music Collection, the Sheridan Libraries, Johns Hopkins University)

A triumphant return to an idealized place of origin—few dreams loomed larger in the antebellum imagination. One of the most popular songs of the early 1850s was "Home, Sweet Home," which owed much of its success to master showman P. T. Barnum. As promoter of the most spectacular concert tour in U.S. history, Barnum had suggested that his star attraction, the famous diva Jenny Lind, should perform the tune at an 1850 performance in Washington, D.C. So haunting was her rendition that the audience—which included then-president Fillmore and his family, along with many other dignitaries—sat silently after the last note faded, wiping tears from their eyes. (Fillmore reportedly described it as the most exciting thing that had happened to him since arriving at the White House.)

The song became a huge hit, once again demonstrating Barnum's brilliance at intuiting the American psyche. In an ever more mobile and unsettled society, convulsed by massive farm-to-city population shifts, record increases in immigration, manic western expansion, and rising sectional divisions, "Home, Sweet Home" evoked the idea of an unchanging, always welcoming place of return. To a nation filled with the kind of roaming exiles described in the song, it was a profoundly comforting fantasy.

Strang's own homelife was becoming extraordinarily complex and nomadic as he shuttled back and forth between two families. On Beaver Island, both of his plural wives were due to give birth the following month, Elvira to her second child and Betsy to her first. The prophet was also now visiting Mary and their three children in Voree with some regularity, though unsurprisingly the relationship with his lawful wife was strained. Their nine-year-old son, William, would remain bitter into adulthood about his father's additional marriages and the children those relationships produced.

Given the complicated world Strang had created for himself, with its myriad entanglements, resentments, and annoyances, it's not hard to imagine why he might have occasionally yearned for something simpler. As he was soon to discover, however, the mythic home of the antebellum imagination was often a more forgiving place than the real one.

On the morning after one of his lectures in Randolph, Strang found himself at a reception hosted by a former associate, Dr. Frederick Larkin. Back in the old days, the two men, who had shared adjacent offices, both were atheists. After Strang's departure, the physician remained "callous to the great truths of the gospel," as he sarcastically put it. Nonetheless he kept in touch with the prophet, who in one letter credited Larkin with souring him on traditional Christianity for good. "It is you that paved the way for the position I occupy," Strang wrote, adding that "since I became a Mormon a flood of light has burst upon my darkened vision." He expressed a hope that the same journey might prove possible for Larkin. "Come to us, my friend," he urged, "and we will lead you to the living truth."

The truth, it turns out, was precisely what Strang's skeptical host now hoped to determine at this gathering, which he would describe in newspaper articles years later. Larkin began by insisting to the prominent citizens of Randolph who had assembled at his office that they were "highly honored by the presence of the prophet." Then, to the obvious surprise of their eminent guest, he informed them that they were about to witness a miracle. Larkin then turned to a local physician and asked the man how much strychnine would be required to kill ten men.

That must have sent a collective shudder through the room. Strychnine, "that terrible poison," as *Scientific American* called it in 1856, was a feared if familiar product in antebellum households, where it was used to kill rats, crows, wolves, and sometimes humans. Those who consumed it could expect painful muscle spasms, difficulty breathing, and a racing heartbeat, with the possibility of death resulting from asphyxiation, cardiac arrest, brain damage, or multiple-organ failure.

In that tense moment Strang must have had second thoughts about his earlier boast that Mormons were immune to the effects of poison. As his old friend Larkin produced a fatal dose of strychnine and dared Strang to swallow it, perhaps the prophet recalled the story of a similar trial by poison that had taken place not far from Randolph, more than two decades earlier. And maybe he remembered, too, that it had left a Mormon missionary dead. A silence must have filled the room as everyone—including, no doubt, Strang himself—wondered what the prophet would do next.

"The test was one that Strang had not expected and he tried in every manner to evade a trial," an article based on Larkin's recollections later explained. At first the prophet asserted that "the days of miracles were past," but Larkin reminded him of his recent letter, in which Strang had claimed to be able to "handle serpents, heal the sick, cast out devils, and eat deadly poison." Finally, Strang gave up, denouncing the onlookers as "all unbelievers anyway." Nothing he could do, he said, would change their views.

"To the disgust of all present," Larkin noted, "no miracle was performed."

Strang emerged from that gathering with his life, but he was once again a local laughingstock. Meanwhile, a suddenly calamitous homecoming was about to get even worse.

———

Within days, the *New York Tribune* and other newspapers were reporting that "the celebrated Mormon teacher, J. J. Strang," had suddenly vanished from his former hometown. The story, which first appeared in the *Randolph Whig,* explained that after a local resident attempted to collect on "a debt of long standing," the prophet "disappeared 'between two days'"—a euphemism for a silent departure under the cover of darkness.

Indeed, Strang seems to have fled Randolph so hastily that he left behind a number of his belongings, which the local constable seized. "Among the novelties," the article reported, "was a revolver, a brace of pistols, and a very singular machine, which we have not time to describe, by the use of which he is enabled to peep into futurity." But what are we to make of this final item? Could that "very singular machine" be the Urim and Thummim, the miraculous contraption Strang claimed to have received from the "hands of an angel" in order to read and translate the Rajah Manchou plates? Had he invented some other sort of divination device? Or was the whole thing just a fabrication, a practical joke by the anonymous author of the article, who, like so many other people of his time, had taken pleasure in blurring the line between fact and fiction?

The writer went so far as to claim that the mysterious machine had enabled the prophet to "guide the destinies of the Mormon people." Without it, the story speculated, Strang "may become as enfeebled in this respect as Samson with his locks shaven!" Although the analogy seems to have been intended as humor, it would prove oracular. Like Samson, the Old Testament hero who suddenly lost his superhuman strength, Strang left town a diminished man, drained of much of his recent magic. Nonetheless, he clung to the hope that President Pierce would award him the Utah governorship. For years, after all, Strang had turned every dream, no matter how far-fetched, into reality. Was his luck—and with it his confidence—finally beginning to fade?

———

"The rush for offices is tremendous. There are thousands of hungry office hunters here," a top Mormon official in the nation's capital wrote to Brigham Young on March 10, 1853, a few days after the incidents in Randolph. But of all these office seekers, the correspondent mentioned only one by name. "James J. Strang of Beaver Island notoriety," he reported, "is among the applicants for the governorship of our Territory." The official—Utah's territorial delegate to Congress, John Bernhisel—apparently took seriously the threat of a Strang candidacy. In that same letter, he sounded an ominous warning for Young: "There will be a strong effort made to procure your removal from office, but with what success remains to be seen. It is almost superfluous to add that I shall spare neither pains nor effort to avert so great a calamity."

But the "calamity" did not come to pass. Brigham Young would remain governor until 1858, leaving office only when about 2,000 U.S. troops arrived in Salt Lake City to install a replacement sent by Washington. For reasons that are largely lost to posterity, Strang's efforts to win the job went nowhere. It's not even certain that he made it all the way to Washington before turning around and skulking back to Beaver Island. His clothing, books, papers, and firearms remained in Randolph where he had abandoned them, along with that mysterious time machine, the secrets of which were lost to scientists and theologians forever. Never again would Strang pose a credible challenge to Brigham Young for control of the Mormon church, nor would he ever achieve higher office.

But as he celebrated his fortieth birthday on March 21, 1853, the prophet was far from defeated. On Beaver Island he could still boast a solid grip on power and a growing royal family, as he looked ahead to welcoming his fifth and sixth children the next month. In the state capital of Lansing, no enemy of the prophet could "measure swords with Strang in debate," according to the *Detroit Advertiser*. His local foes were similarly frustrated, with all their recent attempts to bring the king to justice or check his power having been "as usual...signally defeated," as the *Northern Islander* gleefully put it. And although Strang had suffered a painful humiliation in his hometown and fallen on his face attempting to secure the governorship of Utah, he still had an almost magical ability to impose his will on the world. Soon, in fact, he would make a man disappear from jail.

Twenty

In which a legend appears, and a horse thief departs

There is nothing so certain to succeed as imposture, if boldly managed.

—*Buffalo Courier, 1851*

PERRYSBURG DOES NOT OFTEN HAVE THE HONOR OF A VISIT from any of the great folks whose fame fills the world," observed the editor of a small-town paper from northwest Ohio. "Whenever we do, however, the event deserves to be duly chronicled. Be it known, then, that during the week past, KING STRANG, the Mormon chief of Beaver Island, was here." It was October of 1853, seven months after the prophet had made that hasty exit from his own hometown followed by his failed attempt at the Utah governorship. Now he was on the road again, having just paid a visit to this village along the banks of the Maumee River near Toledo. The editor offered readers a detailed, if far from flattering, portrait of the King of Earth and Heaven:

> Strang is a man of medium size, of light, active build...smooth-faced, a little bald and a little stoop shouldered. He does not show the slightest symptom of being a man of talent; but low cunning is strongly developed in every lineament of his countenance. He is doubtless shrewd and sharp, and can slip through as narrow a place as any other man. He seems to be wide awake, and may have acquired something

of the blended air of a sanctimonious rascal from the sharp vicissitudes with which his nomadic habits of life have made him acquainted.

In the seven months since his failed attempt to gain the governorship of Utah, Strang had become the father of two more children, with Betsy and Elvira each giving birth to a baby girl within weeks of each other in April 1853. But whatever joy he took from those infant daughters, Evangeline and Evaline, Strang had gone through a difficult summer, one marked by strife and violence. He had not come to this Ohio town of roughly 1,000 residents to save souls. He had not come to recruit new pilgrims to Beaver Island. Nor had he come to carry out official business as a member of the Michigan legislature. It so happened that one of the prophet's most important followers was on trial for horse theft, and it was this development, the editor of that local paper explained, that "doubtless brought the saintly Strang among us."

Although Strang had worked hard to recast himself as an upright public servant, allegations persisted that he led a double life as the head of a "piratical band of desperadoes," in the words of one newspaper. In August of 1852, for example, as the prophet was gearing up for his run for the state legislature and pressuring his enemies to leave the island, a man "connected with the Mormons" broke out of jail in Woodstock, Illinois, where he had been "committed for breaking into a store," according to a local paper. The escapee was recaptured a couple of days later on the pier in Racine, Wisconsin, about to board a ship to Beaver Island. Just three months after that, with Strang having won the election, officials in Chicago announced the arrest of six other Mormons from the island who had been "on a marauding expedition," according to the *Chicago Journal*, which added that "a large quantity of stolen goods was found upon them and many articles have already been identified by our citizens as having been purloined by these 'model saints.'" In December, five of the men were convicted of robbery and each was sentenced to a year in the penitentiary.

The following May, not long after Strang's fruitless trip east, additional allegations of theft appeared in the *Detroit Free Press*, the same paper that had so fiercely defended the prophet during his federal trial two years earlier. Back then, the paper had maintained, Beaver Islanders "were branded as felons and murderers...without one particle of proof." Now, however, the *Free Press* had changed its tune, running an article about "daily recurring instances of robberies, burglaries, and other depredations committed by the Mormons of Beaver Island," both "along the shores and upon the waters of Lake Michigan."

The *Free Press* story, reprinted in papers throughout the United States and in England, claimed that Mackinac fishermen had faced an almost impossible task in attempting to guard their property against the "piratical trade" of Beaver Island. When the fishermen set their nets far offshore, hanging them vertically from buoys on the surface of the lake, Strang's men would swoop in with "small boats which move very rapidly," snatch up the equipment, and disappear. At night these same raiders would "make their descent upon the land [to] steal, rob and burn what they can find." The Mormons' motivation for such mischief was clear. "They intend," the *Free Press* concluded, "to monopolize these fishing grounds."

Strang, of course, adamantly denied all such allegations. "Candidly, I most truly believe the story of the stealing was hatched up by some dishonest fishermen, as an excuse for not paying up their arrears with the traders who supplied them," he wrote in a letter to the *New York Tribune*, published a few months before his visit to Ohio. His followers, he insisted, were the victims of a massive smear campaign:

At different times they have been made the subject of legal investigation, and in every instance the result has vindicated the uprightness and intelligence of the Mormons. Yet so greedy is the public ear for some tale of Mormon corruption, that it seems scarcely possible to invent so barefaced and incredible a lie that it shall not find a place in some respectable paper, and believers among its readers.

But what about the accused horse thief now sitting in the Perrysburg jail, the man Strang had come all this way to visit? Was he too the victim of just such a lie?

Stealing horses was considered a particularly serious crime in antebellum America, where the expensive animals were crucial to agriculture, transportation, public entertainment, and the conduct of war. Thieves were often organized into gangs, stealing the horses in one area and selling them hundreds of miles away, usually across state lines. For such operations, stolen horses simultaneously served "as a source of capital, a means of exchange, and a means of transportation," in the words of one historian.

According to the *Perrysburg Journal,* horse thieves were already doing a "brisk business" in this northern Ohio community when four of the animals disappeared from a field ten miles south of town on July 27, 1853. The owners, the paper reported, immediately issued handbills offering a large reward for the recovery of the horses and the arrest of the thieves, and several men set off in pursuit. After following the criminals for about ninety miles, the original pursuers hired a group of vigilante trackers—sometimes known as regulators—to continue the chase across state lines into Indiana. The second group eventually hunted the horses down in Boone County, Kentucky, near Cincinnati, and subsequently apprehended one of the thieves, who "gave his name as Jonathan Pierce, a Mormon of Strang's band...from Beaver Island," according to the Perrysburg paper. The accused rustler was described as "an athletic, stalwart fellow, 6 feet 3, and well proportioned [with] black, curly hair and saturnine temperament." While Pierce was locked up—awaiting trial at the next term of the court, in late September—he apparently sent word to Strang, hopeful that the prophet would rescue him through some sort of intervention, human or divine.

———

Back on Beaver Island, Pierce commanded great respect and even greater fear. He and his older brother, Isaac, served as Strang's storm troopers. "Hard-fisted men"—that's how one nineteenth-century chronicler remembered the siblings, who hailed from the same rural county of southwestern Ohio as the prophet's third wife, Betsy McNutt. Like members of her clan, they might have been recruited into the sect by the magnetic preacher and actor George J. Adams, who, before his bitter split with the prophet, had been an enthusiastic supporter of "consecration" raids on non-Mormon communities.

In 1851, one disaffected resident of Beaver Island claimed that the Pierce brothers were part of a "band of consecrators" involved in horse-theft operations and other marauding forays. The brothers and their cronies, he wrote, "make it their sole and only business to rove around in bands, and steal and plunder everything they can lay their hands on." Another former island resident would later recall them as "large and powerful men" who headed "a band of forty thieves" with a hideout on the island to stash their spoils. "All these goods were new," this observer wrote, "and did not seem to have been damaged."

Strang also used the siblings as his bodyguards and enforcers, devoted henchmen who were not afraid to do his dirty work by pointing a gun at someone's temple—and, if necessary, pulling the trigger. Indeed, in the months leading up to Jonathan Pierce's arrest, he and his brother had been involved in a pair of violent confrontations that received national press coverage. The first of these was in May 1853, when Strang boarded a steamboat bound for Buffalo accompanied by one of the Pierce brothers—newspaper accounts did not supply a first name. When the vessel stopped at Mackinac and word got out that the prophet was a passenger, a deputy sheriff came aboard and tried to arrest him on an old warrant (a move that constituted an attempted kidnapping "by a gang of rowdies," in the subsequent view of the *Northern Islander*). The ship pulled away from the wharf with the officer still trying to apprehend Strang, who had barricaded himself in his stateroom and, according to one press report, "threatened to shoot the first man who entered."

The standoff lasted until the steamboat reached the mouth of the St. Clair River, a waterway dividing the United States from Canada, with Michigan on the western banks and Ontario to the east. Despite protests from the deputy sheriff, the captain decided to dock on the Canadian side to replenish its stock of wood for fuel. This was Strang's big chance. Knowing the lawman couldn't arrest him on foreign soil, he burst from the stateroom, with Pierce next to him, and attempted a leap to safety. But the officer, as one newspaper subsequently reported, "seized him by the collar as he was springing over the rail." It was then that "Pierce, stepping up, presented a revolver." He offered a stark choice: release the king or die.

But the sheriff had other ideas. "The officer at once drew *his* pistol," according to the account, "and, presenting toward the breast of Pierce, pulled the trigger." The gun, however, misfired. "Strang, taking advantage of the *melee,* and jerking himself loose from the grasp of the Sheriff, sprang ashore, and was soon lost in the wilds of Canada," the paper reported, adding that his bodyguard was also able to flee.

As if that weren't enough excitement, the Pierce brothers were soon involved in another armed showdown with their enemies in northern Michigan. The second confrontation took place two months later, in mid-July, at a settlement on the mainland about twenty-five miles southeast of Beaver Island. Then known as Pine River (and now as Charlevoix), it was home to fishermen and other refugees who'd been forced from Strang's colony in recent years. Along with their allies in Mackinac and other nearby areas, residents of Pine River had grown steadily more hostile toward their Mormon neighbors, trading accusations and threats with them all spring and summer. By the afternoon of July 13, when the Pierce brothers and thirteen other Mormon men rowed up to the Pine River beach in a pair of boats, tensions were at the breaking point. "Let words cease and deeds begin," the *Northern Islander* had declared two weeks earlier. "We prefer peace; but if war must come, let it be upon us and not upon our children. We shall not yield."

The ostensible reason for the visit was a seemingly routine legal matter: the Mormons, with control of the local courts, were there to summon three Pine River men for jury duty. But residents of the settlement suspected that the true intent was to arrest the men. Vowing to resist what they called "Mormon law" at all costs, the men raced to the beach with weapons. Though the Mormons were also armed, it was obvious from the start that they had no hope of matching their opponents' firepower. After a jittery half-hour stand-off, they returned to their vessels and prepared to depart.

The two sides offered greatly divergent accounts of what happened next. According to one version, the last Mormons were climbing into their boats when an enraged Jonathan Pierce, frustrated by the decision to leave, declared, "We are running away like a set of damned cowards. I'll let them know that I'm not afraid." With that, he reportedly took out his horse pistol—a large handgun normally carried in a holster on the side of a horse—and shot at the Pine River residents on the beach, hitting one man in the leg and setting off a furious barrage of return fire that left six Mormons wounded, including both Pierce brothers.

Bloody and shaken, the Beaver Islanders then attempted a desperate escape across the water, with their Pine River assailants leaping into boats and giving chase, unleashing a steady stream of fire at the fleeing vessels. All fifteen of Strang's men might have perished had a Chicago-bound commercial ship not intervened, offering refuge to the Mormons just as their enemies were closing in for the kill. When the blood-spattered Mormon boats pulled up next to that vessel, the captain noted that "rifle balls had shattered and riddled [them] in picturesque style."

The six wounded men weren't much better off. The captain judged their injuries so severe that he predicted all of them would become "martyrs to their faith." Isaac Pierce, shot through the elbow, had broken two bones and collapsed in the boat from loss of blood. His younger brother came out of the fight with a rifle ball flattened against his hip bone. Thanks in part to the ministrations of Dr. Hezekiah McCulloch, all the injured Mormons survived. Jonathan Pierce recovered so quickly, in fact, that only two weeks passed between the clash in northern Michigan and the day those four horses disappeared from a field near Perrysburg, Ohio.

Since his arrest for that theft, Jonathan Pierce had "seemed entirely unconcerned as to his fate," the *Perrysburg Journal* observed. Perhaps that was because he had been behind bars before—and didn't expect to stay for long. Two years earlier, according to one report, he and his brother had found themselves locked in an Illinois jail. But they managed to break out just in time to go on a marauding mission with some fellow horse thieves. Now, the *Journal* sarcastically surmised, Pierce once again was probably depending upon "his 'extended colleagues' to help him out of his present embarrassments *in some way.*"

———

During Pierce's trial, Strang "made no ostentatious display" of "his greatness," according to the *Perrysburg Journal*. "His advent created no excitement, he was not welcomed with a public reception as he probably would have been in New York where it is the custom; his presence was not even known by many in town till he was gone." The paper conjectured that "the unfortunate position of Pierce, his friend and follower, may have caused this, though saintly pretentions would probably dictate a show of humility."

Pierce was ultimately convicted of the horse theft, but the judge overturned this verdict on a technicality and granted the defense's motion for a new trial. At issue seems to have been the county sheriff's failure to swear in the foreman of the jury, an omission the lawman blamed on the fact that he wasn't present and was instead at home, "confined to bed by sickness." Some local critics suspected behind-the-scenes maneuvering of a less than saintly nature. "We would *meekly* ask our *sick Sheriff* what was the matter with him when the Jury retired in the case of Jonathan Pierce?" wrote an editor for another local paper, the *Northwestern Democrat*. "Was it a *foul stomach*? eh?"

Given the frequent use of wordplay by antebellum newspapers to make cutting innuendos, it seems clear that the editor suspected foul play. Did Strang use bribes, or perhaps even threats, to secure the sheriff's help? The record of the past leaves us with no definitive answers. What's certain is that a new trial kept Pierce out of the Ohio State Penitentiary, and in the local jail, for a few weeks more. And when it comes to getting out of tight scrapes, sometimes a few weeks is all that's required.

———

ESCAPED.—Jonathan Pierce, convicted of horse stealing, but awaiting a new trial, broke jail a week ago last Saturday night, and has not been heard from since. A reward of $100 is offered for his apprehension. He will not probably be re-arrested soon.

—*Perrysburg Journal*, October 31, 1853

In the aftermath of the jailbreak, the county sheriff insisted that any suggestion he had colluded in the escape was "a willful and malicious falsehood" invented by his enemies, "whose vindictive malice is so apparent." At no point, he declared, had he allowed Jonathan Pierce to roam around the jail yard, unshackled and without supervision. Any suggestion to the contrary was nothing other than "mere abuse." Nor was it true that the sheriff had made it possible for Pierce's confederates to gain entry. "The back door of the jail on the night of the escape was unlocked, I admit," he wrote, but the cell door, constructed of solid iron, was bolted shut, as were other doors leading to the lockup. In a letter to the *Perrysburg Journal*, the sheriff offered no explanation of how the prisoner's accomplices had managed to get through those doors, other than an oblique reference to the fact that certain "instruments" must have been used. Still, suggestions that he'd had anything to do with the escape were "too contemptible to merit an answer." The only certain truth, he wrote, was that "Jonathan Pierce, by the aid of his friends, escaped."

But who were those friends? Criminal gangs tend not to leave records, yet circumstantial evidence suggests that one of those involved in the jailbreak was the very same mysterious figure who had shown up on Beaver Island a few years earlier identifying himself as Dr. J. Atkyn. This chameleonic character, one-time rival for the affections of Louisa Pray, had disappeared from Beaver Island in the fall of 1850, around the same time as George J. Adams, but had since paid another visit to the Mormon colony. In 1856, the *Northern Islander* would pinpoint the date of that return as the summer of 1852, when Atkyn reportedly arrived in poor health and claimed the charity of Strang as a fellow member of the Freemasons. According to that article, Atkyn remained on the island for three weeks until his health recovered, at which point the prophet furnished him with money to leave.

Information that Atkyn provided to a Cincinnati newspaper in 1856, however, suggests the actual date of his return was not the summer of 1852 but a year later. Not only did he demonstrate an insider's knowledge of alleged horse-theft operations, telling the paper that "there are nineteen span [i.e., matched pairs] of horses on the island, *eighteen* of which were stolen," but he also offered specific information on the Perrysburg jailbreak. In addition to divulging the exact number of men involved, Atkyn named the ringleader: "J. J. Strang, in 1853, headed in person a gang of seven Mormons to break the prison at Perrysburg, Ohio, to liberate Jonathan Pierce, convicted of horse stealing."

———

In July of 1853—the same month those horses went missing a few miles outside Perrysburg—the *New York Tribune* noted the steady stream of press reports portraying Strang's followers as "deluded and vicious persons, stirrers up of crime and disorder." Nonetheless, the newspaper insisted, the allegations hadn't been proven, and unless Strang's accusers provided "clear evidence" of his follower's crimes, "the public in this quarter will incline to give a verdict in favor of the Beaver Island Mormons."

Given the virulence of anti-Mormon hysteria in the mid-1850s, the *Tribune* was perhaps wise to refrain from unsubstantiated conclusions about Strang and his followers. Indeed, more than a century later, one of the prophet's biographers would continue to insist that "a great amount of unfavorable public opinion about the Beaver Island Mormons was moulded by nineteenth century feature writers from semi-truths and fabrications gleaned from completely biased Gentiles who hated them." But the Perrysburg episode—which seems to have escaped the notice of both contemporary observers and later historians—comes tantalizingly close to supplying that "clear evidence" of criminal activity the *Tribune* had demanded in 1853. In addition to placing the prophet at the scene, it provides strong indications that he traveled all the way to Perrysburg not to offer Pierce moral support but rather to play a direct role in both subverting the criminal-justice system and pulling off the escape.

James J. Strang, innocent target of religious persecution—like all his personae, this one proved to be a mask. Yet it was exactly those masks—those endless layers of ambiguity—that gave the man his charisma, leading newspapers such as the *Perrysburg Journal* to write, only partly in jest:

> Let the bigger cities boast their lions and whiskerandoed 'furriners;' none of them have had a live prophet, a veritable saint in their midst as this many a day. Who cares for...Jenny Lind and Barnum, when Strang is in the field?...You may frequently and in many latitudes, 'see the elephant,' but it is only once in a lifetime that [you] can see Strang!

Strang may or may not have been a real prophet or an actual king or a sincere man of the people or an honest politician, but by 1853 he had become a bona fide celebrity. Venerated by some, derided by others, he embodied a time when Americans had "begun to see fame as being desirable in itself, elevating the well-known and popular into positions of power and authority," in the words of one scholar. In the months to come, he would attempt both to secure his fame and to tighten his grip on power.

Twenty-One

In which the prophet writes a book, and his followers vote like hell

———=≫)(((●))((≪———

> Now and then some one would cry out "humbug" and
> "charlatan," but so much the better for me; it helped to
> advertise me, and I was willing to bear the reputation.
>
> —Phineas Taylor Barnum, *The Life of P. T. Barnum*

IN MID-DECEMBER OF 1854, A NEW YORK PUBLISHING HOUSE released *The Life of P. T. Barnum, Written by Himself*. It was to become one of the most popular autobiographies of the nineteenth century, selling more than a million copies over the next thirty years.

Barnum's book arrived amid a radical shift in public notions of *celebrity*—a word gaining widespread currency in the mid-nineteenth century, along with the theatrical term *star*. In previous eras, fame had been associated with notions of personal virtue, public service, artistic genius, and military heroism. Founding father Alexander Hamilton, for example, described "the love of fame" as "the ruling passion of noble minds," which would "prompt a man to plan and undertake extensive and arduous enterprises for the public benefit." In this worldview, fame was a conservative influence, a "golden cord" that "binds us to our fathers and to our posterity," in the words of one antebellum writer. But by the early decades of the nineteenth century—with the collapse of old social hierarchies and the rise of mass media—the traditional concept of fame had begun to seem like an increasingly elusive goal. "This field of glory is harvested, and the crop is already appropriated," declared a young Abraham Lincoln in 1837. A new kind of celebrity was emerging—one some historians describe as "post-heroic."

Barnum embodied this new ethos. One contemporary critic, for instance, described his book as "the shameless confession of a common impostor, who has taken the money of the public by downright falsehood and vulgar fraud." But what bothered the writer even more was that such a man would become a star. "There was a time," he complained, "when people must have lived lives before they could sell them. It was necessary for them to have been something, or to have done something." Barnum, by contrast, was famous merely for being famous—and even more famous for casually conferring fame upon others. In 1842, for example, the showman had plucked from obscurity a two-foot-tall dwarf, re-named him General Tom Thumb, provided him with a fictitious biography, and transformed him into an international sensation, feted by European royalty and mobbed by adoring fans. Although dismissed by elitist critics as a "little monster," Tom Thumb would be, by the time of his death in 1883, "probably better known than any man in the United States," according to one obituary. He was the ultimate post-heroic hero—superstar of an age endlessly hungry for "human curiosities."

Although J. J. Strang would never outshine P. T. Barnum, he shared much of the legendary impresario's gift for promotion. It's no coincidence that both men spent formative time as newspaper editors, or that both came to prominence in a period of history that had produced the first advertising agencies, the first programmatic efforts to understand mass-persuasion techniques, the first use of *propaganda* to describe the systematic dissemination of information in a biased or misleading way, and the first use of *celebrity* as a noun that connoted a celebrated person, a public character.

Whatever else anyone might have thought of him, Strang was now undeniably a public character. Indeed, at this point the prophet was more famous than Abraham Lincoln, who had just recently reentered politics, launching what would be an unsuccessful bid for a U.S. Senate seat in Illinois. Yet even Strang must have been aware that many Americans saw the prophet less as a statesman than as a sideshow attraction. Take this item about the prophet, published in the *Schenectady Cabinet,* a paper in upstate New York, around the time that Barnum's autobiography was rolling off the press:

RIOT ON BEAVER ISLAND. Strang's Mormons got into an awkward scrape the other day, in this out of the way locality. Several of the Sheriff's Posse, who had gone with him to summons jurors, were fired upon and grievously wounded. They are now doing well, most probably owing to a free use of Lynde's Russian Ointment, the very best remedy in such cases, as it is in all Wounds, Bruises, Burns, Scalds, Felons, Whitlows, &c.

What looked, at first glance, like an actual news story turned out to be a cynical advertisement for a quack medicine—the perfect emblem of the prophet's post-heroic celebrity. The trouble was that Strang never aspired to serve as a huckster for Lynde's Russian Ointment; he had grown up with the old idea of valorous fame, a dream he returned to again and again in the diary of his youth. ("O! If I was King of England I would try my fortune in the bloody field.") It must have gnawed at the prophet to find himself regarded as the religious and political equivalent of a snake-oil salesman.

Anxious about his place in history and perhaps inspired by Barnum and other popular antebellum memoirists, Strang sat down to write his own autobiography around this time. He completed a scant seven pages before breaking off in mid-sentence—apparently distracted by a more pressing matter. The prophet never returned to that manuscript, but he had recently managed to complete a different book with self-serving intentions. Entitled *Ancient and Modern Michilimackinac* and published at the Mormon printing house in St. James in 1854, this forty-eight-page tract appears, at first glance, to be an objective history of Beaver Island and the surrounding area, starting with the arrival of French explorers in the early seventeenth century. Written in a dry and somewhat detached style that would have been familiar to readers of nineteenth-century histories and travel narratives, the volume offers a brief overview of human habitation in each settlement or county, followed by details on the local geography, natural resources, economy, and principal products. The Mormons and their leader don't show up until a third of the way through the book, and even then only as a passing reference. Thereafter, the prophet is referred to as "Mr. Strang," as if the writer hopes to maintain an objective distance from his subject. In fact, writer and subject were one and the same, though most readers wouldn't have known that, since no author was named.

Yet despite its putative tone of impartiality, the volume's real purpose is propaganda. Its villains are the local fishermen and their cohort of "felons and outlaws," whom the anonymous author describes as the "worst class of men." For him they are "wretches with withered and tearless eyes" whose crimes include "robbery, rape and murder." The heroes of the book are the long-suffering Mormons, "persons of limited means, temperate habits, good morals and persevering industry" who "conduct their business as in the best regulated civilized societies." Despite being falsely accused of all manner of crimes, these intrepid Mormon residents of Beaver Island have endured, vowing "to die upon their native soil, rather than flee." In the end, of course, good triumphs over evil. "The tide is now turned.... The dignity and manhood of the Mormons has been vindicated," the author reports, adding that "the same prudence which characterizes their past acts will insure them a glorious future." And thanks to these heroic pioneers, the vast region of northern Michigan including Beaver Island is finally ready for "the greatest enterprises of this enterprising age."

Enterprise—that word appears more than fifty times in the autobiography of P. T. Barnum, who boasted that he had given the public "a larger measure of enjoyment than has ever been derived from the enterprise of any other single individual." Suffused with the jargon of commerce, the memoir attempted to transform Barnum's post-heroic fame into something more respectable, recasting him as the quintessential American entrepreneur. Barnum didn't deny that many of his entertainments were hoaxes designed solely to pique the curiosity—and empty the pockets—of paying customers. But instead of apologizing for such deceptions, he posed them as "needful and proper relaxations and enjoyments" that performed an important public service. Thrift, ingenuity, and philanthropy—not greed or guile—were what drove him, he insisted, along with a determination to combat the "drudging practicalness" of American life.

Strang's book, too, was intended to justify its author's controversial career, as well as to promote "a change of public opinion favorable to the Mormons," as he explicitly declared on the back cover. But if the reception to Barnum's book offered any indication, it wasn't so easy to alter a person's public image. Although some critics bought into the showman's claim to be a paragon of American virtues, praising his self-denial, frugality, industry, and "moral principles," others were far from convinced. "He does not seem to be conscious," wrote one, "that all his professions of piety and religion are utterly negatived by his conduct." Far from being a saint, in this critic's view, Barnum had been proved "by his deeds" to be "a very serious and inveterate sinner."

———

Having added historian to a résumé that included teacher, lawyer, editor, prophet, pirate, state legislator, and King of Earth and

Heaven, the indefatigable Strang was by this time trying his hand at yet another profession: climate scientist.

In the mid-1850s, meteorology was still very much in its infancy. Weather forecasting did not yet exist, and researchers couldn't even figure out if storm systems followed predictable paths. Tornadoes, hurricanes, blizzards, and droughts often seemed like random and unforeseeable events, devastating to crops, deadly to human beings, and crippling to the economy. But the Smithsonian Institution—a federally administered research center established in 1846 "for the increase and diffusion of knowledge"—planned to change all that. The organization's first major scientific undertaking, in one of the earliest examples of what has come to be known as crowdsourcing, was to establish a national network for collecting meteorological data.

Hundreds of volunteer observers in far-flung locales joined in, and Strang, with his uncanny flair for catching a ride on the currents of history, seized the opportunity to take part. But although the prophet's name appeared on official Smithsonian records (sometimes misspelled *Strong*), most of the actual labor fell on his pantaloon-wearing wife Elvira, who once again found herself performing a job normally done by men. According to an account based on her own recollections, Elvira spent years collecting data for the project. Every day at 7:00 a.m., 2:00 p.m., and 9:00 p.m., she meticulously observed weather conditions on Beaver Island and entered them into a special log supplied by the Smithsonian, then submitted her reports to Washington each month by mail. It was no small task, especially for the mother of a fast-growing family that, in addition to three-year-old Charles, now included daughter Evaline and a second son, Clement, who arrived in 1854. But her efforts—along with those of other volunteers across the country—would help scientists understand storm systems and make possible some of the earliest weather forecasts.

While Elvira collected climate data, the prophet's other plural wife, Betsy McNutt, assumed the role of a traditional antebellum homemaker with "magic skill" in the kitchen, as one island resident later recalled. She also took on the laborious task of counting every word on every page of the *Book of the Law,* so as to ensure that no one could produce an unauthorized copy. In 1854, she too gave birth to a son, David James, who lived for only about ten days. As with so many aspects of Strang's private life, the emotional impact of the child's death on Betsy, on Strang, or on the family's complex dynamic is lost to history.

What's certain is that whatever grief the prophet may have endured, it was far from his only worry. In the autumn of 1855, for instance, Strang's aging parents had packed their belongings in western New York to join Mary in Voree. Strang claimed he was now spending about one-quarter of his time in Voree as he traveled back and forth between two families—the ones he had made both before and after becoming King of Earth and Heaven.

But these responsibilities didn't keep the tireless prophet from other pursuits. The Smithsonian, for instance, encouraged its staff of amateur scientists to collect specimens of local fauna, and to study their behavior, habitat, and distribution. Somehow Strang found the time to complete such a project (perhaps with the help of Elvira or others), the results of which are detailed in a paper he wrote entitled "Some Remarks on the Natural History of Beaver Islands, Michigan." To his apparent surprise and obvious delight, the Smithsonian published the study in one of its annual reports, alongside the work of prominent scientists and scholars. Although written in a formal style similar to that of Strang's history of the region, the paper—an inventory of animals native to Beaver Island and its environs, with a special focus on fish—did not seem to serve any immediate propaganda purposes. Perhaps the prophet viewed it as part of a larger effort at self-legitimization, a subtle means of countering his reputation as a con man and religious fanatic. Or perhaps, with his keen intelligence and intense curiosity, this complex man simply found comfort in studying the natural world.

Near the end of that paper, Strang expressed regret that "a thousand avocations and duties constantly pressing upon [him]" often prevented his zoological pursuits. And in the fall of 1854, he again had to turn to a more immediate concern. With his two-year term in the Michigan legislature about to end, Strang was up for reelection. Facing a stiff challenge, the shape-shifting prophet had to change avocations and duties yet again. Gone was the amateur scientist; back once more was the professional fraud.

Ballot-box corruption had deep roots in American politics—but "this old evil took on new proportions during the 1850s," in the words of one historian. Vote buying, vote importing, ballot stuffing, violence, and intimidation—all these forms of fraud had reached epidemic proportions by mid-century, a fact not lost on commentators of the era. "Political morality is an obsolete idea," said one character in Charles Gayarré's satirical novel, *The School for Politics*, published in 1854. "It would be just as out of place now-a-days as the fashion in which our great-grandfathers used to dress—powdered wigs, knee-buckles, and short breeches." Or as a corrupt Maine politician who gleefully indulged in all manner of illegal electioneering put it, "My God, we have voted like hell!"

In the election that took place on November 7, 1854, the people of Beaver Island likewise voted like hell. In his own county, Strang received 695 votes; his opponents received 0. This tally—aided by just 19 total votes from the other parts of his district—was more than enough for a repeat victory in a divided field of opponents. One twentieth-century researcher determined not only that the prophet garnered more votes than there were legal voters in the county, but also that many of his supporters appeared to have cast ballots multiple times. The fraud itself was perpetrated with an absurdist comic sensibility worthy of Phineas T. Barnum. Among those who appeared on an 1854 census listing eligible voters in the county was a certain Napoleon Bonaparte, as well as the prophet's notorious and elusive personal secretary, Charles J. Douglass, gone now for nearly five years.

According to a later account in the *Northern Islander,* the prophet had not originally intended to run for reelection, preferring instead to turn the job over to his longtime ally, Hezekiah D. McCulloch, the cultivated physician from Baltimore. But in the months leading up to the vote, Dr. McCulloch had begun drinking heavily again, prompting Strang to keep his own name on the ballot. Or at least that was the version reported in the *Islander* more than a year after the incidents transpired. One resident, however, insisted that Strang's real motivation was jealousy, born of the fear that the dynamic McCulloch "would supplant him in the leadership."

For now, at least, McCulloch remained in the prophet's inner circle, retaining his position on church councils and, as county clerk, helping Strang execute what papers across the country called the "farce" election on Beaver Island. Publicly he still professed "moderation and good intentions" toward Strang, but privately the doctor had begun to undermine his longtime patron, "never [letting] slip an opportunity of shaking the confidence of a friend, or aggravating the hate of an enemy," as the *Northern Islander* soon put it. In the near future, animosity between the two men would grow into a blood feud—a microcosm of the violent mood overtaking the entire nation.

———

Three weeks after the prophet's reelection, a vote took place in Kansas that made ballot-box irregularities on Beaver Island seem as minuscule as Tom Thumb's pinkie finger. Earlier in 1854, Congress had passed the controversial Kansas-Nebraska Act, which created two new territories but left it up to the citizens of those jurisdictions to determine whether or not to allow slavery within their borders. From the start, however, it was obvious that outside agitators had no intention of allowing local voters to decide the issue for themselves. As the voters of Kansas went to the polls to select a delegate to Congress on November 29, 1854, more than 1,700 residents of neighboring Missouri swarmed into the new territory. Brandishing bowie knives, shotguns, and pistols and vowing to hang any abolitionists who got in their way, they drove away local election judges in an effort to cast bogus ballots for a pro-slavery candidate. This "fraud and outrage," in the phrasing of one abolitionist paper, marked the start of violence that would soon engulf "Bloody Kansas," as Southerners fought to transform the territory into a slave state and Northerners battled to keep it free.

In his first term in the legislature, Strang had generally focused on local issues. But in his second term, the longtime abolitionist would dive into the national debate over slavery. For once, he planned to use his post-heroic celebrity in a heroic cause.

Twenty-Two

In which the prophet, like just about everyone else,
threatens to slaughter all his enemies

━━━◦◦◦◦◦━━━

We are not one people. We are two peoples. We are a people
for Freedom and a people for Slavery. Between the two conflict
is inevitable.

—Anti-slavery editorial in the *New York Tribune*, 1855

To arms! To arms!

—Pro-slavery handbill in Kansas, 1855

DURING THE FIRST WEEK OF 1855, THE WEATHER UNDERWENT a remarkable transformation in Lansing, the seat of Michigan state government. The new year began as "balmy as a southern April day," according to one political correspondent in the city, but within a few days it was freezing cold, "the wind blowing with the fury of a thousand demons." Inside the state capitol—an austere two-story frame structure topped by a tin cupola—an even more dramatic change was brewing. Michigan had become the scene of a stunning political revolution, one with profound and lasting national implications. Just a few months earlier, more than 1,500 abolitionists had gathered in the town of Jackson to protest the Kansas-Nebraska Act, denounce the spread of slavery, and nominate a slate of candidates for state office. "We will cooperate," members of the fledgling organization pledged in their platform, "and be known as REPUBLICANS."

Soon afterward this new Republican Party shocked political observers all over the country by taking control of both houses of the state
legislature, as well as the governor's office. For Strang's Democratic
Party, which had formerly controlled the state, this was nothing short
of a disaster. The *Detroit Free Press,* a longtime mouthpiece of the
Democrats, sneered that the new party's "political faith is furnished by
the insane ravings and incendiary articles" in the abolitionist press, as
well as by "Mrs. Harriet Beecher Stowe's lying romance," *Uncle Tom's
Cabin.* Thanks to such "farcical" politics, the newspaper predicted,
"their days of misrule and misgovernment will be few."

The Hon. J. J. Strang, however, had come to Lansing not to pick
a fight with his new colleagues but to support their cause. Standing
before his fellow lawmakers on January 8, the prophet presented a
petition on behalf of the state's black residents, requesting that free
men of color be granted the right to vote. Such legislative maneuvers
were hardly new to Michigan politics. For more than a decade, African Americans had regularly petitioned the legislature for suffrage
rights—and just as regularly, lawmakers had ignored or denied those
petitions. Nor would Strang's latest move have any lasting impact on
the debate. Nonetheless, the prophet was now such a celebrity that
almost anything he did made the news. The *Free Press* caustically
observed that Strang was "full of tender compassion for the colored
'citizens,' (so he claims negroes to be)," and that he "most eloquently
informed the House that in 'looking for the man he looked not in
his face to see the color of his skin, but to the *soul*!!' "

Though the measure did not pass, Strang was just getting started.
On January 24, two weeks after introducing the suffrage petition, he
took the floor for a full hour and a half to denounce the Fugitive
Slave Act of 1850, which required officials in free states such as
Michigan to assist in the capture and return of runaway slaves. Strang
had long been an opponent of this controversial federal legislation,
declaring in 1851 that fugitive slaves were "heartily welcome" in his

new kingdom, that Beaver Island "would be entirely safe as a place of refuge for oppressed men of color," and that "no force can be brought there sufficiently potent to take them away." In the end, this offer of sanctuary had turned out to be symbolic, since no slaves seem to have sought refuge on the island. But now, as the 1855 legislative session got under way, Strang planned to back up his words with action. Defying fellow Democrats, he voted with the Republican majority on a pair of bills designed to undermine the Fugitive Slave Act by granting various legal protections (including the right of habeas corpus) to accused runaways, penalizing anyone who arrested a free person with the intent to enslave, and prohibiting sheriffs from allowing slave catchers to detain fugitives in local jails.

The Michigan legislation was modeled on similar statutes in other northern states. Known as personal liberty laws, they were "crucial to the understanding of the slavery debate and the secession crisis that preceded the Civil War," wrote one historian, adding that "most Southerners despised the laws, and Michigan's statutes fueled that hatred." As an outspoken supporter of the measures, Strang quickly became a target of that rage, with one Mississippi paper describing him as "a pillar of the bastard Democracy of Michigan." In the debate over slavery, both sides slung the term "bastard democracy" at their enemies while portraying themselves as the guardians of "true" (that is, legitimate) democracy. But in this case, not just southerners questioned the legality of the new Michigan measures. "State after State cannot nullify laws of [the U.S.] Congress, and disregard plain constitutional provisions, without provoking retaliatory action," warned the *Detroit Free Press*. "And when retaliation fairly begins, where will it end?"

In short, Strang, by voting against his own party on the personal liberty laws, was taking a big political risk. But as with his 1849 decision to ordain black men in the Mormon priesthood, he seemed to be driven by principle and conscience. Fellow abolitionist Henry

David Thoreau once argued that each person's ethics could be accurately plumbed, just like the unseen floor of a pond, and that somewhere in the depths there was a "hard bottom...which we can call *reality.*" Opposition to slavery, the prophet's actions suggested, was his hard bottom, beneath which there were no ulterior motives, no hidden schemes, no confidence tricks.

———

Of course, in the prophet's murky world, perhaps nothing was ever truly solid. Later that year, on September 20, the *Northern Islander* reprinted an excerpt from Frederick Douglass's autobiographical slave narrative, *My Bondage and My Freedom,* issued by a New York publishing house the previous month. Given Strang's abolitionist leanings, it's not surprising he was drawn to the writings of "Fred Douglass," as the *Islander*'s byline identified the famous social reformer. But what was striking about the excerpt was the material Strang chose to include—material that may have said as much about the moral climate on Beaver Island in 1855 as it did about the mind-set of slaves in the South. The article outlined the conditions in which it was ethically justifiable to steal.

Douglass explained how he and his family had been given such a small ration of food on one plantation that "it was not enough to subsist upon; and we were, therefore, reduced to the wretched necessity of living at the expense of our neighbors." He recalled his own moral struggles over becoming a thief: "To be sure, this was stealing, according to the law and gospel....I weighed and considered the matter closely, before I ventured to satisfy my hunger by such means." And he described how he came to the conclusion that under slavery people were relieved of "moral responsibility" for their actions:

> I shall here make a profession of faith which may shock some, offend others, and be dissented from by all....I hold that the slave is fully justified in helping himself to the *gold and silver, and the best apparel*

of his master, or that of any other slaveholder; and that such taking is
not stealing in any just sense of that word.

To Strang's followers, Douglass's ethical formulation must have come off less as a condemnation of slavery than as a justification for their own actions. The "right to steal" proposed by Douglass, after all, sounded a lot like the Law of Consecration, which, in the minds of some Mormons, justified theft from nonbelievers as payback, sanctioned by God, for the real and imagined crimes inflicted upon them by their enemies. Was the prophet drawing a moral equivalence between the two? If so, he had a growing number of reasons to insist, as Douglass had done in that passage from his book, that "on the principle of self-preservation, I am justified in plundering in turn."

Three weeks after the prophet published that essay by Frederick Douglass, the *New York Times* carried a story under the headline "Wholesale Robbery by Pirates on Lake Michigan." Reprinted from a paper in the southwestern Michigan town of Allegan, it began:

The people along Lake Michigan, from here north to the Manistee, have been thrown into the most intense excitement by the operations of a gang of marauders, who are reported to be Mormons from Beaver Island, and who have carried on their operations with a boldness, coolness and desperation rarely equaled in the records of highwaymen. They are reported to have burned sawmills and robbed stores north of the Grand River. At Grand Haven they made repeated attempts to break into stores and shops. On Saturday of last week they made their appearance at the mouth of the Kalamazoo, and after looking about some, pushed up south as far as the tanneries in the town of Ganges, and on Saturday night broke open Robinson & Plummer's store, robbed them of $1,600 worth of goods, and made back again down the lake.... There is said to be upwards of twenty in the gang. They sail one small schooner of twenty or thirty tons and two

Mackinaw boats.... There seems to be no question as to the identity of the robbers or their hailing place. They are emissaries from KING STRANG'S realms, and the whole power of the State should be lent to ferret out and bring to justice the perpetrators of such bold crime.

Through the system of exchange papers, this story would soon be republished as far away as Melbourne, Australia. But it was just one of many articles about alleged thefts by Beaver Islanders that appeared in 1854 and 1855. In July of 1854, for example, a Milwaukee paper had reported that "a large and daring band of thieves" with supposed ties to Strang was "perpetrating systematic outrages in Northern Illinois, breaking into houses and taking money, provisions and various other articles," an echo of the armed burglary in Koshkonong, Wisconsin, for which two men with ties to Beaver Island had been convicted a few years earlier. Two months later, in September, an Illinois paper carried a story on a pair of horse thieves caught near Nauvoo, one of whom "finally told his name and said that he lived on Beaver Island—the stronghold of the notorious Strangites." The following month, the *Buffalo Daily Republic* noted:

A rumor has been current for several days on our docks that the schooner *Robert Willis,* whose sudden disappearance on Lake Michigan last fall was noticed at the time, and of which no intelligence was ever afterwards received, had been captured by the Mormons of Beaver Island, her captain and crew massacred, and the vessel unloaded and scuttled.

Several months after that, in February of 1855, came an account from Lapeer, Michigan, where three stores were burglarized, followed by the alleged arrest of one of the prophet's top aides. That summer, in July, the *Pontiac Gazette* carried accusations about a horse-thieving operation by Strang's followers, adding that because of "the isolated position of the Island which they inhabit, it is nearly impossible to bring [them] to justice." Then in September of 1855—the very month in which Strang reprinted the Frederick Douglass excerpt—more allegations about Mormon horse theft appeared in the *Buffalo Morning Express,* followed by a report from a paper in Grand Haven, Michigan, nearly 200 miles south of Beaver Island, that there was "no longer any doubt of there being a gang of desperadoes along this coast, well armed, taking various kinds of goods." Alleging that the marauders were Mormons, the paper added, "We advise the inhabitants, the whole length of this coast, to be on guard when any small boats visit them."

The prophet, of course, denied every single "false and ridiculous tale," many of which he republished verbatim in the *Northern Islander* so that he could pick them apart with lawyerly precision, launching ad hominem attacks against his accusers or dismissing the substance of an allegation by contesting a few isolated facts. Strang suggested that papers all over the Great Lakes were undertaking "a general and simultaneous assault upon the Mormons of Beaver Island," and compared it to what he saw as similar efforts that had sent him into hiding several years earlier, in the months before his federal trial. Now, he feared, there was again "a reasonable prospect" that accounts of Mormon crimes "may be followed by an array of government prosecutions." He was wary, too, of a vigilante invasion, knowing that "when the public vengeance is waked up the law will not protect us, and that among an angry people innocence is no shield." Neither the governor nor the president, he warned, would safeguard Beaver Island against the coming violence.

Yet Strang's response to such a threat, whether perceived or real, was a refusal to be cowed. "Let it come," he sneered. The next time the prophet's enemies dared to set foot on Beaver Island, he vowed, they would receive "a bloody welcome."

They were shutting down now, those utopian colonies. In October of 1855, newspapers all over the country carried stories about the collapse and sale of a high-profile socialist commune in New Jersey, not far from New York City. Over the past few years, ideal societies of all sorts had been calling it quits—Christian, anarchist, communist, transcendentalist. Back in the 1830s and 1840s, countless Americans had believed people could learn to live together in fellowship, peace, and harmony, but something had changed. A new cynicism, perhaps brought on by rising tensions between North and South, was sweeping the land. Utopian communities now seemed "cursed with idiotic theories," as one paper in the nation's capital put it.

On October 7—the very day that article appeared in the *Washington Union*—a former leader of one such colony arrived in Kansas, having traveled from upstate New York in a wagon loaded with revolvers, rifles, ammunition, and broadswords. John Brown was no longer interested in utopias. He was there to kill. Promising to "save" the territory, this self-avowed avenger had come to believe that, in the words of the Scriptures, *without the shedding of blood there is no remission of sin.* Or, as another of his favorite Bible passages put it, *To me belongeth vengeance and recompence; their foot shall slide in due time; for the day of their calamity is at hand.*

As the winter of 1855–56 approached, Strang also must have felt, more than ever before, that a day of calamity was at hand. In late November, four of his followers were lost at sea, presumed to have drowned in a small vessel between St. James and the mainland. Among them was Jonathan Pierce, the accused horse thief who had escaped from that Ohio jail two years earlier. The death of this "hard-fisted" man—who, along with Jonathan's brother, Isaac, served as something of a bodyguard and enforcer for Strang—did nothing to ease the prophet's fears of arrest and mob violence.

Nor were those his only concerns. Earlier that year, his fourteen-year-old daughter, Myraette, had wed her nineteen-year-old first cousin, the curiously named Romeo D. Strang. The prophet made no attempt to hide his disapproval of the marriage, which took place at a Baptist church. Romeo—the son of Strang's brother, David—had hoped to obtain his own farm near Voree, but the prophet refused to help, insisting that he could do nothing for the young man unless he converted to Mormonism and moved to Beaver Island. Romeo stood firm, writing to his father that he would neither become a Mormon "nor engage with them in stealing and destroying the Gentiles."

Adding to the prophet's anxieties was his quickly collapsing stature in the Michigan legislature. At the beginning of the session, the *Detroit Advertiser* had predicted—wrongly, it turned out—that the prophet would wield "more political power than any other one man in the state." But although members of the new Republican majority in the House welcomed his support in fighting the Fugitive Slave Law, they refused to side with the longtime Democrat on other matters. To make things worse, even "the King's friends have had enough of him, and are turning the cold shoulder," noted one observer, who added that "his majesty's weapons" were by now reduced to "words, words, words." Democrats and Republicans joined together to pass, by an overwhelming margin, a redistricting plan that slashed the size of the prophet's legislative district, stripping him of control over any part of mainland Michigan. They also put an end to his dream of establishing a new judicial district, with the ultimate object of placing himself on the bench. As a result, observed the *Jackson American Citizen,* "his projects and hopes are vanishing away."

Nonetheless, the paper noted, Strang remained "a dangerous man to tamper with—of good habits, intelligent, persevering and extremely energetic, yet ambitious, restless, domineering, and possessed of great cunning." In the months to come, this "dangerous man" would need to rely more than ever on these Machiavellian gifts. A civil war was breaking out—not in faraway Kansas but in his own little kingdom on the lake.

Twenty-Three

In which the picture comes into focus

Were you ever daguerreotyped, O immortal man?...And in your zeal not to blur the image, did you keep every finger in its place with such energy that your hands became clenched as for [a] fight?

—Ralph Waldo Emerson, *Journals*

DUE TO THE PHYSICS OF DAGUERREOTYPE PHOTOGRAPHY, THE cameraman always saw an inverted image of his subject. And as the proprietor of the Saint James Daguerrean Gallery prepared to take a picture of Strang, the prophet appeared before him in the camera's glass viewer upside down, as if hanging by a thread. It was late 1855 or early 1856, and Strang had stopped by the island's brand-new photographic studio to have his likeness preserved for posterity. The past few months had found him in an anxious mood. In a recent issue of the *Northern Islander,* for example, he listed all his travails since assuming the throne:

> I have been imprisoned on one charge and another, trumped up
> against me...so many times, that by the utmost stretch of memory
> I cannot count them over....I have sat sixteen days on trial for
> my life, listening to the false tale of each witness against me as
> one would listen in a theatre, without a play bill, have beheld the
> ponderous grates—have walked amidst clanking chains, or gazed
> between bars of iron for sun light, and beheld the ghastly gibbet,

and I yet live beloved of many wise and good, ready to serve or be sacrificed for my fellow men.

Daguerreotype of Strang attributed to J. Atkyn. (Church History Library, The Church of Jesus Christ of Latter-day Saints)

Serve or be sacrificed—self-aggrandizing melodrama aside, Strang seemed keenly aware that his career as prophet-king was approaching a make-or-break moment. Even the royal portrait that the photographer was about to make would seem full of foreboding, with Strang's intense eyes gazing past the camera at something in the distance, as if glimpsing his fate closing in fast. And whether either man understood it then, in the thirty or so seconds it took to make this exposure, the photographer would play a crucial role in bringing about that fate.

Like an angel of death, the drifter who identified himself as Dr. J. Atkyn had come back to Beaver Island once more. After an absence of at least two years, he had reappeared in the summer of 1855, when, according to a later edition of the *Northern Islander*, "he stopped by at different times, well dressed, and professing to be well stocked with money." During the course of those visits, he proposed to open a daguerreotype studio in St. James, offering "numerous examples of what he claimed to be his work," which, according to the *Islander*, were "of superior quality." As with everything he said, Atkyn's claim of expertise as a photographer may have been a complete fabrication. Then again, the profession was notorious for attracting self-inventors. By the 1850s the countryside was crawling with itinerant daguerreotypists, many of whom "styled themselves 'professor,'" one such photographer remembered, but because "the new business of likeness-taking was admitted to be a genteel calling, enveloped in a haze of mystery," the veracity and provenance of these titles were rarely probed.

Likeness men—that was one contemporary term for these rootless photographers, who often wandered from town to town in horse-drawn wagons fitted out as mobile studios. It was a perfect name for Atkyn, who seemed to consist of nothing but an endless series of inconstant appearances, likeness upon likeness upon likeness. In truth, the real reason for his most recent return to Beaver Island may have been to act as a spy. The state's Republican governor, Kinsley S. Bingham, was believed to have planted a secret agent on the island. Although this individual's identity has never surfaced, the ephemeral Dr. Atkyn, with his frequent disappearances and reappearances, seems a likely candidate.

But whatever Atkyn's intentions, when he returned once more in late 1855 to establish a studio, his fortunes had again shifted, and for the worse. He arrived penniless, insisting he had been mugged and robbed on a train near Niagara Falls after being knocked out with chloroform by his assailant. As proof of this misfortune, the doctor produced a newspaper article about the attack, though—conveniently—no victim was named. According to a later report in the *Northern Islander,* Atkyn then claimed that a Philadelphia institution would be providing the necessary capital for him to open his daguerreotype studio. But when—conveniently once more—the approach of winter made transferring this money impossible, poor Atkyn had no choice but to prevail upon a local merchant for credit. That merchant, a former resident of Nauvoo and Voree named James M. Wait, would soon accuse Atkyn of being an "impostor" who "lives on the publick," allegations that were irrefutably true. Atkyn, meanwhile, would declare that Wait was "engaged in horse stealing and other thefts," charges that circumstantial evidence suggests also may have been true.

Before their relations soured, however, Wait furnished the photographer with a gallery on Water Street next door to the office of the *Northern Islander*—which, in its edition of December 6, 1855, offered an enthusiastic endorsement of the Likeness Man's talents:

> We have examined specimens of Daguerreotypes taken by Bro. A. at the Saint James Daguerrean Gallery, and feel fully justified in stating that they are equal to any in the western States, and inferior to none. Whether the Artist is more skillful, his chemicals more scientifically compounded, his apparatus superior, or his sitters better looking, we know not.

Atkyn would later insist that Strang demanded a bribe of fourteen dollars for this positive mention in print, and an additional payoff of four dollars for each time he praised the gallery from the pulpit.

———

Atkyn's arrival coincided with a fragile moment in the king's reign. Facing increased pressure from outside the kingdom and fearing a loss of control within, the prophet had been acting with more determination than ever to assert his authority and impose his will.

In July of 1855, for example, Strang had issued a decree from the pulpit stipulating that all women on the island were henceforth to wear pantaloons. The prophet seemed to view this strict dress code as a means of bolstering his authority. "In order for Strang to maintain control over his followers," historian Gayle V. Fischer observes in *Pantaloons and Power,* "it became important that he suppress individual impulses."

If that was his intent, however, he made a fatal miscalculation. The edict infuriated a number of women on the island, triggering what some historians call the "dress rebellion." Among the most strident dissenters was Sarah McCulloch, wife of Strang's longtime ally Dr. Hezekiah McCulloch, who remained bitter over having been denied the opportunity to take Strang's seat in the Michigan House. By late 1855, according to a later edition of the *Northern Islander,* "it began to be whispered...that Mr. McCulloch was no longer a believer and was only holding on for a chance to make a 'big pile' off of the Mormons, and be off to distant parts." Instead of leaving, however, he decided to stay and fight, joining a ragtag collection of other dissidents—a group that would soon include Dr. J. Atkyn.

The winter of 1855–56 was extremely cold in the northern Great Lakes. In mid-February the temperature on Beaver Island plunged to 19.5 degrees below zero, and as the frigid weather continued, Lake Michigan froze over for forty miles around. With residents stuck on the island until spring, a chill descended upon the collective psyche, with antagonisms crystallizing until one day they were as solid as the two feet of ice that clutched the harbor.

At first, Dr. Atkyn seemed to be happy on the island. "Early in winter he was constantly boring everybody who came in his way with boasting how strong a Mormon he was, and how much a friend of the Prophet," the *Northern Islander* later reported, adding that Atkyn would show off a "letter which he had written and was about to send to influential papers in the east, praising Mormonism generally, and the Beaver Islanders in particular, as by far the most virtuous and intelligent people on earth." According to the *Islander,* Atkyn liked to brag "of his intimacy with the editors" of various papers, as well as his "influence over them."

Notwithstanding Atkyn's praise for the denizens of the island, his boasts soon got him into trouble with Strang, who became irritated by the visitor's insinuation of a close friendship between the two men and viewed Atkyn "as a pretender to a position to which he had no claim," in the words of the *Northern Islander.* This rebuke apparently took place in a public setting, because Atkyn was soon complaining that his business had been ruined by slander, though it apparently didn't help that he "rarely made a good picture, commonly an indifferent, and frequently a very bad one," as the *Islander* put it. According to a later edition of the paper, he began to drink heavily—until, that is, he ran out of alcohol. "The latter half of the winter he was without liquors of any kind, and exhibited himself daily a nuisance and pitiable object finding no society, and complaining daily of living among barbarians, without politeness or brandy." If indeed Atkyn was a spy for the governor, he had apparently become a pretty wretched one. Solace arrived in the form of his fellow outcast, Dr. McCulloch, around whom a group of dissidents had begun to coalesce.

———

Strang spent the winter preparing an expanded edition of the *Book of the Law of the Lord,* the code of conduct that had come from the Ark of the Covenant, as the prophet told his followers. "Polygamy elevates man," this new edition declared, calling plural marriage a spiritual requirement for "all who attain to the life everlasting." This full embrace of the practice followed Strang's decision, at the age of forty-two, to take two more plural wives—seventeen-year-old Sarah Wright, in July of 1855, followed by her nineteen-year-old cousin, Phoebe Wright, in October. He married the teens over the objection of their parents, a fact that suggests he was now operating with an unprecedented sense of impunity. Nonetheless, Sarah would later remember her much older husband as a "very mild-spoken kind man to his family."

Each of Strang's four plural wives, Sarah Wright explained, occupied a separate bedroom, although "all met in prayer—ate at the same table. We had no quarrels, no jealousies that I knew of." Given the close quarters and the inevitable differences in personality, taste, and opinion, the women "made things as pleasant as possible" for one another. Sarah and Phoebe, for example, regularly cared for Elvira's three children, the youngest of whom was only a year old, and for Betsy's two children, including infant Gabriel, born that year. As for the prophet's lawful wife, Mary Strang, "she never came to Beaver Island and I did not know much about her." Her name, Sarah said, "was seldom mentioned."

But if Strang discouraged his followers from talking about Mary, she was nonetheless ever present in their collective consciousness, as unsettling to them as a shriek in the night. Remembering how her marriage had been destroyed by polygamy, many women feared the same thing would happen to theirs, especially now that the practice was officially enshrined in the *Book of the Law*. "I felt worried and I could see that other women were the same, though we dared not talk much together about the King's affairs," one unnamed island resident later explained. Some men supported the new edict, it seems, but the majority remained firm in their opposition to polygamy, even if they were scared to say so publicly. Over time, more and more families began "leading a double life, seemingly good Mormons, but only waiting for the opportunity to get away," the woman recalled, adding that "Strang was losing much control of his people."

Even Elvira later conceded that the practice was never "looked upon favorably" by most islanders, and that "polygamy gradually became more unpopular, and the cause of much dissatisfaction." By the end of 1855, the king had begun to lack "sufficient confidence" among his followers, according to Elvira, who noted an increasingly determined opposition to the practice.

The backlash, as it happened, coincided with a heated anti-polygamy sentiment nationwide. In 1855 and 1856, American publishers cranked out several sensationalistic novels portraying polygamy as a form of white slavery. Modeled on the decade's best-selling book, *Uncle Tom's Cabin*, these narratives described "strong women being forced into polygamy by Mormon patriarchs incapable of distinguishing between their lusts and God's will," according to one modern expert, who observes that the books had "tremendous influence on the nineteenth century's understanding of Mormons and Mormonism."

Perhaps sensing this threat, Strang published a scathing review of one such book in a February 1856 edition of the *Northern Islander*. Since its release the previous year, *Female Life Among the Mormons,* purportedly written by an anonymous "wife of a Mormon elder, recently from Utah," had become a bestseller. "We do not doubt that 100,000 people have read it," the reviewer—apparently Strang himself—wrote, adding, "Whoever [the author] may be, nearly every page of the book bears the most conclusive evidence that she never lived among the Mormons, and is remarkably ignorant, both of their faith, and their history." The book, in the view of the *Islander,* had "utterly outraged truth and sense."

That same issue of the paper contained a sarcastic attack on the new fashion of hoop skirts, garments so wide that women who wore them had trouble passing through doors. The author—once again Strang, it appeared—mockingly challenged the women of the island "who have itching eyes for Gentile customs" to "make speed" in embracing these fashionable skirts, lest they fall behind the times. The message was clear: Mormon women must henceforth eschew all styles worn by outsiders and submit to the king's edicts about clothing. "What a tyrant fashion is," the piece concluded. "How inexorable."

But a growing number of Beaver Islanders were coming to believe that the real tyrant was Strang. By late winter of 1856, a beleaguered prophet had come to see pantaloons as the ultimate symbol of loyalty. Women who refused to wear them—and men who refused to demand that their wives and daughters wear them—were, in the king's mind, an existential threat to his reign. "After it became apparent that some of the women were not disposed to yield," wrote one nineteenth-century chronicler, "Strang declared in public that the law should be obeyed, if he had to wade ankle deep in blood."

At some point amid these rising animosities, Strang visited the Saint James Daguerrean Gallery to have his picture taken—a picture clearly intended as a display of power. By the mid-1850s, one of the most familiar styles of daguerreotypes was the "public portrait" of prominent individuals—politicians, leaders of industry, lawyers, preachers. "The public portrait was understood to work its effects through a magnetic or hypnotic attraction," scholar Alan Trachtenberg observed in *Reading American Photographs*. "Its goal was to stimulate a desire to identify with the qualities represented by the sitter." In a pose typical of such images, Strang appeared in three-quarter view, formally dressed and focusing his stare not directly at the lens but somewhere slightly beyond it. Some public portraits of clergymen of the time show them cradling holy books, but the volume under Strang's arm looks too small to be the Bible or the Book of Mormon. Its dimensions indicate that a more likely possibility is the *Book of the Law of the Lord,* which declared that God had placed the prophet "above the kings of the earth."

But if Strang hoped the daguerreotype would solidify his standing as a giver of laws, just the opposite ended up happening. In retrospect, this portrait marks the point in his reign at which the king lost his uncanny ability to instill confidence. A popular belief still lingered into the 1850s, after all, that the photographic act caused a kind of disembodiment in which one's corporeal being was stripped away from one's spirit. No less an intellectual giant than the novelist Honoré de Balzac once posited that by being photographed, a human body suffered "the loss of one of its ghosts, that is to say, the very essence of which it was composed." Seen in these terms, the mysterious man behind the camera on Beaver Island that day was assuming yet another guise: soul thief.

Even so, as the ice surrounding the island began to melt in the early spring of 1856, Dr. Atkyn appeared to achieve some sort of warming of relations with the prophet. The *Northern Islander* published a story attributing the period of Atkyn's poor-quality photographs to technical problems caused by the frigid climate of recent months. "During the extreme cold of the past winter our neighbour has sometimes failed of a satisfactory picture," the paper conceded, "but the warm weather has returned, and he can show some as perfect pictures as you will see at any city in the State of Michigan."

Perhaps Strang was trying to placate the unpredictable Atkyn—or perhaps the article was simply the result of another fourteen-dollar bribe. In either case, any rapprochement between the two men was short-lived, with Strang almost immediately accusing the daguerreotypist of bamboozling his customers by "charging from four to six times as high as is customary for good work in the best galleries." When they refused to pay, according to the *Northern Islander*, Atkyn threatened to make up his financial losses "by injuring the Mormons." To back up this threat, he produced some "lampooning handbills" of the sort that he had previously used to smear the reputations of "several respectable citizens" of Council Bluffs, Iowa. The Likeness Man then announced, as reported by the paper, that he had given these humiliating handbills "a wide circulation through the mails, boasting that he could find [his victims] anywhere, but they never could retaliate on him because as he assumed a new name once in a few days, and was ever on the move, no one knew where to hit him."

This was blackmail, of course—but by the spring of 1856 it wasn't Strang's biggest worry. Events were moving fast. A plot was now under way to murder the king.

Twenty-Four

In which various people whip their neighbors, bludgeon their colleagues, hack their enemies to death, and bring the United States to the verge of civil war while James Strang insists there's absolutely nothing to worry about

---

Do you see death, and the approach of death?
— Walt Whitman, *Leaves of Grass*, 1856

IN MAY OF 1856, A BRITISH CIVIL ENGINEER NAMED ADAM Dunin Jundzill applied for a patent on a contraption called the kinimoscope, a word he translated as *to see in motion*. Jundzill would never actually build the device—one of the antebellum era's many proto-cinematic contraptions that attempted to create the illusion of moving pictures through a rapid succession of individual fixed images. But in some ways, that spring of 1856—from April through mid-June—would become its own kind of kinimoscope, with events streaming by so fast on Beaver Island and elsewhere in the country that they blurred one after the other into their own dizzying phantasmagoria.

April 1, 1856: Then came a knock on the door. When Thomas Bedford, small and dark-complexioned, peered out into the mild spring night, a man was waiting in the shadows with an urgent message: Brother Strang wished to see Bedford down at the printing office. Despite the lateness of the hour, Bedford, who had grown more at odds with the prophet in recent months, was not surprised by the summons. In truth, he'd only ever been a halfhearted disciple. A fisherman and small-time farmer by trade, the English-born Bedford had resided on Beaver Island since before Strang and his followers arrived. He had converted to Mormonism for the sake of convenience and perhaps for love, marrying one of the flock, a woman twenty years his junior.

Bedford had always refused to embrace basic tenets of the faith—disregarding, for instance, the church's ban on tobacco. But two even graver sins in the eyes of Strang had now placed Bedford on a collision course with the king. The first of those sins was Bedford's open opposition to the dress code for women. Ruth Ann Bedford and her husband had been among the rule's fiercest resisters, despite attempts at intimidation that allegedly included the theft of their personal property. Thomas Bedford blamed Strang's supporters for stealing a pair of his horses, along with ninety fishing nets and two fishing boats, complete with rigging. Yet even this hadn't silenced him. As one nineteenth-century observer put it: "The losses and annoyances to which Bedford was subjected, instead of subduing him, roused his indignation, and he became more outspoken regarding the acts of the Mormons than before."

That candor was Bedford's second grievous sin—the one that had prompted the knock on his door just now. For nearly two months, Lake Michigan had been frozen solid between the mainland and Beaver Island, allowing no ships to come or go. The only way to reach the island had been to cross the ice by sled, meaning there had been little contact with the outside world. But on that day—the first of April—the thermometer had shot up to 48 degrees, the warmest day on the island since mid-November. Along with that pleasant weather arrived a stranger from Garden Island—home of the Ojibwe and Odawa Indians, just north of the colony—who had come to find out if anyone knew anything about a stolen boat. At the general store he ran into Bedford. The boat's owner, the man said, was offering a reward of fifty dollars for its return. Could Bedford help? Yes, Bedford said, he would be only too glad to go to Mackinac and provide information on the boat's whereabouts. Unfortunately for Bedford, someone loyal to Strang overheard the conversation and reported it to the king.

When Bedford walked inside the publishing office that night, the prophet was nowhere to be seen. Instead, Bedford encountered a group of grim-faced men, one of them holding a rawhide horsewhip, the others carrying large hickory rods. "You've been betraying us, telling about stolen property, and we're here to make it right," one man announced. "We have been ordered to shut you up by giving you forty stripes save one."

The men tied Bedford up and began to walk him toward the woods. The punishment they were about to administer was as ancient as it was excruciating. In Jewish law, the maximum number of lashes imposed as a penalty was forty, but since it was believed that this many might kill a man, "forty stripes save one" was often the punishment for crimes that did not carry a death sentence. With his usual flair for merging earthly grievances with scriptural dictates, Strang had adopted this Talmudic punishment in his efforts to impose order on an increasingly rebellious Beaver Island.

The group had walked only about fifty yards when Bedford decided that he wanted to get it over with. "There's plenty of room for this job right here," he said, "so whip away."

With that, the men of Beaver set to the task of thrashing their neighbor, and the crack of the whip followed by the sound of his screams drifted into the warm spring night.

———

May 22, 1856: The man looked up from his seat in the United States Senate to find his assailant standing over him with a gold-handled cane raised high above his head. Before he could react, the cane crashed down onto his skull. He tried to protect himself, but the other man kept bludgeoning him, over and over and over. The attacker would later boast that he "gave him about thirty first rate stripes. Toward the last he bellowed like a calf."

The victim was Charles Sumner, a U.S. senator from Massachusetts and fierce abolitionist. Earlier in the week, he had delivered a two-day speech on the combustible topic of whether Kansas should be admitted to the Union as a free state or a slave state. His tone was apocalyptic. Sumner began by announcing that the decision Congress now faced—whether to ratify a pro-slavery constitution that a bogus territorial government had sent to Congress—was no ordinary legislative matter. At stake was nothing less than "the peace of the whole country, with our good name in history forevermore."

The lawmaker then launched an acerbic personal attack on the supporters of slavery—especially South Carolina senator Andrew P. Butler, whom he accused of taking on "a mistress...who, though ugly to others, is always lovely to him,—though polluted in the sight of the world, is chaste in his sight: I mean," added Sumner, "the harlot Slavery."

The man who was now slamming that cane into Sumner's skull—slamming it so hard that the staff shattered and the gold handle rattled to the floor—was U.S. representative Preston Brooks of South Carolina, a kinsman of Butler's. He had come with two other southern members of the U.S. House to avenge what he saw as Sumner's libels against his state, his region, and his family. In different circumstances, he might have challenged Sumner to a duel. But the southern code of honor—handed down from generation to generation and codified in published pamphlets—made clear that duels could be fought only between two gentlemen. "Vulgar abolitionists" such as Sumner must be treated like dogs—beaten with a whip or, when the situation called for it, a cane.

Before slumping into unconsciousness, the blood-covered victim murmured, "I could not believe that such a thing was possible." But in the spring of 1856, nothing—not even nightmares made real—was off-limits. "The feeling here is wild and fierce," declared South Carolina congressman Laurence Keitt, who had entered the Senate chamber with Brooks and brandished his own cane to prevent bystanders from coming to Sumner's assistance. In the aftermath of the attack, which left the senator clinging to his life, Keitt proclaimed, "The times are stirring. Everybody here feels as if we are upon a volcano."

———

May 22, 1856: On Beaver Island, too, it seemed as if some big explosion was imminent—an anxiety that the editor, publisher, and chief correspondent of the *Northern Islander*, who also happened to be King of Earth and Heaven, hoped to allay. On the same day that Brooks had burst into the Senate chamber to pummel Sumner, Strang published a report that the "two doctors," McCulloch and Atkyn, had recently left the island. While acknowledging rumors that the pair were on "an errand of mischief," he reassured his readers that, given their penchant for drinking, they were "likely to do more mischief to themselves than anybody else."

Despite the dismissive tone of the report, Strang must have been deeply concerned about the pair's departure. Indeed, the prophet often saved his most caustic epithets—*drunk, crook, whore, liar, inbred, idiot,* and so on—for the people he feared the most. It's telling, for instance, that the *Northern Islander* had been giving frequent and sometimes extensive coverage to the comings and goings of that "universal dead-head and common sponge," J. Atkyn. If he really was "unworthy of notice," as one of those articles claimed, why the obsession with him? It might have been true that Atkyn drank too much, but it's also true that he was a shrewd and dangerous man—and that Strang was vividly aware of this fact.

The other doctor posed even more of a threat. In recent weeks,

Hezekiah McCulloch had been locked in a bitter feud with the king, during which "the spirit of murder entered his heart," in the words of a fellow member of the colony. In fact, as if to suggest further incompetence, or division between the two conspirators, the *Islander* would subsequently claim that Atkyn had tried to get back in Strang's good graces by betraying an alleged plot of McCulloch's against the prophet—a charge that the paper said the doctor, perhaps anticipating a reprisal from the prophet and financial repercussions for his general store, had denied "with indignation."

For McCulloch, the breaking point had come in early April, when Strang stripped the physician of his positions on church councils, as well as his political offices: county clerk and register of deeds. "From that day," Strang later wrote in the *Islander,* "he has been known only as an enemy, seeking our injury." McCulloch had gone so far as refusing to hand over government records and other official documents from his former offices. He had also, according to the *Islander,* "falsified publick documents, for the purpose of involving other men in malfeasance in office." And now, furious with his fall from grace, McCulloch had left—for Chicago, by all accounts—threatening to reveal Strang's secrets and, in no uncertain terms, vowing revenge. "Now it is you and I for it; you will destroy me or I shall destroy you," he was reported to have said.

McCulloch, Atkyn, and Thomas Bedford were among the leaders of what had grown into a full-scale conspiracy "to overthrow the Kingdom as it existed on Beaver Island," as a loyal supporter of the prophet named Warren Post would later put it. The plotters, Post wrote, were "determined to take the life of the King." Strang, it seems, was all too cognizant of this threat, which had left him—publicly, at least—in a defiant and righteous mood. According to Mormon theology, the Second Coming will be preceded by a time of wickedness, war, and turmoil. In one of Joseph Smith's revelations, God told his flock, "Be not troubled, for, when all these things shall come

to pass, ye may know that the promises which have been made unto
you shall be fulfilled." Aware that his life and kingdom had never
been more in peril, Strang adopted a similar tone:

> We laugh in bitter scorn at all these threats.... We will neither
> purchase temporary peace and future calamities by dishonor-
> able trafficking with political jugglers, nor will we yield our
> homes to enemies. If we live, here will we live. If we die, here
> will we die, and here shall our bones be buried, expecting in the
> resurrection of the just to possess the land forever, and dwell
> with the righteous during the lifetime of the Eternal.

The same issue of the *Islander* that announced the departure of
Atkyn and McCulloch also described a reception, featuring "the
musick of stringed instruments," held for new converts who had just
arrived in the kingdom. "It was a most happy gathering of cheerful
and believing spirits, congratulating one another on past blessings
and future hopes," the paper reported. The dancing went on into
the night, as the giddy wail of fiddles floated through the streets of
town and then out over the lake, with the "joyousness of the scene
extended to all."

In Chicago, meanwhile, McCulloch was reported to show off a
bullet—the very one, he boasted, that would soon be used to rid the
world of the prophet James Jesse Strang.

———

May 24, 1856: Then came a knock on the door. James Doyle and his
family weren't used to late-night visitors at their shabby cabin along
Pottawatomie Creek in northeastern Kansas. When he climbed out
of bed to see who was there, a group of men burst in, brandishing
pistols and knives. Their leader, a tall man wearing a straw hat and a
black cravat, announced that they were from the "Northern army"
and that they had come to take Doyle and his sons as prisoners.

In recent weeks, long-simmering acrimonies between pro-slavery and anti-slavery factions in Kansas had reached the boiling point. Just three days earlier, a mob of about 1,000 men had ransacked the abolitionist bastion of Lawrence. Many of the attackers were vigilantes from the South who carried banners reading THE SUPREMACY OF THE WHITE RACE; others were Border Ruffians, as pro-slavery raiders from nearby Missouri were known. In Lawrence they destroyed two printing presses, looted buildings, and shot cannons at an establishment called the Free State Hotel before burning it to the ground, along with the house of a leading abolitionist.

The men at James Doyle's cabin had come to avenge that attack. Although Doyle was too poor to own slaves himself, he was a Tennessean, well known in his adopted home as a strong supporter of the Southern cause—a fact not lost on the men who led him and three of his sons out into the bright moonlight. When Doyle's wife begged for them to leave behind their youngest captive, a boy just sixteen years old, they relented to her tearful pleas, then marched the remaining three prisoners away. "My husband and my two boys, my sons, did not come back," the woman later recounted.

The next morning, the sixteen-year-old found his father and brothers dead in the road a couple of hundred yards from their cabin. They had been hacked to death by broadswords, one of them so brutally that his fingers and arms were cut off. Residents soon discovered two other corpses nearby—both of them pro-slavery settlers, both of them sliced apart. The Doyles could not identify the men who killed their family members, but they did get a good look at their faces in the candlelight. "An old man commanded the party," the surviving son recalled. "His face was slim."

The old man with the skeletal face was of course none other than John Brown, who, in the course of a few short years, had transformed himself from a utopian prophet into an abolitionist avenger. He now saw himself as God's instrument—a new Moses, sent to free the slaves from Pharaoh's legions and issue a new and higher law. In this apocalyptic vision, bloodshed against his opponents was not an act of killing but of cleansing, the beginning of a divine judgment that paved the way for a new age.

A day after the murders, one of Brown's sons confronted his father. Although four of the young man's brothers had taken part, he had only just heard about the raid. "Did you have anything to do with the killing of those men on the Pottawatomie?" he asked.

"I did not do it, but I approved of it," Brown answered.

"I think it an uncalled for, wicked act."

"God is my judge," Brown replied. "We were justified under the circumstances."

———

Late May 1856: When Dr. Hezekiah McCulloch returned to Beaver Island, he brought with him several pistols. Since his departure a couple of weeks earlier, McCulloch had been a busy man. After stopping in Chicago, he and Atkyn had gone on to Lansing, the Michigan capital. There, they seem to have successfully lobbied to get state education funding to Beaver Island lowered, based on evidence they presented that Strang had fraudulently overestimated the number of local schoolchildren. The two men may also have met with state officials to discuss—and perhaps to receive logistical support for—their plans to topple the king.

Afterward, McCulloch and Atkyn apparently parted company. The itinerant photographer was last seen heading south, for Ohio, where he would soon fade from history. Back on Beaver Island, the conspirators commenced taking target practice in the woods.

———

June 2, 1856: In the dense fog, Thomas Bedford waited for his chance to assassinate Strang. The U.S.S. *Michigan* had just docked in the St. James harbor. Five years earlier, this same ship had caused a panic when it swept Strang away to face federal charges in Detroit. Since then, however, island residents had grown accustomed to the vessel making regular visits during patrols of the Great Lakes. Bedford knew that Strang would soon make his way down to the ship to pay a courtesy call on the captain. Having positioned himself along the route, Strang's would-be killer readied for the long-anticipated moment when he would squeeze off a shot on his double-barreled shotgun.

Bedford and another conspirator, named Alexander Wentworth had emerged as the group's de facto assassins. Wentworth, a handsome man in his early twenties, had once been devoted enough to take a bullet for the monarch, suffering a flesh wound alongside the Pierce brothers in the 1853 shootout with Strang's enemies at Pine River. But since then Wentworth had become an outspoken critic of polygamy, prompting a sneering rebuke from the prophet. At a public meeting, Strang dismissed Wentworth as an inbred "whose father was his grandfather and whose mother was his sister." This insult, according to one witness, was "the wasp that stung Wentworth," turning him forever against the king.

For several nights running, Bedford and Wentworth had watched for a chance to kill Strang, but thus far the perfect opportunity had not presented itself. Today the time was still not right. When Strang emerged from the fog on his way to the dock, he was arm in arm between two friends, making it impossible for Bedford to get off a clean shot.

———

June 5, 1856: "Don't believe a word of it," the *Northern Islander* said of a rumor that McCulloch was plotting to have Strang murdered. "They who fear the assassination of the Prophet," the paper added, "may as well reserve their tears for awhile."

———

June 7, 1856: *The Leader,* a newspaper in London, published a story about an American who "has been received by a section of his countrymen as a sort of prophet," though the article, it turns out, was about not a preacher but a poet. Although Walt Whitman had sold only a few copies of *Leaves of Grass* and was largely unknown outside the borough of Brooklyn, he was nonetheless "one of the most amazing, one of the most startling, one of the most perplexing, creations of the modern American mind," according to *The Leader,* which couldn't decide whether to call him a "latter-day poet" or a "latter-day prophet."

The author of the unsigned review—a would-be novelist named Mary Ann Evans, soon to become famous under the pen name George Eliot—was not trying to suggest that Whitman was a Mormon. Her point, an extraordinarily prescient one, was that he came from the same strain of improvisational, self-inventing Americans as Joseph Smith and James Jesse Strang. If, as George Eliot wrote, *Leaves of Grass* was a "strange, grotesque and bewildering book," much of which "seems to us purely fantastical and preposterous," then it shared much in common with the Book of Mormon and the *Book of the Law of the Lord.* Whitman himself, in fact, called *Leaves of Grass* the "Bible of the New Religion."

Like the Latter-day Saints, Whitman wanted to witness the coming of a "grand new epoch," as Eliot put it. But there was a crucial difference: the poet's version of utopia had no place for people like Strang. "A new order shall arise and they shall be the priests of man, and every man shall be his own priest," Whitman wrote in the preface to the first edition. It was an idea he would one day expand upon:

> The people, especially the young men and women of America, must begin to learn that Religion, (like Poetry,) is something far, far different from what they supposed. It is, indeed, too important to the power and perpetuity of the New World to be consigned any longer to the churches, old or new, Catholic or Protestant—Saint this, or Saint that.

Those who claimed to speak for God, those who presumed to know the only truth, those who demanded the obedience of others—Whitman thought their days were numbered. "There will soon be no more priests," he wrote. "Their work is done."

———

June 11, 1856: The *Buffalo Express* reported that 204 residents of northern Michigan had signed a petition to Governor Bingham, "praying some relief from the nefarious conduct of their troublesome neighbors" on Beaver Island. "Judging from the statements of the aggrieved inhabitants, the Mormons must be about the most pestiferous, shiftless, thievish, disreputable creatures ever known," the paper concluded, citing allegations of frequent robberies along Lake Michigan. "Strang, their prophet and king, is a shrewd fellow... but the fact probably is that he and his followers are simply a set of land pirates, fitly entitled to state-prison, and, some of them to the gallows."

———

June 16, 1856: Exactly two weeks after its previous visit, at 12:50 p.m., the U.S.S. *Michigan* docked at St. James once more. Given how recently the ship had been at the island, this stop was unexpected. Even as Strang spotted the vessel's smokestack out his window, gossip, speculation, and anxiety were spreading through the tense community.

"They are not coming back for any good purpose," the prophet said.

Strang had often claimed he could peer into the future. Perhaps, then, he knew immediately that this would be the day his luck ran out. Or perhaps, after narrowly avoiding so many disasters, he had come to see himself as invulnerable. As a former member of the church had put it earlier that year, "The notion exists on the island that God will take care of the prophet, no matter what."

For hours the King of Earth and Heaven waited. Then came a knock on the door.

Twenty-Five

In which the king makes his final procession

Our enemies are silent.... Vain are the men who think to defy the Omnipotent.

—*Northern Islander,* June 5, 1856

THE SWASHBUCKLING LIFE STORY OF CHARLES H. MCBLAIR, commander of the U.S.S. *Michigan,* seems straight out of some South Sea adventure tale by Herman Melville. After leaving his home in Baltimore at age fourteen to join the U.S. Navy as a midshipman, McBlair had sailed uncharted areas of the Pacific on the first American man-of-war to visit Hawaii. He later served in the West Indies, as well as in Brazil and off the Barbary Coast of Africa, where his vessel was nearly lost in a storm. Court-martialed for refusing to shake the hand of a commanding officer against whom he reportedly had a "private pique," he was honorably acquitted and rose through the ranks, while also becoming "probably the best French scholar in the navy," as one newspaper put it. A man of "exquisite" literary tastes, the commander was also, according to a fellow officer, "a good writer of both prose and poetry." Despite his lack of formal education, the forty-six-year-old McBlair was, in short, a person of considerable learning and intellectual acuity— much like the man he had come to Beaver Island to confront. And he shared one other important characteristic with Strang: a willingness to use subterfuge to achieve his ends.

When the *Michigan* docked at the St. James harbor, McBlair sent an emissary to Strang, requesting that the prophet come to see him "on business." Now, awaiting his guest, the commander found himself with time to contemplate his surroundings. Having visited countless islands, some of them barely mapped, he was well aware of the strange grip they had on the human imagination, the dangerous allure that such isolated spots held for dreamers and madmen who'd been aroused by the eternal lust to invent new worlds.

As a teenage sailor in 1825, for example, McBlair had been assigned to the U.S.S. *Dolphin*, a schooner sent to some of the world's remotest islands to hunt down the perpetrators of a gruesome mutiny aboard the whaleship *Globe*. As part of that errand, the *Dolphin* rescued two innocent members of the crew, who had been marooned for two years on a tiny atoll more than 2,000 miles southwest of Hawaii. The horrific and grisly stories told by those men and other survivors—accounts of the sleeping captain's skull being nearly severed in two by a hatchet blow, of his corpse being ritually mutilated, and of a long blade being pounded into his bowels until it protruded from his throat—must have stuck in the seaman's memory. No doubt McBlair also remembered the chief mutineer's motivation for committing such atrocities: an "almost uncontrollable urge to break loose, invade an island and establish his own kingdom," in the words of one later account. And perhaps, as he bided his time, McBlair recalled the fate of that head mutineer—gunned down on a lonely beach by his own followers.

———

The prophet's compound had by now grown to consist of a main building connected by a covered walkway to two log houses. In addition to the king, this expanded residence was home to five children aged five and under, as well as to four wives, each of whom was currently pregnant with another of Strang's offspring. When the emissary from the *Michigan*—a civilian pilot by the name of

Alexander St. Bernard—arrived at the door late in the afternoon of June 16, 1856, all four women were at home with the prophet, who received the visitor cordially. The two men were already well acquainted, and St. Bernard considered Strang a "sociable sort of man," as he would later put it.

When the boat pilot told Strang of McBlair's summons, the prophet grabbed his hat, bid his wives farewell, and departed with St. Bernard. While another witness remembered the prophet as "somewhat cast down in mind" that day, St. Bernard found him in excellent spirits. The two joined arms, a common gesture of cordiality among men of the era, and as Strang told stories and jokes, they emerged from the thick grove of trees that surrounded Strang's house and made their way along the bay toward the harbor. There, hidden from view, the assailants Thomas Bedford and Alexander Wentworth lay in ambush.

McBlair would later insist that he had sent for the prophet "with the hope of being able to advise him to abandon his schemes." His sole motivation for calling Strang to the ship, he testified, was to use "all the moral influence of my official position" to dissuade him from continued persecution of enemies on the island and plunder of non-Mormons across the region. That high-minded rhetoric, however, belied the fact that McBlair had been in secret communications with the conspirators for the better part of two weeks. Those contacts seem to have begun in early June, when the battleship stopped at the island as part of a routine patrol. While in St. James, the commander met with several dissident members of the Mormon community, apparently including McCulloch, who by then had returned to the island with guns for his co-conspirators. After this meeting McBlair departed, only to inform the secretary of the U.S. Navy of his concern about "some circumstances arising from the secession of members of the community from mormonism and the malpractice of James Strang the leader and prophet."

On June 5, the *Michigan* arrived in Chicago, where Commander McBlair dispatched an intelligence briefing about the situation on Beaver Island to Governor Bingham. "I have every reason to believe," the officer wrote, "that the greater part of the community has been for a long time engaged in a system of plunder upon the property of fishermen and others who may arrive at the island, and such as may be within reach of boat expeditions to the Michigan and Wisconsin shores." During his stay in Chicago, the commander also met with a pair of the conspirators from Beaver Island, including Hezekiah McCulloch's business partner, a man named Franklin Johnson. Afterward, Johnson headed back to the colony—presumably with messages from McBlair to those involved in the plot—while the commander informed the Navy secretary of his own plans for a return to the island later in the month to render "assistance to those citizens threatened by the hostility of Strang."

But what did McBlair imagine that assistance would involve? His close communication with the conspirators suggests that the officer had prior knowledge of the murder conspiracy, and that he played at least a tacit role in that plot. Even now, as Bedford and Wentworth waited at the foot of the pier with their pistols, they did so among a few dozen other men, some of whom were "marines from the vessel," as Bedford would later recall. If those troops were there to keep the peace, why didn't they report the armed men to their commander? And why didn't McBlair immediately rush ashore to warn the prophet before it was too late?

———

Once, when he was twenty-two years old, Strang fell into a flooded stream. "The water ran furious," he wrote that day in his diary, describing the terror of being dragged along helplessly for more than 150 yards, "carried most of the way underwater." Finally, "by the most desperate exertions," he managed to haul himself out. For a few brief moments, the future King of Earth and Heaven had thought he was going to die. "What a multitude of thoughts were crowded together," he wrote of those terrifying seconds when he pictured "the obsequies of my end," a vision that included "friends sobbing around; my poor heartbroken mother sinking by my pale remains; those who in life had injured me deep as hatred could conceive or malice could invent standing in clusters round talking perhaps that the hand of God had done it, and then offering their consoling (ah! vile) assistance."

In the two decades since that moment, Strang had never lost his tragic gift for making mortal enemies. But the prospect that he might "die unavenged" had not been his only fear as he faced the prospect of drowning. Perhaps even more horrifying to him was the thought "that this was to be the last end of all my hopes and prospects and aspirations."

Ever since escaping that deadly current, Strang had devoted his life to accomplishing those aspirations. Now, on the quarter-mile walk between his house and the waiting ship, he could take pride in the astonishing extent of his success. Hadn't the country boy with "dreams of royalty and power" largely achieved those audacious goals? Hadn't the young fantasizer who vowed to become "a Priest, a Lawyer, a Conqueror and a Legislator" taken on every one of those personae? Wasn't there evidence of his accomplishments everywhere he looked now, strolling through a world he had invented—the tabernacle, the newspaper office, the bustling town, the busy harbor?

At length he reached the dock where the *Michigan* was moored, a narrow passageway lined on both sides with high piles of cordwood, which visiting steamboats purchased for fuel. Wasn't even this mundane thing, the timber, testimony to the prophet's foresight? Hadn't he realized from the start how crucial that commodity would be to the island's economy? Hadn't he included special provisions in the *Book of the Law of the Lord* requiring that "every man who receiveth an inheritance shall preserve a forest thereon," and that "if there be no forest he shall plant one"? Hadn't he assured readers of the *Northern Islander* just days earlier that timber would be a great source of revenue for residents of the kingdom for many years to come?

Perhaps lost in thought as he entered that shadowy tunnel of stacked wood, the prophet failed to notice that two men were now following him at a distance of fifteen or twenty feet, Bedford armed with a horse pistol and Wentworth carrying a revolver.

"I cannot die," Strang had written after nearly perishing in that stream two decades earlier. "If the thing was possible I should not now be among the living." Although he had made this boast in jest, by now perhaps he had come to believe it. Maybe Strang had somehow convinced himself of one of his bold claims from the pulpit: that no bullet could pierce his body. So many of his pronouncements, after all, had come to pass. Hadn't the teenage farm boy written in his diary, using his special code, that because of the tensions between the North and South, "disunion with all the horrors of anarchy and civil war are staring us in the face"? And wasn't the country now on the verge of just such a calamity? And what about the other prediction he'd made back then? *Amidst all the evils of the disturbances of our national affairs there is one consolation: that is if our government is overthrown, some master spirit may form another. May I be the one.* Was that dream so much crazier than all the others? Might there still be time to make it true—to rule it all, transcend it all, be "the one"?

"Brother Strang, they are going to shoot you!" yelled a boy near the ship.

The two men fired together. Wentworth's bullet struck the prophet in the small of his back, while Bedford's ripped through his silk hat and into his skull. As Strang staggered to the ground, Wentworth bolted for the *Michigan,* but his accomplice—who couldn't fire his horse pistol again without reloading—ordered him back to finish the job. This time Wentworth opened up from point-blank range, shooting Strang in the side of the face before rushing into the ship, screaming, "That damned rascal is out of the way!"

"Who?" asked a man who'd just heard the shots.

"Strang, that damned son of a bitch."

Bedford, meanwhile, remained behind, beating the wounded man's head with the butt end of his horse pistol, after which he, too, fled to the *Michigan.* He would later claim that Commander McBlair had witnessed the entire incident but made no attempt to stop it. Alexander St. Bernard, who had accompanied Strang to the dock, was "covered with blood from head to foot." Before long, the waterfront was swarming with people, he later recalled. "Women were crying, some of the men were yelling, others swearing." Prostrate on the warship's gangplank, the King of Earth and Heaven struggled for life, his dreams oozing out of him faster than the blood from his wounds.

Twenty-Six

In which our story ends where it began — with a disappearance

Hail, King! to-morrow thou shalt pass away.
Farewell! there is an isle of rest for thee.
And I am blown along a wandering wind
— Alfred, Lord Tennyson, "The Death of Arthur,"
from *Idylls of the King*, 1856–59

ON JUNE 17, 1856 — THE DAY AFTER STRANG WAS SHOT ON Beaver Island — the first-ever national convention of the Republican Party convened in Philadelphia, where rising star Abraham Lincoln finished second in the voting for vice-presidential nominee and delegates adopted a platform condemning "those twin relics of barbarism, Polygamy and Slavery." That same day, the *New York Daily Herald* described a victory by John Brown's abolitionist guerrillas over a pro-slavery militia in Kansas, a skirmish that one modern scholar has called the "first real battle" of the Civil War. Meanwhile, in Nashville, the *Union and American* newspaper ran a blistering attack on P. T. Barnum, who — in one of the antebellum era's many astonishing swings of fortune — had abruptly gone bankrupt. "While we do not rejoice in the misfortunes of any man, we look upon Barnum's failure as a just retribution for a long course of swindling and imposture," wrote the editors, who hoped the showman's fall would help dispel the myth "that in this country ingenious humbuggery and swindling are the certain avenues to fame and fortune."

And in Cincinnati that day, a man identifying himself as J. Atkyn strolled into the office of the *Daily Gazette* to offer information about the "lawless proceedings of the Mormons of Beaver Island." Accusing the kingdom's residents of horse theft and other crimes, the informant reported that Strang had personally led a jailbreak in Perrysburg, Ohio, in 1853. "I know the whole history of the people," he concluded, "but am dissuaded from attempting to write it, knowing the inadequacy of the English language to portray the infamy of the proceedings." With those last words, J. Atkyn slipped out the door, sauntered into the crowd on the corner of Fourth and Vine, and disappeared forever.

Strang himself, meanwhile, was stubbornly refusing to disappear. Transported to a nearby house right after the shooting, he had somehow survived into the morning hours of June 17. The night had been a chaotic one. As their king lay bleeding, a "howling mob" of steadfast supporters had gathered at the dock, demanding that McBlair turn over the assassins. The commander refused, instead sending ashore marines to protect the families of the shooters and others who might be in danger. "It would have been the last act of inhumanity to have surrendered the prisoners into the hands of the authorities at such time," McBlair later explained. "I would have been giving them up to the rage and fury of a rabble of religious fanatics whose revenge would not have stopped short of their immediate destruction."

Accompanied by fellow officers, McBlair did finally come ashore to check on the wounded man. On that morning's visit, he found the prophet in horrific shape, his body limp, his face bruised and disfigured from the bullet wounds and the pistol-whipping. Yet despite his severe head injuries and paralysis from the waist down, Strang was alert enough to speak with McBlair. Although the commander believed Strang had invited his own fate, he expressed regret that the shooting had happened during the ship's stay in the St. James harbor. Dismissing this show of "feigned" sorrow, in the words of one Mormon eyewitness, the prophet reiterated, in his wasted state, that Wentworth and Bedford must be turned over to island authorities. McBlair would not back down, and the visit ended with a Navy surgeon examining Strang and pronouncing his wounds "mortal," according to the eyewitness.

It was raining heavily during McBlair's walk back to the ship, where he issued an order to prepare for departure. The U.S.S. *Michigan* cast off from the dock about 1:00 p.m., almost exactly twenty-four hours after it had arrived, now carrying seven families from the island, including those of McCulloch, Johnson, and the gunmen. Arriving in Mackinac early that evening, McBlair turned the assassins over to the local sheriff to do with as he saw fit. A gleeful crowd, elated by the murder of the man they saw as the head of a deviant religious sect and dangerous criminal enterprise, awaited the two killers, hailing them with a spontaneous ovation as they stepped off the ship and feting them in jail with cigars, whiskey, and brandy. Someone even brought the prisoners a bed. Fearing that the mob would tear down the jail, the sheriff eventually decided to shelter the prisoners and their families in his own boardinghouse.

The "trial," such as it was, lasted less than an hour, after which the killers were allowed to go free and charged $1.25 in court costs, a fine that Bedford would later boast he never paid. No further charges would be filed against any of the conspirators.

On June 21, five days after the incident, the *New York Daily Herald* reported: "We learn by telegraph that Hon. James J. Strang, commonly called King Strang, the leader and prophet of Mormons located on Beaver Islands, has been shot by two of his followers, and received injuries from which he [is] not likely to recover." As news of the attack spread, readers across the country woke up to headlines such as this:

From the Beaver Islands---A Tragical Occurrence!---Strang, the Mormon Leader, Shot!!

The story traveled not just the country but the globe, with various papers offering contradictory conclusions about the outcome of that shooting. Some reported that Strang had "died of his wounds," while others insisted that he was alive, "with a fair prospect of recovery." Both were overstatements. Strang was in fact still living—but just barely. Unable to eat, he was receiving all his nourishment through a quill, the antebellum era's version of a feeding tube. Even so, many true believers on Beaver Island clung to the conviction that God would miraculously heal their prophet, who would "remain alive on the earth until the coming of Jesus Christ," as one of them put it.

For the short term, however, residents of the kingdom had to concern themselves less with the coming of the Lord than with the coming of a mob. On June 26, ten days after the shooting, a posse that included co-conspirators McCulloch, Wentworth, Bedford, and Johnson burst from a commercial steamboat during its stop on the island. After firing shots, taking Mormon hostages, and threatening to capture the prophet dead or alive, they retreated to the ship, vowing another assault. "The plan," wrote a correspondent for the *Green Bay Advocate,* "now is to return this week if possible, with at least 150 men, properly armed and equipped, and just clear every Mormon from the island—peaceably if possible—but if they won't do that, then at the range of a rifle."

With the threat of greater violence hanging over them, church leaders decided it was necessary to move the ailing prophet off the island at the earliest opportunity. On June 28 he was carried aboard the steamboat *Louisville,* accompanied by two of his wives, Betsy and Phoebe. For Elvira, who planned to remain on Beaver Island for a few more days, the king's last moment in his realm would forever be a bitter memory. Expecting that she would have a few moments for a "regular parting" from the man with whom she had shared so much, a pregnant Elvira glanced up to see Strang already "nearly halfway down to the dock," borne away from her by his entourage. "He never bid us good by," she would later report.

As Elvira stood at that pier, "deserted and forsaken," the ship churned out of the harbor and disappeared from sight. The prophet was on his final journey to Voree, the place where his career as a holy man had started, the place where he had unearthed the Rajah Manchou plates, the place where he had formulated this whole improbable scheme for a utopia on the American frontier. Aboard the ship with him were 1,500 unbound copies of his new edition of the *Book of the Law of the Lord,* the 336-page blueprint for Strang's "everlasting kingdom of God."

Was the angel at his side as that ship carried him home? Did a half-conscious prophet recognize this celestial being as the same one who had visited him near the junction of the Fox and White rivers all those years ago? And if so, what did the two of them—holy man and holy messenger—have to say to each other? Did the angel accuse Strang of being a fraud, or was it the other way around? Picture the two of them on that ship, the light so intense as it streams into the cabin that the dying man looks as ethereal as his winged companion. Listen to the prophet whisper, *I brought you to life. I gave you the power of speech and taught you how to make miracles. I created a whole cosmos in other people's minds. Could an angel do that?*

For years Strang had assured his followers that they were living in the last days, and that they alone were sure to "escape the calamities that await the ungodly." But when the apocalypse finally arrived on Beaver Island, it was nothing like they had pictured it.

On July 3, 1856, a disciple named Wingfield W. Watson was returning from St. James to his home in the countryside when a pair of strangers emerged from the gate of a house, "armed well with whisky," he noticed, "as well as with weapons of war," including bowie knives, pistols, and rifles. The two men demanded to know where he was going. He said he was headed home, six miles down the island.

"Well, God damn ye," one of the men said, "get your things down here to the harbor by one o'clock tomorrow, or your house will be burned over your head."

Watson tried to explain that his wife had just given birth two days earlier and was in no condition to travel.

"That's a God-damn pretty fix you've got into now," the man replied.

After threatening to tie Watson to a cherry tree by the roadside and whip him there and then, the men ordered him to hurry home, where he learned that his wife had already received a visit from other vigilantes. An all-out invasion was under way. As many as seventy men had landed on the west side of the island, expecting a fierce battle. But despite all Strang's chest-thumping over the years about the "bloody welcome" any attackers would receive, the mob was encountering almost no resistance. It was as if the shooting had caused an almost magical transformation on both sides, shattering the islanders' sense of invincibility and emboldening their foes. "The charm that bound the heterogenous mass together is broken," declared the *Detroit Tribune*.

Federal and state authorities had clearly opted not to intervene. After repeatedly failing to bring Strang and his men to account through courts of law, they were now content, it appeared, to let the vigilantes dole out their own brand of frontier justice. And dole it out they did, torching the tabernacle and other buildings, shooting up the prophet's house, and hunting for church leaders, many of whom had already left the island. By now Elvira had also apparently fled, leaving a terrified and pregnant Sarah Wright, just nineteen years old, as the only wife still around when the pillaging ensued. "My friends advised me to keep out of sight," she later recalled. "I was told some rough had said he would like to find Strang's young wife—but I was not found."

Within days, virtually all the Mormons—about 515 people, by Commander McBlair's estimate, though later observers would put the number as high as 2,500—had been herded onto ships at gunpoint, with roughnecks searching them before they left to make sure no one carried away anything of value. On July 8—the sixth anniversary of the King of Earth and Heaven's coronation—a ship from Beaver Island deposited about ninety refugees in Green Bay. One local newspaper described the new arrivals as being "in the most destitute circumstances, having neither money nor provisions, and not even clothes, save the shabby habiliments on their backs." The plight of these exiles, the paper concluded, was "one of the most pitiable cases we have recorded in a long time." In Chicago, where crowds gathered to gawk at another contingent of refugees, authorities reportedly attempted to prevent them from staying, afraid they would become a burden.

At the newspaper office in St. James, meanwhile, the men who had taken control of Beaver Island published a crudely printed proclamation:

The dominion of King Strang is at an end. The band of marauders once occupying the Beaver group of islands, under the administration and direction of Jas. J. Strang, their reputed prophet, have fled at the approach of the sheriff. The land is redeemed; a kingdom no longer exists upon the borders of one of our most populous states...It should be a matter, therefore, of public rejoicing to all persons living contiguous to the lakes that this nest of banditti have been exterminated.

Once their manifesto was off the press, the island's new rulers set about ransacking the printing office, smashing the equipment, and scattering pieces of type like buckshot. By the time they'd finished, "it would have been cheaper to buy a new printing office than to attempt any work of publication at the one left by Strang," boasted Thomas Bedford. As one of Strang's assassins, Bedford knew the prophet well enough to understand that destroying the press was a coup de grâce. From the start, after all, Strang had constructed himself out of words: the coded dreams in his diary, the forged letter of appointment from Joseph Smith, the Rajah Manchou plates, the *Book of the Law,* the newspapers that served as his trumpet to the outside world. His whole career had been a self-invention, a book he crafted with such skill and assurance that many readers failed to realize it was all an elaborate fiction. Maybe he himself had never realized it, either; maybe he came to believe his own words. Whatever the case, the strange book of his life—a truly singular document in American history—was about to slam shut.

In the mythologizing that would begin almost immediately after he was gone, the prophet's time on earth came to a neat and redemptive ending in Voree, the so-called garden of peace. According to this much-repeated version of events, Strang had a "pang of conscience" on his deathbed and begged to see his estranged wife, Mary, who was still living in Voree. She rushed to his side and forgave him for his long list of misdeeds, after which he died tranquilly "in the arms of his first and true wife."

In reality, Mary was not even in Voree. When the final hour came for her husband of twenty years, she was away at her brother's house in Illinois. Also missing was Elvira, who, for reasons that remain unclear, would not arrive until a few days later. Sarah, apparently the last to leave the island, may have already come and gone, paying the prophet a quick visit after fleeing the carnage in Lake Michigan, then hastily departing for another part of Wisconsin to live with her father. Of the prophet's five wives, only Phoebe and Betsy are known to have been in town, along with a number of other close followers and the prophet's mother. It is unclear whether his father was also on hand. By happenstance, only one aide was at his side when death finally began to overtake him on the morning of July 9, a little more than three weeks after he'd been shot.

The man asked Strang if there was "anything he wished to communicate."

"Yes..."

But he never finished the thought. A life built out of words ended with an ellipsis.

"Death of King Strang" read a front-page headline in the *New York Times* a few days later, as papers all over the country rushed to publish details of the prophet's demise. Upon arriving in Voree, however, a grieving Elvira, just twenty-six years old and soon to deliver her fourth child, refused to believe the news. "I just thought he would be raised from the dead," she later recalled. "I had that faith." Struggling with the fear that she might have "nothing to live for any longer," she waited desperately for a miracle. But the weeks came and went, and it slowly began to dawn on her that her husband was gone for good, having left her penniless and then vanishing to parts unknown, a confidence artist to the very end.

Epilogue

In which the ship steams away

⟞⟞⟞⟞⟞◦((◦))◦⟝⟝⟝⟝⟝

Something further may follow this Masquerade.
> —Herman Melville, *The Confidence-Man*

IN THE LATE SPRING AND EARLY SUMMER OF 1856, AS JAMES Strang's story reached its deadly climax, Herman Melville was finishing work on a novel—the last one published during his lifetime. Called *The Confidence-Man: His Masquerade,* it would prove to be the most difficult to classify of all his books, a dark satire about the fevers, delusions, and excesses of antebellum America, a place Melville had recently described as "intrepid, unprincipled, reckless, predatory, with boundless ambition, civilized in externals but a savage at heart."

Published on April Fool's Day of 1857, *The Confidence-Man* is set on a Mississippi riverboat called the *Fidèle*—Faithful—traveling from St. Louis to New Orleans. The title character is a shapeshifting, name-changing swindler, as fluid and murky as the river itself. Assuming various guises, he attempts to worm his way into the pockets of fellow passengers by passing counterfeit currency, unloading stock in failing companies, selling useless herbal medicines, and raising funds for a fraudulent Seminole Widows and Orphans Society. The word *confidence* appears almost 200 times, and as the title character never fails to remind his victims, the way to demonstrate confidence in one's fellow man is to entrust him with one's money.

The book contains pointed references to religious sects, social-reform movements, and utopian colonies, all of which the chameleonic swindler views as opportunities for fraud. Wearing the mask of a kindly businessman, for instance, he attempts to induce a would-be buyer to purchase land in a place he calls New Jerusalem, a "new and thriving city, so called, in northern Minnesota," one that "was originally founded by certain fugitive Mormons." Many scholars have assumed this new and thriving city was an allusion to either Nauvoo or the Mormon settlement in Utah. But Richard Dilworth Rust, an expert on nineteenth-century American literature, has argued that "the northerly location and the reference to 'fugitive' Mormons" mean Melville may have been referring to "an apostate colony at Beaver Island...once designated the New Jerusalem by colony leader James J. Strang, whose assassination in 1856 received national attention."

Among the newspapers offering particularly close coverage of the prophet's murder, in fact, was the *Springfield Republican,* located just fifty miles from Melville's farm in Pittsfield, Massachusetts, where he wrote *The Confidence-Man.* The paper broke the news of Strang's death on July 15, 1856—the very day, it turns out, that Melville was said to be finishing a first draft of his book. All told, the *Republican* ran at least nineteen stories on the prophet, including five about his assassination and its aftermath. Another local paper, the *Albany Evening Journal,* also published stories on the killing.

Melville, in other words, was almost certainly aware of the saga of James J. Strang. But regardless of whether he was indeed alluding to Beaver Island in *The Confidence-Man,* no book of the nineteenth century better evokes the heated culture of that tiny kingdom, with its scoundrels and dreamers, opportunists and innocents. It's even tempting to imagine the fictional *Fidèle* as one of the steamboats that docked in St. James to rescue survivors from the wreckage of Strang's colony. Picture them now as they make their way up the gangplank of that vessel and join the many masqueraders already on deck, turning to wave goodbye to that sad, strange place for the last time. Then the *Fidèle* hoists anchor and steams away, carrying them toward their futures without J. J. Strang.

———

Mary Perce Strang, the prophet's first and lawful wife, remained in Voree after Strang's death, briefly residing next to a house occupied by Elvira Field, Betsy McNutt, and their children. Despite frequent financial difficulties, she stuck around until about 1870, when she moved with her grown son and daughter to Terre Haute, Indiana. Mary died in 1880, at age sixty-one. "A tragic life," wrote her daughter, Myraette. The widow never married again and passed away in such obscure circumstances that her place of death is lost to posterity.

Her father, the corrupt canal contractor William L. Perce, had died at age sixty-two, in 1855, the year before her husband. By then the inexhaustible old flimflammer had managed to land a lucrative contract with the Illinois Central, soon to be the longest railway in the world. In 1854 a farmer sued the railroad, claiming that Perce and his men had, by force of arms, unlawfully removed fifty thousand cubic feet of soil from his property for their own use, leaving the land pockmarked with "mines, pits, shafts and holes of great depth." So strong was the evidence, apparently, that not even the railroad's talented attorney, Abraham Lincoln, was able to win the case.

———

In the aftermath of the prophet's murder, Elvira Field Strang lived for a few years with her sister-wife Betsy McNutt, as the two women and their children moved around to various spots in Wisconsin with other former members of Strang's sect. Around 1859, she decided to return home to be with her widowed mother near Lansing, Michigan; once there, however, she found herself destitute. After contracting a serious and untreated illness, possibly typhoid fever, the desperate young woman placed an ad in a local newspaper, asking for people to take in her children. Three years passed before she earned enough money to get the oldest three back, but she never regained custody of her youngest son, James Jessie Jr., the prophet's namesake, born after his father's death. Eventually, at age thirty-five, she married a non-Mormon—a man "far inferior to her first love"—and went on to live a long and largely uneventful life, dying at the age of eighty, a full decade into the new century. "She sometimes feared that James had been over tempted to self-glorification," one of her sons later recalled, "and that the calamities were his punishments."

—

Betsy McNutt Strang, the prophet's second plural wife, never married again. After the demise of the kingdom, she led a restless and generally unhappy existence, moving from Wisconsin to Indiana to Wisconsin to an island in the U.S. waters of Lake Huron to a nearby island in Canada to Wisconsin and finally to Iowa, where she died in 1897 at the age of seventy-seven. Gabriel Strang—the middle of her three surviving children, whom one researcher described as having his father's intellectual ability, intuitiveness, and memory—served a pair of prison terms for horse theft, a trade he had learned from close associates of the late prophet. He also seems to have shared with his father what one newspaper account called a "Jekyll-Hyde life." According to a 1910 story out of Grand Rapids, Michigan, Gabriel Strang possessed a "puzzling dual personality," stealing horses and getting into shoot-outs with police while at the same time paying the expenses of "a young girl who was anxious to secure an education, but whose family was unable to send her to college." The benevolent Strang and the nefarious Strang: "police assert both men lived in the same body," the story explained.

———

In order to "appear less conspicuous before the world," Phoebe Wright Strang—nineteen years old and, like Strang's three other plural wives, pregnant at the time of her husband's assassination—changed her name. For the short run, she planned to go by *Phoebe Jesse,* a pseudonym she derived from the prophet's middle name. In the near future, however, she expected his kingdom to return in all its glory, at which time she would once again assume the sanctified name of *Strang.* She was still waiting fifty-eight years later, when she passed away in Tacoma, Washington, at the age of seventy-eight, without having taken another husband.

———

Of all the prophet's widows, the one who led the most adventurous life was Phoebe's cousin, Sarah Wright Strang, who in November of 1856 gave birth to James Phineas Strang, her only child by the prophet. Within three years she was married again, this time to a frontier physician who turned out to be a scoundrel equal to almost any who had resided on Beaver Island. Having abandoned two previous wives and divorced a third, he was already a secret bigamist before his marriage to Sarah, after which he converted to Mormonism and dragged her off to Utah, where he wed six additional women in a span of just four years and made a considerable fortune prospecting for gold.

By the early 1870s, Sarah had decided to leave both her husband and the church. But refusing to depart Utah, this remarkable mother of seven somehow transformed herself into a respected doctor, earning as much as $2,500 a year and bringing hundreds of newborns into the world. She rarely talked about Strang, but in 1920—three years before her death, at eighty-seven—she decided to break her silence. "I had faith that James was a prophet of God and would not do wrong," she told a correspondent. "I don't believe today that God ever speaks to any men."

After his bitter departure from Beaver Island in 1850, George J. Adams, the Shakespearean actor and minister of God, only added to his reputation as "the most consummate, bold and plausible deceiver that ever went unjailed," in the words of a contemporary account. In 1853, for example, newspapers all over the United States and England carried a report that the tragedian had died. Reprinting this obituary, the *Sauk County Standard* of Baraboo, Wisconsin, informed its readers that the dead man was "the same old Adams who, a year or two ago, opened in this village, what he called a 'Legitimate Dramatic Exhibition,' but not meeting with very flattering success, paid his bills with 'I promise to pay,' which the holders reserve, probably, as a memento to beware in the future of all straggling humbugs." It would turn out, however, that the straggling humbug in question was still very much alive, having planted the obituary himself in order to escape his notorious past (and perhaps also his creditors).

In 1860 Adams arrived in Springfield, Massachusetts, where, with his usual charisma, he soon attracted a large and devoted following to a new congregation called the Church of the Messiah. When skeptics in town presented evidence of his past life "in dramatical and Mormon circles," the preacher "persistently denied being the Adams that everybody said he was, asserting that the Adams they meant died several years ago," according to the *Springfield Republican,* which concluded that "a more debased and unblushing villain, a more shameless and unprincipled impostor than he, has never come to our notice."

Forced to flee Springfield, he eventually moved the Church of the Messiah to Maine, where he hit on the idea of establishing a colony in Palestine to await the Second Coming. Somehow he convinced more than 150 followers to sell all their possessions and make the transatlantic pilgrimage with him in 1866. Arriving at Jaffa that

September, they set up a squalid camp of improvised huts and tents on the beach. Within a year, eighteen of them were dead from cholera and starvation, as well as from the drunkenness and ineptitude of their leader. "The colony was a failure, and Christ did not come," wrote Mark Twain, who happened to be on a U.S.-bound ship that rescued about forty miserable survivors of the colony. Twain eventually wrote about the fiasco in his travel narrative, *The Innocents Abroad,* describing members of the church as having been "shamefully humbugged by their prophet." One scholar has argued, moreover, that Twain also used Adams as his model for the King, the inebriated con artist and itinerant actor in *Huckleberry Finn.* Indeed, Huck's comment on the King's fraudulent schemes serves as an apt summation of Adams's entire career: "It was enough to make a body ashamed of the human race."

—

Adams was not the only former crony of Strang's to outlive his own obituary. In 1850, Brigham Young alleged that John C. Bennett—the prophet's colorful right-hand man in Voree—had died in a California slum during the Gold Rush, his body "dragged out with his boots on, put into a cart, hauled off, and dumped into a hole a rotten mass of corruption."

In fact, Bennett was not dead—though perhaps he could not attribute his health to the quack medicines he was then producing, such as the Grains of Paradise and Dr. Bennett's Dysenteric Drops. Medical doctor, abortionist, university president, mayor, military leader, lobbyist, coiner of the term *spiritual wife,* and tomato expert, he spent some of his later years as a poultry farmer. But even in this prosaic profession, he soon attracted allegations of fraud, with fellow breeders accusing Bennett of attempting to "deceive the uninitiated" by passing off common fowl as exotic imports with "humbug, long, jaw-cracking names." Before the fall of Strang's kingdom, some of those chickens had even wound up on Beaver Island, a coronation gift from Bennett, who perhaps hoped to get back into the king's good graces. In the invasion of the island, members of the mob seem to have taken out their rage on the poor birds, when, according to one account of the melee, the king's "poultry-yard was made a shooting-mark for all."

———

The man who had helped orchestrate that raid, Dr. Hezekiah D. McCulloch, returned to Beaver Island a few months later to run for the state legislature. His dream of avenging himself on the prophet by taking Strang's old seat in the Michigan House, however, quickly fizzled. Receiving only eighteen votes, the disgraced physician left the island for good and eventually wound up on the Minnesota frontier, dying there seven years later. He left behind his wife, Sarah, and two teenage sons.

———

A few years after the assassination, one of Strang's killers returned to the island to "see how things were prospering," according to the proprietor of a boardinghouse where Alexander Wentworth resided during his visit. By then there was already something of a local tourist industry for "people who came to see King Strang's Island," as the proprietor put it, and Wentworth liked to show his fellow visitors around. "Alec, as they always called him, was their guide to show them the best fishing streams and take them to hunt ducks and wild pigeons." In the Civil War, Wentworth joined the Union Army, rising to the rank of first sergeant before his death from illness, in 1863, near Vicksburg, Mississippi. "I have never yet regretted what I did," he once said of the murder.

———

Wentworth's fellow gunman, Thomas Bedford, remained on Beaver Island until 1864, when he allegedly committed another killing. This time it was not a decree about pantaloons or a flogging that triggered his rage but a game of cards, after which, the story goes, Bedford attempted to conceal the corpse of his victim underneath a milk cupboard. Apparently allowed to enlist in the Army rather than face charges, the forty-nine-year-old joined the 19th U.S. Infantry and headed south in the waning months of the Civil War, too late to take part in General William Tecumseh Sherman's sack of Atlanta but not too late, it was rumored, to kill a fellow soldier.

Although he liked to boast of his body count, Bedford was never put on trial for any of the killings. And whereas his wife, Ruth Ann, continued to live on Beaver Island, he settled down in a separate residence near Lansing, Michigan. In the 1880 census, Ruth Ann listed herself as a widow, possibly to help her husband, who was still very much alive, avoid prosecution. Never returning to the island, he died at age seventy-four on July 5, 1889. That same day, a newspaper in Kansas published an article about another Civil War veteran of sorts, the legendary abolitionist John Brown, whose failed 1859 raid on the federal arsenal at Harper's Ferry, Virginia, had served as a grisly catalyst to the conflict. The piece included an interview with a surviving witness to Brown's hanging, who claimed his final words were "Isn't this a beautiful country?"

———

In an almost incredible bit of irony, George C. Bates, the U.S. district attorney who led the Navy's assault on Beaver Island and spent months attempting to put "King James and his infatuated brethren" behind bars, wound up in Utah, working as a lawyer for the Mormon Church. "If reason be judge," wrote Herman Melville in *The Confidence-Man,* "no writer has produced such inconsistent characters as nature herself has."

———

Finally, there is the king of all inconsistent characters, James Jesse Strang. In Melville's novel, passengers on the *Fidèle,* constantly encountering different incarnations of an amorphous confidence man, find themselves "at a loss to determine where exactly the fictitious character had been dropped, and the real one, if any, resumed." Anyone attempting to make sense of Strang's life must invariably confront the same dilemma. Was he a holy man or demagogue? Did he break the laws in order to save the faith or did he fabricate the faith in order to break the laws? Did God speak through him, or was the whole thing—the letter of appointment from Joseph Smith, the Rajah Manchou plates, the *Book of the Law of the Lord,* the visions, the covenants, everything that he wrote and said and did—one giant and elaborate hoax?

Perhaps such questions miss the point. In *The Confidence-Man,* Melville observed that every now and then someone comes along like an intense beam of light, "raying away from itself all round it—everything is lit by it, everything starts up to it." He called this kind of person "an original":

> As for original characters in fiction, a grateful reader will, on meeting with one, keep the anniversary of that day. True, we sometimes hear of an author who, at one creation, produces some two or three score such characters; it may be possible. But they can hardly be original in the sense that Hamlet is, or Don Quixote, or Milton's Satan....In short, a due conception of what is to be held for this sort of personage in fiction would make him almost as much of a prodigy there, as in real history is a new law-giver, a revolutionizing philosopher, or the founder of a new religion.

Seer, swindler, idealist, impostor, saint, thief, genius, clown—at one time or another all described James Jesse Strang, a true American original. He did not name a successor. For his followers, there could never be one. Within a few years of his death, his kingdom on Lake Michigan began to fade from popular memory, like an evanescing island in some ancient myth. Soon, Strang himself was relegated to the stuff of legend, his exploits sounding as outrageous and implausible to future generations as those of Johnny Appleseed or Paul Bunyan, and eventually the facts of his life faded into obscurity.

But people like James Strang never really vanish. When the time is right, they reappear, wearing a new guise, exploiting new fears, offering new dreams of salvation. Americans are fixated on such figures, especially in periods of profound social and economic upheaval. And so it is that Elvira's desperate hope for her husband to return from the dead has come true. So it is that the King of Confidence lives on.

Acknowledgments

In writing this book, I often found myself thinking about Edgar Allan Poe's short story "A Man of the Crowd." As that tale opens, the narrator sits at the window of a coffeehouse, watching people stroll past and feeling "a calm but inquisitive interest in everything." In the busy street outside, he observes a broad cross-section of nineteenth-century society—merchants, attorneys, and tradesmen; organ-grinders, coal-sweeps, and "exhausted laborers of every description"; pickpockets, gamblers, and "gentlemen who live by their wits." Suddenly, from amid the bustle, he spots a man who "at once arrested and absorbed my whole attention," a man whose face is unlike any he's ever seen, a man whose enigmatic expression seems to speak of "vast mental power, of caution, of penuriousness, of avarice, of coolness, of malice, of blood-thirstiness, of triumph, of merriment, of excessive terror, of intense—of supreme despair." Overcome by the thought of "how wild a history" this stranger must have had, the narrator grabs his coat, hat, and cane, and dashes after the man, feeling "aroused, startled, [and] fascinated."

Those were pretty much my own emotions when I began looking into the wild history of James J. Strang. And for that, I owe a massive debt of gratitude to Ben George, senior editor at Little, Brown and Company, who in 2015 contacted me out of the blue to inquire whether I might be interested in writing a book about the murder of a nineteenth-century prophet whose name I barely recognized. Although Ben and I had never met, we soon became close collaborators, and I am immeasurably thankful for the vast amount of talent, time, attention, and inspiration he poured into this project. To pundits who claim hands-on, old-school editors in the mold of Maxwell Perkins no longer exist, I reply: Meet Ben George. The book was his brainchild, and he has been a brilliant mentor at every step of the creative process. The same is true of my agent, the wise and unflappable Sloan Harris, who took a risk on an unproven writer two decades ago and has stuck with him, through good times and bad. As with every great literary adventure I've been blessed to undertake, this one never would have happened without Sloan.

My hunt for Strang was a journey through both time and space, and like the narrator of Poe's story, I found myself "utterly amazed at his behavior" and determined that "we should not part until I had satisfied myself in some measure respecting him." Although the mysterious stranger sometimes seemed to escape around a corner, I never quite lost track of him, thanks to the many individuals who contributed to my search, providing wisdom and pointing to clues.

Chief among these guides were three of Strang's previous biographers. Milo M. Quaife helped revive interest in the prophet with his groundbreaking 1930 work, *The Kingdom of Saint James,* while Roger Van Noord and Vickie Cleverley Speek both wrote fascinating books that contained crucial new research. Although I came at Strang's story from a different angle than my predecessors, viewing him as a kind of lightning rod for all the fierce enthusiasms and vibrant social movements of the antebellum era, I am deeply grateful to these fine biographers and am honored by the opportunity to expand upon their work.

I also want to thank my good friend and brother-in-law Chris Carr, who happened to grow up in Burlington, Wisconsin, former home of the Voree colony. Chris gave me a tour of the place by canoe, allowing me to view Voree through nineteenth-century eyes, ospreys swooping overhead as we paddled the White River to visit various sites. His mother, the wonderful Joan Carr, arranged for me to meet with Don Vande Sand, archivist at the Burlington Historical Society, and William Shepard, an elder in Strang's small but surviving offshoot of the Mormon Church. I am grateful to all of them for their wisdom and hospitality. My gratitude and thoughts also go to the late Sandra Birdsall, an extraordinary woman with an impressive career in law, government, and politics, who led me on an invaluable expedition around Beaver Island.

Pointing the way in my hunt for the prophet were librarians and archivists around the country, including Mary Ellen Budney, Ellen Doon, Matthew Mason, Ève Bourbeau-Allard, Molly Bailey-Dillon, Anne Marie Menta, Rebecca Aldi, and Jessica Tubis at Yale; Kendel Joy Darragh and Diane Donham at the Library of Michigan; Annakathryn Parker Welch at the Archives of Michigan; Mark Bowden at the Detroit Public Library's Burton Historical Collection; Maureen Maryanski at the New-York Historical Society; the archives reference staff at the Library of Virginia; Rachel Killebrew at the Community of Christ Archives; Vickie Allan at the Maryland State Archives; Allender Sybert at the Maryland Genealogical Society; Richard Baranowski at the Way Public Library in Perrysburg, Ohio; Nancy Nixon Ensign at the Patterson Library in Westfield, New York; Barbara Cessna and Sharon Terwilliger at the Fenton History Center; Janet Curtiss and Barbara King at the St. Clair County Library in Port Huron, Michigan; Madeleine Bradford at the University of Michigan's Bentley Historical Library; Edith A. Sandler at the Manuscript Division of the Library of Congress; Lori Taylor-Blitz at the Beaver Island Historical Society; and the entire library staff at DePaul University. I would like to offer special thanks to John Fierst of Central Michigan University's Clarke Historical Library, for his guidance on Native American habitation of Beaver

Island, as well as to Tim Lindholm of the Daguerrean Society, Sarah
Weatherwax of the Library Company of Philadelphia, and Gary W.
Ewer of "The Daguerreotype" web archive for their expertise on
early photography. I am, moreover, much indebted to Terryl Givens,
a preeminent scholar of Mormonism, who kindly agreed to read
several passages of this text in order to ensure their accuracy.

Additionally, I am grateful to DePaul University for providing two
research grants that greatly aided me in my work, and to my colleagues in the English department, a gifted, energetic, and supportive
group of scholars and writers with whom I feel blessed to conspire. I
am also thankful to the talented students who helped with research:
Julia Berger, Samantha Garfinkel, Chris Lyons, Sara McCall, Tyler
Noe, and Cari Zwolinski. And I'm colossally appreciative of Kaitlin
Lounsberry and Brittany Schmitt, trusted former graduate students
who, in an early draft of this book, undertook the monumental
copyediting task of changing 400 pages of verbs from present to past
tense, for which I am, was, will be, much obliged.

Like the narrator of Poe's story, who follows the object of his obsession into shadowy and labyrinthine neighborhoods, I often began to
feel lost during my work on this book. Luckily, fellow writers were
there to save me from blind alleys of my own making. I'm profoundly
grateful to Scott Blackwood and Bill Lychack for their superb advice,
and to the members of my writers' group—Doro Boehme, Maria
Finitzo, Peter Handler, Gwen Macsai, Francesca Royster, Gail Louise
Siegel, and Andrew White—for their invaluable input on various
fragmentary first drafts. And to Lauren Cowen, a perceptive and
honest reader of my work for thirty-five years, a special thanks for
making me see the necessity of a major restructuring.

Tapadh leat to Amelia Hunt, along with her associates, Gnipper
and Hexi, and her parents, Richard and Laura, for their wonderful
hospitality on the River Tweed. No writer has ever undertaken the
dreary task of compiling endnotes in a more beautiful setting—or

among better company. I'd also like to thank Allan Fallow (an exacting copyeditor with the ear of a poet), Pamela Marshall, Gregg Kulick, Marie Mundaca, Holly Hartman, Deborah Jacobs, and the ever-patient Evan Hansen-Bundy at Little, Brown, as well as Julie Flanagan at ICM. Additional thanks go to the Venerable Congress of New Year's Celebrants, the Village, the Al & Andy's crew and the *Gruppe von Männern,* as well as to Caitlin Stephenson, Barbara Madison, Kevin Davis, Dave Cullen, Robert Kurson, Alex Kotlowitz, Richard Cahan, Tom Krainz, Michael Paterniti, Sara Corbett, Cammie McGovern, Charles Baxter, Tom Clynes, Donovan Hohn, Eileen Pollack, Matthew Harvey, and Richard "It's a Miracle!" Cohen.

My children, Zooz and J, became young adults during the writing of this book. I find myself in awe of these smart, talented, hilarious human beings—and so very grateful to (and for) them. Finally, to Rengin Altay, adored wife and fellow creative soul, thanks for the lush, lovely, chaotic island we've shared for the past quarter century. It's no paradise, but most of the time it sure comes close.

In the end of Poe's story, the narrator gives up on his hunt, as I must do now. The stranger drifts away, an enigma to the last, like a book that does "not permit itself to be read." This book, too, ends with an unfinished search and with far more questions than answers. Yes, but it was such a joy to write...

Notes

PROLOGUE

3 **"I don't blame anyone"**: Quoted in Alex Beam, *American Crucifixion: The Murder of Joseph Smith and the Fate of the Mormon Church* (New York: PublicAffairs, 2014), p. 283.

3 **more than 100 strong**: Many of the details of Smith's murder are from an eyewitness account, "The Statement of William R. Hamilton," in *History of Hancock County,* Charles J. Scofield, ed. (Chicago: Munsell Publishing Co., 1921), pp. 845–846.

4 **"I am a dead man"**: Quoted in Beam, *American Crucifixion,* p. 179.

4 **"O Lord, my God"**: Quoted in ibid., p. 181.

4 **"indolent," "ignorant," "prevaricating," and "shiftless"**: Richard Lyman Bushman, *Joseph Smith: Rough Stone Rolling* (New York: Knopf, 2005), pp. 90, 127; Alice Felt Tyler, *Freedom's Ferment: Phases of American Social History from the Colonial Period to the Outbreak of the Civil War* (New York: Harper & Row, 1962), p. 87.

5 **2,000 times**: Robert Vincent Remini, *Joseph Smith* (New York: Viking, 2002), p. 74. Other commentators put the number closer to 1,400.

5 **("chloroform in print")**: Mark Twain, *Roughing It,* Harriet E. Smith, Edgar Marquess Branch, Lin Salamo, and Robert Pack Browning, eds. (Berkeley: University of California Press, 1993), p. 107.

5 **25,000 converts**: Beam, *American Crucifixion,* p. 21.

5 **10,000 residents**: Ibid., p. 14.

5 **rivaled Chicago**: Richard E. Bennett, Susan Easton Black, and Donald Q. Cannon, *The Nauvoo Legion in Illinois: A History of the Mormon Militia, 1841–1846* (Norman: Arthur H. Clark Co./University of Oklahoma Press, 2010), p. 127.

6 **"most ragged, lazy fellow"**: Quoted in Tyler, *Freedom's Ferment,* p. 87.

6 **as many as forty women:** Laurie Goodstein, "It's Official: Mormon Founder Had Many Wives," *New York Times* (November 11, 2014), p. 1.

7 ***What hath God wrought?:*** Quoted in Daniel Walker Howe, *What Hath God Wrought: The Transformation of America, 1815–1848* (New York: Oxford University Press, 2007), p. 1.

7 **time would stop:** Dan Erickson, "Mormon Millennialism: The Literalist Legacy and Implications for the Year 2000," *Dialogue: A Journal of Mormon Thought* 30, no. 2 (Summer 1997): pp. 1–32; Glen M. Leonard, "Early Saints and the Millennium," *Ensign* 9, no. 8 (August 1979): web; The Book of Mormon, 2nd Nephi, 28: pp. 16–23.

7 **"reign personally upon the earth":** Joseph Smith's "Articles of Faith" was originally published in the *Times and Seasons* newspaper, Nauvoo, Ill. (March 1, 1842), vol. 3, no. 9, pp. 703–718. This quotation is from p. 710.

7 **"having bodies of flesh and bones":** Church of Jesus Christ of Latter-day Saints, *The Doctrine and Covenants of the Church of Jesus Christ of Latter-day Saints* (Salt Lake City, Utah: Church of Jesus Christ of Latter-day Saints, 1981), Section 129, verse 1.

7 **"once a man like us":** Beam, *American Crucifixion*, p. 29.

7 **half the paper money:** Stephen Mihm, *A Nation of Counterfeiters: Capitalists, Con Men, and the Making of the United States* (Cambridge, Mass.: Harvard University Press, 2007), p. 6.

8 **1.3 million acres:** James Edward Davis, *Frontier Illinois* (Bloomington: Indiana University Press, 1998), p. 202.

8 **(It wouldn't become known as the "Midwest"):** James R. Shortridge, *The Middle West: Its Meaning in American Culture* (Lawrence: University Press of Kansas, 1989), pp. 13–26.

9 **"God blesseth thee":** John J. Hajicek, ed., *Chronicles of Voree, 1844–1849* (Burlington, Wis.: J. J. Hajicek, 1992), pp. 10–11.

9 **"larceny grew not only respectable, but genteel":** James G. Baldwin, *The Flush Times of Alabama and Mississippi* (New York: D. Appleton & Co., 1854), p. 85.

CHAPTER 1

10 **"Ours is an age of suicide":** *Arcturus: A Journal of Books and Opinion* 1, no. 3 (February 1841): p. 17.

10 **"two hundred and fifty dollars":** Quoted in Edward J. Balleisen, *Navigating Failure: Bankruptcy and Commercial Society in Antebellum America* (Chapel Hill: University of North Carolina Press, 2001), p. 80.

11 **William Miller:** Tyler, *Freedom's Ferment*, pp. 70–78, and Howe, *What Hath God Wrought*, pp. 289–292.

11 "rather small but very bright": Quoted in Roger Van Noord, *Assassination of a Michigan King: The Life of James Jesse Strang* (Ann Arbor: University of Michigan Press, 1988), p. 185.

11 "as though they could bore": Ibid.

11 "the soul of trade": *Hunt's Merchants' Magazine and Commercial Review* (August 1839), vol. 1, no. 2, p. 155.

11 "commerce between man and man": Herman Melville, *The Confidence-Man: His Masquerade—An Authoritative Text, Contemporary Reviews, Biographical Overviews, Sources, Backgrounds, and Criticism*, second ed., Hershel Parker and Mark Niemeyer, eds. (New York: W. W. Norton, 2006), p. 133.

12 "pretended to own in the interior of Ohio": *Mayville Sentinel* (March 19, 1846). Strang vehemently denied the allegations in this article, which was published more than two years after his departure from the area. All the quotes about Strang's alleged frauds and subsequent departure are from that March 19 piece.

12 "the greatest scoundrel": Ibid.

13 no region of the United States: Whitney R. Cross, *The Burned-Over District: The Social and Intellectual History of Enthusiastic Religion in Western New York, 1800–1850* (Ithaca, N.Y.: Cornell University Press, 1950), p. 56.

13 "psychic highway": Quoted in Ronald E. Shaw, *Erie Water West: A History of the Erie Canal, 1792–1854* (Lexington: University of Kentucky Press, 1966), p. 219.

13 "the greatest revival of religion": Charles G. Finney, *Memoirs of Rev. Charles G. Finney* (New York: A. S. Barnes & Co., 1876), p. 300.

14 "You could not go": Quoted in Paul E. Johnson, *A Shopkeeper's Millennium: Society and Revivals in Rochester, New York, 1815–1837* (New York: Hill & Wang, 1978), p. 95.

14 "all real men": Quoted in Paul E. Johnson and Sean Wilentz, *The Kingdom of Matthias: A Story of Sex and Salvation in 19th-Century America* (New York: Oxford University Press, 1995), pp. 93–94.

14 "Here and there in the midst of American society": Alexis de Tocqueville, *Democracy in America*, trans. Henry Reeve, rev. Francis Bowen (Ware, Hertfordshire: Wordsworth, 1998), p. 240.

15 "blasphemous work": *Rochester Daily Advertiser and Telegraph* (April 2, 1830).

15 "miserable impostor": *Fredonia Censor* (May 25, 1831). A transcription appears in "Uncle Dale's Old Mormon News Articles," prepared by Dale R. Broadhurst, web.

15 "It is all a mere mock": James J. Strang, *The Diary of James J. Strang;*

Deciphered, Transcribed, Introduced and Annotated by Mark A. Strang (East Lansing: Michigan State University Press, 1961), pp. 10–11.

15 **"pray and talk"**: Ibid., p. 10.

15 **"a perfect atheist"**: Ibid., p. 21.

16 **"a kind of creeping sensation"**: James J. Strang, fragmentary autobiography, in Michigan Historical Commission, *Michigan Historical Collections,* vol. 32 (Lansing, Mich.: Robert Smith Printing Co., 1903), p. 202.

16 *My mind has always been filled:* Strang, *Diary*, p. 19.

16 **"I shall try"**: Ibid.

17 **"a Priest, a Lawyer, a Conqueror"**: Ibid., p. 22.

17 **Amidst all the evils**: Ibid., p. 32.

17 **"those principles of duplicity"**: Louis Antoine Fauvelet de Bourrienne, *The Life of Napoleon Bonaparte* (Philadelphia: Carey and Lea, 1832), p. 279.

17 **"the insincerity with which he could use words"**: Walter Scott, *The Life of Napoleon* (Philadelphia: E. L. Carey and A. Hart, 1839), p. 449.

17 **"bright garden-isles"**: Percy Bysshe Shelley, *Queen Mab,* in *Shelley's Poetry and Prose: Authoritative Texts, Criticism,* Donald H. Reiman and Neil Fraistat (New York: W. W. Norton, 2002), p. 63.

17 **"green woods"**: Shelley, Ibid.; p. 63.

17 *the* **inspirational underground text"**: Joss Marsh, *Word Crimes: Blasphemy, Culture, and Literature in Nineteenth-Century England* (Chicago: University of Chicago Press, 1998), p. 104.

17 **"There is no God!"**: Shelley, *Queen Mab,* p 54.

18 **"human dupes"**: Ibid.

18 **"commerce of good words and works"**: Ibid., p. 48.

18 **"human things"**: Ibid., p. 69.

18 **"When poverty and wealth"**: Ibid., p. 48.

18 **"Fame, fame alone"**: Strang, *Diary,* p. 49.

19 **"governed by inheritance"**: Paul E. Johnson, *Sam Patch: The Famous Jumper* (New York: Hill & Wang, 2003), p. 163.

19 **"I leave this rule"**: Davy Crockett, *Narrative of the Life of Davy Crockett* (Philadelphia: E. L. Carey and A. Hart, 1834), epigraph on title page.

19 **"go-ahead" spirit**: See Scott A. Sandage, *Born Losers: A History of Failure in America* (Cambridge, Mass.: Harvard University Press, 2006), pp. 25–26, 83–85.

19 **"He possessed a wonderful memory"**: William Adams, ed., *Historical Gazetteer and Biographical Memorial of Cattaraugus County, N.Y.* (Syracuse, N.Y.: Lyman, Horton and Co., 1893), pp. 321–322. The editor notes that information on the prophet was supplied by Strang's contemporary Frederick Larkin.

20 "an excellent vantage point": Richard R. John, *Spreading the News: The American Postal System from Franklin to Morse* (Cambridge, Mass.: Harvard University Press, 1995), p. 124.

20 he owed the government $14.41: Auditor of the Treasury Elisha Whittlesey to Strang, May 17, 1841, James Jesse Strang Collection, Yale Collection of Western Americana, Beinecke Rare Book and Manuscript Library.

20 "inclined to a certain evil": Strang, *Diary,* p. 12.

20 One affair with an older woman: Van Noord, *Assassination of a Michigan King,* pp. 13–15.

20 "violent passions": Strang to William L. Perce, September 22, 1836, Strang Collection, Beinecke.

20 "when we meet again": Strang, *Diary,* pp. 62–63.

20 "ushered in by rain": Myraette Strang, "Perce Family History," Library of Michigan, p. 1.

21 72,000 square miles: Alasdair Roberts, *America's First Great Depression: Economic Crisis and Political Disorder After the Panic of 1837* (Ithaca, N.Y.: Cornell University Press, 2012), p. 32.

21 "mania for obtaining land": *Ohio State Journal* (June 25, 1836), quoted in ibid., p. 32.

21 land prices rose 150 percent: John Opie, *The Law of the Land: Two Hundred Years of American Farmland Policy* (Lincoln: University of Nebraska Press, 1994), p. 51.

21 One tract in Buffalo: Roger Whitman, *The Rise and Fall of a Frontier Entrepreneur,* Scott Eberle and David A. Gerber, eds. (Syracuse, N.Y.: University of Syracuse Press, 1996), p. 101.

22 a bank note from a bank that no longer existed: Lot Clark to Strang, August 30, 1841, Strang Collection, Beinecke.

22 offered a probable route: Draft of a letter to Wilson & Co., January 29, 1841, ibid.

22 "HOW TO MAKE MONEY": *Randolph Herald* (May 30, 1843), p. 4.

22 "The next that was heard of him": *Mayville Sentinel* (March 19, 1846).

CHAPTER 2

23 "Out of old materials": Melville, *The Confidence-Man,* p. 185.

23 "The wolves": The "letter of appointment" is published in full in Milo M. Quaife, *The Kingdom of Saint James: A Narrative of the Mormons* (New Haven, Conn.: Yale University Press, 1930), pp. 235–237.

23 "one of the most important": Van Noord, *Assassination of a Michigan King,* p. 7.

24 "fraud and profusion": Andrew B. Dickinson to his fellow lawmakers,

March 28, 1843, *Journal of the Senate of the State of New York* (Albany: E. Mack, 1843), p. 351. Dickinson, a Whig, was attempting to embarrass Democratic politicians linked to canal corruption. He identified Perce as "Pierce," a frequent misspelling of the name.

25 **"not being able to procure bail"**: New York Attorney General Greene C. Bronson, "Report of the Attorney-General, in the Case of William L. Perce and the County of Cayuga," February 20, 1830, *Legislative Documents of the Senate and Assembly of the State of New York* (Albany: E. Croswell, 1830), vol. 2, no. 193, pp. 1–2.

25 **a year and a half after his arrest:** Ibid. The February 1830 report notes that in August of 1828, Perce was committed to jail, "where he still remains."

25 **"getting rich"**: Strang, draft of letter to Benjamin Perce, August 24, 1836, Strang Collection, Beinecke.

25 **took the money and ran:** In August of 1837, the company reported that "William L. Perce, contractor for Section 52, has left the line of the Canal and his force has disbanded." Given his prior history, there was "sufficient reason to believe that said Perce will not return and finish his work." "James River and Kanawha Company. Records, 1835–1881. Accession 36327, Business records collection, The Library of Virginia, Richmond, Virginia," August 10, 1837.

25 **"simply to let numerous strangers"**: *Ottawa Free Trader* (July 11, 1845), p. 2. The paper later retracted its allegation that Perce was guilty of criminal conduct with regard to his work on the Illinois and Michigan Canal. See *Ottawa Free Trader* (September 26, 1846), p. 2.

26 **two-year suspension:** See John Lamb, *Historical Essays on the Illinois & Michigan Canal,* Michael P. Conzen, ed. (Romeoville, Ill.: Lewis University, 2009), pp. 24–25. See also *New York Tribune* (July 31, 1846), which reprints a story from the *Rochester Daily Democrat,* in which the correspondent describes a conversation with Strang: "I learned that he...removed to Illinois several years ago to take charge as contractor, engineer or something of the kind, of a portion of the Illinois canal; but as its construction was soon suspended, he sought other employment."

26 **a champion of "universal liberty"**: Abner Hazeltine to Strang, January 30, 1837, Strang Collection, Beinecke.

26 **assisting escaped slaves:** See Vickie Cleverley Speek, *"God Has Made Us a Kingdom": James Strang and the Midwest Mormons* (Salt Lake City, Utah: Signature Books, 2006), p. 17.

26 **Benjamin Perce:** Van Noord, *Assassination of a Michigan King,* p. 32.

27 **"great shrewdness"**: Judge William Penn Lyon, quoted in Henry E. Legler, *A Moses of the Mormons: Strang's City of Refuge and Island*

Kingdom (Milwaukee: Parkman Club Publications, 1897), nos. 15–16, p. 119, note 8.

27 **required him to travel to Ottawa:** Elvira Field Strang and Charles J. Strang, "Biographical Sketch of James J. Strang," unpublished manuscript, Library of Michigan, p. 5.

27 **"seemed to wear heavily":** Myraette Losee, quoted in Van Noord, *Assassination of a Michigan King,* p. 32.

27 **"an inveterate unbeliever":** *New York Tribune* (July 31, 1846), which reprints details of an interview with Strang from the *Rochester Daily Democrat.*

27 **"growing like a mushroom":** Mormon settler George Miller, quoted in Robert Bruce Flanders, *Nauvoo: Kingdom on the Mississippi* (Urbana: University of Illinois Press, 1965), p. 51.

28 **"sturdy self-asserter":** Josiah Quincy Jr., *Figures of the Past: From the Leaves of Old Journals* (Boston: Roberts Brothers, 1888), pp. 377, 399.

28 **"a mixture of shrewdness":** Charles Francis Adams, quoted in Van Noord, *Assassination of a Michigan King,* p. 5.

28 **"a great egotist":** Charlotte Haven, quoted in Beam, *American Crucifixion,* p. 23.

28 **"a compound of ignorance":** Benjamin Franklin Morris, quoted in ibid.

28 **"contended with Smith":** *New York Tribune* (July 31, 1846), p. 4.

28 **"puny arm in rebellion":** Myraette Strang to James J. Strang, May 16, 1840, Strang Collection, Beinecke.

29 **"Their aim":** Isaac Scott, "James J. Strang in Voree," *Saints' Herald,* vol. 35, no. 815 (December 29, 1888), p. 832.

29 **he was baptized by Joseph Smith:** Hajicek, ed., *Chronicles of Voree,* p. 6.

29 **"a great military despotism":** *New York Sun* (September 4, 1843), quoted in Flanders, *Nauvoo: Kingdom on the Mississippi,* p. 278.

30 **"false and damnable doctrines":** *Nauvoo Expositor* (June 7, 1844), p. 2.

31 **a forgery:** Charles Eberstadt, "A Letter That Founded a Kingdom," *Autograph Collectors' Journal* (October 1950): pp. 2–5, 32.

31 **no other examples are known to exist:** Dale L. Morgan, quoted in Van Noord, *Assassination of a Michigan King,* p. 55 and p. 287, note 33.

31 **"bears no slightest resemblance":** Eberstadt, "A Letter That Founded a Kingdom," p. 4.

31 **"the greatest curiosity in the world":** Barnum promotional notice, quoted in James W. Cook, *The Arts of Deception: Playing with Fraud in the Age of Barnum* (Cambridge, Mass.: Harvard University Press, 2001), p. 84.

31 **this "fabulous creature":** Pamphlet promoting the mermaid, quoted in ibid., p. 100.

32 **"I requested my naturalist's opinion"**: Phineas Taylor Barnum, *The Life of P. T. Barnum* (New York: Redfield, 1855), p. 231.

CHAPTER 3

33 **"In commercial affairs"**: Charles Dickens, *The Life and Adventures of Martin Chuzzlewit* (New York: Penguin Books, 2004), p. 261.

33 **"possessed a remarkable inventive genius"**: Charles Edward Weller, *The Early History of the Typewriter* (La Porte, Ind.: Chase & Shepard, printers, 1918), p. 4.

33 **"the gentleman alluded to"**: *Southport Telegraph* (September 30, 1845), p. 2.

33 **Florence, Michigan**: Hajicek, ed., *Chronicles of Voree*, p. 13; Quaife, *Kingdom of Saint James*, p. 15; Van Noord, *Assassination of a Michigan King*, p. 9.

34 **"false spirit"**: Crandell Dunn, "Letter from Elder Dunn to Elder Appleby, of Philadelphia," *Latter-day Saints' Millennial Star*, vol. 8, no. 6 (October 15, 1846), p. 93.

34 **"carried on its face"**: Norton Jacob, quoted in Van Noord, *Assassination of a Michigan King*, p. 9.

34 **"I am delivered over"**: Strang to Louisa Sanger, December 5, 1844, quoted in ibid., p. 11.

34 **"much talk"**: *Southport Telegraph* (September 30, 1845), p. 2.

34 **"it had been revealed to him"**: Sholes published the men's testimony in ibid.

35 **an angel had loaned him**: By the time he led his followers to those plates, the putative prophet had been visited by two angels. The first came to him as he worked alone in a field near Burlington on June 27, 1844, at 5:30 p.m.—just as Joseph Smith was shot dead in Illinois. The second had led him to that hillside, showing him "an earthen casement...buried in the ground as deep as to a man's waist," in Strang's own words. Inside that underground chamber, which "I beheld it as a man can see a light stone in clear water," were three brass plates. See Hajicek, ed., *Chronicles of Voree*, pp. 10–12, 21–24.

35 **miraculous devices**: Strang's testimony about the Urim and Thummim appears to contradict itself. He originally reported that on September 1, 1845, immediately after using the seer stones to gaze beneath the soil and find out where the plates were buried, "I returned the Urim and Thummim to the Angel of the Lord." Later, however, he said he used the Urim and Thummim to translate the plates on September 18. Ibid. pp. 23, 30.

36 "My people are no more": Strang's translation of the Rajah Manchou of Vorito plates is published in full in Speek, *God Has Made Us a Kingdom*," p. 361.

37 "Is it not surprisingly strange": Quoted in Van Noord, *Assassination of a Michigan King*, p. 39.

37 ("wicked liar") and ("pretended"): Quoted in ibid.

38 "the spot from which they purport to have been taken": *Southport Telegraph* (September 30, 1845), p. 2.

38 some 900 newspapers: David Paul Nord, *Communities of Journalism: A History of American Newspapers and Their Readers* (Urbana: University of Illinois Press, 2001), p. 94.

39 fewer than a dozen subscribers: Van Noord, *Assassination of a Michigan King*, p. 38.

39 "The whole nation is impressed": *New York Herald* (May 12, 1845), p. 2.

39 "every printer of newspapers may send one paper": Richard B. Kielbowicz, "Postal Acts of 1792, 1845, 1879," *Encyclopedia of American Journalism*, Stephen L. Vaughan, ed. (New York: Routledge, 2008), pp. 399–401.

39 364 exchanges in a single month: Richard B. Kielbowicz, *News in the Mail: The Press, Post Office, and Public Information, 1700–1860s* (New York: Greenwood Press, 1989), p. 149.

40 "a vast national conversation": John Nerone, "Representing Public Opinion: US Newspapers and the News System in the Long Nineteenth Century," *History Compass* (September 2011), vol. 9, no. 9, p. 749.

40 "The city of Voree": The version I quote here is from the *Green Mountain Freeman* (July 9, 1846), p. 3. In the original text, this Montpelier, VT, newspaper misspelled the prophet's name as *Strange*.

40 "The 'city of Voree,' for aught we know": *American Freeman* (August 4, 1846), p. 2.

40 "manufacture of public opinion": Hezekiah Niles, quoted in Nerone, "Representing Public Opinion," p. 749.

41 "a shrewd, active, well-informed man": *Milwaukee Sentinel* (May 22, 1846), p. 2.

42 200 Mormon buildings torched: Flanders, *Nauvoo: Kingdom on the Mississippi*, p. 328.

42 persuading the Mormons to leave: Thomas Ford, *A History of Illinois, from Its Commencement as a State in 1818 to 1847* (Chicago: S. C. Griggs & Co., 1854), p. 410.

42 more than 300 men: Flanders, *Nauvoo: Kingdom on the Mississippi*, p. 329.

42 "It was decided": Brigham Young, quoted in ibid., p. 332.

42 "the El Dorado of their hopes": *State Indiana Sentinel* (May 7, 1846), p. 3.

43 "We are a little wild": Ralph Waldo Emerson to Thomas Carlyle, October 30, 1840, in Charles Eliot Norton, ed., *The Correspondence of Thomas Carlyle and Ralph Waldo Emerson, 1834–1872* (Boston: James R. Osgood and Co., 1883), vol. 1, p. 308.

43 Ceresco: James Weinstein, *The Long Detour: The History and Future of the American Left* (Boulder, Colo.: Westview Press, 2003), p. 12.

43 "Our ulterior aim": Charles Dana, quoted in Chris Jennings, *Paradise Now: The Story of American Utopianism* (New York: Random House, 2016), p. 210.

43 "We would err to dismiss these aspirations": Howe, *What Hath God Wrought*, p. 292.

43 "mal-administration": Strang, *Voree Herald* (March 1846), p. 1.

44 "hardly possible": *Voree Herald* (January 1846), p. 4.

44 "Many of you are about to leave": Ibid., p. 3.

44 "saving their daughters": *Voree Herald* (February 1846), p. 4.

44 incorrectly, as it happened: Explorer John C. Frémont's map depicted the Great Salt Lake and Utah Lake as a single body of water. Seymour I. Schwartz and Ralph E. Ehrenberg, *The Mapping of America* (New York: Harry N. Abrams, 1980), p. 271.

45 "A church without a Prophet": *Voree Herald* (January 1846), p. 4.

45 "a lie—a forgery": Brigham Young, quoted in Quaife, *Kingdom of Saint James*, p. 23.

45 "imperatively necessary" to head west: Quoted in Flanders, *Nauvoo: Kingdom on the Mississippi*, p. 337.

45 "many are turning away": Isaac Chauncey Haight, *The Journal of Isaac Chauncey Haight*, Paul Jones, ed. (Raleigh, N.C.: Lulu Press, 2013), p. 22.

45 many Mormons were "filled with the notion": Isaac Paden, quoted in Richard E. Bennett, *Mormons at the Missouri Winter Quarters, 1846–1852* (Norman: University of Oklahoma Press, 1987), p. 19.

46 "an earnest, energetic manner": *New York Tribune* (July 31, 1846), p. 4.

46 "in his rapid manner": Hajicek, ed., *Chronicles of Voree*, p. 52.

46 "was not able to contend": Ibid., p. 52.

46 300 new recruits: Ibid., p. 57.

46 "considerably bewildered": Quoted in Beam, *American Crucifixion*, p. 247.

47 "The clear authority exercised": Karen Halttunen, *Confidence Men and Painted Women: A Study of Middle-Class Culture in America, 1830–1870* (New Haven, Conn.: Yale University Press, 1982), p. 23.

47 **German physician Franz Anton Mesmer:** Erika Janik, *Marketplace of the Marvelous: The Strange Origins of Modern Medicine* (Boston: Beacon Press, 2014), pp. 147–181.

47 **"meridian of its glory":** *Boston Medical and Surgical Journal* 29, no. 23 (January 10, 1844): p. 466.

48 **"the path between reality and their souls":** Walt Whitman, *Leaves of Grass,* 1st ed. (Brooklyn, N.Y.: Fowler & Wells, 1855), p. v.

48 **"Are you the new person drawn toward me?":** Ibid., 4th ed. (New York: Wm. E. Chapin & Co., 1867), pp. 129–130.

49 **"ancient appearance":** Scott, "James J. Strang in Voree," *Saints' Herald* (December 29, 1888), p. 832.

49 **"owner of a large tract":** *Voree Herald* (May 1846), p. 4.

50 **"a mine of Golden Hope":** Charles Dickens, *American Notes and Pictures from Italy* (New York: Oxford University Press, 1987), p. 171. The other quotations in this passage can be found on pp. 245–246.

51 **500 followers:** Van Noord, *Assassination of a Michigan King,* p. 48.

51 **"like an encampment":** *Voree Herald* (July 1846), p. 1.

51 **"dwell in plain houses":** *Voree Herald* (September 1846), p. 4.

51 **"the place is more prosperous":** Ibid.

51 **were "in destitute condition":** *Louisville Daily Courier* (September 26, 1846), p. 3. The original source of this article apparently was the *St. Louis Republican.*

52 **"destined to make a flourishing town":** *Voree Herald* (September 1846), p. 4.

CHAPTER 4

53 **"Methinks an island":** Nathaniel Hawthorne, *The American Notebooks,* Randall Stewart, ed. (New Haven, Conn.: Yale University Press, 1932), p. 25.

53 **Odawa and Ojibwe:** George A. Anthony, *The Elders Speak: Reflections on Native American Life Centering on Beaver Island, Michigan, in the Nineteenth and Twentieth Centuries* (Beaver Island, Mich.: Beaver Island Historical Society, 2009), pp. 1–3, 39–41, 47, 61–67, 129–132, 139–140; Michael McDonnell, *Masters of Empire: Great Lakes Indians and the Making of America* (New York: Hill & Wang, 2015), pp. 318–327; Charles E. Cleland, *Rites of Conquest: The History and Cultures of Michigan's Native Americans* (Ann Arbor: University of Michigan Press, 1992), pp. 225–230; Charles Garrad, "Some Notes on the Ojibwa (Chippewa) of the Beaver Islands," *Journal of Beaver Island History,* vol. 3, pp. 7–11.

54 **a small community of them still lived there:** James J. Strang, *Ancient*

and Modern Michilimackinac: Including an Account of the Controversy Between Mackinac and the Mormons (St. James, Mich., 1854), p. 21.

54 **"When my eyes"**: Elizabeth Whitney Williams, *A Child of the Sea, and Life Among the Mormons* (New York: J. E. Jewett, 1905), p. 61. Williams was a child on Beaver Island during the time of Strang's colony. According to this account, apparently based on stories she heard while growing up, Strang became aware of the island when the steamer he was on went there to take shelter from a storm.

54 **"alarming progress"**: Quaife, *Kingdom of Saint James*, p. 44.

54 **discussed the island with associates**: Andrew F. Smith, *The Saintly Scoundrel: The Life and Times of Dr. John Cook Bennett* (Urbana: University of Illinois Press, 1997), p. 153.

54 **not to waste their money**: Ibid.

55 **"I do not doubt"**: Charles Darwin, *Journal of Researches into the Natural History and Geology of the Countries Visited During the Voyage of H.M.S. Beagle Round the World, Under the Command of Capt. Fitz Roy, R.N.*, vol. 2 (New York: Harper & Brothers, 1846), p. 310. The book is now better known as *The Voyage of the Beagle*.

55 **"the heart-burnings, the jealousies"**: Herman Melville, *Typee: Complete Text with Introduction, Historical Contexts, Critical Essays*, Geoffrey Sanborn, ed. (Boston: Houghton Mifflin, 2004), p. 126. Other quotes in this passage are from pp. 37 and 39.

57 **"I came to the conclusion"**: Reuben Miller, *James J. Strang, Weighed in the Balance of Truth, and Found Wanting* (Burlington, Wisconsin Territory, 1846), p. 4.

57 **"The whole landscape"**: Melville, *Typee*, p. 57.

57 **"Melville's version of [the] American dream"**: Andrew Delbanco, *Melville: His World and Work* (New York: Vintage Books, 2006), p. 80.

57 **"greatest scamp in the western country"**: Ford, *A History of Illinois*, p. 263.

57 **"bare-faced impudent corruption"**: *New York Daily Herald* (December 26, 1848), p. 2.

58 **granted himself the titles**: *Western Medical Reformer*, extra ed. (October 27, 1845), p. 4.

58 **"gilded hopes"**: Ibid., extra ed. (September 8, 1845), p. 7.

58 **health benefits of the tomato**: Smith, *Saintly Scoundrel*, pp. 34–42.

58 **"savor[ed] of the most arrant quackery"**: *American Agriculturist*, quoted in ibid., pp. 38–39.

58 **the country's first "diploma mill"**: Ibid., pp. 13–25.

58 **"time and energies to the advancement of the cause"**: Bennett, quoted in ibid., p. 55.

58 **2,000 men:** *New York Herald* (June 17, 1842), p. 2.

58 **"the Prophet's great gun":** Ibid.

58 **may have written himself:** Smith, *Saintly Scoundrel,* pp. 72, 212. The article, written by an anonymous "Officer in the Artillery," offered gushing praise for Bennett and was written with his characteristic hyperbole. Some researchers have also ventured that the unnamed author was future Confederate general Robert E. Lee.

59 **"J. C. Bennett, Prince":** Ibid., p. 29.

59 **Already married to someone in Ohio:** Ibid., pp. 78–81.

59 **a term he seems to have introduced:** Brian C. Hales, "John C. Bennett and Joseph Smith's Polygamy: Addressing the Question of Reliability," *Journal of Mormon History* 41, no. 2 (April 2015): pp. 159–160.

60 **"guilty of infidelity, deism, atheism":** John C. Bennett, *The History of the Saints; or, An Exposé of Joe Smith and Mormonism* (Boston: Leland & Whiting, 1842), p. 257.

60 **"a heap of monstrosities"; "too stupid…anybody":** Smith, *Saintly Scoundrel,* pp. 122–128.

60 **to stoke anti-Mormon passions:** Ibid., pp. 134–136.

60 **Bennett was in Cincinnati:** Ibid., pp. 144–146.

60 **"western dolts":** *Boston Medical and Surgical Journal* 30, no. 12 (April 24, 1844): p. 246.

60 **"that notorious personage":** *Western Medical Reformer* 5, no. 1 (June 1845): p. 4.

61 **"I have not been myself":** Bennett to Strang, March 31, 1846, Strang Collection, Beinecke.

61 **"possessed power":** Bennett, *History of the Saints,* p. 10.

61 **"glorious movement":** Bennett to Strang, March 31, 1846, Strang Collection, Beinecke.

61 **"Crowned Imperial Primate":** Ibid.

61 **"one great thing":** Strang, *Diary,* p. 15.

61 **"dreams of empire":** Ibid.

61 **"In person, Strang":** *New York Tribune* (July 31, 1846), p. 4.

62 **"ever to conceal":** quoted in Van Noord, *Assassination of a Michigan King,* which offers a good overview of the Order of the Illuminati, pp. 48–51.

62 **founding a Masonic Lodge in Nauvoo:** Smith, *Saintly Scoundrel,* pp. 75–77. See also John L. Brooke, *The Refiner's Fire: The Making of Mormon Cosmology, 1644–1844* (New York: Cambridge University Press, 1994), pp. 248–253.

62 **"illicit intercourse with a Master Mason's wife":** Smith, *Saintly Scoundrel,* p. 111.

63 "the supreme Law": Quoted in ibid., p. 151.

63 "picking out his victims": *The New Era and Herald of Zion's Watchmen*, vol. 1, no. 2 (February 1847), as transcribed in "Uncle Dale's Old Mormon News Articles," prepared by Dale R. Broadhurst, web.

63 "abject slavery": Quoted in Van Noord, *Assassination of a Michigan King*, p. 62.

63 sex with a fifteen-year-old girl: Smith, *Saintly Scoundrel*, p. 155.

63 "teaching false doctrine": Quoted in ibid.

64 "damning, soul-destroying doctrines": *Voree Herald* (April 1846), p. 4.

64 "destroy a man of distinguished talent": *Zion's Reveille* (December 1846), p. 2. Between November of 1846 and November of 1847, Strang changed the name of his newspaper from the *Voree Herald* to *Zion's Reveille*.

65 "And lo, I beheld a land": *Zion's Reveille* (January 14, 1847), p. 1.

65 "establish a mission among the Indians": *Voree Herald* (October 1846), p. 2.

66 "a significant role in building that new city": Leonard, "Early Saints and the Millennium," *Ensign* 9, no. 8 (August 1979): web.

66 "in the absence of authorized occupation": Acting Commissioner to the General Land Office James H. Piper to John C. Bennett, October 14, 1846, as quoted in Smith, *Saintly Scoundrel*, p. 153.

66 "the vigorous prosecution of the wooding business": *Zion's Reveille* (June 8, 1847), p. 3.

67 "perfect security": Edgar Allan Poe, "Narrative of A. Gordon Pym," in *The Complete Tales and Poems of Edgar Allan Poe* (New York: Vintage Books, 1975), p. 782.

67 Great Dismal Swamp along the Virginia: Richard Grant, "Hell and High Water," *Smithsonian* 47, no. 5 (September 2016): pp. 68–77.

67 "a large number of counterfeiters": *Ottawa Free Trader* (August 27, 1841), p. 2.

67 "repeated instances of their passing": *Vicksburg Daily Whig* (December 10, 1841), p. 2.

68 "placed them on board a trading boat": *Boon's Lick Times* (August 28, 1841), p. 2.

68 "cast upon the bosom": *Mississippi Free Trader* (August 16, 1841), p. 2.

68 "The daring impunity": *North Alabamian* (August 28, 1841), p. 3.

68 "along geographical and political fault lines": Mihm, *Nation of Counterfeiters*, p. 198. Other quotations from this passage can be found on pp. 198 and 159.

69 "Bennett managed matters well": Ford, *A History of Illinois*, p. 263.

69 state legislator named Abraham Lincoln: Smith, *Saintly Scoundrel*, pp. 58–59.

69 "a happy hunting ground": Tyler, *Freedom's Ferment*, p. 103.

69 "thieves, robbers, bogus makers": Daniel Spencer, quoted in Kenneth W. Godfrey, "Crime and Punishment in Mormon Nauvoo, 1839–1846," *BYU Studies Quarterly* 32, no. 1 (Winter and Spring 1991), article 14: p. 213.

69 "a set of fanatics": *New York Tribune* (January 27, 1844), p. 1.

69 known as the Law of Consecration: Godfrey, "Crime and Punishment," pp. 195–227; Michael S. Riggs, "From the Daughters of Zion to the 'Banditti on the Prairies': Danite Influence on the Nauvoo Period," *Restoration Studies* 7 (1998): pp. 95–106; Bill Shepard, "Stealing at Mormon Nauvoo," *The John Whitmer Historical Association Journal* 23 (2003): pp. 91–110.

70 "right to steal": Hyrum Smith, quoted in Shepard, "Stealing at Mormon Nauvoo," p. 94.

70 "Look to thyself, priest": Shelley, *Queen Mab*, p. 41.

70 paradise of peace: Ibid., p. 24.

71 "with less than two days [of] provisions": Strang, *Ancient and Modern Michilimackinac*, p. 22.

71 "The advantages": *Zion's Reveille* (June 1, 1847), p. 3.

CHAPTER 5

72 "'Old man,' said the young one": Mark Twain, *Adventures of Huckleberry Finn* (New York: Charles L. Webster and Co., 1885), p. 162.

72 "I have received information": *Zion's Reveille* (June 1, 1847), pp. 3–4. The notice is signed by Strang and dated May 26.

73 "has been removed from all official standing": *Zion's Reveille* (July 8, 1847), p. 4.

73 "delivered over to the buffetings": Hajicek, ed., *Chronicles of Voree*, p. 157.

73 "qualified to take the position": *New York Times* (August 19, 1867), p. 6.

73 "deceiver of the first class": *New York Times* (March 20, 1867), p. 2.

73 Trained as a tailor: For background on the life of this colorful rogue, see Reed M. Holmes, *Dreamers of Zion: Joseph Smith and George J. Adams* (Portland, Ore.: Sussex Academic Press, 2003), pp. 72–74, as well as Peter Amann, "Prophet of Zion: The Saga of George J. Adams," *New England Quarterly* 37, no. 4 (December 1964): pp. 477–500.

73 "Methodist exhorter": *New York Times* (August 19, 1867), p. 6.

74 nearly 3,000 British converts: Flanders, *Nauvoo: Kingdom on the Mississippi*, p. 71.

75 **"begging money"**: Wilford Woodruff, quoted in Terryl L. Givens and Matthew J. Grow, *Parley P. Pratt: The Apostle Paul of Mormonism* (New York: Oxford University Press, 2011), p. 230. Adams's partners in crime during this spree were Joseph Smith's black-sheep brother William, who later briefly became a member of Strang's church, and Samuel Brannan, who later moved to California—where, after getting kicked out of the Mormon Church, he became the state's first millionaire during the Gold Rush.

75 **"the Kissing Women spiritual wife" doctrine**: Ibid.

75 **nine wives**: Jeffery Ogden Johnson, "Determining and Defining 'Wife': The Brigham Young Households," *Dialogue: A Journal of Mormon Thought* 20, no. 3 (Fall 1987): pp. 57–70.

75 **"diabolical conduct"**: Young, quoted in Holmes, *Dreamers of Zion*, p. 86.

75 **in St. Louis, managing a theater**: Van Noord, *Assassination of a Michigan King*, p. 64.

75 **"the vile, polluted"**: *Illinois Register* (July 7 and 14, 1843), as quoted in Smith, *Saintly Scoundrel*, p. 137.

75 **"first in all things"**: Bennett to Strang, March 24, 1846, Community of Christ Archives, Independence, Mo.

76 **"a base phalshood"**: Adams to Strang, March 27, 1846, Strang Collection, Beinecke.

76 **"all fire"**: John A. Eaton in *The Prophet,* a short-lived Mormon newspaper published in New York (October 12, 1844), p. 1.

76 **"when he came to dwell"**: *Dollar Weekly Bostonian* (June 11, 1842), as transcribed in "Uncle Dale's Old Mormon News Articles," prepared by Dale R. Broadhurst, web.

76 **shared the pulpit**: *Voree Herald* (August 1846), p. 2.

76 **"I am glad"**: Adams to Strang, July 19, 1847, as republished in *Zion's Reveille* (August 19, 1847), p. 4.

76 **"a certain rattle brained Elder"**: Silas Estabrook, *Estabrook's Great Public Chowder: A Journal of Entertainment for the People* (May 8, 1847), p. 1.

77 **"cold, stern, uncommunicative"**: Strang to unknown woman, n.d., Strang Collection, Beinecke.

77 **preached thirty-one sermons**: *Zion's Reveille* (August 19, 1847), p. 3.

77 **had traveled over 16,000 miles**: *Zion's Reveille* (August 12, 1847), p. 3.

77 **(casting his own young son)**: George Clinton Densmore Odell, *Annals of the New York Stage* (New York: AMS Press, 1970), vol. 5, p. 359.

77 **"shining light Shakespearean"**: Philadelphia *Public Ledger* (December 20, 1847), p. 2.

77 **"deemed a better preacher than an actor"**: *New York Herald* (February 10, 1848), p. 4.

77 **"feeling greatly scandalized"**: *Boston Mail,* quoted in Estabrook, *Public Chowder* (May 8, 1847), p. 1.

77 **horsewhipped the man**: The victim of this assault, which made headlines across the country, was Silas Estabrook, a newspaper editor and brilliant satirist. Although he was "handled rather roughly" by Adams, Estabrook continued to skewer his nemesis in print in the aftermath of the attack. Ibid., pp. 1, 3.

77 **"Grand Temperance Rally"**: *Baltimore Sun* (September 15, 1848), p. 2.

78 **opened a saloon**: *Baltimore Sun* (August 21, 1848), p. 2.

78 **the manager of a theater**: *Baltimore Sun* (June 17, 1848), p. 2. See also David L. Rinear, *Stage, Page, Scandals, and Vandals: William E. Burton and Nineteenth-Century American Theatre* (Carbondale: Southern Illinois University Press, 2004), pp. 111–112. The cavernous Front Street Theatre in Baltimore was operated by Burton, a famous impresario, who sometimes turned over its management to visiting performers. This appears to be what happened in the case of Adams.

78 **Junius Brutus Booth**: *Baltimore Sun* (May 29, 1848), p. 3.

78 **"made all sorts of promises"**: *Baltimore Sun* (May 31, 1848), p. 2.

78 **("confined for debts")**: *Baltimore Sun* (June 17, 1848), p. 2.

78 **manager of another theater**: *Baltimore Sun* (August 8, 1848), p. 3.

78 ***Cobb v. Cobb:*** Laurel Thatcher Ulrich, *A House Full of Females: Plural Marriage and Women's Rights in Early Mormonism, 1835–1870* (New York: Knopf, 2017), pp. 105–106, 213–221.

78 **"would lead to the devil"**: Quoted in *Buffalo Commercial* (December 6, 1847), p. 2.

78 **"unmitigated scoundrel"**: *Richmond Weekly Palladium* of Richmond, Ind. (May 14, 1843), p. 2, and *Boston Post* (May 4, 1843), p. 1. An entire book could be written about the exploits of Dr. Charles W. Appleton, temperance lecturer, "besotted vagabond," inventor of elixirs such as "Dr. Appleton's Great Remedy for Deafness," serial seducer, sidekick to George J. Adams, and—for a brief time—convert to James J. Strang's brand of Mormonism. For an overview of his career, see Connell O'Donovan, *Early Boston Mormons and Missionaries, A–C: 1831–1860* (n.p.: 2008), pp. 47–59. See also the *Cincinnati Enquirer* (April 22, 1843), p. 2, and *The Advocate* of Buffalo, N.Y. (May 20, 1852), p. 1, as well as these 1849 issues of the *Gospel Herald:* April 19, p. 3; June 28, pp. 5–6; August 2, pp. 1–2; and August 23, pp. 2–3.

78 **"lecture on love"**: Ad in *Baltimore Sun* (March 8, 1849), p. 2.

78 **"lecture on the passions"**: Ad in *Baltimore Sun* (March 20, 1849), p. 2.

78 **"I long to be with you"**: Adams to Strang, September 8, 1847, as republished in the *Gospel Herald* (October 7, 1847), p. 3. In September

of 1847, Strang changed the name of his newspaper once again—from *Zion's Reveille* to the *Gospel Herald*.

79 **"I am preaching here"**: Adams to Strang, December 28, 1847, as republished in the *Gospel Herald* (January 20, 1848), p. 8.

79 **"Beaver Island, in Lake Michigan"**: *Louisville Daily Courier* (November 30, 1847), p. 2.

79 **full of excommunications**: Hajicek, ed., *Chronicles of Voree*, pp. 143–161.

80 **only 400 people remained**: The *Rock River Pilot* of Watertown, Wisc. (November 24, 1847), p. 2.

80 **"Well, brother, do you wish"**: *Gospel Herald* (October 21, 1847), p. 4.

80 **"several families moved to the Island"**: Strang, *Ancient and Modern Michilimackinac*, p. 22.

80 **"harbor melancholy"**: Lydia Perce to James and Mary Strang, February 23, 1838, Strang Collection, Beinecke.

81 **"wifely relations"**: Speek, *"God Has Made Us a Kingdom,"* p. 63.

81 **three children to be baptized**: Ibid., pp. 62, 266.

81 **lost his close childhood friend**: Ibid., p. 63.

81 **Perce died in Boston**: "Record of the Deaths and Burials in the City of Boston," September 19, 1847, *Massachusetts, Town and Vital Records, 1620–1988*, Ancestry.com, web.

81 **his "mind was dark"**: *Gospel Herald* (November 25, 1847), p. 8.

81 **"an almost universal apprehension"**: David N. Lord, "A Discourse on the Millennial State of the Church," *Theological and Literary Journal* 2, no. 4 (April 1850): p. 657.

CHAPTER 6

82 **"It needs a wild steersman"**: Nathaniel Hawthorne, *The Blithedale Romance: An Authoritative Text, Backgrounds and Sources, Criticism*, Seymour Gross and Rosalie Murphy, eds. (New York: W. W. Norton, 1978), p. 132.

82 **verge of an apocalypse**: Gail E. Husch, *Something Coming: Apocalyptic Expectation and Mid-Nineteenth-Century American Painting* (Hanover, N.H.: University Press of New England, 2000), pp. 1–25.

82 **killed more than a million people**: Howe, *What Hath God Wrought*, p. 823.

82 **death toll of almost 13,000**: Page Smith, *The Nation Comes of Age: A People's History of the Ante-Bellum Years* (New York: McGraw-Hill, 1981), p. 236.

83 **$97 million**: Ibid.

83 **"Events are occurring"**: Albert Barnes, *The Casting Down of Thrones:*

A Discourse on the Present State of Europe (Philadelphia: William Sloanaker, May 1848), pp. 3–4.

83 **"a universal impression exists":** D.C.E., "The Approach of the Millennium Argued from the Signs of the Times," *Christian Review,* vol. 13, pp. 249, 250.

83 **"ominous":** *Gospel Herald* (July 28, 1848), p. 4.

83 **"Let me warn you":** *Zion's Reveille* (August 26, 1847), p. 4.

84 **"Come up to the places":** Ibid.

84 **a huge sea serpent:** *Gospel Herald* (June 8, 1848), p. 4. The brief article did not specify the size of the monster supposedly spotted off Beaver Island. But it compared the serpent to "the kraken, the enormous Norwegian sea monster" mentioned in an accompanying piece. See also pp. 3–4.

84 **many such sightings:** For example, reports about the "Nahant Serpent" off the Massachusetts coast in the *Lancaster Examiner* (January 20, 1847), p. 2, and *Arkansas Intelligencer* (August 7, 1847), p. 2. See also reports of a "Great Sea-Serpent" spotted by the crew of the H.M.S. *Daedalus* in the South Atlantic, which appear in the London *Times* (October 10, 1848), p. 5, and *Zoology: A Popular Miscellany of Natural History,* vol. 6 (1848), pp. vii–xiii, 2307–2324.

84 **"degenerate kingdoms of the wicked world":** Joseph Smith, April 8, 1843, Church of Jesus Christ of Latter-day Saints, *History of the Church of Jesus Christ of Latter-day Saints,* vol. 5 (Salt Lake City, Utah: *Deseret News,* 1909), p. 341.

85 **sixty true believers:** Strang, *Ancient and Modern Michilimackinac,* p. 22.

85 **"destined to have a greater":** Fritz J. Raddatz, *Karl Marx: A Political Biography,* Richard Barry, trans. (Boston: Little, Brown and Co., 1978), pp. 80–81.

85 **"uninterrupted disturbance":** Karl Marx, *The Communist Manifesto: Annotated Text,* Frederic L. Bender, ed. (New York: W. W. Norton, 1988), p. 58. Other quotes can be found on pp. 68 and 84.

86 **another two years:** "Preface to the German Edition of 1872," ibid., p. 46.

86 **"not against the despotism":** *Gospel Herald* (June 29, 1848), p. 1.

86 **"money business":** Strang, *Diary,* p. 59.

87 **"the proletarians have nothing":** Marx, *Communist Manifesto,* p. 86.

87 **the Order of Enoch:** Van Noord, *Assassination of a Michigan King,* pp. 76–78.

87 **150 members:** Ibid., p. 77.

87 **Spartan life:** Speek, *"God Has Made Us a Kingdom,"* pp. 56–57.

87 **left almost as soon:** Ibid., pp. 57–58.

88 **"slow to enter":** *Gospel Herald* (September 21, 1848), p. 6.

88 **"I admonish you to come"**: Ibid. (February 3, 1848), p. 5.

88 **"the historical record"**: E. Mansell Pattison and Robert C. Ness, "New Religious Movements in Historical Perspective," in *Cults and New Religious Movements: A Report from the American Psychiatric Association* (Washington, D.C.: American Psychiatric Association, 1989), p. 59.

88 **Eric Jansson** [spelled "Janson"]: Tyler, *Freedom's Ferment,* pp. 132–139.

88 **"All authority has been given"**: Ibid., p. 134.

89 **at public auction in 1849**: Lindsay Swift, *Brook Farm: Its Members, Scholars, and Visitors* (New York: Macmillan, 1900), p. 25.

89 **its glory days**: Jennings, *Paradise Now,* pp. 189–237.

89 **"rather keep bachelor's hall"**: Thoreau, quoted in ibid., p. 195.

89 **"not put forward"**: Hawthorne, *The Blithedale Romance,* p. 1. Other quotes from the book (in order of their appearance) can be found on pp. 51, 65, 19, and 34.

90 **"men of iron"**: A. N. Kaul, "Community and Society," in ibid., p. 307.

91 **"respectable, princely, bold"**: *New York Daily Herald* (July 11, 1849), p. 1.

91 **"a man of genteel appearance"**: Ibid. (July 8, 1849), p. 2.

91 **"great object of universal devotion"**: Washington Irving, "Creole Village: A Sketch from a Steamboat," *The New-Yorker* (November 12, 1836), p. 115.

92 **("If you ever perceive")**: Poe, "The Business Man," *The Complete Tales and Poems of Edgar Allan Poe,* p. 413.

92 **"ubiquitous personage"**: *Boston Evening Transcript,* quoted in Johannes Dietrich Bergmann, "The Original Confidence Man," *American Quarterly* 21, no. 3 (Autumn 1969): p. 576.

92 **"Arrest of the Confidence Man"**: *New York Daily Herald* (July 8, 1849), p. 2.

92 **"ingenious man of persuasion"**: *New York Daily Herald* (July 14, 1849), p. 1.

92 **"And so,"** writes: Maria Konnikova, *The Confidence Game: Why We Fall for It…Every Time* (New York: Viking, 2016), p. 8.

92–93 **"Samuel Thompson, alias Thomas"**: *New York Daily Herald* (October 10, 1849), p. 4.

93 **two and a half years in state prison**: See *New York Daily Herald* (October 18, 1849), p. 1.

93 **"the commandment to gather"**: *Gospel Herald* (November 8, 1949), p. 4.

93 **a "thunderstruck" victim**: *New York Daily Herald* (October 9, 1849), p. 1.

CHAPTER 7

94 **"Who knows, my dear sir"**: Melville, *The Confidence-Man*, p. 27.

94 **"In our great cities"**: T. S. Arthur, "American Characteristics: No V.—The Daguerreotypist," *Godey's Lady's Book*, vol. 39 (May 1849): p. 352.

94 **"All you have to do"**: *Niles' National Register* (May 30, 1840), vol. 58, p. 208. Exposure times had sped up between 1840, when the quoted article was written, and 1849, when Charles J. Douglass posed for a picture. But as of 1853, "the time usually occupied in what is generally called, 'taking a likeness,' is from fifteen to twenty seconds and upwards," according to the *New York Tribune* (April 30, 1853), p. 6.

95 **"Creating man's perfect image"**: Henry Fitz, *The Layman's Legacy, or Thirty-Five Sermons on Important Subjects; Containing the Conclusion of the Whole Matter*, vol. 2 (New York: P. Price, 1840), p. 316.

95 **new tabernacle**: Strang, *Ancient and Modern Michilimackinac*, pp. 23–24.

95 **"while so many are homeless"**: *Gospel Herald* (May 3, 1849), p. 2.

96 **"a more favorable impression"**: Strang, *Ancient and Modern Michilimackinac*, p. 23.

96 **approximately 250 souls**: See Van Noord's calculation of the population at this time in *Assassination of a Michigan King*, p. 73.

96 **"We left things prospering"**: *Gospel Herald* (October 11, 1849), p. 3.

96 **baptism for the dead**: Ibid. (August 30, 1849), p. 3.

96 **a life expectancy**: Herbert S. Klein, *A Population History of the United States* (New York: Cambridge University Press, 2004), p. 101.

96 **"from the bathing-pool"**: Hajicek, ed., *Chronicles of Voree*, p. 195.

96 **James K. Polk**: *Gospel Herald* (August 30, 1849), p. 3.

97 **Reuben Miller and other enemies**: See Richard Lloyd Anderson, "Reuben Miller, Recorder of Oliver Cowdery's Reaffirmations," *BYU Studies Quarterly* 8, no. 3 (July 1968): pp. 277–293. Miller sold his farm near Voree on June 10, 1848, and departed the area on September 12. He made his way to the Salt Lake Valley and assumed a prominent role in Brigham Young's branch of the church.

97 **"a traveling friend"**: Strang to John Ursbruck, November 20, 1849, Strang Collection, Beinecke.

97 **"I am informed"**: Gilbert Watson to Strang, February 11, 1850, as quoted in Speek, *"God Has Made Us a Kingdom,"* p. 73.

98 **practically everyone aboard**: *Gospel Herald* (September 27, 1849), p. 2.

98 **that he would help with the childcare**: Mary Strang to James Strang, January 9, 1850, Strang Collection, Beinecke.

98 **one-third of all white children**: Howe, *What Hath God Wrought*, p. 37.

98 **"I have had two of them"**: Mary Strang to James Strang, January 9, 1850, Strang Collection, Beinecke.

98 **"in constant reddiness"**: Mary Strang to James Strang, December 1849, ibid.

99 **"Do write something"**: Mary Strang to James Strang, January 9, 1850, ibid.

99 **to cut her off from the outside world**: See Mary Strang to James Strang, December 1849, ibid., in which she adds an especially poignant postscript: "I have heard nothing from home or from my relations since I left home."

99 **"There exists in the minds of men"**: S. Margaret Fuller, *Woman in the Nineteenth Century* (New York: Greeley & McElrath, 1845), p. 22.

99 **"first statement of American feminism"**: Smith, *Nation Comes of Age*, p. 726.

99 **was "so narrow"**: Fuller, *Woman in the Nineteenth Century*, p. 62.

99 **"Male and female"**: Ibid., p. 103.

100 **"Charley's a gal!"**: James and Clarissa Canney to James Strang, June 16, 1850, Strang Collection, Beinecke. Various correspondents also spelled the name *Charlie*. For the sake of consistency, I use *Charley* in all references.

100 **"from the crown of his head"**: Peter Hess to Strang, November 22, 1849, ibid. Hess was reporting on another man's conclusions, which he didn't want to believe.

100 **"a mess of bloody cloths"**: James and Clarissa Canney to James Strang, June 16, 1850, ibid.

100 **"Don't you know"**: Strang to John Ursbruck, November 20, 1849, ibid.

101 **"I now say distinctly"**: *Zion's Reveille* (August 12, 1847), p. 4.

101 **to "sound out" Elvira**: Speek, *"God Has Made Us a Kingdom,"* pp. 67–68; Quaife, *Kingdom of Saint James*, pp. 100–101.

101–102 **a "frigging spree"**: Gilbert Watson to Strang, October 7, 1849, as quoted in Van Noord, *Assassination of a Michigan King*, p. 83.

102 **"expert in the use of a rifle"**: "In Memoriam: Mrs. Elvira E. Baker," Strang Collection, Library of Michigan.

102 **only a dollar a week**: Ibid., as well as *History of Wages in the United States from Colonial Times to 1928* (Washington, D.C.: United States Government Printing Office, 1934), pp. 133, 136.

102 **viewed his proposition as a command from God**: Speek, *"God Has Made Us a Kingdom,"* p. 68.

103 **"discovered to be a disguised woman"**: "William Newcomb [*sic*]," Record of Service Card, Mexican War, 1846–1847, Office of Adjutant General, box 62, reel s00912, Missouri State Archives.

103 **"the fatigues of the campaign"**: New Orleans *Times-Picayune* (January 8, 1848), p. 4. The original source for this article seems to be the *St. Louis Republican.*

103 **400 women**: Gayle V. Fischer, *Pantaloons and Power: A Nineteenth-Century Dress Reform in the United States* (Kent, Ohio: Kent State University Press, 2001), p. 148.

103 **"Anecdotal evidence"**: Ibid., p. 147.

103 **six or seven petticoats**: Ibid., p. 20.

103 **"There never was a period"**: James Laver, quoted in ibid.

103 **"a woman achieved 'true womanhood'"**: Ibid., p. 24.

104 **"entrenched ideas"**: Ibid., p. 148.

104 **"We would have every arbitrary barrier"**: Fuller, *Woman in the Nineteenth Century*, p. 26.

104 **"wore disguises"**: Julia Ward Howe, *The Hermaphrodite*, Gary Williams, ed. (Lincoln: University of Nebraska Press, 2004), p. 121.

104 **"He is quite anxious"**: A. J. Graham to Strang, January 22, 1850, Strang Collection, Beinecke.

CHAPTER 8

106 **"I am eternally tired"**: Quoted in David S. Reynolds, *John Brown, Abolitionist: The Man Who Killed Slavery, Sparked the Civil War, and Seeded Civil Rights* (New York: Knopf, 2005), p. 159.

106 **"no food, no gun"**: R. H. Dana Jr., "How We Met John Brown," *Atlantic Monthly*, vol. 28, no. 165 (July 1871), pp. 1–9. All of Dana's recollections of the encounter are from this essay.

107 **100,000 slaves**: Andrew Delbanco, *The War Before the War: Fugitive Slaves and the Struggle for America's Soul from the Revolution to the Civil War* (New York: Penguin, 2018), p. 25. Delbanco points out that there are no firm statistics on escapes and that all estimates are largely a matter of guesswork.

107 **a ship called the *Pearl***: Ibid., pp. 213–215, as well as Manisha Sinha, *The Slave's Cause: A History of Abolition* (New Haven, Conn.: Yale University Press, 2016), pp. 401–403.

107 **"unfortunate slaves"**: *Gospel Herald* (June 21, 1848), p. 1.

107 **great American bestseller**: Brenda Wineapple, *Ecstatic Nation: Confidence, Crisis, and Compromise, 1848–1877* (New York: HarperCollins, 2013), pp. 47–48; and Michael Winship, "Two Early American Bestsellers: Rowson's *Charlotte Temple* and Stowe's *Uncle Tom's Cabin*," *Common-Place: The Interactive Journal of Early American Life*, vol. 9, no. 3 (April 2009), web.

108 **"There are thousands"**: Henry David Thoreau, *Civil Disobedience, and Other Essays* (New York: Dover Publications, 1993), pp. 4, 5, 7.

109 **his support for "universal liberty"**: Strang's original letter has apparently not survived, but Hazeltine quotes this phrase in his response. See Abner Hazeltine to Strang, January 30, 1837, Strang Collection, Beinecke.

109 **into the hands of people in the South**: Hazeltine did not specifically mention where the newspapers were to be circulated, but it's clear that he was referring to an ongoing campaign to smuggle abolitionist literature into the South, where distributing such materials was sometimes punished by death. See Sinha, *The Slave's Cause*, pp. 250–251.

109 **counted on slave labor**: Gary Robertson, "Canal Was Carved with Slave Labor—Waterway's Construction Was a Demanding Task," *Richmond Times-Dispatch*, city ed. (September 26, 1999), p. A-1.

110 **"The cause of so much sickness here"**: Strang to W. L. Perce, July 2, 1837, Strang Collection, Beinecke.

111 **"because of their iniquity"**: The Book of Mormon, 2nd Nephi, 5:21.

111 **"have souls & are subjects"**: Smith, quoted in W. Paul Reeve, *Religion of a Different Color: Race and the Mormon Struggle for Whiteness* (New York: Oxford University Press, 2015), p. 127.

111 **"If they were far away"**: Young, quoted in John G. Turner, *Brigham Young, Pioneer Prophet* (Cambridge, Mass.: Belknap Press of Harvard University Press, 2012), p. 222.

111 **"the Negro is cursed"**: John W. Gunnison, quoted in Reeve, *Religion of a Different Color*, p. 147.

111 **"involuntary labor"**: Ibid.

111 **"a firm believer in slavery"**: Young, quoted in Turner, *Brigham Young*, p. 225.

111 **"negroes shall not rule us"**: Ibid., p. 226.

111 **American Moral Reform Society**: Eric Rose, "American Moral Reform Society," in *Encyclopedia of African American History*, vol. 1, Leslie M. Alexander and Walter C. Rucker, eds. (Santa Barbara, Calif.: ABC-CLIO, 2010), pp. 309–310. See also Howard H. Bell, "The American Moral Reform Society, 1836–1841," *Journal of Negro Education* 27, no. 1 (Winter 1958): pp. 34–40.

112 **"visionary in the extreme"**: Samuel E. Cornish, editor of *The Colored American*, quoted in Bell, "The American Moral Reform Society," p. 36.

112 **(seconded by Walker)**: *Early Negro Writing, 1760–1837*, Dorothy Parker, ed. (Baltimore: Black Classics Press, 1995), p. 219.

112 **later joined a Protestant congregation**: In 1860, Walker was listed as the sexton of the Bethesda Congregational Church in New York City, where he worked alongside abolitionist pastor Charles B. Ray. See *Trow's New*

York City Directory: For the Year Ending May 1, 1861, vol. 74 (New York: John F. Trow, 1860), p. 13.

112 "the impression had gone forth": *Gospel Herald* (November 15, 1849), p. 5.

112 129 years before Brigham Young's branch: The church did not lift its ban on the ordination of African Americans until 1978 and did not issue a comprehensive disavowal of its past racism until 2013. See Robert A. Rees, "Long-Awaited Day Has Finally Arrived for Mormons," *Oakland Tribune* (December 14, 2013).

112 "the theories advanced in the past": Statement of the church, quoted in ibid.

113 a new name—Harriet Tubman: Sinha, *The Slave's Cause,* pp. 438–439.

113 "the year of remarkable slave escapes": Ibid., p. 438.

114 made Henry "Box" Brown famous: Delbanco, *War Before the War,* p. 215.

114 "originally and radically distinct": Josiah C. Nott, quoted in Alexander Tsesis, *We Shall Overcome: A History of Civil Rights and the Law* (New Haven, Conn.: Yale University Press, 2008), p. 54.

114 "the attention and homage": William Craft, *Running a Thousand Miles for Freedom; or, The Escape of William and Ellen Craft from Slavery* (London: William Tweedie, 1860), p. 52.

114 "an incident of courage": Wendell Phillips, quoted in William Lloyd Garrison's abolitionist newspaper the *Liberator* (February 2, 1849), p. 3.

116 "some rather lonesome evenings": "C. J. Douglass" to Strang, February 4, 1850, Strang Collection, Beinecke.

116 "Her death has shocked me": Mary Strang to James Strang, January 9, 1850, ibid.

116 "I have not been well": James Strang, draft of a letter to Mary Strang, January 25, 1850, ibid.

117 obsession with "not sinking": Tocqueville, *Democracy in America,* p. 250.

117 "cannot safely remain in the union": Calhoun to James H. Hammond, February 16, 1850, *Correspondence of John C. Calhoun,* vol. 2, part 1 (Washington, D.C.: Government Printing Office, 1900), p. 781.

117 "slavery can only end in blood": Frederick Douglass, *The Life and Times of Frederick Douglass, Written by Himself* (Hartford, Conn.: Park Publishing Co., 1882), p. 342.

117 "for the emancipation of the negro race": Quoted in Tony Horwitz, *Midnight Rising: John Brown and the Raid That Sparked the Civil War* (New York: Henry Holt, 2011), p. 31.

117 "It would have been past belief": Dana, "How We Met John Brown," p. 7.

119 **"We felt very bad"**: Abigail Strang to James Strang, May 1850, Strang Collection, Beinecke.

CHAPTER 9

120 **"But the emperor has nothing"**: Hans Christian Andersen, "The Emperor's New Clothes." The version I use in this chapter is from the *Brooklyn Daily Eagle*, edited by a young Walt Whitman (December 31, 1847), p. 1. It appears to have been adapted from Charles Boner's translation of the story, published in *The Nightingale and Other Stories* (London: Joseph Cundall, 1846).

120 **coronation of Queen Victoria**: Helen Rappaport, *Queen Victoria: A Biographical Companion* (Santa Barbara, Calif.: ABC-CLIO, 2003), pp. 359–360; Julia Baird, *Victoria the Queen: An Intimate Biography of the Woman Who Ruled an Empire* (New York: Random House, 2017), pp. 73–83; Marc Alexander, *Britain's Royal Heritage: An A to Z of the Monarchy* (Stroud, U.K.: History Press, 2001), p. 61; Philip Schwyzer, *Shakespeare and the Remains of Richard III* (New York: Oxford University Press, 2013), p. 106; "Westminster Abbey," *The Hutchinson Unabridged Encyclopedia with Atlas and Weather Guide* (2018), web; "Westminster Abbey," History.com, web; "Stone of Scone," *Encyclopedia Britannica* (April 30, 2018), web; "Golden Coach Fit for a King," CNN.com (June 4, 2002), web.

120 **coronation of King James**: Stephen Post, "Account of travel to Beaver Island for conference," Stephen Post papers, Church History Library, pp. 14, 16–18.

121 **people who "dream by day"**: Edgar Allan Poe, "Eleonora," *The Works of the Late Edgar Allan Poe: With Notices of His Life and Genius,* vol. 1, Rufus Wilmot Griswold, ed. (New York: J. S. Redfield, 1850), p. 446.

122 **a "regular tearer"**: *Kenosha Telegraph* (June 7, 1850), p. 2.

122 **"for the purpose of breaking up"**: Quoted in Speek, *"God Has Made Us a Kingdom,"* p. 118.

122 **"A dozen men"**: Strang, *Ancient and Modern Michilimackinac,* p. 24.

123 **"no longer submit to injury"**: Elvira Field Strang and Charles J. Strang, "Biographical Sketch of James J. Strang," p. 22.

123 **"a piece of lead"**: Post, "Account of travel to Beaver Island," p. 12.

123 **"not a little alarmed"**: See Strang's later account in the *Northern Islander* (March 2, 1854), p. 1. He also described his acts of sabotage in this piece.

123 **the entire crisis was manufactured**: Van Noord, *Assassination of a Michigan King,* pp. 103–104.

123–124 **"There was a curtain drawn"**: Chauncy Loomis, "Experience on Beaver Island with James J. Strang," *Saints' Herald,* vol. 35, no. 45 (November 10, 1888), p. 718.

124 **"One day a couple of swindlers"**: Andersen, "The Emperor's New Clothes," *Brooklyn Daily Eagle* (December 31, 1847), p. 1.

125 **235 lonely souls**: Van Noord, *Assassination of a Michigan King,* p. 106.

125 **"did not attend"**: Williams, *Child of the Sea,* p. 137.

126 **"towered over the short-statured King"**: Cecelia Hill, "Mrs. Cecelia Hill's Recollections," in Legler, *A Moses of the Mormons,* pp. 163–164. Hill was about fifteen years old at the time of the coronation.

126 **lineage traced directly back to David**: Van Noord, *Assassination of a Michigan King,* p. 106.

126 **one of David's descendants would rule**: Victor L. Ludlow, "David, Prophetic Figure of Last Days," in *Encyclopedia of Mormonism,* Daniel H. Ludlow, ed. (New York: Macmillan, 1991), pp. 360–361.

126 **"were made to resemble"**: Post, "Account of travel to Beaver Island," p. 17.

126 **"large numbers of lady saints**: *Kenosha Telegraph* (June 7, 1850), p. 2.

126 **"dressed in drawers & skirts"**: Post, "Account of travel to Beaver Island," journal entry for July 3, 1850, pp. 7–8.

127 **Amelia Bloomer**: Fischer, *Pantaloons and Power,* pp. 79–83.

127 **"ten or fifteen pounds of petticoat"**: Bloomer, quoted in the *Brooklyn Daily Eagle* (April 14, 1851), p. 2.

127 **the Oneida Community**: Fischer, *Pantaloons and Power,* pp. 53–62.

128 **"semi-masculine attire"**: Harriet Noyes Skinner, quoted in ibid., p. 59.

128 **"social control"**: Ibid., p. 70.

128 **"Standardized apparel enabled Strang"**: Ibid., p 71.

128 **"in preference to the laws"**: "Book of the Covenant," quoted in Speek, *"God Has Made Us a Kingdom,"* p. 116.

128 **"with uplifted hands"**: Warren Post, quoted in ibid., p. 122. This witness was the brother of Stephen Post, who also supplied an account of the event.

128 **"testimony to the nation"**: This document was published in the *Gospel Herald* (June 6, 1850).

129 **"Long live James"**: Post, "Account of travel to Beaver Island," p. 19.

129 **used *cognitive dissonance* to describe**: See Joel Cooper, *Cognitive Dissonance: Fifty Years of a Classic Theory* (Los Angeles: SAGE, 2007), pp. 2–5.

129 **"But the emperor and the courtiers"**: Andersen, "The Emperor's New Clothes," *Brooklyn Daily Eagle* (December 31, 1847), p. 1.

CHAPTER 10

130 **"Was [he], then, a pirate"**: James Fenimore Cooper, *The Sea Lions; or The Lost Sealers* (New York: Stringer & Townsend, 1849), p. 67.

130 **God had given**: Post, "Account of travel to Beaver Island for conference," p. 20. See also James J. Strang, *The Book of the Law of the Lord, Consisting of an Inspired Translation of Some of the Most Important Parts of the Law Given to Moses, and a Very Few Additional Commandments, with Brief Notes and References* (St. James, Mich.: Printed by command of the King, at the Royal Press, 1851), pp. 50–51. Strang's sweeping code of conduct for his followers contains a revelation he received on the day of his coronation: "I have appointed the islands of the great lakes for the gathering of the saints, saith the Lord God."

130 **to purchase a boat**: Van Noord, *Assassination of a Michigan King*, p. 99.

131 **perfect vessels of pirates**: David Corrodingly, *Under the Black Flag: The Romance and Reality of Life Among the Pirates* (New York: Random House, 2006), pp. 168–171.

131 *Get rich quick:* Although the *Oxford English Dictionary* records this phrase as entering the lexicon only in 1891, numerous examples can be found in antebellum newspapers. See, for example, the *Nashville Union and American* (December 28, 1855), p. 2, in which one correspondent describes his experiences in the California Gold Rush: "I wanted to get rich quick and would not pursue any business that did not promise an immediate yield."

131 **$42 million worth of gold**: Malcolm J. Rohrbough, *Days of Gold: The California Gold Rush and the American Nation* (Berkeley: University of California Press, 1997), p. 35. Federal expenditures for that year were around $40 million. See Richard F. Selcer, *Civil War America, 1850 to 1875* (New York: Facts on File, 2006), p. 77.

131 **"The frenzy continues to increase"**: George Templeton Strong, quoted in Smith, *The Nation Comes of Age*, p. 456.

131 **"The coming of the Messiah"**: Unnamed newspaper, quoted in ibid.

131 **"surrounded by desperadoes"**: *Gospel Herald* (March 8, 1849), p. 1.

132 **"men, women & children"**: Gilbert Watson to Strang, November 30, 1849, as quoted in Speek, *"God Has Made Us a Kingdom,"* p. 98.

132 **90,000 gold-seekers**: Kevin Starr and Richard J. Orsi, eds., *Rooted in Barbarous Soil: People, Culture, and Community in Gold Rush California* (Berkeley: University of California Press, 2000), p. 57.

132 **"Our enemies think"**: Benjamin Wright to Strang, January 29, 1850, as quoted in Speek, *"God Has Made Us a Kingdom,"* p. 102.

133 **"The 'consecrating' of 'Gentile' property"**: Morgan Lewis Leach, *A*

History of the Grand Traverse Region, Published in the Grand Traverse Herald (Traverse City, Mich: n.p., 1883), p. 31.

133 "We are going into the gentiles": Adams to Strang, February 18, 1850, Strang Collection, Beinecke.

133 "plundering operations": Leach, *History of the Grand Traverse Region,* p. 31.

134 "weather beaten hulk": *Oswego Palladium* (December 30, 1876), p. 4. All of the old sailor's recollections are from this same article.

135 with a seated Lady Liberty: This description is based on surviving U.S. half dollars minted in 1850.

136 "He wanted men to go off": Deposition of Daniel S. Wheelock, *United States v. James J. Strang,* June 19, 1851, James J. Strang Papers, Burton Historical Collection, Detroit Public Library.

136 "church and state were united": Elvira Field Strang and Charles J. Strang, "Biographical Sketch of James J. Strang," unpublished manuscript, Library of Michigan, p. 21.

136 the 1850 census: Speek, *"God Has Made Us a Kingdom,"* p. 114.

136 "He made a great joke of this": Williams, *Child of the Sea,* p. 79.

136 "lewd woman": Post, "Account of travel to Beaver Island," p. 7.

137 "hidden truths": *Gospel Herald* (September 27, 1849), p. 1. Strang began mentioning the existence of these plates as early as February of 1849. See *Gospel Herald* (March 1, 1849), p. 2.

137 "defer my species-paper": Darwin to J. D. Hooker, October 12, 1849, in Charles Darwin, *Charles Darwin's Letters: A Selection, 1825–1859,* Frederick Burkhardt, ed. (Cambridge: Cambridge University Press, 1996), p. 111.

138 "Different islands": Darwin, *Journal of Researches,* vol. 2, p. 166.

138 "a little world within itself": Ibid., p. 145.

138 "the sincere believers": Leach, *History of the Grand Traverse Region,* p. 30. The other descriptions of factions on the island can be found on pp. 30–31.

CHAPTER 11

140 "Does all the world act?": Melville, *The Confidence-Man,* p. 40.

140 as an "eccentric genius": *Brooklyn Daily Eagle* (August 31, 1850), p. 2.

140 "was taken suddenly drunk": *New York Times* (August 19, 1857), p. 6.

141 "was anything but pleasing": Helen Mar Whitney, "Scenes and Incidents in Nauvoo," *Woman's Exponent,* vol. 11, no. 12 (November 15, 1882), p. 90. The author of this article was one of Joseph Smith's many plural wives. Marrying the prophet when she was only fourteen years old, she

performed in *Pizarro* with Adams, whom she called "a very good actor," when she was fifteen.

141 **"The discipline of the Church":** "King of the Saints," *New York Times* (September 3, 1882), p. 10. Elvira and her son Charles provided much of the information for this article, which credits the manuscript biography that Charles Strang compiled, as well as "data furnished by his mother."

142 **"one of the best women":** Adams to Strang, January 15, 1850, Strang Collection, Beinecke.

142 **a letter from Caroline Adams:** This letter—dated May 7, 1850—appears, apparently in full, in an extraordinary document that Strang published shortly after Adams fled the kingdom. Entitled "Traveling Theatre Royal, Late from Beaver Island. Adams' New Drama," the broadside presents itself as the plot summary of a play, "The Famous Original Five Act Drama 'Improving the Household,' by Mr. G. J. Adams, Author, Manager and Star Actor." For more background, see Richard L. Saunders, ed., *Dale Morgan on the Mormons: Collected Works, Part 1, 1939–1951* (Norman: The Arthur H. Clark Co., University of Oklahoma Press, 2012), pp. 422–423.

142 **"she breathed her last":** Letter from Margaret Duff to Adams, August 27, 1850, reprinted in "Theatre Royal, Late from Beaver Island," Strang Collection, Beinecke.

142 **the woman's real identity was Louisa Pray:** Strang described her as "a woman of indifferent fame in Boston, by the name of Louisa Pray, *alias* Louisa Cogswell." *Northern Islander* (December 12, 1850), p. 2.

142 **"graceful and popular danseuse":** *Chicago Tribune* (November 19, 1857), p. 1.

142 **"the gambler, the thief":** The author of this exposé, *Dashes at City Life* (Boston: Berry and Co., 1853), went by the pseudonym *Our Ned*. See pp. 5 and 79.

143 **swindled out of a paycheck:** *Baltimore Sun* (May 31, 1848), p. 2.

143 **"a literary embarrassment":** Julie A. Carlson, "Trying Sheridan's *Pizarro*," *Texas Studies in Literature and Language* 38, no. 3/4 (Fall/Winter 1996): p. 359.

144 **the first Mormon theatrical production:** Stanley W. Kimball, "Discovery: Also Starring Brigham Young," *Ensign* 5, no. 10 (October 1975): pp. 51–52.

144 **"a most irresistibly ludicrous account":** *New York Daily Tribune* (June 5, 1844), p. 1. The piece originated in the *Warsaw Signal,* an anti-Mormon publication in Illinois.

144 **"At times nearly the whole audience":** Whitney, "Scenes and Incidents," p. 90.

144 **Mormon audiences:** See Noel A. Carmack, "A Note on Nauvoo Theatre," *BYU Studies Quarterly* 34, no. 1 (1994): pp. 94–100. See also Jeremy Ravi Mumford, "The Inca Priest on the Mormon Stage: A Native American Melodrama and a New American Religion," *Common-place: The Interactive Journal of Early American Life,* vol. 5, no. 4 (July 2005), web.

145 **"Mormon national play":** Selena Couture and Alexander Dick's introduction to Richard Brinsley Sheridan, *Pizarro* (Peterborough, Ontario: Broadview Press, 2017), p. 55.

145 **"youth...loveliness":** Richard Brinsley Sheridan, *Pizarro: A Play, in Five Acts,* adapted from the German of Augustus von Kotzebue (New York: Samuel French & Son, 1850), p. 23. This version is the source of all the quotations from the play used in this chapter.

145 **(Neither of the two people):** Depositions of Daniel S. Wheelock and Asa C. B. Field, *United States v. James J. Strang,* June 19, 1851, Strang Papers, Burton Historical Collection. Wheelock, who played violin in the production of *Pizarro,* said he "did not recollect Miss Field being there." Field, whose relation to Elvira, if any, is unclear, also made no mention of her being in the play.

146 **"one man shall have but one wife":** Post, "Account of travel to Beaver Island," p. 19.

147 **"extremely feeble":** Deposition of Hezekiah McCulloch, *United States v. James J. Strang,* June 20, 1851, Strang Papers, Burton Historical Collection.

147 **"The exterior life is but a masquerade":** Mrs. Harrison Smith, "Who Is Happy?" *Godey's Lady's Book,* vol. 18 (May 1839), p. 214.

148 **"corrupt men":** Benjamin Wright to Strang, August 1, 1850, as quoted in Speek, "*God Has Made Us a Kingdom,*" p. 126.

148 **"Oh! James":** Adams to Strang, August 1, 1850, Strang Collection, Beinecke.

149 **"the obscurest man of letters":** Nathaniel Hawthorne, *Twice-Told Tales,* vol. 1, new ed. (Boston: Ticknor and Fields, 1865), p. iii.

149 **"like a man talking to himself":** Quoted in Norman Holmes Pearson, "Elizabeth Peabody on Hawthorne," *Essex Institute Historical Collections,* vol. 94, no. 3 (July 1958), p. 261.

149 **sold out an initial press run:** Brenda Wineapple, *Hawthorne: A Life* (New York: Knopf, 2003), p. 216.

149 **"the inmost Me":** Nathaniel Hawthorne, *The Scarlet Letter and Other Writings: Authoritative Texts, Contexts, Criticism,* Leland S. Person, ed., Norton Second Critical Edition (New York: W. W. Norton, 2017), p. 7.

149 **"No man, for any considerable period":** Ibid., p. 129.

150 **"putting off one exterior":** Hawthorne, *The House of Seven Gables,* p. 155.

150 **"continually changing his whereabout":** Ibid., p. 155.

150 **"Though now but twenty-two years old":** Ibid., p. 154–155.

151 **("assumed a new name"):** *Northern Islander* (June 19, 1856), p. 2.

151 **"Look Out for the ScoundreL":** New Orleans *Times-Picayune* (December 6, 1845), p. 3.

152 **"He is a mirror":** Henry Ward Beecher, *Lectures to Young Men, on Various Important Subjects* (Salem, Mass.: John P. Jewett & Co., 1846), p. 125.

152 **"jealous of Dr. Akenside":** Strang, "Theatre Royal, Late from Beaver Island."

152 **"My Sufferings":** Ibid.

153 **her life would be in danger:** According to a later account in Strang's newspaper, Louisa claimed the prophet had told her that if she did not leave the island he would ride her out backward on the back of a black ram—a traditional ritual for shaming prostitutes. *Northern Islander* (February 2, 1854), p. 1.

153 **she produced a bowie knife:** Speek, *"God Has Made Us a Kingdom,"* p. 128.

153 **"gross slander and personal insult":** *Detroit Advertiser* (June 6, 1851), p. 2.

153 **"May disease rot my bones":** Quoted in Van Noord, *Assassination of a Michigan King,* p. 113.

153 **"the church would not countenance":** Quoted in ibid.

154 **"war of extermination":** Testimony of James M. Greig, *United States v. James J. Strang, Detroit Advertiser* (July 9, 1851), p. 3.

154 **"obtained a precarious subsistence":** *Northern Islander* (June 19, 1856), p. 2.

154 **"a continually shifting apparition":** Hawthorne, *The House of the Seven Gables,* p. 81.

CHAPTER 12

155 **"I was not born to fortune":** Strang, *Diary,* p. 55.

155 **"I was just an apprentice":** Fillmore to Day O. Kellogg, July 24, 1872, Raab Collection site, web.

155 **"Sir, The melancholy":** Secretary of State John M. Clayton et al. to Millard Fillmore, July 9, 1850, in James D. Richardson, ed., *A Compilation of the Messages and Papers of the Presidents,* vol. 6 (New York: Bureau of National Literature, 1917), p. 2589.

156 **"My advice has neither"**: Quoted in Robert J. Scarry, *Millard Fillmore* (Jefferson, N.C.: McFarland & Co., 2001), p. 167.

156 **"The shock is so sudden"**: Ibid., p. 154.

156 **"His Majesty"**: *Detroit Free Press* (May 28, 1851), p. 2.

156 **"His Accidency"**: *Brooklyn Daily Eagle* (September 14, 1850), p. 2.

157 **"self-confessed impostor"**: See Loomis, "Experience on Beaver Island," p. 718.

157 **"more like a gang of pirates"**: Mackinac resident Isaac Whicher, in a letter to the *Detroit Advertiser* (July 16, 1851), p. 2.

157 **"THE MORMON COMMOTION"**: *Baltimore Sun* (November 9, 1850), p. 1.

157 **"your ignorance has shielded me"**: Quoted in *Northern Islander* (December 12, 1850), p. 3.

158 **"a brilliant public speaker"**: Michigan Historical Commission, "George C. Bates," in *Michigan Historical Collections,* vol. 9 (Lansing, Mich.: Throp & Godfrey, 1886), p. 87.

158 **"a decided favorite with the ladies"**: Robert B. Ross, *Early Bench and Bar of Detroit from 1805 to the End of 1850* (Detroit: Richard P. Joy and Clarence M. Burton, 1907), p. 26. The descriptions of Bates's appearance, personality, and speaking style are from pp. 25–27.

159 **"this Mormon element"**: George C. Bates, "The Beaver Island Prophet," in Michigan Historical Commission, *Michigan Historical Collections,* vol. 32, p. 226.

159 **"credibly informed"**: Bates to Crittenden, March 16, 1851, quoted in Van Noord, *Assassination of a Michigan King,* p. 128.

159 **Millard Fillmore "means well"**: *New York Tribune* (April 1, 1852), p. 4.

159 **"God knows that I detest slavery"**: Quoted in Scarry, *Millard Fillmore,* p. 181.

160 **"man of hesitation"**: Quoted in Frederick W. Seward, ed., *Seward at Washington, as Senator and Secretary of State: A Memoir of His Life, With Selections from His Letters, 1846–1861* (New York: Derby and Miller, 1891), p. 145.

160 **"Being a very cautious, cold, and calculating man"**: Bates, "Beaver Island Prophet," p. 227.

160 **"a pack of outlaws"**: Mormon emissary Almon W. Babbitt, quoted in Wayne K. Hinton, "Millard Fillmore, Utah's Friend in the White House," *Utah Historical Quarterly* 48, no. 2 (Spring 1980): p. 118.

160 **"Because God told me so"**: Quoted in Stanley P. Hirshson, *The Lion of the Lord: A Biography of Brigham Young* (New York: Knopf, 1969), p. 111.

161 **"a religious tolerance few possessed"**: Angus E. Crane, "Millard Fillmore and the Mormons," in *Journal of the West* 34 (January 1995): p. 70.

161 **Young had admitted to having "only" twenty-six wives:** The source of this report is somewhat unclear, given that Young didn't officially acknowledge the practice of polygamy in the church until 1852.

161 **"This is the Governor of Utah":** *Vermont Journal* (May 9, 1851), p. 2.

161 **"some of the opposition presses":** *Hartford Courant* (July 18, 1851), p. 2.

161 **"lend the power":** Bates, "Beaver Island Prophet," p. 227.

162 **"eight or ten drunken Irishmen":** *Northern Islander* (May 1, 1851), p. 2.

162 **"war and annihilation":** Strang, *Ancient and Modern Michilimackinac,* p. 29.

162 **a harrowing escape:** Ibid., pp. 29–30.

162 **a $300 reward:** Ibid., p. 30.

162 **"interchange of civilities":** *Buffalo Commercial* (May 17, 1851), p. 2.

162 **"it would seem probable":** Frank H. Severance, ed., *Millard Fillmore Papers,* vol. 1 (Buffalo, N.Y.: Buffalo Historical Society, 1907), p. 344.

163 **were the two Cabinet members:** *Buffalo Commercial* (May 17, 1851), p. 2.

163 **"The *Michigan* reached":** Ibid.

CHAPTER 13

164 **"I am no bird":** Charlotte Brontë, *Jane Eyre,* Signet Classic (New York: Penguin Group, 2008), pp. 257–258.

164 **(My spirit bows before thee):** James Strang to Mary Perce Strang, December 5, 1836, Strang Collection, Beinecke.

165 **"seemed very affectionate":** Williams, *Child of the Sea,* pp. 89, 91.

166 **"kept in the Ark":** Strang, *Book of the Law of the Lord,* 1st ed., p. 4.

166 **"the Swedish work":** Speek, *"God Has Made Us a Kingdom,"* pp. 147–148.

166 **"rising early and sitting up late":** Court records, quoted in ibid., p. 149.

166 **"a complete framework":** Quaife, *Kingdom of Saint James,* p. 138.

167 **"over the princes and rulers":** Strang, *The Book of the Law of the Lord,* 1st ed., p. 37.

167 **"A more centralized autocracy":** Quaife, *Kingdom of St. James,* p. 138.

167 **as a "master spirit":** Strang, *Diary,* p. 32.

167 **"She was very sweet":** Williams, *Child of the Sea,* p. 91.

168 **"We did not like to declare":** *New York Tribune* (January 23, 1851), p. 6.

168 **"piteously degrading" marriage market:** Quoted in Claire Harman, "Author Charlotte Brontë Was an Uncompromising Feminist Trailblazer," *Independent* (October 22, 2015): web.

168 **"wretched bondage":** Quoted in Claire Harman, *Charlotte Brontë: A Fiery Heart* (New York: Knopf, 2016), p. 103.

168 "suffer from too rigid a restraint": Brontë, *Jane Eyre*, p. 111.

169 "that come up and fill me with wonder": Elvira Field Strang, quoted in Speek, *"God Has Made Us a Kingdom,"* p. 266.

169 "never tried to bring": Ibid., p. 266.

169 ("an eye to the beautiful"): Quoted in "An Interview with One of the Saints," Milwaukee *Daily Free Democrat* (November 20, 1850), p. 2.

169 she "was always mad" about them: Charles Strang, quoted in Speek, *"God Has Made Us a Kingdom,"* p. 115.

169–170 "ought to confine themselves": Brontë, *Jane Eyre*, p. 111.

170 "having no faith in the revelations": Williams, *Child of the Sea*, p. 62.

170 appointed Mary to his governing council: Graham to Strang, July 10, 1851, Strang Collection, Beinecke.

170 allowed women into high-level leadership: Brady McCombs, "Mormon Women Named to Three Councils Previously Reserved for Men," Associated Press (August 19, 2015): web.

170 "huddle up like frightened sheep": *Northern Islander* (April 3, 1851), p. 2.

171 "the enormities which have been": James Strang to Clement Strang, May 19, 1851, Strang Collection, Beinecke. This letter was enclosed in the note the prophet sent to Mary Strang.

171 "I don't feel at all well about going": James Strang to Mary Strang, May 19, 1851, ibid.

CHAPTER 14

172 "Those grand fresh-water seas of ours": Herman Melville, *Moby-Dick; or The Whale,* Harrison Hayford, Herschel Parker, and G. Thomas Tanselle, eds. (Evanston, Ill.: Northwestern University Press, 1988), p. 244.

172 "the missing link": Bradley A. Rodgers, *Guardian of the Great Lakes: The U.S. Paddle Frigate Michigan* (Ann Arbor: University of Michigan Press, 1996), p. 1. Other descriptions of the ship come from pp. 4, 5, and 166, note 32.

173 "well armed and equipped": Bates, "Beaver Island Prophet," p. 228.

174 "paramilitary bands to rally voters": Aaron Astor, "Partisanship Is an American Tradition—and Good for Democracy," *Washington Post* (July 12, 2017): web.

174 "The U.S. steamer *Michigan*": *Detroit Advertiser* (May 22, 1851), p. 2.

174 "We were certain": *Detroit Free Press* (May 28, 1851), p. 2.

175 "devotee of Venus and Bacchus": Ross, *Early Bench and Bar of Detroit*, p. 26.

175 **second-largest manufacturing industry:** Eric Rutkow, *American Canopy: Trees, Forests, and the Making of a Nation* (New York: Scribner, 2012), pp. 108–109.

175 **$1 billion greater:** Bruce A. Rubenstein and Lawrence E. Ziewacz, *Michigan: A History of the Great Lakes State*, 5th ed. (Hoboken, N.J.: John Wiley & Sons, 2014), p. 184.

175 **a crucial role in the westward expansion:** William Cronon, *Nature's Metropolis: Chicago and the Great West* (New York: W. W. Norton, 1991), pp. 151–159.

175 **"green gold":** Rubenstein and Ziewacz, *Michigan: A History*, p. 184.

175 **"fast becoming epidemic":** Rodgers, *Guardian of the Great Lakes*, p. 43.

176 **"purchased goods":** New Orleans *Times-Picayune* (June 30, 1851), p. 1.

176 **"the boldest and most far fetched":** Strang, letter to the *Detroit Advertiser* (July 16, 1851), p. 2.

176 **"King James and his infatuated brethren":** Bates, "Beaver Island Prophet," p. 226.

177 **Originally built by the British:** See Walter Havighurst, *Three Flags at the Straits: The Forts of Mackinac* (Englewood Cliffs, N.J.: Prentice Hall, 1996), pp. 96–100.

177 **"the goat-like craggy guns":** Melville, *Moby-Dick,* p. 244.

178 **a "half musket shot":** Bates, "Beaver Island Prophet," p. 229. Other accounts of Greig's apprehension can be found on pp. 228–230.

179 **"Crazy Ahab":** Melville, *Moby-Dick,* p. 184.

179 **"a strange sort of book":** Melville to Richard Henry Dana Jr., May 1, 1850, quoted in Delbanco, *Melville: His World and Work,* p. 122.

179 **Melville's stature…was "horrible":** Melville to Nathaniel Hawthorne, June 1851, quoted in Erik Hage, *The Melville-Hawthorne Connection: A Study of the Literary Friendship* (Jefferson, N.C.: McFarland & Co., 2014), p. 149.

180 **"driven forth":** Melville to Evert Duyckinck, February 25, 1850, quoted in Delbanco, *Melville: His World and Work,* p. 141.

180 **barely $500 in American sales:** Ibid., p. 178.

180 **"a disease specific to a society":** Michael Paul Rogin, *Subversive Genealogy: The Politics and Art of Herman Melville* (Berkeley: University of California Press, 1983), p. 118.

180 **"Ahab embodied the dangers facing America":** Ibid., p. 124.

180 **"the personification of the very essence":** Delbanco, *Melville: His World and Work,* p. 166.

CHAPTER 15

181 "Where is that viper": William Shakespeare, *The Tragedy of Othello*.

181 "entered into a short engagement": *Detroit Free Press* (May 23, 1851), p. 3.

182 "should be bound to swing him": Bates, "Beaver Island Prophet," p. 230.

183 "draftsman": This is how Greig identifies himself on the surviving manuscript map, housed at the State Archives of Michigan.

184 "a long hewn log building": Bates, "Beaver Island Prophet," p. 231.

185 shouting, "Kill him!": *Northern Islander* (August 14, 1851), p. 2.

185 "covered with clotted blood": Bates, "Beaver Island Prophet," p. 231.

185 "The papers are aboard": Strang, *Ancient and Modern Michilimackinac*, p. 31.

185–186 the first "foreign potentate": *Northern Islander* (October 11, 1855), p. 3.

186 performance of the "great attraction": Advertisement, *Detroit Free Press* (May 23, 1851), p. 2.

186 "that insatiate want of human nature": Phineas Taylor Barnum, *Struggles and Triumphs; or, Forty Years' Recollections of P. T. Barnum*, rev. ed. (Buffalo, N.Y.: Warren, Johnson & Co., 1873), p. 71.

186 "perhaps the most exciting pageant on record": *Detroit Free Press* (June 5, 1851), p. 3. See also the advertisement for "Huff's Grand Moving Panoramic Mirror," p. 2. Another ad in the same issue trumpets a dance performance by "Mademoiselle Louise," possibly George Adams's paramour, Louisa Pray.

186 the "well-proportioned" man: *Detroit Advertiser* (May 27, 1851), p. 2.

187 the "hardy looking" newcomer: *Detroit Free Press* (May 28, 1851), p. 2.

187 "expressed themselves": *Northern Islander* (June 5, 1851), p. 2.

187 "the streets were lined": Bates, "Beaver Island Prophet," p. 232.

CHAPTER 16

188 "In every community": "Discovery of the Source of the Rochester Knockings," *Buffalo Medical Journal and Review* 6, no. 10 (March 1851): p. 629.

188 "Mrs. McCulloch, you are": Bates quoted this entire conversation—or at least his recollection of it—in "Beaver Island Prophet," p. 233. For clarity's sake, this passage includes one or two minor changes in punctuation.

189 feeling "utterly abashed": Ibid., p. 234.

189 The daughter of a military officer: She was the daughter of Major Josiah

Green, who fought in the War of 1812. See her obituary in the *Baltimore Sun* (February 24, 1911), p. 13.

189 **public lectures on chemistry:** *Baltimore Sun* (October 22, 1838), p. 2; (October 27, 1838), p. 4.

190 **the Fox sisters:** Karen Abbott, "The Fox Sisters and the Rap on Spiritualism," blog post, *Smithsonian* (October 30, 2012), web; Edward White, "In the Joints of Their Toes: The Ruse That Gave Rise to the Spiritualist Movement," blog post, *Paris Review* (November 4, 2016), web.

190 **"If ever the world":** "Lights and Shade of Sense and Nonsense," *Scientific American,* vol. 5, no. 41 (June 29, 1850): p. 325.

190 **"exploded across the nation":** Randolph Roth, *American Homicide* (Cambridge, Mass.: Belknap Press of Harvard University Press, 2009), p. 299.

190 **a "growing disposition":** Lincoln, quoted in Richard Maxwell Brown, *Strain of Violence: Historical Studies of American Violence and Vigilantism* (New York: Oxford University Press, 1975), p. 3.

191 **"Let the first blow be the signal":** Quoted in Reynolds, *John Brown, Abolitionist*, p. 122.

191 **"aggression and vitriolic language":** Roth, *American Homicide*, p. 301.

191 **"killed each other over card games":** Ibid., p. 312.

191 **"one of the most singular":** *Hartford Courant* (October 25, 1851), p. 2.

191 **a "morbid excitement":** Ibid.

192 **convicted of assault:** *Baltimore Daily Commercial* (January 28, 1846), p. 2.

192 **a pair of foreclosure suits:** *David Carlisle vs. Hezekiah D. McCulloch,* May 5, 1848, Maryland State Archives, Chancery Court (Chancery Papers), No. 6850, MSA S512-6850; Location: 01/37/03/077. See also *David Carlisle vs. Hezekiah D. McCulloch,* April 25, 1849, Maryland State Archives, Chancery Court (Chancery Papers), No. 7004, MSA S512-7004; Location: 01/37/03/091.

192 **"intemperate habits":** William E. Curtis, *"King Strang's Home,"* in S. E. Wait and W. S. Anderson, eds., *Old Settlers of the Grand Traverse Region* (Traverse City, Mich.: n.p., 1918), p. 55.

192 **a deadly cholera epidemic:** Rodgers, *Guardian of the Great Lakes,* pp. 41–42. Strang boasted that Beaver Island remained "remarkably healthy," whereas the disease hit his enemies, the local fishermen, because of their "vicious habits and filthy living." See *Northern Islander* (July 29, 1852), p. 3. There may have been truth to this. Island resident Elizabeth Whitney Williams later reported that at the height of the epidemic in 1852, there were fifty-two deaths from the disease on Mackinac Island and only three on Beaver Island. Williams, *Child of the Sea*, p. 141.

192 **should be "excluded from the streets":** McCulloch to the Baltimore

City Council, March 28, 1844, in *Journal of the Proceedings of the First Branch of the City Council of Baltimore,* January Session, 1844 (Baltimore: Joseph Robinson: 1844), pp. 330–331.

193 **"a preeminent position in the Church"**: *Northern Islander* (June 19, 1856), p. 3.

193 **"Americans could no longer coalesce"**: Roth, *American Homicide,* p. 300.

194 **Having fled Beaver Island**: Strang, *Ancient and Modern Michilimackinac,* p. 21.

194 **vowed "to have the life of Mr. Strang"**: *Northern Islander* (April 3, 1851), p. 2.

194 **"mark my words"**: *Detroit Advertiser* (June 21, 1851), p. 2.

194 **"that Bennett was the cause of much of the disturbance"**: Testimony of Edward Kanter, *Documents Accompanying the Journal of the House of Representatives of the State of Michigan, at the Biennial Session of 1857* (Lansing: Hosmer & Fitch), p. 12.

194 **three dozen**: The dead man's brother, Samuel Bennett, put the number at sixty. *Detroit Advertiser* (June 21, 1851), p. 2.

194 **"told them we would not obey"**: Ibid.

195 **sharply divergent stories**: See Van Noord's useful summary of these events, *Assassination of a Michigan King,* pp. 145–150.

195 **"FURTHER OUTRAGES"**: *Detroit Advertiser* (June 12, 1851), p. 2.

195 **accused McCulloch of "butchery"**: *Detroit Advertiser* (June 16, 1851), p. 2.

195 **"Blood was then scooped"**: Ibid.

195 **dismissed as "slanderous reports"**: New Orleans *Times-Picayune* (August 26, 1851), p. 1.

196 **"a prophet, gifted by divine inspiration"**: *Detroit Advertiser* (June 24, 1851), p. 2.

197 **smuggling disaffected followers off the island**: Williams, *Child of the Sea,* p. 141.

197 **"Mary was jeopardizing Strang's hold"**: Van Noord, *Assassination of a Michigan King,* p. 164.

197 **"Mary tried to kill the writer"**: Speek's fascinating analysis of this note appears in *"God Has Made Us a Kingdom,"* pp. 135–136.

197 **"I write you under"**: Strang to Governor John S. Barry, June 12, 1851, quoted in Don Faber, *James Jesse Strang: The Rise and Fall of Michigan's Mormon King* (Ann Arbor: University of Michigan Press, 2016), p. 108.

198 **in his "under advisement" box**: Ibid.

CHAPTER 17

199 **"The plan of 'counting the chickens'"**: Barnum, *Life of P. T. Barnum*, p. 395.

199 **Strang stood before a jury**: The surviving record is spotty, but it appears that Strang addressed the jury on the final day of the trial. Prosecutor George C. Bates described this speech, emphasizing its importance to the outcome of the case, but he did not provide a date. His summary does not seem to match descriptions of a speech Strang made earlier in the trial. See Van Noord, *Assassination of a Michigan King*, pp. 159–160.

199 **twelve codefendants**: *Northern Islander* (July 24, 1851), p. 2.

199 **"would have control of the mail"**: Quoted in Van Noord, *Assassination of a Michigan King*, p. 156.

200 **an ambush on the frozen lake**: Ibid., pp. 154–156.

200 **"The evidence was quite clear"**: Bates, "Beaver Island Prophet," p. 234.

200 **"of the fervid, impassioned sort"**: Ludlow P. Hill, "Narrative of Ludlow P. Hill," in Legler, *A Moses of the Mormons*, p. 162.

200 **"Strang's speech to the jury"**: Bates, "Beaver Island Prophet," pp. 234–235.

201 **"the question of King Strang's gifts"**: *Detroit Free Press* (July 10, 1851), p. 2.

201 **"The evidence was of the most dim"**: Ibid.

201 **"the timber theft charges"**: David Gardner Chardavoyne, *United States District Court for the Eastern District of Michigan: People, Law, and Politics* (Detroit: Wayne State University Press, 2012), p. 53.

201 **dropped all remaining federal charges**: Dockets for *United States v. James J. Strang* and associated cases, Strang Papers, Burton Historical Collection.

202 **"a systematic effort"**: *Detroit Free Press* (July 10, 1851), p. 2.

202 **"While one of the ruffians stood over the bed"**: *Democratic State Register* of Watertown, Wisc. (October 20, 1851), p. 3.

202 **"The proof against these men"**: *Watertown Chronicle* (October 22, 1851), p. 2.

203 **"I heard that you was to be hanged"**: David Heath to Strang, July 22, 1851, Strang Collection, Beinecke.

204 **and sentenced to four years**: *Watertown Chronicle* (November 19, 1851), p. 2.

204 **"the Mormons are continually"**: *Watertown Chronicle* (November 26, 1851), p. 2.

204 **one of Strang's fiercest opponents**: Moore, who signed the article *E.J.M.*, was a central figure in the case against Strang, urging the federal

government to indict the prophet, then testifying against him on charges of obstructing the U.S. mail.

204 **"in search of another place of refuge"**: *Watertown Chronicle* (November 26, 1851), p. 2.

204 **he had been on an "exploring expedition"**: James J. Strang to David Strang, October 25, 1851. A typescript copy of this letter can be found in box 2, item 10, Strang Collection, State Archives of Michigan.

CHAPTER 18

206 **"Beaver Island is a very handsome spot"**: Story from the *Erie Chronicle,* reprinted in the *Northern Islander* (August 12, 1852), p. 2.

206 **"Is it possible"**: Leo Tolstoy, "The Raid," Ronald Wilks, trans., in *The Death of Ivan Ilyich and Other Stories* (New York: Penguin, 2008), p. 17.

206 **"This is my revenge"**: James J. Strang to David Strang, November 25, 1852, Clarke Historical Library.

206 **all 165 votes**: Van Noord, *Assassination of a Michigan King,* pp. 179–180.

207 **a sense of "triumph"**: James J. Strang to David Strang, November 25, 1852, Clarke Historical Library.

207 **of his "most violent persecutors"**: Strang, *Ancient and Modern Michilimackinac,* p. 65.

207 **"everyone whom he didn't like"**: Ludlow P. Hill, "Narrative of Ludlow P. Hill," in Legler, *A Moses of the Mormons,* p. 157.

207–208 **state legislation passed a year earlier**: Van Noord, *Assassination of a Michigan King,* pp. 171–173.

208 **by approximately 1,000 to 20**: *Northern Islander* (September 9, 1852), p. 3.

208 **Even "the blindest can see"**: *Northern Islander* (August 14, 1851), p. 2.

208 **"refused to affiliate with Mormondom"**: *Green Bay Spectator* (July 13, 1852).

209 **"Within twenty-four hours"**: Williams, *Child of the Sea,* p. 142. Other descriptions of the family's ordeal come from pp. 142–144.

209 **"armed and hunting me"**: *New York Tribune* (July 2, 1853), p. 3.

210 **Elizabeth "Betsy" McNutt**: Speek, *"God Has Made Us a Kingdom,"* pp. 156–159.

210 **"poisonous arrows of slander"**: Strang associate Samuel Graham, quoted in ibid., p. 159.

210 **"lived in a log house"**: Samuel T. Douglass, quoted in ibid., p. 161.

210 **"At first it was talked of"**: "King of the Saints," *New York Times* (September 3, 1882), p. 10.

210 "Does not the constitution": *Northern Islander* (March 4, 1852), p. 3.

211 Betsy took over: Speek, *"God Has Made Us a Kingdom,"* pp. 159–160.

211 a bearded man in a dress: *Yankee Notions,* vol. 1, no. 9 (September 1852): p. 278.

211 a "new costume for males": *Harper's New Monthly Magazine,* vol. 4, no. 20 (January 1852): p. 285.

211 "The Great Bloomer Prize Fight": Free-standing lithograph, J. L. Magee, 1851.

213 "has taken the sacred marriage vow": Lucy Stone, September 8, 1852, quoted in *The Proceedings of the Woman's Rights Convention, Held at Syracuse, September 8th, 9th & 10th, 1852* (Syracuse, N.Y.: J. E. Masters, 1852), p. 20.

214 "the implication that my first wife": *Northern Islander* (October 11, 1855), p. 3.

214 "it is forgotten": James J. Strang to David Strang, November 25, 1852, Clarke Historical Library

214 "unsteady minded": David Strang to James Strang, January 31, 1837, Strang Collection, Beinecke.

214 "Frankly, brother, I intend": James J. Strang to David Strang, November 25, 1852, Clarke Historical Library.

214 One expert argues: Van Noord, *Assassination of a Michigan King,* p. 181.

215 "the faithful were commanded to vote": The version quoted here is from the *Buffalo Commercial* (December 9, 1850), p. 1, which reprinted the original *Detroit Advertiser* story.

215 "unanimity probably nowhere": *Northern Islander* (November 11, 1852), p. 2.

215 "'King Strang' pled": *Jackson Citizen* (February 10, 1853), quoted in Strang, *Ancient and Modern Michilimackinac,* p. 49.

216 "Mr. Strang's course": *Detroit Advertiser* (February 10, 1853), quoted in ibid.

CHAPTER 19

217 "There's no place like home!": John Howard Payne (lyrics) and Sir Henry Bishop (music), "Home, Sweet Home" (1823).

217 "Hon. J. J. Strang": This news item appeared in a Washington, D.C., publication, the *Daily Republic* (March 19, 1853), p. 3. It originated in a Michigan paper, the *Adrian Watchtower* (March 8, 1853).

217 "There never were before": *Hartford Courant* (March 9, 1853), p. 2.

218 "It is considered a settled matter": John Bernhisel, quoted in Turner, *Brigham Young: Pioneer Prophet,* p. 203.

218 **"the most talented and ready debater"**: *Temperance Advocate* (February 10, 1853), quoted in Strang, *Ancient and Modern Michilimackinac*, p. 49.

218 **"the uprooting of Brighamite Mormonism"**: "King of the Saints," *New York Times* (September 3, 1882), p. 10.

219 **"a delicate matter"**: *Battle Creek Journal* (January 28, 1853), quoted in Van Noord, *Assassination of a Michigan King*, p. 194.

219 **prodigal son had returned**: See *Randolph Register* (March 6, 1885). This story—apparently written by Dr. Frederick Larkin—does not supply a precise date for Strang's visit but notes that it happened in the spring after his first session in the Michigan legislature. The timing makes clear that the stop took place on his trip to Washington.

219 **"there are many there who look on me"**: James J. Strang to David Strang, November 25, 1852, Clarke Historical Library.

219 **"the hero of the hour"**: *Randolph Register* (January 5, 1898). This article, which supplies the most detailed account of Strang's visit, seems to have been based largely on the memories of the "venerable Dr. Larkin, who still resides here."

219 **"he claimed that the true believers"**: *Randolph Register* (March 6, 1885).

219 **"to secure any converts"**: *Randolph Register* (January 5, 1898).

220 **"Home, Sweet Home"**: See Rosa Pendleton Chiles, "John Howard Payne: American Poet, Actor, Playwright, Consul and the Author of 'Home, Sweet Home,'" *Records of the Columbia Historical Society, Washington, D.C.*, vol. 31/32, pp. 209–297. See also James M. Volo and Dorothy Denneen Volo, *The Antebellum Period* (Westport, Conn.: Greenwood Press, 2004), pp. 274–275.

220 **the most exciting thing**: *Volo and Volo: The Antebellum Period*, p. 275.

221 **bitter into adulthood**: See Speek, *"God Has Made Us a Kingdom,"* pp. 243–244.

221 **"callous to the great truths"**: *Randolph Register* (March 6, 1885).

221 **"It is you that paved the way"**: Quoted in *Randolph Register* (January 5, 1898).

222 **"highly honored by the presence"**: Ibid.

222 **"that terrible poison"**: *Scientific American*, vol. 11, no. 37 (May 24, 1856): p. 1.

222 **left a Mormon missionary dead**: In January of 1832, Mormon elder Joseph Brackenbury wound up dead "from the effects of poison secretly administered by his opposers." See Samuel Morris Brown, *In Heaven as It Is on Earth: Joseph Smith and the Early Mormon Conquest of Death* (New York: Oxford University Press, 2012), p. 45.

222 **"The test was one"**: *Randolph Register* (January 5, 1898).

223 "To the disgust of all present": *Randolph Register* (March 6, 1885).

223 "the celebrated Mormon": *New York Tribune* (March 14, 1853), p. 3.

224 "The rush for offices": John Bernhisel to Brigham Young, March 10, 1853, Brigham Young office files, 1832–1878 (bulk 1844–1877); Utah Delegate Files, 1849–1872; John M. Bernhisel to Brigham Young, 1849–1866; 1853; John M. Bernhisel, letter, Church History Library.

225 "measure swords": *Detroit Advertiser* (February 5, 1853), as quoted in the *Northern Islander* (May 5, 1853), p. 2.

225 "as usual...signally defeated": Ibid.

CHAPTER 20

226 "There is nothing so certain": *Buffalo Courier* (September 4, 1851), p. 2.

226 "Perrysburg does not": *Perrysburg Journal* (October 3, 1853), p. 2.

227 a "piratical band": Quoted in the *Northern Islander* (September 2, 1852), p. 2. The source is a Buffalo newspaper, *Rough Notes* (July 27, 1852).

227 a man "connected with the Mormons": *Weekly Wisconsin* (September 1, 1852), p. 2.

227 "on a marauding expedition": *Chicago Journal* (November 20, 1852), p. 2.

227–228 five of the men were convicted: *Watertown Chronicle* (December 29, 1852), p. 2.

228 "were branded as felons": *Detroit Free Press* (July 10, 1851), p. 2.

228 "daily recurring instances": *Detroit Free Press* (May 24, 1853), p. 2.

228 "Candidly, I most truly believe": *New York Tribune* (July 2, 1853), p. 3.

229 "as a source of capital": Mihm, *A Nation of Counterfeiters*, p. 90. See also Brown, *Strain of Violence*, p. 99.

229 doing a "brisk business": *Perrysburg Journal* (August 22, 1853), p. 2.

230 "Hard-fisted men": Leach, *History of the Grand Traverse Region*, p. 33.

230 same rural county: The Pierce brothers apparently hailed from Preble County, Ohio, where Betsy McNutt grew up. The county seat is Eaton, where Jonathan Pierce was arrested for the horse theft in Perrysburg. The Pierce brothers do not appear to have been directly related to Strang's father-in-law, William L. Perce, whose name was sometimes spelled *Pierce*.

230 might have been recruited: Speek, *"God Has Made Us a Kingdom,"* pp. 156–157.

230 a "band of consecrators": *Watertown Chronicle* (November 26, 1851), p. 2.

230 "large and powerful men": Williams, *Child of the Sea*, pp. 129, 196–197.

231 "by a gang of rowdies": *Northern Islander* (April 13, 1854), p. 1.

231 "threatened to shoot": *Buffalo Daily Republic* (May 21, 1853), p. 2. The story appears to have originated in the *Detroit Tribune* (May 19, 1853).

232 **Pierce brothers and thirteen other Mormon men:** Strang, *Ancient and Modern Michilimackinac,* p. 40.

232 **"Let words cease":** *Northern Islander* (June 30, 1853), p. 3.

232 **"We are running away":** Quoted in Leach, *History of the Grand Traverse Region,* p. 33. In *Ancient and Modern Michilimackinac,* pp. 40–41, Strang denied that the Mormons fired first; in fact, he claimed (wrongly) that they were unarmed. See Williams, *Child of the Sea,* pp. 148–153.

233 **"rifle balls had shattered":** *New Orleans Crescent* (July 29, 1853), p. 1. The source of this article is the *Chicago Journal.*

233 **"martyrs to their faith":** Ibid. The captain, E. S. Stone, later offered a more complete account of the episode in Legler, *A Moses of the Mormons,* pp. 165–168.

233 **a rifle ball flattened against his hip bone:** A list of the men's injuries appears in a one-page extra edition of the *Northern Islander* (July 14, 1853).

233 **"seemed entirely unconcerned":** *Perrysburg Journal* (August 22, 1853), p. 2.

233 **locked in an Illinois jail:** *Watertown Chronicle* (November 26, 1851), p. 2.

233 **"his 'extended colleagues'":** *Perrysburg Journal* (August 22, 1853), p. 2.

233 **"made no ostentatious display":** *Perrysburg Journal* (October 3, 1853), p. 2.

234 **the judge overturned this verdict:** Ibid.

234 **"confined to bed by sickness":** *Perrysburg Journal* (November 7, 1853), p. 2.

234 **"We would *meekly* ask":** *Northwestern Democrat* (November 7, 1853), p. 2.

234 **"ESCAPED.—Jonathan Pierce":** *Perrysburg Journal* (October 31, 1853), p. 2.

234 **"a willful and malicious falsehood":** *Perrysburg Journal* (November 7, 1853), p. 2.

235 **pinpoint the date of that return:** *Northern Islander* (June 19, 1856), p. 2.

236 **"there are nineteen span":** *Cincinnati Daily Gazette* (June 18, 1856).

236 **"deluded and vicious persons":** *New York Tribune* (July 2, 1853), p. 4.

236 **"a great amount of unfavorable public opinion":** Doyle Fitzpatrick, *The King Strang Story: A Vindication of James J. Strang, the Beaver Island Mormon King* (Lansing, Mich.: National Heritage, 1979), p. ix.

237 **"Let the bigger cities boast":** *Perrysburg Journal* (October 3, 1853), p. 2.

237 **had "begun to see fame"**: David Haven Blake, *Walt Whitman and the Culture of American Celebrity* (New Haven, Conn.: Yale University Press, 2008), p. 196.

CHAPTER 21

238 **"Now and then"**: Barnum, *Life of P. T. Barnum, Written by Himself* (Buffalo, N.Y.: Courier Co., 1888), p. 65. This passage did not appear in the first edition of the autobiography. It is from a later edition of the book, which Barnum revised several times.

238 **a million copies**: Neil Harris, *Humbug: The Art of P. T. Barnum* (Chicago: University of Chicago Press, 1981), p. 207.

238 **the theatrical term *star***: Blake, *Walt Whitman and the Culture of American Celebrity*, p. 29.

238 **"the love of fame"**: Hamilton, quoted in ibid., p. 31.

238 **"golden cord"**: Rufus Choate, quoted in George B. Forgie, *Patricide in the House Divided: A Psychological Interpretation of Lincoln and His Age* (New York: W. W. Norton, 1979), p. 57.

239 **"This field of glory"**: Lincoln, quoted in ibid., p. 65.

239 **"post-heroic"**: Ibid., p. 55.

239 **"the shameless confession"**: Severn Teackle Wallis, "Barnum and Mrs. Stowe," *Writings of Severn Teackle Wallis*, vol. 2 (Baltimore: John Murphy & Co., 1896), p. 83. This review originally appeared in the *Southern Literary Messenger*.

239 **"There was a time"**: Ibid., p. 72.

239 **a "little monster"**: *London News*, quoted in Eric D. Lehman, *Becoming Tom Thumb: Charles Stratton, P.T. Barnum, and the Dawn of American Celebrity* (Middletown, Conn.: Wesleyan University Press, 2013), p. 38.

239 **"probably better known"**: *Daily Los Angeles Herald*, quoted in ibid., p. ix.

239 **the first advertising agencies**: Blake, *Walt Whitman and the Culture of American Celebrity*, p. 24.

239 **the first programmatic efforts**: Ibid.

239 **first use of *propaganda***: "propaganda, n. 3," *OED Online*, Oxford University Press, June 2019, web.

239 **first use of *celebrity***: P. David Marshall, *Celebrity and Power: Fame in Contemporary Culture* (Minneapolis: University of Minnesota Press, 1997), p. 5. See also Blake, *Walt Whitman and the Culture of American Celebrity*, pp. 27–34.

240 **"Riot on Beaver Island"**: *Schenectady Cabinet* (December 5, 1854), p. 3

240 ("O! If I was King of England"): Strang, *Diary*, p. 34.

241 his own autobiography: The fragmentary manuscript was published in Michigan Historical Commission, *Michigan Historical Collections*, vol. 32, pp. 202–206.

241 "felons and outlaws": Strang, *Ancient and Modern Michilimackinac*, p. 13.

241 "worst class of men": Ibid., p. 12.

241 "wretches with withered": Ibid., p. 42.

241 "persons of limited means": Ibid., p. 13.

241 "to die upon their native soil": Ibid., p. 42.

241 "The tide is now turned": Ibid., p. 43.

242 "a larger measure of enjoyment": Barnum, *Life of P. T. Barnum*, p. 400.

242 "needful and proper": Ibid., p. 399.

242 "a change of public opinion": Strang, *Ancient and Modern Michilimackinac*, back cover.

242 some critics bought into: A. H. Saxon, *P. T. Barnum: The Legend and the Man* (New York: Columbia University Press, 1989), pp. 12–13.

242 "He does not seem": *Blackwood's Edinburgh Magazine*, vol. 77, no. 512 (February 1855), p. 193.

243 first major scientific undertaking: James Rodger Fleming, *Meteorology in America, 1800–1870* (Baltimore: Johns Hopkins University Press, 2000), pp. 75–93.

243 Smithsonian records: *Annual Report of the Board of Regents of the Smithsonian Institution, Showing the Operations, Expenditures, and Condition of the Institution for the Year 1868* (Washington, D.C.: Government Printing Office, 1869), p. 76.

243 her own recollections: "In Memoriam: Mrs. Elvira E. Baker." This obituary, housed in the Library of Michigan, maintains that Elvira collected weather data for five years. Smithsonian records suggest her work went on for four years, from 1853 to 1856.

243 Every day at 7:00 a.m., 2:00 p.m., and 9:00 p.m.: Fleming, *Meteorology in America, 1800–1870*, p. 82.

244 "magic skill": Quoted in Speek, *"God Has Made Us a Kingdom,"* p. 158.

244 one-quarter of his time: *Northern Islander* (October 11, 1855), p. 3.

244 such a project: James J. Strang, "Some Remarks on the Natural History of Beaver Islands, Michigan," *Ninth Annual Report of the Board of Regents of the Smithsonian Institution, Showing the Operations, Expenditures and Condition of the Institution up to January 1, 1855* (Washington, D.C.: Beverly Tucker, 1855), pp. 282–288.

245 "a thousand avocations": Ibid., p. 288.

245 "this old evil": Mark Wahlgren Summers, *The Plundering Generation: Corruption and the Crisis of the Union, 1849–1861* (New York: Oxford University Press, 1987), p. 56.

245 "Political morality": Charles Gayarré, *The School for Politics: A Dramatic Novel,* 2nd ed. (New York: D. Appleton and Co., 1855), p. 79.

245 "My God, we have": Political operative William H. Dickey, quoted in Summers, *The Plundering Generation,* p. 52.

245 more votes than there were legal voters: Van Noord, *Assassination of a Michigan King,* pp. 210–213.

246 McCulloch had begun drinking: *Northern Islander* (June 19, 1856), p. 3.

246 "would supplant him in the leadership": Thomas Bedford, one of Strang's assassins, quoted in the *Detroit News* (July 7, 1882).

246 the "farce" election: *Baltimore Sun* (December 2, 1854), p. 1.

246 "moderation and good intentions": *Northern Islander* (June 19, 1856), p. 3.

246 "never [letting] slip": Ibid.

247 1,700 residents of neighboring Missouri: Reynolds, *John Brown, Abolitionist,* p. 141.

247 "fraud and outrage": *Green-Mountain Freeman* of Montpelier, Vt. (December 21, 1854), p. 2.

CHAPTER 22

248 "We are not one people": *New York Tribune* (April 12, 1855), p. 4.

248 "To arms!": Quoted in Reynolds, *John Brown, Abolitionist,* p. 146.

248 "balmy as a southern": *Detroit Free Press* (January 9, 1855), p. 1.

248 more than 1,500 abolitionists: William McDaid, "Kinsley S. Bingham and the Republican Ideology of Antislavery, 1847–1855," *Michigan Historical Review* 16, no. 2 (Fall 1990): p. 68.

248 "We will cooperate": "Michigan Republican Platform, 1854," in John W. Quist, ed., *Michigan's War: The Civil War in Documents* (Athens: Ohio University Press, 2019), pp. 14–16.

249 the new party's "political faith": *Detroit Free Press* (January 17, 1855), p. 1.

249 on behalf of the state's black residents: *Journal of the House of Representatives of the State of Michigan,* 1855 (Lansing: Hosmer & Fitch, 1855), p. 32.

249 regularly petitioned the legislature: Hanes Walton Jr., Sherman C. Puckett, and Donald R. Deskins Jr., *The African American Electorate: A Statistical History* (Los Angeles: CQ Press/SAGE Publications, 2012), pp. 152–155. See also Ronald P. Formisano, "The Edge of Caste: Colored

NOTES 363

Suffrage in Michigan, 1827–1861," *Michigan History* 56 (Spring 1972): pp. 19–41.

249 **"full of tender compassion"**: *Detroit Free Press* (January 10, 1855), p. 2.

249 **"heartily welcome"**: *North American and United States Gazette* (May 5, 1851), p. 1.

249 **a full hour and a half**: *Detroit Democrat* (January 26, 1855), p. 2.

250 **he voted with the Republican majority**: *Journal of the House of Representatives of the State of Michigan*, 1855, p. 606.

250 **"crucial to the understanding"**: Matthew R. Thick, "'The Exploded Humbug': Antebellum Michigan, Personal Liberty Laws, and States' Rights," *Michigan Historical Review* 42, no. 2 (Fall 2016): p. 56.

250 **"a pillar of the bastard Democracy"**: *Vicksburg Daily Whig* (October 2, 1855), p. 2.

251 **"State after State"**: *Detroit Free Press* (April 15, 1855), p. 2.

251 **a "hard bottom"**: Henry David Thoreau, *Walden; Or, Life in the Woods* (New York: Dover Publications, 1995), p. 64.

251 **reprinted an excerpt**: Frederick Douglass, *My Bondage and My Freedom* (New York and Auburn: Miller, Orton & Mulligan, 1855), pp. 188–191.

251 **"it was not enough"**: *Northern Islander* (September 20, 1855), p. 3.

252 **"Wholesale Robbery by Pirates"**: *New York Times* (October 10, 1855), p. 2.

253 **Melbourne, Australia**: *The Age* (January 7, 1856), p. 3.

253 **"a large and daring band of thieves"**: *Milwaukee Daily Free Democrat* (July 8, 1854), p. 3.

253 **"finally told his name"**: *Alton Weekly Telegraph* (September 14, 1854), p. 1.

253 **"A rumor has been current"**: *Buffalo Daily Republic* (October 13, 1854), p. 3.

253 **three stores were burglarized**: *St. Louis Luminary* (February 17, 1855), republished in the *Northern Islander* (May 31, 1855), p. 1.

254 **"the isolated position"**: *Pontiac Gazette*, republished in the *Northern Islander* (July 26, 1855), p. 2. The front page of this edition of the *Islander* appears to be misdated July 25, an error corrected on the second page.

254 **more allegations about Mormon horse theft**: *Buffalo Morning Express and Illustrated Buffalo Express* (September 1, 1855), p. 3.

254 **"no longer any doubt"**: *Grand River Times* (September 26, 1855), republished in the *Northern Islander* (October 18, 1855), p. 2.

254 **"false and ridiculous tale"**: *Northern Islander* (December 6, 1855), p. 1.

254 **there was again "a reasonable prospect"**: Ibid., p. 3.

254 **"Let it come"**: Ibid., p. 1.

254 "a bloody welcome": Ibid., p. 3.

255 "cursed with idiotic theories": *Washington Union* (October 7, 1855), p. 3. This article originally appeared in the *New York Express*.

255 arrived in Kansas: Reynolds, *John Brown, Abolitionist*, p. 136.

255 *without the shedding of blood:* Ted A. Smith, *Weird John Brown: Divine Violence and the Limits of Ethics* (Stanford: Stanford University Press, 2015), p. 166.

255 *To me belongeth vengeance:* Horwitz, *Midnight Rising*, p. 47.

255 lost at sea: *Northern Islander* (January 24, 1856), p. 3.

256 Romeo D. Strang: Speek, *"God Has Made Us a Kingdom,"* pp. 239–242.

256 "nor engage with them": Quoted in ibid., p. 240.

256 the prophet would wield "more political power": Detroit Advertiser (November 22, 1854), quoted in Van Noord, *Assassination of a Michigan King*, p. 211.

256 even "the King's friends": *Niles Republican* (February 10, 1855), quoted in ibid., p. 217.

256 stripping him of control: Ibid., pp. 216–218.

256 "his projects and hopes": *Jackson American Citizen* (February 7, 1855), quoted in ibid., p. 217.

CHAPTER 23

257 "Were you ever daguerreotyped": Ralph Waldo Emerson, *Journals of Ralph Waldo Emerson, with Annotations*, vol. 6, Edward Waldo Emerson and Waldo Emerson Forbes, eds. (Boston: Houghton Mifflin, 1911), p. 100.

257 "I have been imprisoned": *Northern Islander* (October 11, 1855), p. 3.

259 "he stopped by at different times": *Northern Islander* (June 19, 1856), p. 2.

259 "styled themselves 'professor'": James Fitzallan Ryder, *Voigtländer and I in Pursuit of Shadow Catching; A Story of Fifty-Two Years' Companionship with a Camera* (Cleveland: Cleveland Printing & Publishing Co., 1902), p. 14.

259 *Likeness men:* Ibid., p. 32.

259 planted a secret agent: Leach, *History of the Grand Traverse Region*, p. 39.

260 to prevail upon a local merchant: *Northern Islander* (October 11, 1855), p. 3.

260 of being an "impostor": *Northern Islander* (June 5, 1856), p. 2.

260 "engaged in horse stealing": Ibid.

260 circumstantial evidence suggests: Dry-goods stores on Beaver Island may

have been used to fence stolen goods. For example, on November 11 of 1852, amid systematic confiscation of non-Mormon property and charges of Mormon raiding expeditions on towns along Lake Michigan, the *Northern Islander* ran a notice announcing that Wait "has just returned with a large assortment" of dry goods, which he was selling "cheaper than the cheapest." *Northern Islander* (November 11, 1852), p. 3.

260 **"We have examined specimens":** *Northern Islander* (December 6, 1855), p. 3.

260 **Strang demanded a bribe:** *Cincinnati Daily Gazette* (June 18, 1856).

261 **a decree from the pulpit:** Strang announced his edict "concerning the apparel of the sisters" on July 10 during a church conference on Beaver Island. *Northern Islander* (August 9, 1855), p. 3.

261 **"In order for Strang to maintain control":** Fischer, *Pantaloons and Power,* p. 72.

261 **the "dress rebellion":** Ibid., p. 71, and Leach, *History of the Grand Traverse Region,* p. 39.

261 **"it began to be whispered":** *Northern Islander* (June 19, 1856), p. 3.

261 **19.5 degrees below zero:** *Northern Islander* (March 13, 1856), p. 2; (April 3, 1856), p. 2.

261 **"Early in winter":** *Northern Islander* (June 19, 1856), p. 2.

262 **"as a pretender":** Ibid.

262 **"rarely made a good picture":** *Northern Islander* (May 22, 1856), p. 1.

262 **"The latter half of the winter":** *Northern Islander* (June 19, 1856), p. 2.

262 **"Polygamy elevates man":** James J. Strang, *The Book of the Law of the Lord: Being a Translation from the Egyptian of the Law Given to Moses in Sinai, with Numerous and Valuable Notes* (Burlington, Wisc.: Voree Press, 1991), pp. 327–328. This expanded edition had not been bound by the time of Strang's death in 1856. An online version can be found here: http://www.strangite.org/Law.htm.

263 **"very mild-spoken kind man":** Sarah Wright, quoted in Speek, *"God Has Made Us a Kingdom,"* p. 196.

263 **"I felt worried":** Island resident identified as "Mrs. H.," quoted in Williams, *Child of the Sea,* pp. 165–166.

263 **"leading a double life":** Ibid., p. 174.

263 **was never "looked upon favorably":** *New York Times* (September 3, 1882), p. 10.

263–264 **"polygamy gradually became more unpopular":** Elvira Field Strang and Charles J. Strang, "Biographical Sketch of James J. Strang," p. 39.

264 **several sensationalistic novels:** Michael Austin, "'As Much as Any Novelist Could Ask': Mormons in American Popular Fiction," in J. Michael Hunter, ed., *Mormons and Popular Culture: The Global Influence*

of an American Phenomenon, vol. 2 (Santa Barbara, Calif.: Praeger, 2013), p. 5.

264 **"strong women being forced into polygamy"**: Ibid.

264 **"tremendous influence"**: Ibid.

264 **"We do not doubt"**: *Northern Islander* (February 14, 1856), p. 3.

264 **"who have itching eyes"**: Ibid.

265 **"After it became apparent"**: Leach, *History of the Grand Traverse Region,* p. 38.

265 **"The public portrait was understood"**: Alan Trachtenberg, *Reading American Photographs: Images as History, Mathew Brady to Walker Evans* (New York: Hill & Wang, 1989), p. 32.

265 **Its dimensions indicate:** The aspect ratio of the book pictured in the daguerreotype appears to be almost precisely that of the 1851 edition of *The Book of the Law of the Lord,* which measures 17.8 centimters by 11.4 centimeters.

265 **"above the kings of the earth"**: Strang, *The Book of the Law of the Lord* (1851 edition), p. 35. The 1856 edition was still in production when the daguerreotype was taken.

266 **"the loss of one of its ghosts"**: Quoted in Barry Sanders, *Unsuspecting Souls: The Disappearance of the Human Being* (Berkeley, Calif.: Counterpoint, 2009), p. 41. Balzac made this statement to photographer Félix Nadar, who recalled it in his memoir.

266 **"During the extreme cold"**: *Northern Islander* (May 1, 1856): p. 2.

267 **"charging from four to six times"**: *Northern Islander* (June 19, 1856): p. 2.

267 **"a wide circulation through the mails"**: Ibid.

CHAPTER 24

268 **"Do you see death"**: Walt Whitman, *Leaves of Grass,* 2nd ed. (Brooklyn, N.Y.: Fowler & Wells, 1856), p. 276. Although *Leaves of Grass* was published in 1855, the line quoted here is from "Poem of Remembrances for a Girl or a Boy of These States," which was added in the 1856 edition.

268 **Adam Dunin Jundzill:** Richard J. Leskosky, "Phenakiscope: 19th Century Science Turned to Animation," *Film History* 5, no. 2 (June 1993): p. 181. For documents relating to Jundzill's patent application for the kinimoscope, see *Patents for Inventions: Abridgements of Specifications Relating to Photography* (London: George E. Eyre and William Spottiswoode, 1861), p. 61, as well as "Specification of Adam Dunin Jundzill: Giving Motion to Stereoscopic Figures," in Great Britain Patent Office,

Specifications of Inventions…,vol. 16, no. 1245 (London: George E. Eyre and William Spottiswoode, 1856): pp. 1–2.

268 **April 1, 1856:** Van Noord, *Assassination of a Michigan King,* p. 315, note 10.

268 **Brother Strang wished to see:** Bedford's account of these events appeared in the *Detroit Evening News* (July 7, 1882).

269 **"The losses and annoyances":** Leach, *History of the Grand Traverse Region,* p. 39.

269 **48 degrees:** *Northern Islander* (April 3, 1856), p. 2.

270 **"You've been betraying us":** *Detroit News* (July 7, 1882).

270 **"There's plenty of room for this job":** Ibid.

271 **"gave him about thirty":** Preston Brooks, quoted in Eric H. Walther, *The Shattering of the Union: America in the 1850s* (Wilmington, Del.: Scholarly Resources, Inc., 2004), p. 99.

271 **"the peace of the whole country":** Charles Sumner, *Charles Sumner: His Complete Works,* vol. 5 (Boston: Lee and Shepard, 1900), p. 138.

271 **taking on "a mistress":** Ibid., p. 144.

271 **"Vulgar abolitionists":** Walther, *The Shattering of the Union,* p. 100. Several other details of the attack come from this source, pp. 97–100.

272 **"I could not believe":** Ibid., p. 99.

272 **"The feeling here is wild and fierce":** Keitt, quoted in Stephen W. Berry, *That Makes a Man: Love and Ambition in the Civil War South* (New York: Oxford University Press, 2003), p. 249.

272 **"an errand of mischief":** *Northern Islander* (May 22, 1856), p. 4.

272 **"universal dead-head":** *Northern Islander* (June 19, 1856), p. 2.

273 **"the spirit of murder":** James Hutchins to George A. Smith, September 19, 1870, George A. Smith papers, 1834–1877; General Correspondence; Incoming letters, H, 1870; Church History Library. Hutchins was a follower of Strang and a resident of the island. The recipient of the letter, George A. Smith, was the official Mormon church historian in Salt Lake City.

273 **had denied "with indignation":** *Northern Islander* (June 5, 1856), p. 1.

273 **"From that day":** *Northern Islander* (June 19, 1856), p. 3.

273 **"falsified publick documents":** Ibid.

273 **"Now it is you and I for it":** Quoted in Leach, *History of the Grand Traverse Region,* p. 39.

273 **"to overthrow the Kingdom":** Warren Post, "James J. Strang," in *Journal of History,* Reorganized Church of Latter Day Saints, vol. 3, no. 1 (January 1910): p. 74.

273 **"Be not troubled":** Church of Jesus Christ of Latter-day Saints, *Doctrine and Covenants,* Section 45, verse 35. Smith had this revelation on March 7, 1831.

274 "We laugh in bitter scorn": *Northern Islander* (June 5, 1856), p. 3.

274 "the musick of stringed instruments": *Northern Islander* (May 22, 1856), p. 3.

274 to show off a bullet: James Hutchins to George A. Smith, September 19, 1870, George A. Smith papers, 1834–1877, Church History Library.

274 a straw hat and a black cravat: Reynolds, *John Brown, Abolitionist*, p. 171.

274 "Northern army": Horwitz, *Midnight Rising*, p. 50.

275 a mob of about 1,000 men had ransacked: Walther, *The Shattering of the Union*, pp. 90–91.

275 "THE SUPREMACY OF THE WHITE RACE": Ibid., p. 90.

275 "My husband and my two boys": Mahala Doyle, quoted in Horwitz, *Midnight Rising*, p. 50.

275 found his father and brothers dead: Ibid., p. 52.

275 "An old man commanded the party": Ibid., pp. 50–51.

276 "Did you have anything to do": Quoted in ibid., p. 53.

276 Late May, 1856: The exact date of McCulloch's return to the island is unclear, but it appears to have been in late May, around the time his co-conspirator Atkyn was reported to be in Detroit. Beaver Island resident James Hutchins recalled that McCulloch returned "two or three weeks" after his departure, which would put him back on the island between May 20 and May 27. See James Hutchins to George A. Smith, September 19, 1870, George A. Smith papers, 1834–1877, Church History Library.

276 several pistols: Warren Post, "James J. Strang," in *Journal of History*, p. 74. Post, a follower of Strang, lived on the island.

276 had gone on to Lansing: Leach, *History of the Grand Traverse Region*, p. 39, as well as *Northern Islander* (June 5, 1856), p. 3. See also Van Noord, *Assassination of a Michigan King*, pp. 240–242.

276 taking target practice in the woods: Post, "James J. Strang," p. 74.

276 June 2, 1856: Recalling the event more than twenty-five years later, Bedford described it as taking place "about the first of June." But Roger Van Noord, using the log of the *Michigan*, places it on the morning of June 2 in a dense fog. See Van Noord, *Assassination of a Michigan King*, pp. 244 and 317, note 51.

277 suffering a flesh wound: one-page extra edition of the *Northern Islander* (July 14, 1853).

277 an inbred "whose father": Strang follower Wingfield Watson, quoted in Van Noord, *Assassination of a Michigan King*, p. 237.

277 "the wasp that stung": Ibid.

277 "Don't believe a word of it": *Northern Islander* (June 5, 1856), p. 1.

277 **"has been received"**: "Transatlantic Latter-Day Poetry," *The Leader* 7 (June 7, 1856), pp. 547–548, available on the *Whitman Archive,* web.

278 **a would-be novelist named Mary Ann Evans**: Jessica DeSpain, "Transatlantic Book Distribution," in *Walt Whitman in Context,* Joanna Levin and Edward Whitley, eds. (Cambridge: Cambridge University Press, 2018), p. 180.

278 **the "Bible of the New Religion"**: Quoted in Michael Robertson, *Worshipping Walt: The Whitman Disciples* (Princeton, N.J.: Princeton University Press, 2008), p. 16.

278 **"A new order shall arise"**: Walt Whitman, *Leaves of Grass,* 1st ed. (Brooklyn, N.Y.: Fowler & Wells, 1855), p. xi.

278 **"The people, especially"**: Walt Whitman, *Two Rivulets: Including Democratic Vistas, Centennial Songs, and Passage to India,* author's ed. (Camden, N.J.: n.p., 1876), p. ix.

279 **"There will soon be no more priests"**: Walt Whitman, *Leaves of Grass,* 1st ed., p. xi.

279 **"praying some relief"**: *Buffalo Morning Express and Illustrated Buffalo Express* (June 11, 1856), p. 3.

279 **"They are not coming back"**: The prophet's son Gabriel Strang, letter to John Wake Jr., April 10, 1929, quoted in Speek, *"God Has Made Us a Kingdom,"* p. 217.

279 **"The notion exists"**: Stephen Post to Warren Post, February 8, 1856, quoted in Van Noord, *Assassination of a Michigan King,* p. 243.

CHAPTER 25

280 **"Our enemies are silent"**: *Northern Islander* (June 5, 1856), p. 1.

280 **life story of Charles H. McBlair**: Much of the biographical information in this section comes from an obituary in the New Orleans *Times-Picayune* (November 23, 1890), p. 7.

280 **"private pique"**: *Army and Navy Chronicle,* vol. 10, no. 20 (May 14, 1840): pp. 311–312, and *Boston Post* (May 22, 1840), p. 2.

280 **"probably the best"**: New Orleans *Times-Picayune* (November 23, 1890), p. 7.

281 **to see him "on business"**: McBlair to Secretary of the Navy James C. Dobbin, June 19, 1856, quoted in Rodgers, *Guardian of the Great Lakes,* p. 72.

281 **mutiny aboard the whaleship *Globe***: David F. Long, *"Mad Jack": The Biography of Captain John Percival, USN, 1779–1862* (Westport, Conn.: Greenwood Press, 1993), pp. 55–66; James A. Michener and A. Grove Day, *Rascals in Paradise* (New York: Random House, 1957), pp. 7–43;

and Edouard A. Stackpole, *The Sea-Hunters: The New England Whale-men During Two Centuries, 1635–1835* (Philadelphia: Lippincott, 1953), pp. 413–433.

281 **nearly severed in two:** Long, *"Mad Jack,"* p. 58, as well as Michener and Day, *Rascals in Paradise,* p. 23.

281 **an "almost uncontrollable urge":** Ibid., p. 8.

281 **each of whom was currently pregnant:** Speek, *"God Has Made Us a Kingdom,"* pp. 247–248, 375–377.

282 **a "sociable sort of man":** St. Bernard, interview with the *Detroit Free Press* (June 30, 1889), p. 8.

282 **"somewhat cast down in mind":** Warren Post, "James J. Strang," in *Journal of History,* p. 75.

282 **found him in excellent spirits:** *St. Clair Republican* (March 8, 1882), Clarke Historical Library.

282 **a common gesture of cordiality:** D. Michael Quinn, "Male-Male Intimacy Among Nineteenth-Century Mormons: A Case Study," in *Dialogue: A Journal of Mormon Thought* 25, no. 4 (Winter 1995): p. 110.

282 **as Strang told stories and jokes:** Speek, *"God Has Made Us a Kingdom,"* p. 217.

282 **"with the hope":** McBlair to Dobbin, September 24, 1856, quoted in Rodgers, *Guardian of the Great Lakes,* p. 76.

283 **his concern about "some circumstances":** McBlair to Dobbin, June 6, 1856, quoted in ibid., p. 73.

283 **"I have every reason to believe":** McBlair to Governor Kinsley S. Bingham, June 6, 1856, quoted in ibid., p. 71.

283 **"assistance to those citizens":** McBlair to Dobbin, June 6, 1856, quoted in ibid., p. 74.

284 **"marines from the vessel":** Bedford, *Detroit News* (July 7, 1882).

284 **"The water ran furious":** Strang, *Diary,* p. 60.

284 **"What a multitude of thoughts":** Ibid., p. 61.

285 **"dreams of royalty and power":** Ibid., p. 19.

285 **"a Priest, a Lawyer":** Ibid., p. 22.

285 **"every man who receiveth":** Strang, *Book of the Law of the Lord,* 1st ed., pp. 62–63.

285 **timber would be a great source:** "Wood Trade at Beaver Island," *Northern Islander* (June 19, 1856), p. 4. This issue of the paper apparently went to press shortly before the prophet's murder.

285 **"I cannot die":** Strang, *Diary,* p. 59.

285 **no bullet could pierce his body:** Williams, *Child of the Sea,* p. 175.

285 **"disunion with all the horrors":** Strang, *Diary,* p. 24.

286 *Amidst all the evils:* Ibid., p. 32.

286 "Brother Strang, they are going to shoot you": Quoted by James Hutchins in his letter to George A. Smith, September 19, 1870, George A. Smith papers, 1834–1877, Church History Library.

286 "That damned rascal": Quoted by Warren Post, "James J. Strang," in *Journal of History,* p. 75.

286 made no attempt to stop it: *Detroit News* (July 7, 1882).

286 "covered with blood": Quoted in the *Port Huron Daily Times* (February 26, 1881), p. 1.

CHAPTER 26

287 "Hail, King!": Alfred, Lord Tennyson, *Idylls of the King,* James Martin Gray, ed. (London: Penguin, 2004), p. 289.

287 convened in Philadelphia: Sidney Blumenthal, *All the Powers of Earth: The Political Life of Abraham Lincoln, 1856–1860* (New York: Simon & Schuster, 2019), pp. 229–235.

287 Abraham Lincoln finished second: Ibid., pp. 234–235.

287 "those twin relics": Ibid., p. 231.

287 described a victory: *New York Daily Herald* (June 17, 1856), p. 8.

287 "first real battle" of the Civil War: Reynolds, *John Brown, Abolitionist,* p. 187.

287 "While we do not rejoice": *Nashville Union and American* (June 17, 1856), p. 2.

288 "lawless proceedings of the Mormons": *Cincinnati Daily Gazette* (June 18, 1856).

288 a "howling mob": St. Bernard, quoted in the *Detroit Free Press* (June 30, 1889), p. 8.

288 "It would have been the last act": McBlair to Dobbin, September 24, 1856, quoted in Rodgers, *Guardian of the Great Lakes,* p. 74.

289 Dismissing this show of "feigned" sorrow: Warren Post, "James J. Strang," in *Journal of History,* pp. 75–76.

289 A gleeful crowd: Ibid, p. 76, as well as Leach, *History of the Grand Traverse Region,* p. 40.

289 The "trial," such as it was: *Detroit News* (July 7, 1882).

289 "We learn by telegraph": *New York Daily Herald* (June 21, 1856), p. 4.

290 "From the Beaver Islands—": *Lake Superior Miner* of Ontonagon, Mich. (June 28, 1856), p. 2.

290 "died of his wounds": *Baltimore Sun* (June 25, 1856), p. 2, and *Morning Chronicle* of London, England (June 28, 1856), p. 5.

290 "fair prospect of recovery": *Detroit Free Press* (June 28, 1856), p. 1.

290 his nourishment through a quill: *New York Times* (July 4, 1856), p. 2.

290 "remain alive on the earth": Warren Post, "James J. Strang," in *Journal of History*, p. 76.

290 to capture the prophet dead or alive: Ibid.

290 "The plan": *Green Bay Advocate* (July 3, 1856), quoted in Van Noord, *Assassination of a Michigan King*, p. 255.

291 a "regular parting": Elvira Field, quoted in Speek, *"God Has Made Us a Kingdom,"* p. 248.

291 1,500 unbound copies: Van Noord, *Assassination of a Michigan King*, p. 256.

291 "everlasting kingdom of God": Strang, *The Book of the Law of the Lord*, 1st ed., p. ii.

292 "escape the calamities": *Northern Islander* (October 18, 1855), p. 4.

292 "armed well with whisky": Wingfield W. Watson's written account of these events was republished verbatim in Leach, *History of the Grand Traverse Region*, pp. 40–42.

292 "The charm that bound": *Detroit Tribune* (July 8, 1856), quoted in Van Noord, *Assassination of a Michigan King*, p. 262.

293 "My friends advised me": Quoted in Speek, *"God Has Made Us a Kingdom,"* p. 228.

293 about 515 people: See Van Noord, *Assassination of a Michigan King*, p. 245.

293 as high as 2,500: See, for example, Faber, *James Jesse Strang*, p. 142.

293 "in the most destitute": *Green Bay Advocate* (July 17, 1856), quoted in Van Noord, *Assassination of a Michigan King*, p. 264.

293 In Chicago: Wingfield W. Watson, "The Autobiography of Wingfield Watson," available online at the Livingston-Watson Family Association site, web. See also James Hutchins to George A. Smith, September 19, 1870, George A. Smith papers, 1834–1877, Church History Library.

293 "The dominion of King Strang": Quoted in the New Orleans *Times-Picayune* (July 31, 1856), p. 1.

294 "it would have been cheaper": *Detroit News* (July 7, 1882), as republished in the *Cincinnati Enquirer* (July 15, 1882), p. 10.

294 "pang of conscience": See Speek, *"God Has Made Us a Kingdom,"* p. 223.

294 "in the arms": *Detroit Free Press* (June 30, 1889), p. 8.

294 Mary was not even in Voree: Speek, *"God Has Made Us a Kingdom,"* p. 223.

295 "anything he wished to communicate": Strang follower Edward Chidester, quoted in ibid., p. 224.

295 "Death of King Strang": *New York Times* (July 15, 1856), p. 1.

295 "I just thought": Quoted in Faber, *James Jesse Strang*, p. 144.

295 "nothing to live for any longer": Ibid.

EPILOGUE

296 "Something further may follow": Melville, *The Confidence-Man*, p. 251.

296 "intrepid, unprincipled": Melville, *Israel Potter: His Fifty Years of Exile* (New York: G. P. Putnam & Co., 1855), p. 197.

297 a "new and thriving city": Melville, *The Confidence-Man*, p. 58.

297 either Nauvoo or: See, for example, H. Bruce Franklin's observations in an edition of *The Confidence-Man* he edited and annotated (Champaign, Ill.: Dalkey Archive Press, 2007), p. 70, note 10.

297 "the northerly location": Richard Dilworth Rust, " 'I Love All Men Who Dive': Herman Melville and Joseph Smith," in *BYU Studies Quarterly* 38, no. 1, article 13 (1999): p. 154.

297 finishing a first draft: Watson Branch, Hershel Parker, and Harrison Hayford, with Alma A. MacDougall, "Historical Note," in Melville, *The Confidence-Man* (Evanston, Ill.: Northwestern University Press, 1984), p. 277.

297 five about his assassination: *Springfield Republican* (June 21, 1856), p. 5; (June 24, 1856), p. 1; (July 3, 1856), p. 1; (July 8, 1856), p. 2; and (July 15, 1856), p. 3.

298 "A tragic life": Myraette Strang, quoted in Speek, *"God Has Made Us a Kingdom,"* p. 8.

298 lost to posterity: Ibid., p. 243, note 21.

298 William L. Perce, had also died: "Perce Family History," Library of Michigan, family tree on p. 11.

298 a farmer sued the railroad: *Allen v. Illinois Central Railroad et al.*, in *The Papers of Abraham Lincoln: Legal Documents and Cases*, vol. 3, Daniel W. Stowell, ed. (Charlottesville: University of Virginia Press, 2008), pp. 1–23.

298 "mines, pits, shafts and holes": Ibid., p. 3.

298 Elvira Field Strang lived for a few years: Speek's superb account of Elvira's life after Strang's murder in *"God Has Made Us a Kingdom,"* pp. 259–271.

299 "far inferior to her first love": Elvira's son Clement, quoted in ibid., p. 271.

299 "She sometimes feared that James": Ibid., p. 270.

299 Betsy McNutt Strang: Ibid., pp. 273–275.

299 having his father's intellectual ability: Ibid., p. 276.

299 a pair of prison terms: Ibid., pp. 311, 313.

299 a "Jekyll-Hyde life": The version quoted here appeared in the *Sheboygan Press* (March 5, 1910), p. 3, but the article appeared in a number of papers, including the *Los Angeles Herald* (January 27, 1910), p. 16.

300 "appear less conspicuous": Quoted in Speek, *"God Has Made Us a Kingdom,"* p. 297.

300 she passed away in Tacoma: Ibid., p. 301.

300 Sarah Wright Strang: Ibid., pp. 287–295.

300 "I had faith that James was a prophet": Quoted in ibid., p. 294.

301 as "the most consummate": *Springfield Republican* (February 19, 1861), p. 2.

301 "the same old Adams who": *Sauk County Standard* (August 3, 1853), p. 2.

301 "in dramatical and Mormon circles": *Springfield Republican* (February 19, 1861), p. 2.

301 the preacher "persistently denied": *Springfield Republican* (February 23, 1861), p. 4.

301 "a more debased and unblushing villain": Ibid.

301 establishing a colony in Palestine: Holmes, *Dreamers of Zion,* pp. 127–178, and Amann, "Prophet of Zion," pp. 477–500.

302 eighteen of them were dead: Amann, "Prophet of Zion," p. 488, note 21.

302 "The colony was a failure": Mark Twain, "The American Colony in Palestine," *New York Tribune* (November 2, 1867), p. 2.

302 "shamefully humbugged": Mark Twain, *The Innocents Abroad* (New York: Signet Classic, 1980), p. 459.

302 his model for the King: Robert P. Weeks, "The Captain, the Prophet, and the King: A Possible Source for Twain's Dauphin," *Mark Twain Journal* 18, no. 1 (Winter 1975–1976): pp. 9–12.

302 "It was enough": Mark Twain, *Adventures of Huckleberry Finn,* p. 210.

302 "dragged out with his boots on": Quoted in Smith, *Saintly Scoundrel,* p. 166.

302 Grains of Paradise and Dr. Bennett's Dysenteric Drops: Ibid.

302 "deceive the uninitiated": *New England Cultivator* (August 1852), as quoted in ibid., p. 176.

303 the king's "poultry-yard was made": Elvira Field Strang and Charles J. Strang, "Biographical Sketch of James J. Strang," p. 49.

303 only eighteen votes: See the official vote tally in *Documents Accompanying the Journal of the House of Representatives of the State of Michigan at the Biennial Session of 1857* (Lansing: Hosmer & Fitch, 1857), p. 13.

303 on the Minnesota frontier: *Baltimore Sun* (May 20, 1863), p. 2.

303 "see how things were prospering": Williams, *Child of the Sea,* p. 212.

303 his death from illness: Van Noord, *Assassination of a Michigan King,* p. 270.

303 "I have never yet regretted": Quoted in Williams, *Child of the Sea,* p. 212.

303 **another killing:** Van Noord, *Assassination of a Michigan King,* p. 271, and Speek, *"God Has Made Us a Kingdom,"* p. 268.

304 **to kill a fellow soldier:** Speek, *"God Has Made Us a Kingdom,"* p. 268.

304 **he liked to boast of his body count:** Ibid.

304 **"Isn't this a beautiful country?":** John R. Entwistle, quoted in the *Assaria Argus* (July 5, 1889), p. 1. Biographer David S. Reynolds relates a similar story in *John Brown, Abolitionist,* p. 395.

304 **lawyer for the Mormon Church:** Ross, *Early Bench and Bar of Detroit,* p. 27.

304 **"If reason be judge":** Melville, *The Confidence-Man,* p. 75.

304 **"at a loss to determine":** Ibid., p. 224.

305 **"raying away from itself":** Ibid., p. 238.

305 **"As for original characters in fiction":** Ibid., p. 237.

Bibliography

MANUSCRIPT SOURCES

Beinecke Rare Book & Manuscript Library, Yale University
Burton Historical Collection, Detroit Public Library
Church History Library, the Church of Jesus Christ of Latter-day Saints (online
  collections)
Clarke Historical Library, Central Michigan University
Community of Christ Archives, Independence, MO
LaSalle County Clerk, Ottawa, IL
Library of Michigan
Library of Virginia
Maryland State Archives
State Archives of Michigan

NINETEENTH-CENTURY NEWSPAPER AND JOURNAL SOURCES

American Antiquarian Society, Worcester, MA
Beinecke Rare Book & Manuscript Library, Yale University
Burlington Historical Society, Burlington, WI
Burton Historical Collection, Detroit Public Library
Center for Research Libraries, Chicago
Chicago History Museum Research Center
Chronicling America
Clarke Historical Library, Central Michigan University
Early American Newspapers (Series 2)
Fenton History Center, Jamestown, NY
Fultonhistory.com
Google Books

HathiTrust Digital Library
Internet Archive
Newberry Library, Chicago
NewspaperArchive.com
Newspapers.com
St. Clair County Library, Port Huron, MI

SELECT BIBLIOGRAPHY

Adams, William, ed. *Historical Gazetteer and Biographical Memorial of Cattaraugus County, N.Y.* Syracuse, NY: Lyman, Horton, 1893.

Amann, Peter. "Prophet in Zion: The Saga of George J. Adams." *New England Quarterly* 37, no. 4 (December 1964): 477–500.

Anderson, Richard Lloyd. "Reuben Miller, Recorder of Oliver Cowdery's Reaffirmations." *BYU Studies Quarterly* 8, no. 3 (July 1968): 277–93.

Anthony, George A. *The Elders Speak: Reflections on Native American Life Centering on Beaver Island, Michigan, in the Nineteenth and Twentieth Centuries.* Beaver Island, MI: Beaver Island Historical Society, 2009.

Austin, Michael. "'As Much as Any Novelist Could Ask': Mormons in American Popular Fiction." In *Mormons and Popular Culture: The Global Influence of an American Phenomenon.* Edited by J. Michael Hunter. Vol. 2, 1–22. Santa Barbara, CA: Praeger, 2013.

Baldwin, Peter G. *The Flush Times of Alabama and Mississippi.* New York: D. Appleton, 1854.

Balleisen, Edward J. *Navigating Failure: Bankruptcy and Commercial Society in Antebellum America.* Chapel Hill: University of North Carolina Press, 2001.

Barnes, Albert. *The Casting Down of Thrones: A Discourse on the Present State of Europe.* Philadelphia: William Sloanaker, 1848.

Barnum, Phineas Taylor. *The Life of P. T. Barnum: Written by Himself.* New York: J.S. Redfield, 1854.

_____. *Life of P. T. Barnum, Written by Himself, Including His Golden Rules for Money-Making. Brought up to 1888.* Rev. ed. Buffalo, NY: Courier, 1888.

_____. *Struggles and Triumphs; or, Forty Years' Recollections of P. T. Barnum.* Rev. ed. Buffalo, NY: Warren, Johnson, 1873.

Bates, George C. "The Beaver Island Prophet." *Michigan Historical Collections* 32 (1903): 225–35.

Beam, Alex. *American Crucifixion: The Murder of Joseph Smith and the Fate of the Mormon Church.* New York: PublicAffairs, 2015.

Beecher, Henry Ward. *Lectures to Young Men, on Various Important Subjects.* Salem, MA: J. P. Jewett, 1846.

Bennett, Richard E., Susan Easton Black, and Donald Q. Cannon. *The Nauvoo Legion in Illinois: A History of the Mormon Militia, 1841–1846.* Norman: Arthur H. Clark / University of Oklahoma Press, 2010.

Berry, Stephen William. *All That Makes a Man: Love and Ambition in the Civil War South.* New York: Oxford University Press, 2003.

Blake, David. *Walt Whitman and the Culture of American Celebrity.* New Haven, CT: Yale University Press, 2008.

Blumenthal, Sidney. *All the Powers of Earth: The Political Life of Abraham Lincoln, 1856–1860.* New York: Simon & Schuster, 2019.

Bringhurst, Newell G., and John C. Hamer, eds. *Scattering of the Saints: Schism Within Mormonism.* Independence, MO: John Whitmer Books, 2007.

Brontë, Charlotte. *Jane Eyre.* New York: Penguin, 2008.

Brooke, John L. *The Refiner's Fire: The Making of Mormon Cosmology, 1644–1844.* New York: Cambridge University Press, 1994.

Brown, Richard Maxwell. *Strain of Violence: Historical Studies of American Violence and Vigilantism.* New York: Oxford University Press, 1975.

Brown, Samuel Morris. *In Heaven as It Is on Earth: Joseph Smith and the Early Mormon Conquest of Death.* New York: Oxford University Press, 2012.

Bushman, Richard L. *Joseph Smith: Rough Stone Rolling.* New York: Alfred A. Knopf, 2005.

Carlyle, Thomas, and Ralph Waldo Emerson. *The Correspondence of Thomas Carlyle and Ralph Waldo Emerson, 1834–1872.* Boston: J. R. Osgood, 1883.

Carmack, Noel A. "A Note on Nauvoo Theatre." *BYU Studies Quarterly* 34, no. 1 (1994): 94–100.

Chardavoyne, David Gardner. *The United States District Court for the Eastern District of Michigan: People, Law, and Politics.* Detroit: Wayne State University Press, 2012.

Cleland, Charles E. *Rites of Conquest: The History and Culture of Michigan's Native Americans.* Ann Arbor: University of Michigan Press, 1992.

Cook, James W. *The Arts of Deception: Playing with Fraud in the Age of Barnum.* Cambridge, MA: Harvard University Press, 2001.

Craft, William. *Running a Thousand Miles for Freedom; or, The Escape of William and Ellen Craft from Slavery.* London: William Tweedie, 1860.

Crane, Angus E. "Millard Fillmore and the Mormons." *Journal of the West* 34 (January 1995): 70–76.

Crockett, Davy. *A Narrative of the Life of David Crockett of the State of Tennessee, Written by Himself.* Philadelphia: E. L. Carey and A. Hart, 1834.

Cronon, William. *Nature's Metropolis: Chicago and the Great West.* New York: W.W. Norton, 1991.

Cross, Whitney R. *The Burned-Over District: The Social and Intellectual History of Enthusiastic Religion in Western New York, 1800–1850.* Ithaca, NY: Cornell University Press, 1950.

Cumming, John, and Audrey Cumming. "The Saints Come to Michigan." *Michigan History* 49, no. 1 (March 1965): 12–27.

Dana, Richard Henry. "How We Met John Brown." *Atlantic Monthly* 28, no. 165 (July 1871): 1–9.

Darwin, Charles. *Charles Darwin's Letters: A Selection, 1825–1859.* Edited by Frederick Burckhardt. Cambridge: Cambridge University Press, 1996.

_____. *Journal of Researches into the Natural History and Geology of the Countries Visited During the Voyage of H.M.S. Beagle Round the World, Under the Command of Capt. Fitz Roy, R.N.* Vol. 2. New York: Harper & Brothers, 1846.

Delbanco, Andrew. *Melville: His World and Work.* New York: Vintage, 2006.

_____. *The War Before the War: Fugitive Slaves and the Struggle for America's Soul from the Revolution to the Civil War*. New York: Penguin, 2018.

Dickens, Charles. *American Notes and Pictures from Italy*. New York: Oxford University Press, 1987.

_____. *The Life and Adventures of Martin Chuzzlewit*. London: Penguin, 2004.

Dinius, Marcy. *The Camera and the Press: American Visual and Print Culture in the Age of the Daguerreotype*. Philadelphia: University of Pennsylvania Press, 2012.

Douglass, Frederick. *The Life and Times of Frederick Douglass, Written by Himself*. Hartford, CT: Park Publishing, 1881.

_____. *My Bondage and My Freedom*. New York and Auburn: Miller, Orton & Mulligan, 1855.

Eberstadt, Charles. "A Letter That Founded a Kingdom." *Autograph Collectors' Journal* (October 1950): 2–5, 32.

Emerson, Ralph Waldo. *Journals of Ralph Waldo Emerson with Annotations*. Vol. 6. Boston: Houghton Mifflin, 1911.

Erickson, Dan. "Mormon Millennialism: The Literalist Legacy and Implications for the Year 2000." *Dialogue: A Journal of Mormon Thought* 30, no. 2 (summer 1997): 1–32.

Faber, Don. *James Jesse Strang: The Rise and Fall of Michigan's Mormon King*. Ann Arbor: University of Michigan Press, 2016.

Fischer, Gayle V. *Pantaloons and Power: A Nineteenth-Century Dress Reform in the United States*. Kent, OH: Kent State University Press, 2001.

Fitzpatrick, Doyle C. *The King Strang Story: A Vindication of James J. Strang, the Beaver Island Mormon King*. Lansing, MI: National Heritage, 1970.

Flanders, Robert Bruce. *Nauvoo: Kingdom on the Mississippi*. Urbana: University of Illinois Press, 1965.

Fleming, James Rodger. *Meteorology in America, 1800–1870*. Baltimore: Johns Hopkins University Press, 2000.

Fluhman, J. Spencer. *"A Peculiar People": Anti-Mormonism and the Making of Religion in Nineteenth-Century America*. Chapel Hill: University of North Carolina Press, 2012.

Ford, Thomas. *History of Illinois, from Its Commencement as a State in 1818 to 1847*. Chicago: S. C. Griggs, 1854.

Forgie, George B. *Patricide in the House Divided: A Psychological Interpretation of Lincoln and His Age*. New York: W. W. Norton, 1979.

Foster, Lawrence. *Women, Family, and Utopia: Communal Experiments of the Shakers, the Oneida Community, and the Mormons*. Syracuse, NY: Syracuse University Press, 1991.

Fuller, S. Margaret. *Woman in the Nineteenth Century*. New York: Greeley & McElrath, 1845.

Givens, Terryl. *The Book of Mormon: A Very Short Introduction*. New York: Oxford University Press, 2009.

_____. *The Viper on the Hearth: Mormons, Myths, and the Construction of Heresy*. New York: Oxford University Press, 1997.

Givens, Terryl, and Matthew J. Grow. *Parley P. Pratt: The Apostle Paul of Mormonism*. New York: Oxford University Press, 2011.

Godfrey, Kenneth W. "Crime and Punishment in Mormon Nauvoo, 1839–1846." *BYU Studies Quarterly* 32, no. 1–2 (1992): 195–227.

Goodstein, Laurie. "It's Official: Mormon Founder Had Many Wives." *New York Times,* November 11, 2014.

Gutjahr, Paul C. *The Book of Mormon: A Biography.* Princeton, NJ: Princeton University Press, 2012.

Hage, Erik. *The Melville-Hawthorne Connection: A Study of the Literary Friendship.* Jefferson, NC: McFarland, 2014.

Hajicek, John J., ed. *Chronicles of Voree, 1844–1849.* Burlington, WI: J. J. Hajicek, 1992.

Hales, Brian C. "John C. Bennett and Joseph Smith's Polygamy: Addressing the Question of Reliability." *Journal of Mormon History* 41, no. 2 (April 2015): 131–81.

Halttunen, Karen. *Confidence Men and Painted Women: A Study of Middle-Class Culture in America, 1830–1870.* New Haven, CT: Yale University Press, 1982.

Harman, Claire. *Charlotte Brontë: A Fiery Heart.* New York: Alfred A. Knopf, 2016.

Harris, Neil. *Humbug: The Art of P. T. Barnum.* Chicago: University of Chicago Press, 1981.

Hawthorne, Nathaniel. *The Blithedale Romance: An Authoritative Text, Backgrounds and Sources, Criticism.* New York: W. W. Norton, 1978.

———. *The House of the Seven Gables.* New York: Barnes & Noble Classics, 2007.

———. *The Scarlet Letter and Other Writings: Authoritative Texts, Contexts, Criticism.* New York: W. W. Norton, 2017.

Hinton, Wayne K. "Millard Fillmore, Utah's Friend in the White House." *Utah Historical Quarterly* 48, no. 2 (1980): 112–28.

Hirshson, Stanley P. *The Lion of the Lord: A Biography of Brigham Young.* New York: Alfred A. Knopf, 1969.

Holmes, Reed M. *Dreamers of Zion: Joseph Smith and George J. Adams: Conviction, Leadership and Israel's Renewal.* Portland, OR: Sussex Academic Press, 2003.

Horwitz, Tony. *Midnight Rising: John Brown and the Raid That Sparked the Civil War.* New York: Henry Holt, 2011.

Howe, Daniel Walker. *What Hath God Wrought: The Transformation of America, 1815–1848.* New York: Oxford University Press, 2007.

Howe, Julia Ward. *The Hermaphrodite.* Lincoln: University of Nebraska Press, 2004.

Husch, Gail E. *Something Coming: Apocalyptic Expectation and Mid-Nineteenth-Century American Painting.* Hanover, NH: University Press of New England, 2000.

Janik, Erika. *Marketplace of the Marvelous: The Strange Origins of Modern Medicine.* Boston: Beacon Press, 2014.

Jennings, Chris. *Paradise Now: The Story of American Utopianism.* New York: Random House, 2016.

Jensen, Robin S. "Gleaning the Harvest: Strangite Missionary Work, 1846–1850." MA diss., BYU ScholarsArchive, Paper 591, 2005.

John, Richard R. *Spreading the News: The American Postal System from Franklin to Morse.* Cambridge, MA: Harvard University Press, 1995.

Johnson, Paul E. *Sam Patch, the Famous Jumper.* New York: Hill & Wang, 2003.

———. *A Shopkeeper's Millennium: Society and Revivals in Rochester, New York, 1815–1837.* New York: Hill & Wang, 1978.

Johnson, Paul E., and Sean Wilentz. *The Kingdom of Matthias: A Story of Sex and Salvation in Nineteenth-Century America*. New York: Oxford University Press, 1995.

Kielbowicz, Richard B. *News in the Mail: The Press, Post Office, and Public Information, 1700–1860s*. Westport, CT: Greenwood Press, 1989.

Konnikova, Maria. *Confidence Game: Why We Fall for It...Every Time*. New York: Viking, 2016.

Lasch, Christopher. *The World of Nations: Reflections on History, Politics, and Culture*. New York: Alfred A. Knopf, 1973.

Leach, Morgan Lewis. *A History of the Grand Traverse Region, published in the Grand Traverse Herald*. Traverse City, MI: n.p., 1883.

Legler, Henry E. "A Moses of the Mormons: Strang's City of Refuge and Island Kingdom." *Parkman Club Publications* no. 15–16 (May 11, 1897): 115–47.

_____. "Narrative of Ludlow P. Hill." *Parkman Club Publications* no. 15–16 (May 11, 1897): 153–63.

Lehman, Eric D. *Becoming Tom Thumb: Charles Stratton, P. T. Barnum, and the Dawn of American Celebrity*. Middletown, CT: Wesleyan University Press, 2013.

Leonard, Glen M. "Early Saints and the Millennium." *Ensign* 9, no. 8 (August 1979): web.

Leskosky, Richard. "Phenakiscope: 19th Century Science Turned to Animation." *Film History* 5, no. 2 (June 1993): 176–89.

Lewis, David Rich. "'For Life, the Resurrection and the Life Everlasting': James J. Strang and Strangite Mormon Polygamy." *Wisconsin Magazine of History* 66, no. 4 (1983): 274–91.

Long, David F. *"Mad Jack": The Biography of Captain John Percival, USN, 1779–1862*. Westport, CT: Greenwood Press, 1993.

Loomis, Chauncy. "Experience on Beaver Island with James J. Strang." *Saints' Herald* 35, no. 45 (November 10, 1888): 718–19.

Lord, David N. "A Discourse on the Millennial State of the Church." *Theological and Literary Journal* 2, no. 4 (April 1850): 656–98.

Marsh, Joss. *Word Crimes: Blasphemy, Culture, and Literature in Nineteenth-Century England*. Chicago: University of Chicago Press, 1998.

Marx, Karl. *The Communist Manifesto: Annotated Text*. New York: W. W. Norton, 1988.

McDaid, William. "Kinsley S. Bingham and the Republican Ideology of Antislavery, 1847–1855." *Michigan Historical Review* 16, no. 2 (1990): 42–73.

McDonnell, Michael A. *Masters of Empire: Great Lakes Indians and the Making of America*. New York: Hill & Wang, 2015.

Melville, Herman. *The Confidence-Man: His Masquerade; An Authoritative Text, Contemporary Reviews, Biographical Overviews, Sources, Backgrounds, and Criticism*. 2nd ed. New York: W. W. Norton, 2006.

_____. *Israel Potter: His Fifty Years of Exile*. New York: G. P. Putnam, 1855.

_____. *Moby-Dick: or, The Whale*. Evanston, IL: Northwestern University Press, 1988.

_____. *Typee: Complete Text with Introduction, Historical Contexts, Critical Essays*. Boston: Houghton Mifflin, 2004.

Michener, James A., and A. Grove Day. *Rascals in Paradise*. New York: Random House, 1957.

Michigan Historical Commission. "George C. Bates." *Michigan Historical Collections* 9 (1886): 87.

Mihm, Stephen. *A Nation of Counterfeiters: Capitalists, Con Men, and the Making of the United States.* Cambridge, MA: Harvard University Press, 2007.

Miller, Reuben. *James J. Strang, Weighed in the Balance of Truth, and Found Wanting.* Burlington: Wisconsin Territory, n.p., 1846.

Mumford, Jeremy Ravi. "The Inca Priest on the Mormon Stage: A Native American Melodrama and a New American Religion." *Common-place* 5, no. 4 (July 2005): web.

Nerone, John. "Representing Public Opinion: US Newspapers and the News System in the Long Nineteenth Century." *History Compass* 9, no. 9 (2011): 743–59.

Newhall, Beaumont. *The Daguerreotype in America.* New York: Duell, Sloan & Pearce, 1961.

Nord, David Paul. *Communities of Journalism: A History of American Newspapers and Their Readers.* Urbana: University of Illinois Press, 2006.

Pattison, E. Mansell, and Robert C. Ness. "New Religious Movements in Historical Perspective." In *Cults and New Religious Movements: A Report of the American Psychiatric Association,* 43–83. Washington, DC: American Psychiatric Association, 1989.

Poe, Edgar Allan. *The Complete Tales and Poems of Edgar Allan Poe.* New York: Vintage, 1975.

Porter, Dorothy, ed. *Early Negro Writing: 1760–1837.* Baltimore: Black Classics Press, 1995.

Post, Warren. "James J. Strang." *Journal of History* 3, no. 1 (January 1910): 72–79.

Quaife, Milo Milton. *The Kingdom of Saint James: A Narrative of the Mormons.* New Haven, CT: Yale University Press, 1930.

Raddatz, Fritz J. *Karl Marx: A Political Biography.* Boston: Little, Brown, 1978.

Reeve, W. Paul. *Religion of a Different Color: Race and the Mormon Struggle for Whiteness.* New York: Oxford University Press, 2015.

Remini, Robert V. *Joseph Smith.* New York: Viking, 2002.

Reynolds, David S. *John Brown, Abolitionist: The Man Who Killed Slavery, Sparked the Civil War, and Seeded Civil Rights.* New York: Alfred A. Knopf, 2005.

Riegel, O. W. *Crown of Glory: The Life of James J. Strang, Moses of the Mormons.* New Haven, CT: Yale University Press, 1935.

Riggs, Michael S. "From the Daughters of Zion to the 'Banditti on the Prairies': Danite Influence on the Nauvoo Period." *Restoration Studies* 7 (1998): 95–106.

Rinear, David L. *Stage, Page, Scandals, and Vandals: William E. Burton and Nineteenth-Century American Theatre.* Carbondale: Southern Illinois University Press, 2004.

Roberts, Alasdair. *America's First Great Depression: Economic Crisis and Political Disorder After the Panic of 1837.* Ithaca, NY: Cornell University Press, 2013.

Robertson, Gary. "Canal Was Carved with Slave Labor—Waterway's Construction Was a Demanding Task." *Richmond (VA) Times-Dispatch,* September 26, 1999.

Rodgers, Bradley A. *Guardian of the Great Lakes: The U.S. Paddle Frigate* Michigan. Ann Arbor: University of Michigan Press, 1996.

Rogin, Michael Paul. *Subversive Genealogy: The Politics and Art of Herman Melville.* Berkeley: University of California Press, 1983.

Rohrbough, Malcolm J. *Days of Gold: The California Gold Rush and the American Nation*. Berkeley: University of California Press, 1997.

Ross, Robert Budd. *The Early Bench and Bar of Detroit: From 1805 to the End of 1850*. Detroit: Richard P. Joy and Clarence M. Burton, 1907.

Roth, Randolph. *American Homicide*. Cambridge, MA: Belknap Press of Harvard University Press, 2009.

Rubenstein, Bruce A., and Lawrence E. Ziewacz. *Michigan: A History of the Great Lakes State*. 5th ed. Hoboken, NJ: John Wiley & Sons, 2014.

Rust, Richard Dilworth. " 'I Love All Men Who Dive': Herman Melville and Joseph Smith." *BYU Studies Quarterly* 8, no. 31 (1999): 151–69.

Rutkow, Eric. *American Canopy: Trees, Forests, and the Making of a Nation*. New York: Scribner, 2012.

Ryder, J. F. *Voigtländer and I in Pursuit of Shadow Catching: A Story of Fifty-Two Years' Companionship with a Camera*. Cleveland: Imperial Press, 1902.

Sandage, Scott A. *Born Losers: A History of Failure in America*. Cambridge, MA: Harvard University Press, 2006.

Sanders, Barry. *Unsuspecting Souls: The Disappearance of the Human Being*. Washington, DC: Counterpoint, 2009.

Saxon, A. H. *P. T. Barnum: The Legend and the Man*. New York: Columbia University Press, 1989.

Scarry, Robert J. *Millard Fillmore*. Jefferson, NC: McFarland, 2001.

Scott, Isaac. "James J. Strang in Voree." *Saints' Herald* 35, no. 52 (December 29, 1888): 831–33.

Shaw, Ronald E. *Erie Water West: A History of the Erie Canal, 1792–1854*. Lexington: University of Kentucky Press, 1966.

Shelley, Percy Bysshe. "Queen Mab." In *Shelley's Poetry and Prose: An Authoritative Texts Criticism*. 2nd ed. New York: W. W. Norton, 2002.

Shepard, William, and H. Michael Marquardt. *Lost Apostles: Forgotten Members of Mormonism's Original Quorum of Twelve*. Salt Lake City, UT: Signature Books, 2014.

Sheridan, Richard Brinsley. *Pizarro: A Tragedy in Five Acts*. Peterborough, ON: Broadview Press, 2017.

Shipps, Jan. *Mormonism: The Story of a New Religious Tradition*. University of Illinois Press, 1987.

Sinha, Manisha. *The Slave's Cause: A History of Abolition*. New Haven, CT: Yale University Press, 2016.

Smith, Andrew F. *The Saintly Scoundrel: The Life and Times of Dr. John Cook Bennett*. Urbana: University of Illinois Press, 1997.

Smith, Joseph. *An American Prophet's Record: The Diaries and Journals of Joseph Smith*. Salt Lake City, UT: Signature Books, 1987.

Smith, Page. *The Nation Comes of Age: A People's History of the Ante-Bellum Years*. New York: McGraw-Hill, 1981.

Smith, Ted A. *Weird John Brown: Divine Violence and the Limits of Ethics*. Stanford, CA: Stanford University Press, 2015.

Speek, Vickie Cleverley. *"God Has Made Us a Kingdom": James Strang and the Midwest Mormons*. Salt Lake City, UT: Signature Books, 2006.

Sperber, Jonathan. *Karl Marx: A Nineteenth-Century Life*. New York: Liveright, 2013.

Stackpole, Edouard A. *The Sea-Hunters: The New England Whalemen During Two Centuries, 1635–1835*. Philadelphia: Lippincott, 1953.

Stowell, Daniel W., ed. *The Papers of Abraham Lincoln: Legal Documents and Cases*. Vol. 3. Charlottesville: University of Virginia Press, 2008.

Strang, Charles J. "Elvira Field Strang Baker Memorial Book." 1910.

Strang, Elvira Field, and Charles J. Strang. "Biographical Sketch of James J. Strang." Unpublished, n.d.

Strang, James J. *Ancient and Modern Michilimackinac: Including an Account of the Controversy Between Mackinac and the Mormons*. St. James, MI: n.p., 1854.

_____. *The Book of the Law of the Lord: Being a Translation from the Egyptian of the Law Given to Moses in Sinai, with Numerous and Valuable Notes*. Rev. ed. Burlington, WI: Voree Press, 1991.

_____. *The Book of the Law of the Lord, Consisting of an Inspired Translation of Some of the Most Important Parts of the Law Given to Moses, and a Very Few Additional Commandments, with Brief Notes and References*. 1st ed. St. James, MI: Printed by command of the King, at the Royal Press, 1851.

_____. *The Diary of James J. Strang. Deciphered, Transcribed, Introduced, and Annotated*. East Lansing: Michigan State University Press, 1961.

_____. "Some Remarks on the Natural History of Beaver Islands, Michigan." In *Ninth Annual Report of the Board of Regents of the Smithsonian Institution, Showing the Operations, Expenditures and Condition of the Institution up to January 1, 1855, 282–88*. Washington, DC: Beverly Tucker, 1855.

_____. "Strang's Autobiography." In *Michigan Historical Collections* 32 (1903): 202–206.

_____. "Traveling Theatre Royal, Late from Beaver Island. Adams' New Drama. The Famous Original Five Act Drama, 'Improving the Household,' by Mr. G. J. Adams, Author, Manager and Star Actor." St. James, MI: Cooper & Chidester, 1850.

Summers, Mark W. *The Plundering Generation: Corruption and the Crisis of the Union, 1849–1861*. New York: Oxford University Press, 1987.

Taves, Ann. *Fits, Trances, and Visions: Experiencing Religion and Explaining Experience from Wesley to James*. Princeton, NJ: Princeton University Press, 1999.

Tennyson, Alfred, Lord. *Idylls of the King*. London: Penguin, 2004.

Thick, Matthew R. " 'The Exploded Humbug': Antebellum Michigan, Personal Liberty Laws, and States' Rights." *Michigan Historical Review* 42, no. 2 (Fall 2016): 53–65.

Thoreau, Henry David. *Civil Disobedience and Other Essays*. Mineola, NY: Dover, 1993.

_____. *Walden: or, Life in the Woods*. Mineola, NY: Dover, 1995.

Tocqueville, Alexis de. *Democracy in America*. Ware, Hertfordshire: Wordsworth Editions, 1998.

Tolstoy, Leo. "The Raid." In *The Death of Ivan Ilyich and Other Stories*. New York: Penguin, 2008.

Trachtenberg, Alan. *Reading American Photographs: Images as History, Mathew Brady to Walker Evans*. New York: Hill & Wang, 1989.

Turner, John G. *Brigham Young, Pioneer Prophet*. Cambridge, MA: Harvard University Press, 2012.

Twain, Mark. *Adventures of Huckleberry Finn*. New York: Charles L. Webster, 1885.

_____. *The Innocents Abroad*. New York: Signet Classic, 1980.

_____. *Roughing It.* Berkeley: University of California Press, 2011.

Tyler, Alice Felt. *Freedom's Ferment: Phases of American Social History from the Colonial Period to the Outbreak of the Civil War.* New York: Harper & Row, 1962.

Ulrich, Laurel Thatcher. *A House Full of Females: Family and Faith in Nineteenth-Century Mormon Diaries.* New York: Alfred A. Knopf, 2017.

Van Noord, Roger. *Assassination of a Michigan King: The Life of James Jesse Strang.* Ann Arbor: University of Michigan Press, 1997.

Walther, Eric H. *The Shattering of the Union: America in the 1850s.* Wilmington, DE: Scholarly Resources, 2004.

Walton, Hanes, Donald Richard Deskins, and Sherman C. Puckett. *The African American Electorate: A Statistical History.* Vol. 1. Washington, DC: CQ Press, 2012.

Weeks, Robert W. "The Captain, the Prophet, and the King: A Possible Source for Twain's Dauphin." *Mark Twain Journal* 18, no. 1 (1975): 9–12.

_____. "A Utopian Kingdom in the American Grain." *Wisconsin Magazine of History* 61, no. 1 (1977): 3–20.

Weinstein, James. *The Long Detour: The History and Future of the American Left.* Boulder, CO: Westview, 2003.

Weller, Charles Edward. *Early History of the Typewriter.* La Porte, IN: Chase & Shepard, 1918.

Whitman, Walt. *Leaves of Grass.* 1st ed. Brooklyn, NY: Fowler & Wells, 1855.

_____. *Leaves of Grass.* 2nd ed. Brooklyn, NY: Fowler & Wells, 1856.

_____. *Leaves of Grass.* 4th ed. New York: Wm. E. Chapin, 1867.

_____. *Two Rivulets: Including Democratic Vistas, Centennial Songs, and Passage to India.* Author's ed. Camden, NJ: n.p., 1876.

Williams, Elizabeth Whitney. *A Child of the Sea; and Life Among the Mormons.* New York: J. E. Jewett, 1905.

Wineapple, Brenda. *Ecstatic Nation: Confidence, Crisis, and Compromise, 1848–1877.* New York: HarperCollins, 2013.

_____. *Hawthorne: A Life.* New York: Alfred A. Knopf, 2003.

Yacovazzi, Cassandra L. *Escaped Nuns: True Womanhood and the Campaign Against Convents in Antebellum America.* New York: Oxford University Press, 2018.

Index

Note: Italic page numbers refer to illustrations. The abbreviation JJS refers to James Jesse Strang.

About the Author

Miles Harvey is the author of the national and international best-seller *The Island of Lost Maps* and the recipient of a Knight-Wallace Journalism Fellowship at the University of Michigan. His book *Painter in a Savage Land* was named a *Chicago Tribune* Best Book of the Year and a *Booklist* Editors' Choice. He teaches creative writing at DePaul University in Chicago, where he is a founding editor of Big Shoulders Books.